THE SENSE OF HEARING

The Sense of Hearing is a truly accessible introduction to auditory perception, addressing the fundamental aspects of hearing. Thoroughly revised throughout, this edition reflects recent discoveries in the field, and includes additional coverage of the neural basis of hearing. The book introduces the nature of sound and the spectrum, and the anatomy and physiology of the auditory system, before discussing basic auditory processes including frequency selectivity, loudness and pitch perception, temporal resolution, and sound localization. Subsequent chapters show how complex processes such as perceptual organization, speech perception, and music perception are dependent on the initial analysis that occurs when sounds enter the ear. The book concludes with coverage of how hearing impairment can provide an insight into disorders of the auditory system.

Featuring student-friendly features including an overview of research techniques, an extensive glossary of technical terms, and over 150 original illustrations, *The Sense of Hearing* offers a clear introduction and an essential resource for students and educators involved in this challenging field.

Christopher J. Plack was educated at Christ's College, University of Cambridge, where he obtained a BA in Natural Sciences in 1987 and a PhD in 1990. He worked as a postdoctoral research fellow for two years at the University of Minnesota and for two years at the University of Sussex before being awarded a Royal Society University Research Fellowship in 1994. He moved to the University of Essex in 1998 and was promoted to Chair in 2001. He moved again to Lancaster University in 2005 before obtaining his present position of Ellis Llwyd Jones Professor of Audiology at the University of Manchester in 2008. He also holds a 50 % position as Professor of Auditory Neuroscience at Lancaster University. He has published over 100 peer-reviewed journal articles, 14 book chapters, and two edited volumes. In 2003, he was elected a Fellow of the Acoustical Society of America.

THE SENSE OF HEARING

Third Edition

CHRISTOPHER J. PLACK

Routledge
Taylor & Francis Group

LONDON AND NEW YORK

Third edition published 2018
by Routledge
2 Park Square, Milton Park, Abingdon, Oxon, OX14 4RN

and by Routledge
711 Third Avenue, New York, NY 10017

Routledge is an imprint of the Taylor & Francis Group, an informa business

First edition published by Lawrence Erlbaum Associates 2005
Second edition published by Psychology Press 2014

British Library Cataloguing-in-Publication Data
A catalogue record for this book is available from the British Library

Library of Congress Cataloging-in-Publication Data
Names: Plack, Christopher J., author.
Title: The sense of hearing / Christopher J. Plack.
Description: Third edition. | Abingdon, Oxon; New York, NY: Routledge, 2018. |
    Includes bibliographical references and index.
Identifiers: LCCN 2018004726 | ISBN 9781138632585 (hb: alk. paper) |
    ISBN 9781138632592 (pb: alk. paper) |
    ISBN 9781315208145 (ebk)
Subjects: LCSH: Hearing.
Classification: LCC BF251 .P57 2018 | DDC 152.1/5—dc23
LC record available at https://lccn.loc.gov/2018004726

ISBN: 978-1-138-63258-5 (hbk)
ISBN: 978-1-138-63259-2 (pbk)
ISBN: 978-1-315-20814-5 (ebk)

Typeset in Joanna MT
by Apex CoVantage, LLC

Printed and bound in Great Britain by
TJ International Ltd, Padstow, Cornwall

Contents

Preface

The aim of the first edition of this book was to provide a basic introduction to hearing, one that would be appropriate for undergraduate and master's-level students taking introductory courses on the topic. The aim was to provide an account that would be accessible to students approaching the subject for the first time. The book was focused on explaining human perceptions rather than on providing a comprehensive description of auditory anatomy and physiology. However, details of anatomy and physiology were included where they were considered important to an understanding of the function of the auditory system.

The feedback on the first edition, particularly from students, was quite positive, although I also received some constructive suggestions for improvements. The second edition was a major update, with two new chapters, on music and on hearing impairment, and an appendix on research methodologies. For the third edition, in addition to incorporating new discoveries where relevant throughout, I have attempted to clarify sections that some readers have found difficult. Following advice, I have also added more information on the neural mechanisms of auditory perception across several chapters, most notably Chapter 10 on auditory scene analysis and Chapter 11 on speech.

I would like to express my gratitude to some of the individuals who have helped, directly or indirectly, in the production of this book. First, I have been lucky enough to work for and with some of the brightest and best in the field. In chronological order, Brian Moore, Neal Viemeister, Bob Carlyon, Chris Darwin, Andrew Oxenham, Ray Meddis, Enrique Lopez-Poveda, Hedwig Gockel, Deb Hall, Colette McKay, and Kevin Munro. I owe special thanks to Brian, who was the best PhD supervisor a boy could ask for and has given me support and guidance ever since. Bob was largely responsible for getting me the original book deal, so I probably still owe him a beer or two. Several experts in the field made invaluable comments and suggestions on earlier drafts of the first edition. Three readers were anonymous, but I can name Bob Carlyon, who made some good suggestions for Chapters 1 and 12, and Chris Darwin, who put me straight with respect to auditory scene analysis and speech perception. I also received useful feedback on the first edition from Deb Fantini, Dave McAlpine, Brian Moore, Tassos Sarampalis, Rebecca Watkinson, and Ifat Yasin. For the preparation of the second edition, I am indebted to Bruce Goldstein for some great advice on clarity for Chapter 4; Peter Pfordresher, whose expert suggestions greatly improved Chapter 12 ("Music"); Mike Maslin, likewise for Chapter 13 ("Hearing Impairment"); and Karolina Kluk-de Kort, who inspired and provided invaluable comments on the Appendix. This third edition benefitted greatly from the constructive comments of three anonymous reviewers, and from the advice of my PhD student Hannah Guest.

1 INTRODUCTION

Our senses provide us with the information that allows us to interact with the world in a meaningful way. Hearing is the sense that obtains information about the world using the pressure fluctuations in the air (i.e., sounds) that are produced by vibrating objects. In most situations in which we find ourselves, the air is full of sound, and it is therefore full of information. Much of this information is generated, directly or indirectly, by other life-forms. The ear evolved to make use of that information, to make us better at coping with the "struggle for existence," as Charles Darwin (1859) put it. In this chapter, I explain why I think that hearing is a worthwhile subject for study and give an overview of the delights to follow in this volume.

1.1 WHY STUDY HEARING?

In most undergraduate psychology courses, the study of hearing is neglected in favor of the study of vision. Is this bias justified? I argue that it is not. Hearing is a crucial sense for humans. Speech is the main means by which we communicate with one another. Music is one of the most important forms of entertainment and recreation, as well as being an important form of communication itself – it allows the expression of powerful emotions. Hearing is, therefore, *central* to the interaction of human beings with other human beings. Hearing is also of importance to our interactions with our environment. Sounds warn us of danger: In many situations, we hear an approaching car before we see it. Sounds are also used in our interactions with objects. They wake us up in the morning and provide information about the operation of machines, from car engines to smartphones.

We study hearing to understand how the ear and the brain make sense of these stimuli, which are such an integral part of our daily lives. Despite the importance of knowledge in itself for our culture (and the promise that "pure" research will eventually lead to useful applications), hearing research is not driven by curiosity alone. If we understand how the auditory system responds to sounds, then we can use that knowledge to help design sound-producing devices, such as telecommunication systems, entertainment systems, and devices that produce auditory alerts and warnings. We can use that knowledge to design buildings and plan towns and cities, to give their inhabitants a more intelligible, and beneficial, acoustic environment. We can also use our knowledge of how the human auditory system works to design artificial devices that mimic aspects of this system, such as speech recognition programs that enable us to talk to our machines. Last but not least, this knowledge helps us to understand and manage hearing disorders. About one in six people are hearing impaired. The development of diagnostic techniques and interventions such as hearing aids is dependent on perceptual research.

There is a great deal of ignorance about hearing, probably more than there is regarding vision. Many people are aware of how the eye works, at least in general terms. They know that light from an object is focused by the lens onto the retina. How many people know what happens to sounds in the ear? Very few, on the basis of my experience. Even if you believe that vision is the most important sense and that this should be reflected in teaching practices, I hope you will agree that we should not neglect hearing. If you are approaching this subject for the first time, I would like to convince you that auditory science is not only *important* but also *fascinating*.

1.2   ABOUT THIS BOOK

This book provides an introduction to human auditory perception; it explains how sounds are represented and analyzed in the auditory system and how these processes cause the sensations that we experience when we listen to sounds. The description will mostly be a mix of *auditory psychophysics* (or *psychoacoustics*), which is the study of the relations between sounds and sensations, and *auditory anatomy and physiology*, which is the study of the biological hardware involved. To start, however, a little background is needed for readers who are not familiar with the physics of sound. Chapters 2 and 3 are devoted to physical acoustics and describe the nature of sound and introduce the spectrum – a very important concept for understanding the function of the ear. Resonance, sound propagation, and signal processing are also discussed, as a familiarity with these topics will be of benefit later. Chapter 4 provides an overview of the anatomy and physiology of the auditory system, explains how the cochlea separates sound into different frequency components, and describes the transduction process by which vibrations are converted into electrical impulses in the auditory nerve. The crucial topic of frequency selectivity is explored further in Chapter 5, in which our sensations are related to processes in the cochlea and at other stages in the auditory system.

The next few chapters cover auditory sensations that should be familiar to most readers. Our perception of sound magnitude, or loudness, is discussed in Chapter 6. Our perception of sound periodicity, or pitch, is presented in Chapter 7. Chapter 8 describes temporal aspects of hearing, the ability to respond to rapid changes in sounds, and the ability to combine acoustic information over time. Chapter 9 explains how we determine the location of sound sources. In Chapters 6–9, our sensations are explained, whenever possible, in terms of what we know about the underlying physiological mechanisms. The next three chapters move on to higher level aspects of perception involving extremely complex and, in some cases, little understood, brain processes. The remarkable ability of the auditory system to separate sounds from different sources (e.g., a single talker at a noisy party) is described in Chapter 10. The main end result of hearing – deriving meaning from sounds – is discussed in Chapter 11, with a description of speech perception, and in Chapter 12, with a description of music perception. Chapters 10, 11, and 12 show how the complex auditory processes make use of the more basic analysis mechanisms described in the previous chapters. Hearing impairment is one of the most significant health burdens for humans, particularly for the elderly. The need to improve the diagnosis and management of hearing loss is the main driver for auditory research. Chapter 13 describes the physiological bases and perceptual consequences of hearing loss, as well as the diagnostic techniques and management options that are available. To conclude, Chapter 14 summarizes what we know and what we do not know about auditory perception, and the Appendix provides an overview of the experimental methodologies that we use to study the auditory system.

2 THE NATURE OF SOUND

Before we begin a discussion of the physiological and psychological aspects of auditory perception, we must look at what sound is, how it is produced, and how it can be modified and analyzed. After attempting to get all this information into one chapter, I gave up and split it into two. I think this level of coverage is justified, since a firm understanding of the physical characteristics of acoustic information is required before we can make sense of our perceptions. The present chapter will introduce the basic characteristics of sound and look at some typical sound waves. The important concept of the *spectrum* will be introduced. The next chapter will cover more advanced topics, such as resonance, sound propagation, and signal processing. Some mathematical knowledge is useful here, but I hope that the main ideas can be understood without the reader spending too much time bogged down in equations.

2.1 WHAT IS SOUND?

2.1.1 Static pressure

The matter around me, the chair I sit on, the air I breathe, and the vodka martini I drink – all are composed of tiny particles called *atoms*. These atoms are typically arranged into larger groups called *molecules*. For example, the water that dilutes the alcohol in my drink is composed of many billions of billions of molecules, each of which is made up of two atoms of hydrogen and one atom of oxygen. Molecules and atoms in liquids and gases are free to move, as the bonds between them are weak. In contrast, the molecules and atoms in solids are held together tightly to produce a dense structure. In my chair (which is composed of solids), the molecules are quite densely packed, whereas in the air (which is composed of gases), the molecules are spaced relatively far apart.

Molecules in the air are constantly moving about, and this exerts a *static pressure* on any material that is in contact with the air, caused by the constant bombardment of billions of air molecules. On a much larger scale, a fast-moving tennis ball pushes hard back on the racket as its momentum is transferred. Although air molecules are tiny in comparison, there are a very large number of them striking an object at a given time, and the cumulative effect of these tiny collisions from all directions is to squeeze objects as if they were grasped in an all-enveloping hand. This pressure depends on the density of the air (the more molecules there are per unit volume, the greater the number of collisions and the greater the pressure) and the temperature of the air (the higher the temperature, the faster the air molecules move, and the more force they exert with each collision).

As a result of the earth's gravity, the air molecules near the surface of the earth have been squashed together to create a pressure of about 100,000 newtons per square meter (N/m²), also known as *atmospheric pressure*. A newton is a unit of force (the weight of a 100-gram mass – a small apple – is approximately 1 newton). A square meter is a unit of area, so pressure is measured in terms of the *force per unit area*. Hence, for a constant force, the larger the area, the smaller the pressure. The density of air decreases with altitude, which is why helium balloons increase in size at high altitudes, as the air outside the balloon exerts less pressure allowing the balloon to expand due to the internal pressure of the helium atoms.

2.1.2 Pressure variations

If you drop a pebble in a still pond, the water is disturbed, and ripples will spread across the surface. Similarly, if air is disturbed by the movement or vibration of an object (the *sound source*), then the air density will show a fluctuation. As the vibrating object moves out, the nearby air molecules are pushed away and squeezed together, creating a slight *increase* in density and pressure called *condensation*. As the vibrating object moves in, the air molecules spread out to fill the space vacated, creating a slight *decrease* in density and pressure called *rarefaction*. These pressure variations are called *sound waves*. Sound waves are composed of alternating condensation and rarefaction. As we will discover later on (Section 2.2.3), the pressure variations we normally experience as sound are very tiny (usually less than 0.01% of atmospheric pressure). The pressure variations produced by a sound source propagate through the air in a (broadly) similar way to the way ripples produced by dropping a stone in a pond travel through water. However, there are important differences. Whereas water waves on a flat pond propagate only in two dimensions, across the surface of the pond, sound waves can propagate in all directions, in three-dimensional space. In addition, in water waves the molecules oscillate up and down in a circular motion. Sound waves, on the other hand, are *longitudinal* waves. The particles transmitting the wave (e.g., the molecules in the air) oscillate backward and forward in the direction of the movement of the wave.

One way of thinking about this is to imagine the air as a line of golf balls connected by springs (this analogy is borrowed from Howard and Angus, 2001). If the golf ball at the left end is pushed to the right, then the spring will be compressed (condensation), which causes the next golf ball to move to the right, which will cause the next spring to be compressed, and so on down the line of golf balls. Similarly, if the golf ball at the end is pulled to the left, then the spring will be stretched (rarefaction) causing the next golf ball to move to the left, which causes the next spring to be stretched, and so on. Following this pattern, if a golf ball is moved from side to side, then the pattern of oscillation will *propagate* down the line (see Figure 2.1). This is, essentially, how sound waves are transmitted through a material. In air, which is composed of gases, the molecules are not connected by anything like springs, but the effect of billions of molecules bashing into each other and passing on their momentum can be represented in this way. Anyone who has played with a bicycle pump by blocking off the air nozzle and working the piston will know that the air certainly feels springy (technically *elastic*) when it is compressed.

As a more concrete example, a loudspeaker (as found in hi-fi speaker cabinets, radios, and mobile phones) converts electric potential variations into sound waves. The loudspeaker pushes and pulls at the air, squeezing the air molecules together then stretching them apart. This causes alternate condensation (the high pressure produced when the speaker cone moves outward) and rarefaction (the low pressure produced when the speaker cone moves inward). Figure 2.2

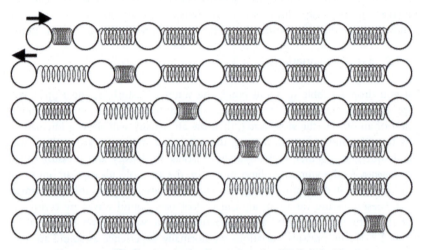

Figure 2.1 The propagation of a disturbance along a line of golf balls linked by springs. Seven successive time frames are shown from top to bottom.

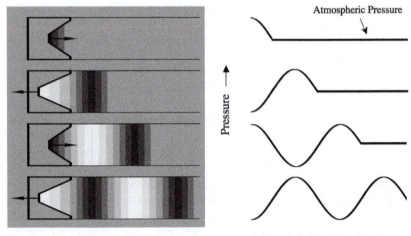

Figure 2.2 An illustration of successive snapshots of a loudspeaker producing sound waves down a hollow tube. Dark shades represent high pressure (condensation); light shades represent low pressure (rarefaction). To the right of the picture is a plot of the pressure variations in the tube as a function of the distance from the loudspeaker. The horizontal lines represent atmospheric pressure.

illustrates the (somewhat unusual) situation of a loudspeaker producing sound waves that travel down a hollow tube. The dark shades indicate regions of high pressure, and the light shades indicate regions of low pressure. The pattern of pressure variations is shown in a sequence, from when the loudspeaker first starts moving (top panel) to the time at which it has completed almost two cycles (bottom panel). To return to the water analogy, you can imagine producing a similar sequence of waves by moving your hand up and down at one end of a long, rectangular fish tank. In this case, the dark shades in Figure 2.2 represent high water, and the light shades represent low water.

2.1.3 The speed of sound

Sound waves travel from their source through the air at a certain speed, depending on the temperature of the air. At 20° Celsius (68° Farenheit) the speed of sound is about 343 meters per second (m/s), 767 miles per hour, or Mach 1. So sound travels quickly compared to our everyday experience of moving objects, but compared to light, which travels at a blistering 671 million miles per hour, sound is very sluggish indeed. The relatively slow journey of sound through air produces the irritating effect at large pop concerts, where fans clapping to the rhythm at the front are out of time with fans clapping to the rhythm at the back because of the time delay.

I have discussed sound waves in terms of the medium with which they are most associated – the air. However, sound can be produced in any material: Producing a pressure change at a given point will cause that pressure change to propagate at a speed that depends on the density and stiffness of the material (think of the golf balls and springs). The denser the material, the slower the speed, because heavy objects take longer to accelerate. The stiffer the material, the higher the speed, because stiff springs generate more force (and acceleration) for a given displacement. For example, sound travels through steel (very stiff) at a speed of 5,200 m/s, whereas sound travels through vulcanized rubber (dense and not very stiff) at a speed of only 54 m/s. We are familiar with sound produced in water. It is used by many sea mammals for communication and can be used to identify objects underwater by the means of reflection (sonar). Although water is denser than air, which tends to make the speed of sound slower, it is much stiffer than air, and this results in a much faster speed. Sound travels through water at a speed of about 1,500 m/s.

2.2 A TONE FOR YOUR SINS

2.2.1 Frequency and phase

From an acoustician's viewpoint, the simplest sound wave is the *pure tone*. The sound produced by the loudspeaker in Figure 2.2 is a pure tone. The sound produced when you whistle is almost a pure tone. For a pure tone, the pressure varies *sinusoidally* with time, and hence its pressure at a given time is given by the following equation:

$$x(t) = A\sin(2\pi ft + \Phi), \tag{2.1}$$

where $x(t)$ is the pressure at time t, A is the peak amplitude (or pressure), f is the frequency of the pure tone, and Φ is the starting phase. I will discuss the meaning of these terms over the next few paragraphs. The sinusoidal function ("sin") produces a waveform that varies up and down, over time, between plus and minus one. The symbol π is pi, the well-known constant, defined as the ratio of the diameter of a circle to its circumference (3.14159265. . .). Sinusoidal motion is the simplest form of oscillation. It is observed in the displacement, over time, of a simple oscillator, such as a weight moving up and down on the end of a spring. In this situation, the maximum acceleration (change in speed) occurs when the displacement of the weight is at its largest (the spring is most stretched or compressed). To visualize a pure tone more directly, water waves, at least the simple ripples you get if you drop a stone in a still pond, are also close to sinusoidal.

Sound *frequency* refers to the number of repeats or *cycles* of the pure tone (alternate condensation and rarefaction) that occur at a given location during a given length of time. High frequencies are popularly associated with treble (or *bright* sounds), and low frequencies are associated with bass (or *warm* sounds). The frequency of a sound is measured in cycles per second, or *hertz* (abbreviated Hz). That is, the frequency of a pure tone in hertz corresponds to the number of times in each second the air pressure changes from high to low and back again. For high-frequency sounds, it is sometimes convenient to measure frequency in terms of thousands of hertz, or kilohertz (kHz).

Imagine that you are standing a fixed distance from a loudspeaker, with sound waves propagating out toward you from the loudspeaker. The number of wave peaks (peaks in pressure) that pass by you every second is equal to the frequency of the sound. Because the speed of sound is constant, the more rapidly the speaker cone moves in and out, the higher the frequency of the sound waves that are produced. This is illustrated in Figure 2.3. The figure also shows a graph illustrating how the pressure in the air varies with distance from the speaker cone and how the pressure varies in time (because sound travels at a constant speed, the shapes of the waveforms will be the same whether measured as a function of distance or time). The frequency of a sound in hertz corresponds to the number of times in every second the speaker cone moves in and out. To

Figure 2.3 A loudspeaker producing pure tones at two different frequencies (the frequency in the lower picture is twice that in the upper picture). To the right of each picture is a plot of the pressure variation over distance or time.

reproduce the frequency of the low E string on a double bass or a bass guitar, which vibrates at 41.2 Hz, the speaker cone must move in and out 41.2 times every second. To reproduce middle C, the speaker cone must move in and out 261.6 times per second. To reproduce sounds across the whole range of human hearing, the speaker cone must be able to move in and out at rates up to 20,000 times per second. It is demonstrated in Section 2.3 that the definition of frequency given here is oversimplified, but this will suffice for the time being.

The *period* of a pure tone is the inverse of the frequency; that is, it is the time taken for the pure tone to complete one cycle of alternating condensation and rarefaction. Because the speed of sound is constant in a given medium, the *wavelength* of the sound – that is, the physical distance that is covered by a complete cycle of the sound wave – is a simple function of the frequency of the sound. Specifically, the wavelength is the speed of sound divided by the frequency of the sound wave: The higher the frequency, the shorter the wavelength, and vice versa. The period and wavelength of a pure tone are shown in Figure 2.4. Two pure tones with different frequencies (and therefore different periods and different wavelengths) are shown in Figure 2.5.

Another important concept that we should address at this juncture is that of *phase*. The phase of a pure tone is the point reached on the pressure cycle at a particular time. Phase covers a range of 360 degrees, or 2π radians, for one cycle of the waveform (see Figure 2.6). (Some readers may notice that phase is measured in the same way as the angle around a circle; 360 degrees or 2π radians correspond to a complete rotation around the circle. This is not a coincidence: The sine function and the circle are linked mathematically. Height as a function of time for a point on an upright circle that is rotating at a constant speed is a sine function.) You can think of phase in terms of pushing someone on a swing. If you push at just the right time – that is, at just the right *phase* – during each

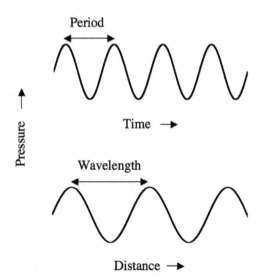

Figure 2.4 The pressure variation over time and distance for a pure tone. The figure illustrates the measures of *period* and *wavelength*.

Two pure tones with the same
starting phase and amplitude
but with different frequencies

Two pure tones with the same
frequency and amplitude but
with different phases

Two pure tones with the same
frequency and phase but with
different amplitudes

Pressure →

Time →

Figure 2.5 Each panel shows the pressure variations over time for two pure tones (superimposed). The figure illustrates the effects of varying frequency, phase, and amplitude.

Positive Zero Crossing   Peak Pressure

Pressure →

0   π/2   π   3π/2   2π   5π/2   3π   7π/2   4π

Phase

Figure 2.6 The phase of different points on the waveform of a pure tone measured in radians relative to the positive zero crossing on the far left of the curve. Notice that each complete cycle of the waveform corresponds to a phase interval of 2π. Also shown is the peak amplitude or pressure of the waveform. Based on Moore (2012).

cycle, then you increase the height of the oscillations. Measurements of phase are *relative*. In other words, we can specify that one pure tone has a phase delay of π compared to another pure tone at a particular time, so if the first pure tone is at a peak in its waveform cycle, the second is at a trough. In Equation 2.1, starting phase (Φ) refers to the phase at time zero ($t = 0$). Time zero does not refer to the beginning of the universe. It is a reference to the start of the waveform, or to the start of the vibration of the sound source. Starting phase is measured relative to the phase when the waveform crosses zero and is rising (also known as a *positive*

Two pure tones added in phase: Two pure tones added when out of phase by π:

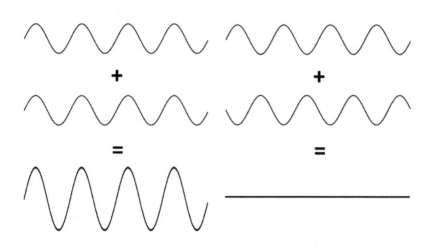

Figure 2.7 An illustration of how the effect of adding sound waves depends on their phase, or alignment in time, relative to each other.

zero crossing; see Figure 2.6). If a pure tone starts at a positive zero crossing, it has a starting phase of zero. If it starts at a peak, it has a starting phase of $\pi/2$. Two pure tones with different starting phases are shown in Figure 2.5.

Phase is important to hearing because the effect of adding two sounds together depends on their relative phase. If we add two pure tones with the same frequency that have no phase delay between them ("in-phase" addition), then the peaks of the waveforms will coincide, and the result will be a combined waveform that has a high amplitude (see Figure 2.7, left panel). If, however, one pure tone is delayed by π – that is, half a cycle – then dips in one waveform will coincide with peaks in the other waveform, and vice versa. If the peak amplitudes of the two tones are equal, then the peaks and dips will cancel out to give no response (see Figure 2.7, right panel). This principle is used in "noise cancellation" headphones, in which sound is generated that is an inverted version of the external sound measured from the environment using a microphone. Adding this generated sound has the effect of canceling the external sound, so that almost all that is left is the sound signal traveling down the wires to the headphones. The result is a less corrupted listening experience. For practical reasons, however, noise cancellation works well only at low frequencies.

2.2.2 Amplitude and intensity

The *amplitude* of a sound wave is the magnitude of the pressure variations, measured with respect to the deviation from atmospheric pressure. A sound wave with a higher amplitude sounds louder. Two pure tones with different amplitudes are shown in Figure 2.5. Pressure can be measured at a given time to provide an *instantaneous* amplitude, which varies with the waveform cycle. However, amplitude is often used to refer to the pressure at the peak of the waveform cycle (*A* in Equation 2.1). In addition, amplitude can be used to refer to the *square root* of the *average over time* of the individual pressure variations *squared*. This is called the *root mean squared* (rms) pressure. Think of the rms pressure as a sort of average pressure, with more weight given to times of extreme pressure (highest and lowest values) and with negative pressures made positive (*rectified*). (If the pressure was just averaged, then the negative and positive pressures would cancel and the result for all waveforms would be zero.) For a pure tone, the rms pressure is equal to $1/\sqrt{2}$ (i.e., 0.707) times the peak pressure.

The amplitude, or pressure, of a sound wave produced by a loudspeaker is proportional to the velocity of the speaker cone. The higher the velocity, the higher the pressure that is produced in the air. The velocity depends on the distance the speaker cone moves during each cycle and the number of times it has to make this movement every second. Clearly, if the speaker cone is vibrating very rapidly to produce a high-frequency sound, then it has to move faster, *for the same speaker cone displacement*, than if it is vibrating at a lower frequency. This means that, if the speaker cone always moves the same distance during each cycle, high-frequency sounds will have a higher pressure – and will tend to sound louder – than low-frequency sounds. Conversely, to reproduce a low-frequency sound with the same pressure amplitude as a high-frequency sound, the speaker cone has to move a greater distance during each cycle. This is why it is possible to see, or feel with your hands, a speaker cone moving when it tries to produce low frequencies and is one of the reasons why woofers (low-frequency loudspeakers) are usually much larger than tweeters (high-frequency loudspeakers). A tweeter trying to produce an intense low-frequency sound would fail, and perhaps be blown apart, because it cannot move a large enough distance to produce the required pressure changes.

Although pressure is a useful measure, it is also common in acoustics to refer to the *intensity* of a sound wave. Intensity is defined as the sound energy passing through a unit area (e.g., a square meter of air) every second. *Power* is defined simply as the energy transmitted per second. The units of intensity are watts (units of power) per square meter (W/m^2). The intensity of a sound wave is proportional to the square of the rms pressure so that

$$I = kP^2, \tag{2.2}$$

where I is the intensity, P is the rms pressure, and k is a constant.

2.2.3 The decibel scale

A problem with using pressure or intensity as a measure is that the sounds we encounter cover such an enormous range of pressures and intensities. A sound near the pain threshold is approximately one million million times as intense (or one million times greater in terms of pressure) as a sound near the absolute threshold of hearing (the quietest sound we can hear). Clearly, if we had to use units of pressure or intensity to describe sounds, we would end up dealing with huge and unwieldy numbers. Instead, we specify intensity in logarithmic units called *decibels* (dB). A sound intensity expressed in decibels is called a sound *level*. The number of decibels is a measure of the *ratio* between two intensities, specifically, 10 times the natural logarithm of the intensity ratio. Because decibels express a ratio (sound A compared to sound B, for example), if you want to use decibels to refer to an absolute level for a sound you need something to compare it to. In other words, you need a *reference* intensity or pressure:

$$\text{Sound level in dB} = 10 \times \log_{10}\left(I / I_o\right)$$
$$= 10 \times \log_{10}\left(P^2 / P_o^2\right) = 20 \times \log_{10}\left(P / P_o\right), \quad (2.3)$$

where I is intensity, I_o is a reference intensity, P is rms pressure, and P_o is a reference pressure. Conventionally, sound level in air is expressed relative to a reference pressure of 0.00002 newtons per square meter (2×10^{-5} N/m²), which corresponds to a reference intensity of 10^{-12} watts per square meter (W/m²). A sound level expressed relative to this reference point is called a sound pressure level (SPL). A sound wave at the reference pressure ($P = P_o$) has a level of 0 dB SPL (by definition) because the logarithm of 1 is zero. In fact, the reference pressure was chosen because 0 dB SPL is close to the lowest level we can hear (absolute threshold) at a frequency of 1000 Hz.

Let us reflect on these numbers. We have learned that atmospheric pressure is 10^5 N/m² and that the softest sound we can hear corresponds to a pressure fluctuation of about 2×10^{-5} N/m². It follows that we can hear a sound wave with pressure fluctuations that are less than one *billionth* of atmospheric pressure. This is equivalent, in scale, to a wave one millimeter high on an ocean 1,000 kilometers deep! Even a sound at 120 dB SPL, a sound that would cause you pain and damage your ears if you were foolish enough to listen to it for any length of time, has pressure fluctuations with an amplitude 5,000 times less than atmospheric pressure. The pressure variations of the sound waves we encounter in everyday life are very tiny indeed.

In addition to dB SPL, another popular measure of absolute sound level is dB(A), or "A-weighted" dB. This measure is based on the intensity of the sound weighted across frequency according to the normal sensitivity of the ear, which decreases at low and high frequencies. Specifically, the weighting is based on the variation with frequency in the *loudness* (i.e., *perceived* magnitude) of a sound relative to a 40-dB SPL, 1000-Hz pure tone (see Section 6.2.2). For a 1000-Hz pure tone, the dB(A) and dB SPL values are identical, but for a 200-Hz pure tone, the dB(A) value is less than the dB SPL value, reflecting the reduced sensitivity of the ear at 200 Hz compared to 1000 Hz. Environmental noise is often measured in dB(A), for example, to determine if the noise in a factory is likely to harm the hearing of the workers.

Figure 2.8 shows how the intensity scale maps onto the decibel scale. Logarithms and decibels take some getting used to, but the most important point to remember is that a change in level by a constant number of decibels corresponds to a constant *multiplication* of the sound intensity. For example, a useful property of the decibel scale is that an increase of 10 dB corresponds to an increase by a factor of 10 in intensity (hence 20 dB is a factor of 100, 30 dB is a factor of

Figure 2.8 The left panel shows how intensity ratios map onto the decibel scale. The right panel shows the levels of some familiar sounds in dB SPL.

1,000, etc.) and 3 dB is (approximately) a doubling of intensity. Now the range of numbers we have to deal with when describing sounds is reduced from a factor of about 1,000,000,000,000 (in units of intensity) to a range from about 0 to 120 dB SPL. That is much less frightening! Incidentally, I once heard Ozzy Osbourne (the legendary rocker) state that he was hard of hearing because he had been listening to 30 billion dB all his life (or something to that effect). Thirty billion dB SPL corresponds to an intensity of $10^{2999999988}$ (i.e., a 1 with almost 3 billion zeros after it) watts per square meter: That is enough power to destroy the universe, never mind Ozzy's ears. Figure 2.8 shows a scale of sound levels from 0 to 120 dB SPL and how some sounds we are familiar with might fit on the scale, including Ozzy Osbourne at maximum attack.

Because a constant change in decibels represents a constant multiplication of the sound pressure or intensity, the decibel scale can be quite useful when talking about the amplification or attenuation of a sound. For instance, a hi-fi amplifier will cause a multiplication of the sound pressure or intensity, and this, for a constant amount of amplification, will correspond to a constant change in decibels, regardless of the starting level of the sound. Similarly, earplugs cause a constant *attenuation* of a given sound, dividing the pressure or intensity by a constant amount (or multiplying by a value less than one), and reducing the sound level entering the ear by a constant number of decibels.

The instantaneous pressure variations produced by two sound waves that overlap in space will sum so that a more complex waveform may be produced. (This is an example of *linear addition*, a topic that is covered in Section 3.3.4.) As in our water analogy, if you drop two pebbles into the water, the waves produced by each will overlap, sometimes producing a high peak, sometimes a deep trough, and sometimes canceling one another to produce flat water. Two different sound waveforms (e.g., two noise sounds or two pure tones of different frequencies) will generally add together so that the *intensities* of the waveforms sum (not the pressures). This is true because the phase relations between the two sounds will usually vary from one moment to the next: Sometimes a peak will match a peak and the pressures will add; sometimes a peak will match a trough and the pressures will cancel. The net effect is that the average *intensities* sum linearly. Two identical waveforms added *in phase* (so that all their peaks coincide) will combine so that the *pressures* sum. In this situation, the intensity of the combined waveform will be greater than a linear sum of the intensities of the two original waveforms.

Returning to our discussion of the decibel scale, try to remember that the decibel levels for two sounds *do not add* when the sounds are combined. A sound with a level of 40 dB SPL added to another sound with a level of 40 dB SPL will not produce a sound with a level of 80 dB SPL. A sound with a level of 80 dB SPL is 10,000 *times* more intense than a 40-dB SPL sound. In fact, these two sounds added together (assuming a random phase relation) will produce a sound with a level of 43 dB SPL.

2.3 THE SPECTRUM

2.3.1 Describing sounds in the frequency domain

Now that we have quantified the basic characteristics of sounds, we move on to perhaps the most important – and difficult – concept in the chapter. The discussion has focused on a simple sound called the pure tone. As noted earlier, a pure tone is (roughly) the sound waveform you produce when you whistle. However, the waveforms of most sounds in the environment are much more complex than this. We look at some idealized examples in the next few sections. The wonderful property of all these waveforms is that they can be produced by *adding together* pure tones of different amplitudes, frequencies, and phases (see Figure 2.9). In fact, *any* waveform can be produced in this way; you just need enough pure tones. The entire concept of frequency is linked to the pure tone. A warm, bass sound (e.g., the beat of a drum) contains low-frequency pure tones. A bright, treble sound (e.g., the crash of a cymbal) contains high-frequency pure tones. Just as you can build up a sound by adding together pure tones, you can break down a sound into a set of pure tones. *Fourier analysis* is the mathematical technique for separating a complex sound into its pure-tone frequency components.

You may be familiar with the concept of spectrum in terms of the separation of light by a prism or by water droplets in a rainbow. When we look at a rainbow, we are looking at the *spectrum* of light emanating from the sun, and we can see the different frequency components of visible light from red (low frequency) to blue (high frequency). Similarly, the spectrum of a sound is a description of the frequency components that make up that sound. The *magnitude spectrum* of a sound is the distribution of the *magnitudes* of the pure-tone components that make up the sound. It can be represented by a plot of the level of each of the pure-tone components as a function of frequency (see Figure 2.9). High-frequency components appear on the right side of the graph and low-frequency components on

Figure 2.9 An illustration of how complex sound waves can be constructed from pure-tone building blocks. The complex waveform at the bottom is produced by adding together three pure tones with different amplitudes, frequencies, and phases. The frequencies of the pure tones required to produce a given waveform are always integer multiples of the inverse of the duration of the waveform that needs to be produced. For example, if the waveform duration is 100 ms, only pure tones with frequencies that are integer multiples of 10 Hz (10 Hz, 20 Hz, 30 Hz, etc.) are required. The *spectrum* of the complex waveform, showing the levels of the components as a function of frequency, is shown on the right.

the left side of the graph. The height of the line corresponding to each frequency component represents its level. The *phase spectrum* of a sound is the distribution of the *phases* (temporal alignments) of the pure-tone components that make up the sound. It can be represented by a plot of the phase of each of the pure-tone components as a function of frequency. The magnitude and phase spectra, taken together, determine precisely the pressure variations of the sound as a function of time. We do not study phase spectra in this volume, but references to magnitude spectra (from now on just "spectra") will be commonplace.

2.3.2   Time-frequency trading and the spectrogram

An important property of this type of analysis limits the resolution, or precision of measurement, we can achieve. A spectrum shows the distribution of pure tones that make up a waveform. Hence, the spectrum of a *continuous* pure tone is a single line at the frequency of the tone. However, the spectrum of a pure tone with a short duration occupies a wider spectral region (Figure 2.10). This is because a range of continuous pure tones is required to make the pure tone itself, and to *cancel out*, to produce the silence before and after the pure tone.

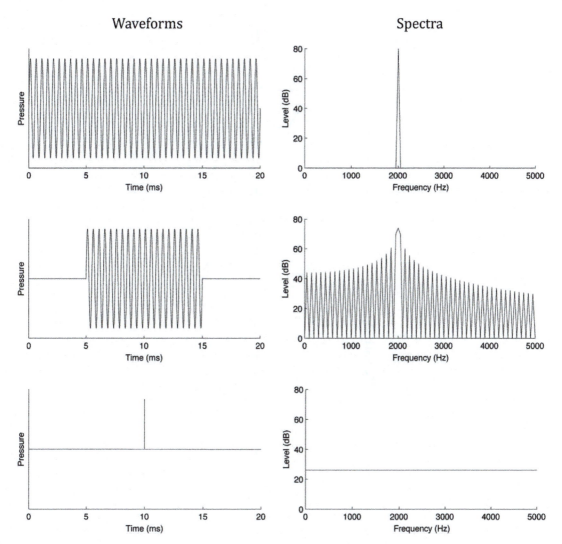

Figure 2.10 The waveforms and spectra of 2000-Hz pure tones with durations of 20 ms (top panel) and 10 ms (middle panel) and the waveform and spectrum of an almost instantaneous impulse (bottom panel). Notice the symmetrical equivalence of the top and bottom plots. In the top plot, the waveform is continuous and the spectrum is a discrete peak. In the bottom plot, the waveform is a discrete peak and the spectrum is continuous.

In *extremis*, an instantaneous impulse or click (like the snap of your fingers) has a spectrum that is completely flat (it contains all frequency components with equal levels). Figure 2.11 shows how an impulse can be constructed by adding together pure tones. The general rule is that an abrupt change in amplitude over frequency (a sharp transition in the spectrum such as that produced by a long pure tone) is associated with a broad spread of amplitude over time, and an abrupt change in amplitude over time is associated with a broad spread of amplitude over frequency. In the latter case, the spectral components generated are known as *spectral splatter*. If a sound is turned off abruptly, you may hear this as a

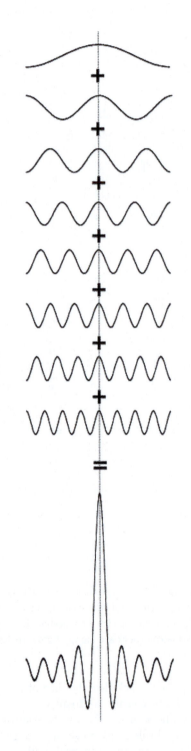

Figure 2.11 How an impulse (bottom) can be constructed by adding up pure tones, with phases aligned so that their peaks are all coincident at the time of the impulse (see dotted line). To produce a perfect impulse of infinitesimal duration, an infinite number of pure tones would be required.

"click" or "glitch." It follows from this relation that the shorter the duration of the stimulus we analyze, the more spread out or "blurred" the representation of the stimulus on the frequency axis will tend to be. There is a *time-frequency trade-off* in our ability to represent the characteristics of a sound: The better the temporal resolution, the worse the spectral resolution, and vice versa.

On occasion, we might want to see how the "short-term" spectrum of a sound changes over time. This is particularly useful when analyzing speech sounds. To see the changes, we can draw a *spectrogram*, which is a quasi-three-dimensional plot showing level as a function of both time and frequency. To collapse the plot onto a two-dimensional page, the spectrogram has time on the horizontal axis, frequency on the vertical axis, and level represented by a gray scale or by different colors. Figure 2.12 shows spectrograms for two of the waveforms from Figure 2.10. The short-term spectrum at a given time is produced by performing a Fourier analysis of a short duration of the waveform centered on that time. The analysis "window" usually applies a weighting so that the waveform near the edges of the window is attenuated relative to the center. The weighting avoids the abrupt changes in amplitude at the beginning and end of the window that would cause pronounced spectral splatter. Essentially, the spectrogram represents a sequence of snapshots of the spectral information in a sound. Because there is a time-frequency trade-off, we can choose to track temporal events very finely, in

Figure 2.12 Waveforms and spectrograms for a continuous pure tone (top) and for an impulse (bottom). The spectrograms show the spectrum of the waveform as a function of time (dark areas indicate high levels). To produce the left-most spectrograms, a series of spectra were calculated using successive 2-ms snapshots of the waveform (weighted according to the window shape on the upper left). This gives good temporal resolution but poor spectral resolution. For the spectrograms on the right, 5-ms snapshots were used. For these spectrograms, the temporal resolution is worse (see spectrogram for impulse, lower right) but the spectral resolution is better.

which case we lose out on spectral detail, or to track the spectrum very finely, in which case we lose out on temporal detail.

In the next few sections, we examine the spectra of some complex sound waves. One thing to look for in these plots is that the faster the pressure oscillations in the waveform, the greater the relative level or proportion of the high-frequency components in the spectrum. Eventually, you may begin to get an almost instinctive feel for what the spectrum of a particular waveform will look like.

2.4   COMPLEX TONES AND NOISE

2.4.1   Complex tones

Thus far, we have looked at pure tones, which have simple sinusoidal waveforms that repeat over time at a rate equal to the frequency of the tone. However, we can imagine that there are more complex patterns of pressure variations that repeat over time. The left side of Figure 2.13 shows three examples of such waveforms. As are pure tones, these waveforms are *periodic*. The *period* of the waveform is the time taken for a complete pattern repetition. Periodic waveforms are very familiar to us: The sounds made by (nonpercussive) musical instruments and vowel sounds in speech are periodic. Periodic waveforms are associated with the sensation of *pitch*. A sound that repeats over time but is *not* sinusoidal is called a periodic *complex tone*. The repetition rate of a complex tone (the number of cycles of the waveform per second) is called the *fundamental frequency* of the tone (measured in hertz). The fundamental frequency is equal to the inverse of the period of the waveform (i.e., one divided by the period): The longer the period, the lower the fundamental frequency.

The right panels of Figure 2.13 show the spectra of the waveforms on the left. Note that the spectra show a series of discrete lines, spaced at regular intervals. These lines indicate that the waveforms are made up of a series of pure tones at specific frequencies. These pure-tone frequency components are called *harmonics*. The first harmonic (the lowest frequency harmonic in Figure 2.13) has a frequency equal to the fundamental frequency (the first harmonic is also sometimes called the *fundamental* component). The frequencies of the harmonics are *integer multiples* of the fundamental frequency (in other words, they have frequencies 1, 2, 3, 4, etc., times the fundamental frequency). It follows that the *frequency spacing* between successive harmonics is equal to the fundamental frequency. So, a guitar playing the A above middle C, which has a fundamental frequency of 440 Hz, will have harmonics as follows:

Harmonic number:	Frequency of harmonic in Hz:
1	440
2	880
3	1320
4	1760
5	2200
6	2640
7	3080

. . . and so on.

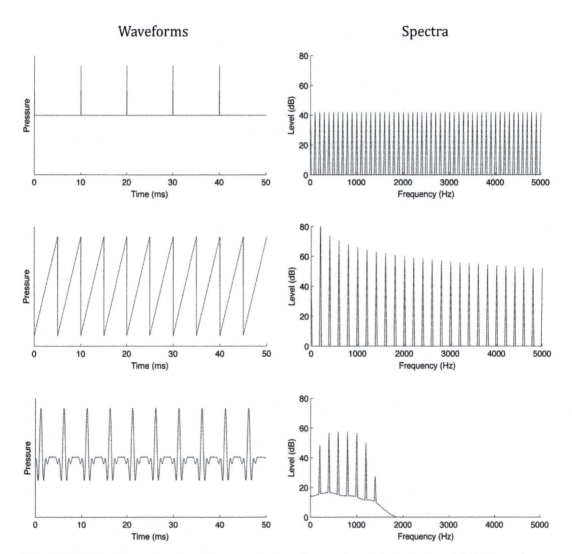

Figure 2.13 The waveforms and spectra of three complex tones. The waveform at the top has a period of 10 ms and a fundamental frequency of 100 Hz. This waveform is a *pulse train*, consisting of a regular sequence of almost instantaneous pressure impulses. The two other waveforms have a period of 5 ms and a fundamental frequency of 200 Hz. The spread of the spectrum in the lower right plot for levels below around 20 dB is an example of spectral splatter, produced in this case by the abrupt beginning and end of the tone.

Any periodic complex tone is composed of a harmonic series similar to this, although not all the possible harmonics need to be present. In fact, the repetition rate or fundamental frequency of the complex would be the same (although the waveform itself would change) even if the fundamental component were to be removed from the series. For any arbitrary group of harmonics, the fundamental frequency can be taken as the largest number that will divide exactly into the frequencies of each of the harmonics. For example, if harmonics are present with frequencies of 550, 600, 700, and 750 Hz, then the fundamental frequency is 50 Hz, as this is the largest number that will divide exactly into each of the harmonic frequencies (11 times into 550, 12 times into 600, etc.).

Figure 2.14 illustrates how a complex tone can be constructed by adding together pure tones at harmonic frequencies. The complex tone second from the bottom is constructed by adding together four pure tones. The fundamental component (labeled 1) is at the top, and the remaining harmonics (labeled 2–4) have frequencies that are integer multiples of the frequency of the fundamental

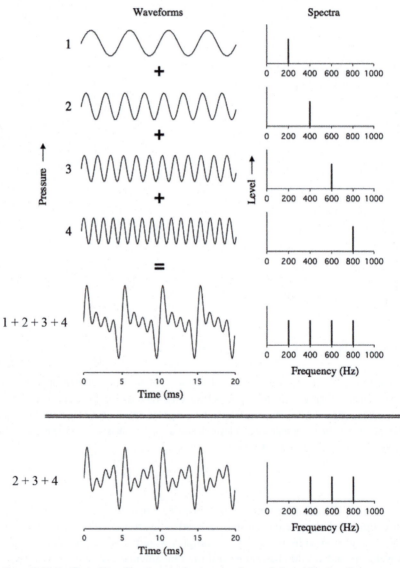

Figure 2.14 An illustration of how a complex tone can be made by adding together pure tones at harmonic frequencies. The bottom panel shows the effect of removing the fundamental component.

(400, 600, and 800 Hz). Note that the repetition rate of the complex waveform (200 Hz) is the same as the repetition rate of the fundamental component. The spectra of the waveforms are shown on the right of the figure. As I said before, the spectrum of a pure tone is a single line. The spectrum of the complex tone at the bottom is simply the sum of the line spectra for each of the pure tones of which it is composed. We see how taking the spectrum of a sound is a convenient way to break a complex sound down into more basic components. We discover in Chapters 4 and 5 how the auditory system uses this technique as a vital first stage in analyzing sounds entering the ear.

Shown at the bottom of Figure 2.14 is the waveform and spectrum produced by adding together the second, third, and fourth harmonics. Although this waveform differs from that directly above it, *the repetition rate is the same*. This illustrates that the fundamental frequency of a complex tone depends on the spacing of the harmonics, not on the frequency of the lowest harmonic present.

It should be noted that the waveforms of the complex tones in Figure 2.14 could be changed by, for example, shifting the waveform of the third harmonic slightly to the right. This action is equivalent to changing the relative phase of the third harmonic: The magnitude spectrum of the complex tone would stay the same. The magnitude spectra given in Figure 2.14 do not unambiguously determine the form of the pressure variations to which they correspond. To form a complete description of the sound, we also need the phase spectrum, which tells us how the different harmonics are aligned in time relative to each other.

2.4.2 Harmonic structure

We come to the question of what differentiates two instruments playing the same musical note or, indeed, two different vowel sounds with the same fundamental frequency. The initial "attack" portion of an instrument's sound is important. However, even if the attack portion is removed along with any other nonperiodic element of the sound, most musical instruments can be distinguished from one another by a trained ear.

Whereas the repetition rate of the pattern of pressure variations determines the pitch of a tone, it is the pattern that is being repeated that characterizes the instrument. This determines the *harmonic structure* and, therefore, the sensation we call *timbre*. (Note that the word timbre, like pitch, refers to the subjective experience, not to the physical characteristics of the sound.) The timbre of a complex tone depends in part on the relative magnitude of the various harmonics of which it is composed. It is this that distinguishes the ethereal purity of a flute, the sound of which is dominated by low harmonics, from the rich tone of a violin, which contains energy across a wide range of harmonics. Instruments that produce intense high-frequency harmonics (e.g., a trumpet) will tend to sound "bright." Instruments that produce intense low-frequency harmonics (e.g., a French horn) will tend to sound "warm" or "dark." These characteristics are evident even if the different instruments are playing the same note. Figure 2.15 shows the waveforms and spectra of two complex tones with the same fundamental frequency but with very different spectra. The tone displayed on the bottom will sound brighter and more "trebly" than the tone displayed on the top, since the magnitudes of the high-frequency harmonics are greater in the former case.

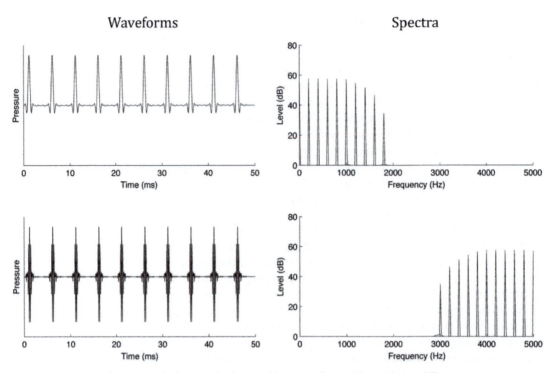

Figure 2.15 Two complex tones with the same fundamental frequency (200 Hz) but with very different spectra.

2.4.3   Noise

A broad definition of *noise* is any unwanted sound. However, in the acoustics lexicon, the word is often used to refer to a sound wave whose pressure varies in a random way over time, and that will be the definition employed here. By "random," I mean that the next pressure variation is not predictable from the one that was just previous. Good examples of noise are radio hiss, the sound of a waterfall, and the sound you make when you go "sssssssssssssss." In our everyday lives, noise is often regarded as an irritating sound, and we try to avoid it when we can. It interferes with our ability to hear sounds that are important to us (e.g., radio hiss interfering with a broadcast). For hearing researchers, however, noise is a most wonderful thing. Many thousands of experiments have been (and are being) designed that use noise as a stimulus.

One property of noise is that it consists of a *continuous* distribution of frequency components. Whereas a complex tone has a series of discrete frequency components (the harmonics), a noise contains every frequency component within a certain range. Wideband *white noise*, for instance, consists of a continuous distribution of frequency components across the entire spectrum. Noises can also contain a more restricted range of frequencies. For example, *low-pass* noise only contains frequency components below a specific frequency. *Band-pass* noise (or *narrowband* noise) contains frequency components between two frequencies: The *bandwidth* of the noise is equal to the difference between these two frequencies.

The waveforms and spectra of three different noises are illustrated in Figure 2.16. The random, nonperiodic nature of the waveforms is clear. The spectra also can be seen to have random fluctuations, although these fluctuations tend to "average out" over time so that the spectrum of a noise with a very long duration is almost smooth. Note that the spectrum of wideband white noise is almost flat, similar to that of an impulse. How can the waveforms of these two sounds be so different when their spectra are the same? The answer relates to *phase*. In an impulse, all the frequency components are aligned so that their peaks sum (see Figure 2.11). At all other times than at this peak, the effect of adding together all these different frequencies is that the waveforms cancel each other out to produce no response. In a noise, the phase relation is random, and the result is

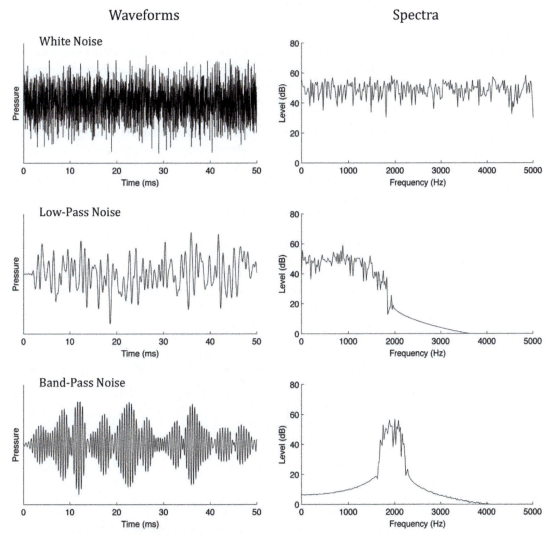

Figure 2.16 The waveforms and spectra of three different noises.

a continuous, random waveform, even though the magnitude spectrum is the same as that for an impulse.

It is sometimes convenient to specify the level of a noise in terms of its spectral density. The *spectrum level* of a noise is the intensity per 1-Hz-wide frequency band expressed in decibels (relative to the reference intensity of 10^{-12} W/m^2). If a noise has a bandwidth of 100 Hz and a spectrum level of 30 dB, then the overall level of the noise is 50 dB SPL. This is true because the spectrum level specifies the level per 1-Hz band, and there are 100 of these in our 100-Hz band of noise. An increase in intensity by a factor of 100 corresponds to an increase in level of 20 dB, so the total level becomes 30 + 20 = 50 dB SPL.

2.5   MODULATED WAVEFORMS

2.5.1   Amplitude modulation

Imagine that you are playing a pure tone over your stereo and you vary the volume control on your amplifier up and down so that the overall level of the tone fluctuates. The sound you would create in this circumstance would be *amplitude modulated*. The original tone is called the *carrier*, and the slow up and down fluctuations are called the *modulator*. It is convenient to distinguish the rapid pressure variations of the carrier from the slower changes in the peak amplitude of these fluctuations caused by the modulator. These two aspects of a signal are sometimes referred to as *temporal fine structure* and *envelope*, respectively (Figure 2.17). Amplitude modulation refers to variations in the envelope of a sound.

Amplitude modulation can be produced by *multiplying* the carrier waveform with the modulator waveform. If the carrier is a pure tone and the modulator is a pure tone, the equation for the modulated waveform is

$$x(t) = A\{1 + m\sin(2\pi f_m t)\} \sin(2\pi f_c t), \tag{2.4}$$

where $x(t)$ is the pressure variation over time t, A is the peak amplitude (or pressure) of the carrier, m is the modulation depth, f_m is the modulation

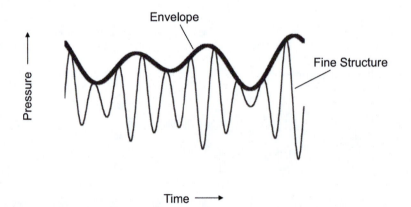

Figure 2.17 A segment of a sound waveform illustrating the temporal fine structure (thin line) and the envelope (thick line).

frequency, and f_c is the frequency of the carrier. (The phases of the modulator and the carrier have been omitted.) Modulation depth usually varies from 0 (no modulation; the equation becomes the same as Equation 2.1) to 1 (100% modulation, where the envelope amplitude goes down to zero). Note that the constant 1 has been added to the sinusoidal modulator. It is added so that the modulator always has a positive amplitude, as long as the modulation depth is no greater than 1. Because the modulator is a pure tone, this equation is an example of *sinusoidal amplitude modulation*.

The top panel of Figure 2.18 shows a 1000-Hz pure tone that has been 100% sinusoidally amplitude modulated, with a modulation frequency of 200 Hz. Modulating a waveform introduces changes to the spectrum, specifically, *spectral sidebands*. For a sinusoidally amplitude-modulated pure tone, there are three components in the spectrum with frequencies equal to $f_c - f_m$, f_c, and $f_c + f_m$ ($f_c - f_m$ and $f_c + f_m$ are the sidebands). In the example in Figure 2.18, the sidebands have frequencies of 800 and 1200 Hz. For 100% modulation, each sideband has a level 6 dB below the level of the carrier. If the depth of modulation is less, the levels of the sidebands are reduced. Note that when the carrier frequency is an integer multiple of the modulation frequency, the effect of the modulation is to produce a three-harmonic complex tone with a fundamental frequency equal to the modulator frequency.

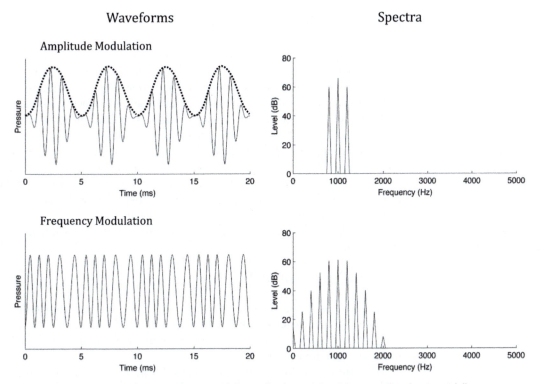

Figure 2.18 The waveforms and spectra of a sinusoidally amplitude-modulated (top panel) and a sinusoidally frequency-modulated (bottom panel) pure tone. In each case, the carrier frequency is 1000 Hz and the modulation frequency is 200 Hz. The envelope of the amplitude-modulated signal is shown by the dotted line.

Amplitude modulation does not require three components. Any two pure tones added together will produce a waveform whose envelope fluctuates at a rate equal to the difference in frequency between the tones. For example, if one tone has a frequency of 2050 Hz and the other has a frequency of 2075 Hz, the envelope will fluctuate at a rate of 25 Hz. These amplitude modulations occur because the frequency difference between the tones means that the phases of the two waveforms drift relative to one another. At regular intervals, the peaks in the fine structure of the tones combine (0 phase difference), producing a maximum in the envelope. Between the envelope maxima, there is a time when a peak in the fine structure of one waveform matches a trough in the other waveform (phase difference of π) and cancellation occurs, producing a minimum in the envelope. We can sometimes hear these amplitude modulations as *beats* (a "fluttering" sensation). I tune my guitar by listening to the beating between the two strings I am comparing. If the rate of amplitude modulation is low, then I know that the strings are almost in tune (the fundamental frequencies of the strings are close to each other so that the difference between them, and hence the rate of amplitude modulation, is small).

Sinusoidal amplitude modulation and the beats produced by the interaction of two tones are just specific examples of simple amplitude modulation. A complex sound wave can have a complex pattern of envelope fluctuations, and in some cases, these envelope fluctuations help us to identify the sound.

2.5.2   Frequency modulation

Whereas amplitude modulation refers to variations in the amplitude of a sound, *frequency modulation* refers to variations in the frequency of a sound. In music, rapid variations in frequency are known as *vibrato*. The sirens used by police cars and ambulances are good examples of frequency modulation. Frequency modulation is also found in speech. Speech contains variations in fundamental frequency over time, and in the frequencies of spectral features over time.

Just as in amplitude modulation, in frequency modulation we can distinguish the carrier, which is the original waveform, from the modulator, which is the waveform that describes the variation in frequency over time. For instance, if the carrier is sinusoidally frequency-modulated, the frequency of the carrier will vary up and down in the pattern of a sine wave or pure tone.

This is the equation for sinusoidal frequency modulation applied to a pure-tone carrier:

$$x(t) = A\sin\left\{2\pi f_c t + \beta\sin\left(2\pi f_m t\right)\right\}, \tag{2.5}$$

where $x(t)$ is the pressure variation over time t, A is the peak amplitude (or pressure), f_c is the frequency of the carrier, β is the modulation index (equal to $\Delta f / f_m$ where Δf is the frequency excursion from the carrier frequency), and f_m is the modulation frequency.

The bottom panel of Figure 2.18 shows the waveform and spectrum of a 1000-Hz pure tone that has been sinusoidally frequency-modulated at a modulation frequency of 200 Hz. One might imagine, because the instantaneous frequency of the waveform varies continuously from moment to moment, that the spectrum would have a more continuous distribution of frequency components. However, this waveform can be produced by adding together a set of sinusoids with discrete frequencies. Sinusoidal frequency modulation consists of more frequency components than sinusoidal amplitude modulation, all spaced at f_m. However, if β is small, the same three components found in sinusoidal amplitude modulation dominate, albeit with different *phases*.

2.6 SUMMARY

From the start of my research career, it took a long time to become comfortable with concepts such as spectrum and phase. The more time I spent playing with sounds and examining their spectra and waveforms, the more natural it became. In some ways, understanding the fundamentals of hearing is much more involved than understanding the fundamentals of vision because the basic visual representation involves features (light, dark, color) in *space*. This is much easier to grasp than the idea of features in the *spectrum*, but unfortunately we have to be able to master this idea if we are to understand how the ear works. Use this chapter partly for reference – to return to when you need reminding of some particular property of sound or of the meaning of a technical term.

1   Sound is composed of *pressure variations* in some medium (e.g., the air). These pressure variations spread outward from the sound source at the speed of sound for that medium.

2   A *pure tone* is a sound with a sinusoidal variation in pressure over time. The *frequency* of a pure tone is determined by the number of alternating peaks and troughs in the sound wave that occur in a given time. The *period* of a pure tone is the time between successive peaks, and the *wavelength* of a pure tone is the distance between successive peaks.

3   The magnitude of a sound wave can be described in terms of its *pressure*, its *intensity* (the square of pressure), or in logarithmic units called *decibels*. A constant change in decibels corresponds to a constant multiplication of sound intensity.

4   Any sound wave can be made by adding together pure tones of different amplitudes, frequencies, and phases. A plot of the *spectrum* of a sound shows the levels of the pure-tone components as a function of frequency. The *spectrogram* of a sound shows the short-term spectrum of a sound as a function of time. Because of the time-frequency trade-off, increasing the resolution in the time domain decreases the resolution in the frequency domain, and vice versa.

5   Periodic *complex tones* have waveforms that repeat over time. The spectra of these sounds have a number of pure-tone components (*harmonics*), with frequencies equal to *integer multiples* of the repetition rate, or *fundamental frequency*.

6   A *noise* sound has random variations in pressure over time. The spectrum of a noise has a continuous distribution of frequency components.

7   *Amplitude modulation* is a variation in the amplitude *envelope* of a sound over time. *Frequency modulation* is a variation in the frequency of a sound over time. Both these manipulations have effects on the spectrum and create a number of additional frequency components.

2.7   READING

Some of the introductory hearing texts provide a good overview of physical acoustics. In particular:

Yost, W.A. (2006). *Fundamentals of hearing: An introduction* (5th ed.). New York: Academic Press.

For more specialist coverage, I recommend:

Everest, F. A., & Pohlmann, K. C. (2014). *The master handbook of acoustics* (6th ed.). New York: McGraw-Hill.
Rossing, T. D., Moore, F. R., & Wheeler, P. A. (2002). *The science of sound* (3rd ed.). San Francisco: Addison-Wesley.

For a mathematical description of sounds and the spectrum:

Hartmann, W.M. (1998). *Signals, sound, and sensation.* New York: Springer-Verlag.

3 PRODUCTION, PROPAGATION, AND PROCESSING

Chapter 2 describes the basic nature of sound and introduces several different sound waves, including pure tones, complex tones, and noise, which are examples of the idealized sound waves that hearing researchers might synthesize in the laboratory. Chapter 3 begins by examining sound production in the real world and includes a discussion of how objects vibrate to produce sound waves in air. The chapter will also consider how sound spreads out, or propagates, from the sound source and how it interacts with other objects in the environment. Finally, this brief introduction to physical acoustics concludes by considering some ways in which sounds, or electronic representations of sounds, can be manipulated to change their characteristics.

3.1 SOUND SOURCES AND RESONANCE

3.1.1 Sound sources

A sound source is an object or an event that produces pressure fluctuations. Most sound sources are located at (or, at least, around) a discrete point in space rather than spread over a wide area or volume. Pressure fluctuations do not occur spontaneously; they require a source of *energy*. We slam a door and the energy of the collision is dissipated, mostly as heat, but partly as sound: The door vibrates to produce sound waves in the air that we can hear. Similarly, a musical instrument does not produce sound on its own; it requires someone to blow, pluck, scrape, or strike the instrument (or to turn on the power in the case of electronic instruments). To offer a more extreme example, a firework explodes in the air, liberates the chemical energy of the gunpowder, and causes a brief but dramatic increase in pressure that may be heard several miles away. For a firework, the explosion of the gunpowder and resulting pressure change in the air is pretty much the end of the story in terms of sound production. For most sound sources, however, the input of energy is just the beginning, because the material that is excited will usually produce a characteristic pattern of oscillation that will determine the sound waves that are produced in the air.

3.1.2 Resonance

Many objects and structures that we encounter in our everyday lives have a *natural frequency* of vibration, also called a *resonant frequency*. A drinking glass, for instance, when struck, may vibrate at a high frequency and produce a "ringing" sound. What causes these oscillations? When an elastic material (glass is technically elastic) is bent out of shape, parts of the material are stretched or compressed. There is, therefore, a force that acts to restore the original shape. When a diver jumps off the diving board, the board tries to spring back to its original shape. However, as it springs back, it overshoots and bends in the opposite direction. In this way, the diving board oscillates back and forth until it comes to rest in its original shape. The frequency of the vibration is determined by the stiffness of the material and by the mass of the material. Stiff, light objects (e.g., a drinking glass) vibrate rapidly and produce high-frequency sound waves. Compliant and heavy objects (e.g., the diving board) vibrate slowly and produce low-frequency sound waves. The standard model for vibrations such as these is a mass attached to a spring that is fixed at the other end. When the mass is pulled away from its resting point and then released, it will oscillate back and forth with a resonant frequency determined by the stiffness of the spring and by the mass (see Figure 3.1). Elasticity (represented by the spring) and inertia (represented by the mass) are the two requirements for a resonant system.

Of course, these oscillations cannot go on forever. There is clearly a difference between a wine glass held lightly by the stem, which may ring for some time after being struck, and a wine glass held by the rim, which will produce only a brief sound. The difference is a consequence of *damping*. If the oscillatory motion is fairly frictionless, it will continue for some time before the energy of vibration is dissipated, mainly as heat in the material. On the other hand, if there is a great deal of friction (*resistance* to the motion), then the oscillation will be brief, and the energy of vibration will dissipate very quickly as heat. That is what happens when the vibration of the glass is damped by touching the rim with a hand, thereby suppressing the oscillations (Figure 3.2).

Most objects have complex structures and, therefore, have complex patterns of vibration with perhaps several different resonant frequencies. Most are quite heavily damped, so, for instance, if we tap a wooden table, it does not usually continue to vibrate for several seconds. However, even if the vibrations are fairly brief, almost every solid object has some sort of characteristic resonance. We can hear the difference between the sound produced by tapping a table and tapping a windowpane, and this is because of the different ways these objects vibrate.

Resonance does not just account for the sounds that an object makes when it is given an impulsive excitation, such as a tap from a finger. An object will respond to the vibrations of the materials with which it is in contact, and these include the air. If an object has a pronounced resonant frequency with little damping, it is also highly tuned to that frequency. If the object receives excitation from a source that is vibrating at the resonant frequency of the object, then the object will vibrate strongly. This is how professional singers can sometimes break a glass with their voice – by producing an intense tone at the resonant frequency of the glass (although this is far from easy and usually requires amplification to reach the necessary sound levels). It is like pushing someone on a swing. If you push at just the right time – that is, if the frequency of your pushes is equal to the frequency of oscillation of the swing – then the swing will go higher and higher. Similarly, if you hold a spring attached to mass and move your hand up and down at the resonant frequency of the system, then the oscillations of the

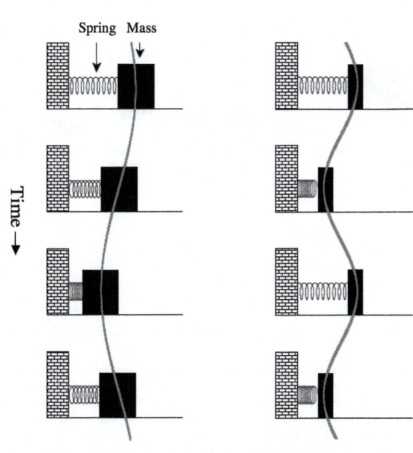

Figure 3.1 The oscillation of a mass attached to a spring that is fixed at the other end. The sinusoidal motion of the mass is indicated by the gray lines. The rate of oscillation is inversely proportional to the square root of the mass (and directly proportional to the square root of the stiffness of the spring) so that if the mass is reduced by a factor of four, the frequency of oscillation doubles (compare left and right illustrations).

mass will build and become quite strong. If you move your hand up and down at a rate lower or higher than the resonant frequency, then the oscillations will be much weaker. In general, if the frequency of excitation is different from the resonant frequency, then the object will vibrate less strongly.

Damped objects have broader patterns of resonance than objects with little damping and, hence, do not respond as strongly to one particular frequency. Large amounts of damping lead to a very broad response that is biased toward low frequencies. In general, damped objects are *less highly tuned* than objects with little damping (compare the spectra in Figure 3.2). This is clarified in the discussion of filters in Section 3.3.1. The important point is that the resonant properties of the object determine its frequency response – that is, how it will modify the spectrum of the oscillations that are passed on to it.

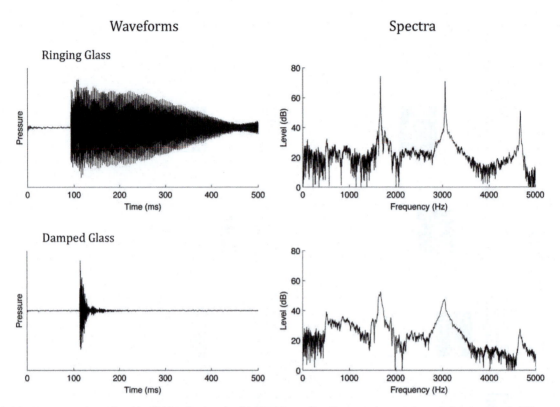

Figure 3.2 Sounds produced by flicking the rim of a drinking glass with a finger. In the upper panel, the glass was held by the stem. In the lower panel, the glass was held by the rim and was therefore highly damped. Shown are the waveforms and the spectra of the sounds produced. The spectra also illustrate the *frequency response* of the drinking glass in each case. Notice that the damped glass is less sharply tuned than the glass without the damping. The latter is highly sensitive to excitation at particular frequencies (1666, 3050, and 4672 Hz).

3.1.3 Enclosed spaces and standing waves

Oscillations can also be produced in an enclosed volume of air. You are probably aware that blowing across the top of a drink bottle can cause the air to resonate and produce a tone. When sound waves are produced in an enclosed space, such as a pipe that is closed at both ends, regions of condensation and rarefaction are reflected back and forth. For a pipe, the fundamental frequency of oscillation is determined by its length, simply because the time taken by the pressure variations to move from one end of the pipe to the other (at the speed of sound) is dependent on its length. When the wavelength of the sound wave is such that the reflected sound wave is in *phase* with the outgoing wave, then the reflected wave and the outgoing wave will combine to produce a large response. In a closed pipe, this will happen when the wavelength of the sound is twice the length of the pipe, so a peak in pressure at one end will be in *phase* with the previous peak that has traveled up and down the pipe. If one end of the pipe is open (like the bottle), however, the sound reaching the open end experiences a *phase reversal* (so

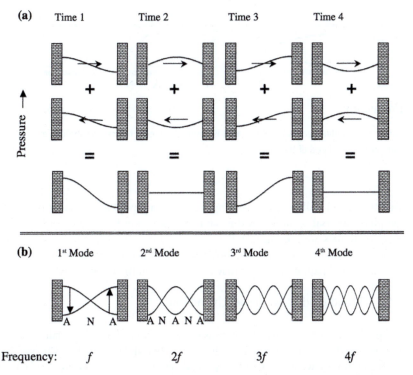

Figure 3.3 Standing waves between two boundaries. (a) The pressure variations for four successive time frames for a pure tone with a wavelength twice the distance between the two boundaries. In the top panel, the sound wave travels left to right; in the middle panel, the sound wave travels right to left. The *addition* of these two components creates a standing wave whose pressure varies according to the bottom panel. (b) The two lines in each plot represent the maximum positive and negative pressure variations for the pure tone from (a) and for pure tones with frequencies that are integer multiples of this fundamental component. The standing waves of the four modes of oscillation have places where the pressure does not vary (nodes, N) and places where the pressure variation is maximal (antinodes, A).

a condensation is reflected back as a rarefaction). This means that for a pipe open at one end, the wavelength of the fundamental resonance is four times the length of the pipe. In general, however, long pipes have lower resonant frequencies than short pipes.

The actual pressure variations in the space will be a combination of all the sound waves as they are reflected back and forth. The combination of sound waves at a resonant frequency moving in opposite directions as they bounce between two boundaries (such as the ends of a closed pipe) creates *standing waves* (Figure 3.3). The space between boundaries contains places where the pressure does not change, called *nodes*, and places where the pressure variations are maximal, called *antinodes*. In addition to the fundamental frequency, the air in a pipe will also resonate at frequencies that are *harmonically related* to the fundamental. As long as the length of the pipe is an integer multiple of half the wavelength of the sound,

Frequency: f   3f   5f

Figure 3.4 Standing waves for a pipe that is open at one end. Notice that there is always a node at the open end of the pipe.

then the sound will set up a standing wave. For a pipe that is open at one end, the phase reversal complicates this, and only odd-numbered (first, third, fifth, etc.) harmonics are present (see Figure 3.4). More complex volumes of air are associated with more complex resonant properties because of the many different reflections and path lengths that may occur between the boundaries.

3.1.4   Sound production in speech and music

The production of both speech and music involves complex and specially evolved and designed structures. Speech production is described in detail in Chapter 11. In this section, I want to provide a general overview and stress the similarities between the way our vocal apparatus works and the way many musical instruments work.

Speech is produced when air is forced from the lungs (source of excitation) past the vocal folds, causing them to vibrate. This action produces a sequence of pressure pulses that can be described as a complex tone with a rich set of harmonics. The sound emanating from the vocal folds is then modified by cavities in the throat and mouth. The vocal tract behaves like a pipe that is open at one end (see Section 3.1.3); the open end in this case is between the lips. The vocal tract has a number of resonances (roughly corresponding to odd-numbered harmonics of the fundamental resonant frequency), and this produces peaks in the spectrum called *formants*. Formants are numbered (F1, F2, F3, etc.) in order of frequency. We can change these resonant frequencies by changing the shape of the vocal tract (mainly by moving the tongue), which enables us to produce the sounds associated with different vowels. In essence, speech production involves a source of periodic pressure fluctuations (the vocal folds) and a resonant structure (the vocal tract; see Figure 3.5).

Tonal musical instruments also have some apparatus that produces oscillations at particular frequencies. These are usually highly tuned resonant systems. Some instruments use strings that vibrate when they are plucked (e.g., guitar), struck (e.g., piano), or scraped with a bow (e.g., violin). The frequency of vibration is inversely proportional to the length of the string: The longer the string, the lower the frequency. You can double the frequency that is produced by halving the length of the string. Like the mass-spring system described in Section 3.1.2, the frequency of vibration of a string is also dependent on the mass of the string (the greater the mass, the lower the frequency). That is why the strings

Figure 3.5 Sound production in speech. The spectrum of the complex tone produced by the vibration of the vocal folds (left) is modified by resonances in the vocal tract (center) to produce the output spectrum associated with a particular vowel sound (right). The spectrum shows three broad peaks corresponding to the first, second, and third formants.

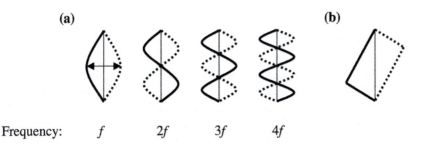

Figure 3.6 The first four modes of vibration of a string that is fixed at both ends (a). The frequency of vibration of the string in each case is equal to 1, 2, 3, and 4 times the fundamental frequency (f). The actual vibration of the string (e.g., b) will be a combination of the individual modes, resulting in a complex tone with a series of harmonics.

on guitars that produce low notes are thicker than the strings that produce high notes. Finally, the frequency is dependent on the tension in the string (the more tension in the string, the higher the frequency). Stringed instruments can be tuned by altering the tension in the string. A vibrating string produces *overtones* at harmonic frequencies (see Figure 3.6), as well as at the fundamental frequency of vibration, so the overall pattern of vibration can be described as a harmonic complex tone.

Instruments can also use vibrating columns of air to produce sound. Wind instruments (flute, saxophone, trumpet, etc.) work in this way. As discussed in Section 3.1.3, the fundamental frequency of vibration is inversely related to the length of the column of air, and there will also be overtones at harmonic frequencies. The length of the air column can be continuously varied (as in the trombone) or modified in jumps (as in the trumpet, tuba, etc.). The effective length of the column can also be changed by opening or closing holes along its length (as in the flute, oboe, etc.). The column of air is excited by forcing air through a specially shaped opening at one end of the pipe, by forcing air past a vibrating reed, or by using the lips as a vibrating source. Brass instruments use the lips as a vibrating source, and the musician can alter the frequency produced by controlling the lip tension. For brass and wind instruments, the resonance of the column of air supports and controls the vibration frequency of the source.

The waveforms and spectra of several musical instruments are shown in Figure 3.7. Like vowel sounds, the sounds made by tonal musical instruments are complex tones with a set of harmonics. Vowel sounds are produced by the combination of a vibrating source (the vocal folds) and resonances in the vocal tract. In the same way, musical instruments often contain a vibrating source (which may be a highly tuned resonator such as a string under tension) and a broadly tuned resonator that modifies the spectrum of the sound (see Figure 3.8). For stringed instruments, the resonator is the body of the instrument. For wind instruments, the resonator is usually the pipe itself, which can have many different shapes leading to different spectral characteristics. It should not be a surprise to discover that the characteristics of the resonator partly determine the characteristic sound of an instrument. Just as vowel sounds can be differentiated in terms of the spectral pattern of the harmonics, so can different musical instruments be characterized by their spectra.

3.2 PROPAGATION

Sound waves from a source often reach us directly with little modification except for a reduction in level. For example, we may be listening to a person standing in front of us. The speech sounds leaving the speaker's mouth are not greatly modified as they pass through the air to our ears. In particular, the frequency composition of the sound waves is little affected by the journey. In some cases, however, the sound waves reaching our ears may not be the same as the sound waves that were produced by the sound source. This is especially likely if the sound waves do not reach us directly but interact with objects in the course of their journey. Such interactions can produce large modifications to the characteristics of the sounds we hear. For instance, if we are listening to someone speak from a different room in the house, the person's voice appears quite different than if the person is in front of us. This section describes some of the ways in which sounds can be modified as they travel from the source to the listener.

3.2.1 The inverse square law

Sound propagates through air in three dimensions. Imagine a sound source radiating sound in all directions, in what is known as the free field (i.e., in an open volume of air). Because the intensity of the sound wave depends on the area through which it is transmitted (intensity equals power divided by area), the intensity of the sound will depend on how far away you are from the source. Specifically, the intensity will vary according to an inverse square law. If you are a certain distance from the source, the power will be spread over a sphere centered on the source. The farther you are from the source, the larger the area of the sphere. Because the area of a sphere is proportional to the radius squared, the intensity of the sound decreases by the square of the distance from the source. The inverse square law means that there is a 6-dB reduction in sound level for every doubling in the distance from the source (6 dB is a factor of four in intensity). Although sound

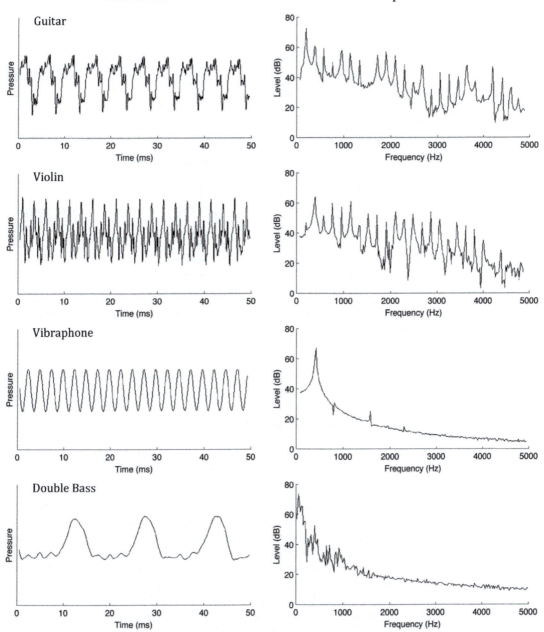

Figure 3.7 The waveforms and spectra of some familiar musical instruments. The guitar and the violin have the same fundamental frequency, but the guitar has a more dominant fundamental component or first harmonic (see first peaks in the respective spectra on the right). Notice that the fundamental (with a period of about 5 ms) is more visible in the waveform for the guitar. The vibraphone has a higher fundamental frequency, and almost all the energy is in the first harmonic. The double base has a much lower fundamental frequency, and the harmonics are clustered in the lower part of the spectrum.

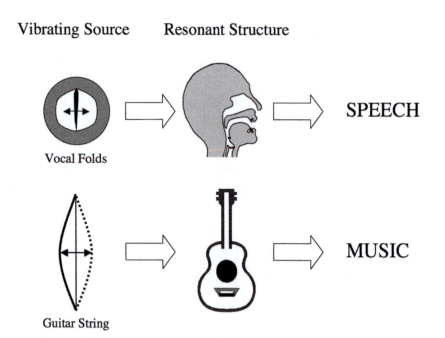

Figure 3.8 Similarities in the production of sound by the vocal apparatus and by a musical instrument.

sources in the real world, such as a loudspeaker or a human voice, are often directional to a certain extent, the inverse square law still applies.

3.2.2 Reflection and reverberation

When sound waves meet a hard boundary (e.g., the wall of a room), they will be reflected. We sometimes hear these reflections as *echoes*. Sound is reflected when the medium carrying the sound waves has a different *impedance* than the medium it encounters. Impedance is a measure of how much a medium resists being moved. Stiff and dense materials have high impedances. The greater the difference between the impedances of the two media, the more sound energy is reflected. When sound waves in a low-impedance medium such as air meet a high-impedance medium such as a wall, much of the energy in the sound wave is reflected back because air is not very efficient at moving a wall. It is similar to throwing a tennis ball against a wall. The tennis ball will bounce back off the wall rather than donating all its energy to the forward motion of the wall.

Sound waves will be reflected off the boundary at an angle depending on the angle of arrival or *incidence*. This is illustrated by the arrows in Figure 3.9. If the sound hits the boundary head on, then it will be reflected straight back toward the source. The angle of reflection is equal to the angle of incidence, just as it is for light waves. Another way to think about this is to imagine throwing a ball at a wall at different angles. The relation between the angle of incidence and the angle at which the ball bounces back is the same for the ball as it is for sound. The sound waves propagate from the boundary *as* if they originate from a *sound image*,

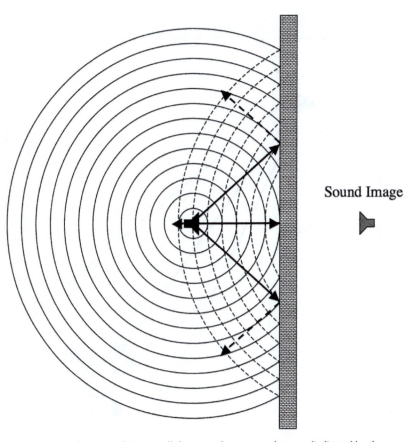

Sound Image

Figure 3.9 Sound waves radiating in all directions from a sound source (indicated by the black loudspeaker symbol) and being reflected from a hard boundary. The continuous lines represent peaks in the direct sound waves. Dashed lines represent peaks in the reflected waves. The arrows show the directions of propagation of the sound waves. The reflected sound waves propagate as if they originated from a *sound image* (indicated by the gray loudspeaker symbol) located the same distance behind the boundary as the sound source is in front of it.

which is behind the boundary – and the same distance from the boundary – as the sound source. It is like looking at yourself in a mirror, when your reflection appears the same distance behind the mirror as you are in front of it.

Now imagine that you are listening to a sound source in an enclosed space, for example, a room in a house. Sound will be reflected off the walls at different angles (see Figure 3.10), and these reflections will themselves be reflected and so on. The end result is a complex mixture of echoes called *reverberation*. Rooms with very reflective walls (e.g., a tiled bathroom) will produce reverberation with a high level. Very large spaces (e.g., a cathedral) will produce very long reverberation times.

As described in Section 3.1.3, enclosed spaces also have resonant properties. The reflections of the sound waves bounce between the walls and may interfere

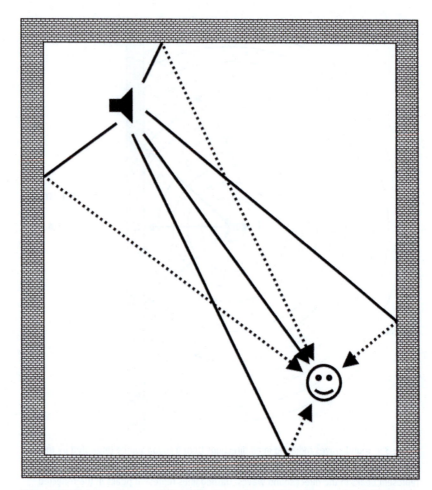

Figure 3.10 The arrows represent the paths of sound waves from a source (top left) to a listener (bottom right). The continuous lines show direct sound; the dotted lines show reflections off the boundaries of a room. The figure shows only the first reflections. In a real room, the reflections will also produce reflections and so on. Since the path lengths are longer, the reflections take longer to arrive at the listener than the direct sound.

constructively to produce peaks at particular frequencies dependent on the dimensions of the room. Standing waves may be set up for these frequencies, and there may be places in the room where the pressure variations are minimal (nodes) and places where the pressure variations are maximal (antinodes). Larger spaces have lower resonant frequencies, and in general, the size of rooms is such that resonance is only significant for frequencies less than a few hundred hertz.

3.2.3   Transmission and absorption

Part of the sound energy that is not reflected by an object may be transmitted through the object. The incident waves produce vibrations in the object that are passed on to the air, or to other materials in contact with the object. However, much of the energy that is not reflected may be *absorbed* by the object. The acoustic energy is converted into thermal energy (heat). This is partly because the energy of the sound wave is transferred to the vibration of the object, which will dissipate as heat due to friction in the material (damping). Wood paneling over a cavity, which is sometimes used as a sound absorber in rooms, has a low resonant frequency and, therefore, absorbs low frequencies better than high frequencies. The interaction of the sound wave with the surface of the material can also cause a loss of acoustic energy. It is in this manner that porous absorbers such as carpets and curtains work. The interaction of the moving air molecules and the fibers in the material produces frictional heat, which dissipates the energy of the sound wave. Porous absorbers are most effective at high frequencies. It is actually quite difficult to insulate rooms from very low frequencies. Even professional soundproof booths can be breached by low rumbles from building work.

3.2.4 Diffraction

Finally, sound bends or *diffracts* around the edge of an object. Diffraction occurs because the pressure variations in the sound wave passing the edge interact with the air that is behind the object. The amount of diffraction of a component depends on its frequency: Low-frequency components diffract more than high-frequency components, so the effect of diffraction can be a reduction in the high-frequency composition of the sound. Two examples are shown in Figure 3.11. You may have seen a similar effect produced when waves from the sea bend around the end of a harbor wall. Sound will also diffract around (and be reflected and absorbed by) isolated objects. If the object is much smaller than the wavelength of the sound wave, then the sound wave will pass the object almost unaffected (you can think of this as maximum diffraction). If the object is larger than the wavelength, then much of the sound energy will be reflected back from, or be absorbed by, the object, and the sound will diffract much less around it. As a result, the object will cast a *sound shadow* behind it, where no sound will be heard. Diffraction is important in hearing because if a low-frequency component is coming from the right, say, it will diffract around the head to reach the left ear. For high-frequency components, the head casts a sound shadow. This has implications for our ability to determine from which direction a sound originates (see Chapter 9).

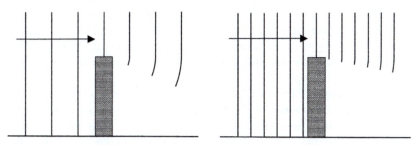

Figure 3.11 Low-frequency sound waves (left) and high-frequency sound waves (right) diffracting around a boundary.

3.3 SIGNAL PROCESSING

A *signal* can be defined as anything that serves to communicate *information*. Sound waves can be signals, as can electric potential variations in electronic circuits, as can the sequences of ones and zeros that are used to store information on a computer or smartphone. In acoustics, we usually think of signals in terms of sound waves, or in terms of their analog, or digital, electronic representations. So when we talk about signal *processing*, we are talking about using a device to modify the sound wave or its representation in some way.

3.3.1 Filters

In general, a *filter* is any device that alters the relative magnitudes or phases of the frequency components in a sound or signal. For example, the bass and treble controls on an amplifier act as *low-pass* and *high-pass* filters, respectively. A low-pass filter allows low frequencies through and reduces or *attenuates* high frequencies. A high-pass filter allows high frequencies through and attenuates low frequencies. A low-pass or high-pass filter can be specified in terms of its *cutoff frequency*. In a low-pass filter, frequency components above the cutoff frequency are attenuated. In a high-pass filter, frequency components below the cutoff frequency are attenuated.

Another way to alter the relative magnitudes of the frequency components in a sound, and hence change the spectrum of a sound, is to use a *band-pass* filter. Band-pass filters only let through a limited range of frequency components, called the *passband* of the filter. A band-pass filter can be characterized by a *center frequency*, which is the frequency to which it is most sensitive (usually near the midpoint of the range of frequencies it lets through), and by a *bandwidth*, which is the size of the frequency range it lets through without significant attenuation. Some of the resonators described in Section 3.1 act as band-pass filters. For instance, the resonances in the vocal tract that produce formants are band-pass filters, with center frequencies equal to the formant frequencies. There are also *band-stop* (or *band-reject*) filters, which are like the opposite of band-pass filters. Band-stop filters attenuate a range of frequencies and let through frequencies lower and higher than this range.

Filters are often described by means of a graph in the frequency domain that shows which of the frequency components in the input sound are attenuated and which are passed unaffected. Figure 3.12 shows the spectral characteristics of a low-pass, a band-pass, and a high-pass filter. The y-axis gives the output level with respect to the input level. In the case of the low-pass filter, this diagram shows that the higher the frequency of the input component above the passband of the filter, the greater the attenuation and, hence, the lower the output level with respect to the input level.

The top panel of Figure 3.13 shows the waveform and spectrum of a complex tone. In the lower two panels, the waveforms and spectra are shown for the same complex tone passed through two band-pass filters with different center frequencies. Note that the repetition rate of the waveform does not change; this is determined by the spacing of the harmonics. The figure shows how filters may

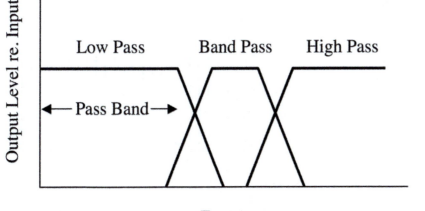

Figure 3.12 The attenuation characteristics of three different filters. The passband is the range of frequencies that are let through with little attenuation, shown here for a low-pass filter.

be used to radically alter the spectra of complex stimuli. Similarly, the low-pass and band-pass noises in Figure 2.16 were produced by passing the wideband noise through low-pass and band-pass filters, respectively.

Filters can be used for modifying sounds in a large variety of applications. Although the discussion here has focused on relatively simple filters, theoretically a filter can have just about any pattern of attenuation with respect to frequency. Filters can also take many different physical forms. There are "analog" electronic filters, which modify the sequence of electric potentials applied to the input. There are digital filters, which use software to modify the sequence of ones and zeros in a digital representation of a signal. There are also resonant physical objects that behave as filters – such as the vocal tract or a musical instrument (see Section 3.1.4).

3.3.2 Quantifying filter characteristics

Figure 3.14 shows the spectral characteristics of a band-pass filter. Here, the output level is plotted in decibels. From this figure, we can deduce that a 200-Hz pure tone, passed through this filter, would be reduced in level by approximately 24 dB. Even the best analog electronic filters cannot totally remove frequency components outside their passbands, although the further the frequency of the component from the passband of the filter, the more its intensity will be attenuated. A filter is said to have *skirts* that determine the attenuation for frequency components outside the passband. The slope of the skirts is usually given in decibels per octave. An octave is equal to a doubling in frequency. If a filter has a passband between 600 and 800 Hz and skirts with a slope of 50 dB per octave, then the level of a pure tone with a frequency of 1600 Hz will be reduced, or attenuated, by 50 dB, compared to a tone with a frequency within the passband

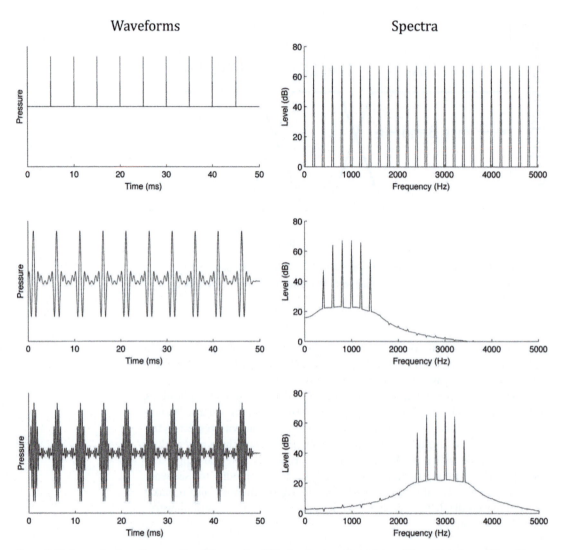

Figure 3.13 A complex tone (top panel) and the results of filtering the tone through two different band-pass filters (lower two panels). (Note that the pressure scale is much larger for the top waveform.)

of the filter. For a more concrete example, imagine that we have an electronic filter with these same characteristics. We plug a microphone into the filter, connect the output of the filter to an amplifier, and connect a pair of loudspeakers to the amplifier. We whistle (almost a pure tone) at 800 Hz into the microphone, and the sound of the whistle comes through loud and clear from the speakers. But if we whistle at 1600 Hz, the speakers will make a much quieter sound, since 50-dB attenuation is a substantial reduction in intensity (by a factor of 100,000).

It is also difficult to construct a filter with a completely flat passband. Therefore, we need a convention for specifying the frequencies where the passband ends so that we can then determine the bandwidth. We define the cutoff frequencies of the passband, arbitrarily, as the frequencies at which the filter attenuation

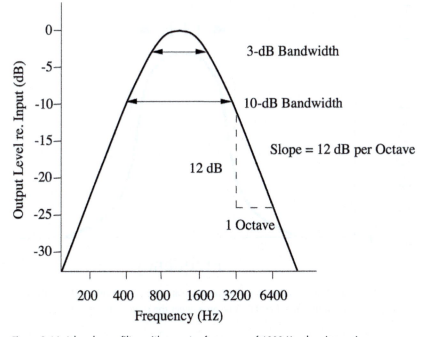

Figure 3.14 A band-pass filter with a center frequency of 1000 Hz, showing various measures of the filter's characteristics. Notice that the frequency axis is *logarithmic*. In other words, a constant distance along the axis represents a constant *multiplication* of frequency.

is a certain number of decibels greater than the minimum attenuation in the passband (i.e., the "peak" of the filter). Two values for this attenuation are often used, 3 dB and 10 dB, which define the *3-dB bandwidth* and the *10-dB bandwidth*, respectively. The 3-dB and 10-dB bandwidths for a representative band-pass filter are shown in Figure 3.14. Another measure you may come across is the Q of a filter. The Q is simply the center frequency of the filter divided by the bandwidth. For example, if the center frequency is 1000 Hz and the 10-dB bandwidth is 400 Hz, then the Q_{10} is 2.5. Note that the higher the Q value, the more sharply tuned is the filter, with respect to its center frequency.

A final measure, beloved of many psychoacousticians, is the *equivalent rectangular bandwidth*, or ERB. The ERB of a filter is the bandwidth of a rectangular filter with the same peak output (minimum attenuation) and the same area (in units of intensity) as that filter (see Figure 3.15). An advantage of the ERB measure is that if you have a stimulus with a flat spectrum (e.g., a white noise) and you know the spectrum level of the stimulus and the ERB and minimum attenuation of the filter, then you automatically know the level of the stimulus at the output of the filter. Assume, for the moment, that the attenuation at the peak of the filter is zero. Because the area under a rectangular filter with a width equal to the ERB is equal to the area under the original filter, the intensity passed is simply the spectral density (intensity per hertz) of the stimulus times the ERB. In decibel units, this means that the output level is equal to the spectrum level plus $10 \times \log_{10}$ (ERB).

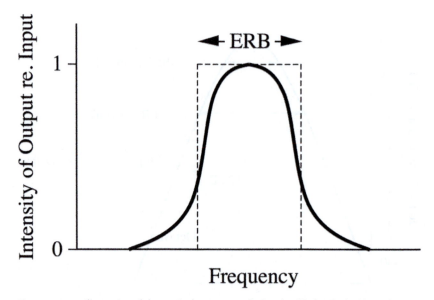

Figure 3.15 An illustration of the equivalent rectangular bandwidth (ERB) of a filter. The rectangular filter (dashed line) has the same area under the curve as the original filter (solid line).

The relation between the 3-dB bandwidth, the 10-dB bandwidth, and the ERB depends on the shape of the filter. Imagine a filter with a very pointy tip going down for 5 dB before ballooning out into very shallow skirts. This filter could have a very small 3-dB bandwidth but a large 10-dB bandwidth and a large ERB. On the other hand, for a perfectly rectangular filter with a flat passband and infinitely steep skirts, the 3-dB bandwidth, the 10-dB bandwidth, and the ERB are the same. We discover in Chapter 4 that the ear behaves somewhat like a bank of band-pass filters. The shape of these filters is such that the 10-dB bandwidth is about twice the 3-dB bandwidth, and the 3-dB bandwidth is a little smaller than the ERB.

3.3.3   The impulse response

An impulse sound is a sudden (theoretically, instantaneous) increase and decrease in pressure. Figure 3.16 shows the waveform and spectrum of an impulse. What happens if we pass an impulse through a filter? The spectrum of the impulse will change, but what about the waveform? The waveform produced when an impulse is passed through a filter is called the *impulse response* of the filter. The *spectrum* of the impulse response is identical to the attenuation characteristics of the filter. This must be the case when you think about it. An impulse has a flat spectrum, so when the impulse is passed through a band-pass filter, the resulting spectrum matches the attenuation characteristics of the filter. The impulse response is the waveform corresponding to that spectrum. Ergo, the spectrum of the impulse response is the same as the filter attenuation characteristics.

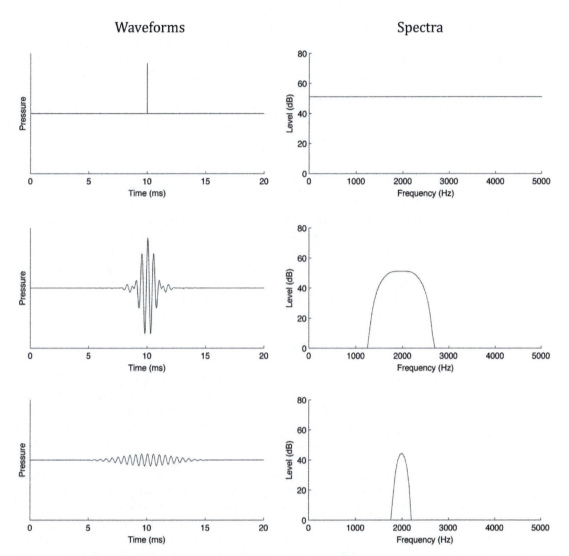

Figure 3.16 The top panel shows the waveform and spectrum for an impulse. The lower two panels show the waveforms (impulse responses) and spectra of the impulse after it has been passed through two different band-pass filters. The spectral characteristics of the filters are the same as the spectra of the impulse responses. Brief impulse responses are associated with broad filters. Sharp filters are associated with long impulse responses.

The impulse response of a band-pass filter usually looks like a pure tone whose envelope rises and decays. The narrower the bandwidth of the filter (in hertz) and the steeper the skirts of the filter, the greater is the duration of the impulse response (see Figure 3.16). One way of thinking about the impulse response is to consider that a filter with an infinitesimally small bandwidth and infinitely steep skirts has the same spectrum as a pure tone. A pure-tone frequency component is continuous, and so is the impulse response of the filter. The wider the bandwidth of the filter, on the other hand, the broader the spectrum of the impulse response. Hence, the impulse response will tend to be briefer. This is just another expression of the time-frequency trade-off rule discussed in Section 2.3.2. A consequence of this is that if *any* signal is terminated abruptly, a sharply tuned filter may continue to respond, or ring, for a significant time afterward, and the more sharply tuned the filter, the longer it will ring. Because filters modify the spectral characteristics of sounds, they *necessarily* modify the temporal characteristics: The spectrum determines the temporal waveform, and vice versa.

We encountered these ideas in the discussion of resonance in Section 3.1.2. A wine glass held by the stem behaves as a sharply tuned filter and will ring for a considerable time if struck. The ringing of the glass is the impulse response of the glass. A glass held by the rim, and hence damped, behaves as a more broadly tuned filter and has a brief impulse response (see Figure 3.2). It is possible to think about many familiar objects in this way. For instance, the springs and dampers (or shock absorbers) on a car act as a type of low-pass filter, filtering out the small bumps and imperfections on the road to produce a smooth ride. When you jump onto the hood, the car will bounce on its springs. This movement is the impulse response of the car. Most physical structures will have some sort of response when struck (and these vibrations will often produce a sound), so filters and impulse responses are all around us.

3.3.4 Linearity and nonlinearity

A *linear system* is a signal processor in which the output is a *constant multiple* of the input, irrespective of the level of the input. For example, if an amplifier is linear, the output voltage will always be a constant multiple of the input voltage. It follows from this property that if two sounds are added together and passed through a linear system, the output is *identical* to what would be produced if the two sounds were passed through the system independently then added together afterward. The upper left graph of Figure 3.17 shows plots of output magnitude against input magnitude for two linear systems. The units on the axes here could be either pressure, for an acoustic device, or electric potential, for an electronic device. The input-output relationship for a linear system is always a straight line passing through the origin on these coordinates. The upper right graph of Figure 3.17 shows these functions plotted in decibel units. Note that the plots are straight lines with a slope of one (an increase in the input by a certain number of decibels causes the same decibel increase in the output). Linear systems always produce an output level in decibels that is the input level in decibels plus a constant number. This is because a constant increment in decibels corresponds to a *constant multiplication*.

The output of a *nonlinear* system is *not* a constant multiple of the input. If two sounds are added together and passed through a nonlinear system, the output is *different* to what would be produced if the two sounds were passed through the system independently then added together afterward. The input-output functions for two nonlinear systems are shown in the lower left graph of Figure 3.17. In both cases, the ratio of output to input magnitude varies with input magnitude; therefore, the functions are not straight lines. The lower right graph of Figure 3.17 shows these functions plotted in decibel units. Anything other than a straight line with a slope of one indicates nonlinearity on these axes.

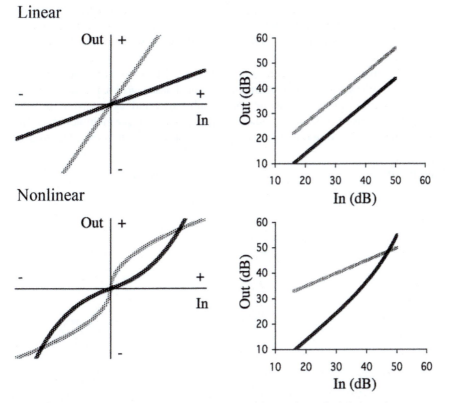

Figure 3.17 Examples of linear and nonlinear functions. The graphs on the left show the input and output of the device plotted in units of pressure or electric potential. The axes cross at the origin (0,0). The graphs on the right show the same functions on a dB/dB scale.

The distinction between linear and nonlinear is extremely important. It is possible to specify the characteristics of any linear system simply by measuring its output in response to pure tones. For example, we might determine the shape of a filter by measuring the attenuation of a pure tone as a function of frequency. From this measurement, we can predict the output of the filter in response to any complex sound. If the filter were nonlinear, however, this prediction would not be valid. Characterizing nonlinear systems can be very difficult indeed. It is often assumed for practical purposes that the ear is linear, although substantial nonlinearities do exist and are the bane – and also sometimes the livelihood – of auditory scientists everywhere.

3.3.5 Distortion

An important characteristic of linear systems is that they never introduce frequency components in the output that were not present in the input. A linear filter might change the relative *magnitude* of frequency components, but it never puts in components that were not there originally. If only 200-Hz and 400-Hz components were present at the input, you will not get a 600-Hz component in the output. Nonlinear systems, on the other hand, introduce frequency components in the output that were not present in the input. These extra frequency components are sometimes called *distortion products*. Distortion is a characteristic of systems that are nonlinear.

Two types of distortion are commonly heard when tones are played through nonlinear systems; *harmonic distortion* and *intermodulation distortion*. Harmonic distortion is a very prominent symptom of nonlinearity and, as the name suggests, only consists of components whose frequencies are integer multiples of the frequency of the component, or components, present in the input. Figure 3.18

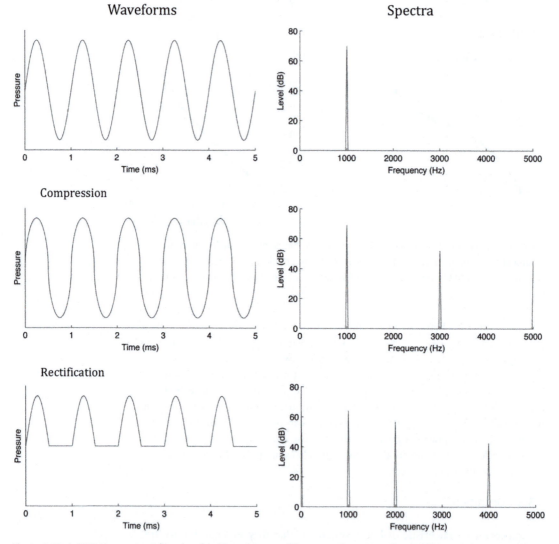

Figure 3.18 A 1000-Hz pure tone (top panel) subjected to two different nonlinearities. The middle panel shows the effect of taking the square root of the waveform in the top panel (using the absolute value then taking the negative of the square root when the pressure is negative). The bottom panel shows the effects of half-wave rectification, in which negative pressures are set to zero.

shows the effects of two types of nonlinearity on the waveform and spectrum of a 1000-Hz pure tone. The harmonic distortion products can be seen to the right of the spectrum. Harmonic distortion does not necessarily sound disagreeable because a complex tone, for example, will produce harmonic distortion with frequencies in the same harmonic series.

When different frequency components are added together and are put through a linear system, they don't interact in any way. The output of the system in response to a complex sound is identical to the sum of the outputs produced by each of the individual frequency components. When these same frequency components are put through a nonlinear system, they interact, generating harmonic and intermodulation distortion products. Intermodulation distortion arises from the interaction of two or more frequency components. One example of intermodulation distortion is the difference tone. The frequency of the difference tone is simply the difference between the frequencies of the two components in the input. For example, if one component has a frequency of 775 Hz and the other has a frequency of 975 Hz, then a difference tone with a frequency of 200 Hz might be generated. Figure 3.19 shows the effects of processing a signal composed of two pure tones with the same two nonlinear functions used in Figure 3.18. The dramatic effects of intermodulation distortion on the spectrum can be seen clearly.

A typical source of distortion is "peak clipping," which occurs when electronic amplifiers are overloaded. Peak clipping can result from a component of the amplifier being unable to produce more than a certain electric potential output. When the input electric potential is too high, it will produce a sound wave with its peaks sheared off. If a pure tone is put through a peak-clipping amplifier, harmonic distortion will be produced with frequencies equal to three, five, seven, nine, and so on times the frequency of the pure tone. If several tones with different fundamental frequencies and a large number of harmonics are put in, the result can be quite complex, to say the least. Not only is harmonic distortion generated from each frequency component present in the mix, but also intermodulation distortion is generated from the interaction of all the different frequency components. The end result can be very messy and leads to the noisiness associated with distorted electric guitars, especially when the musician is playing chords (several notes at once).

Compressors, which are frequently used in recording studios (and found in most modern hearing aids; see Section 13.6), are nonlinear. The purpose of a compressor is to reduce the range of sound intensities in the output. This can be useful for controlling the intensity of instruments in a recording, particularly for vocals, which tend to stray somewhat. An extreme form of limiting is the peak clipping described above. In this case, the intensity of the input is limited by simply preventing the electric potential from exceeding (or being less than) a certain value. Compressors can be a much gentler way of limiting sound. Low intensities may be boosted, and high intensities reduced slightly. However, compressors are nonlinear and will produce a certain amount of distortion, although the effects may be barely noticeable. This is particularly the case if the compression is slow acting so that the amplitude manipulation does not change instantaneously with variations in signal amplitude but varies slowly over time. A high-level sound may be gradually turned down, for example. In this case, very

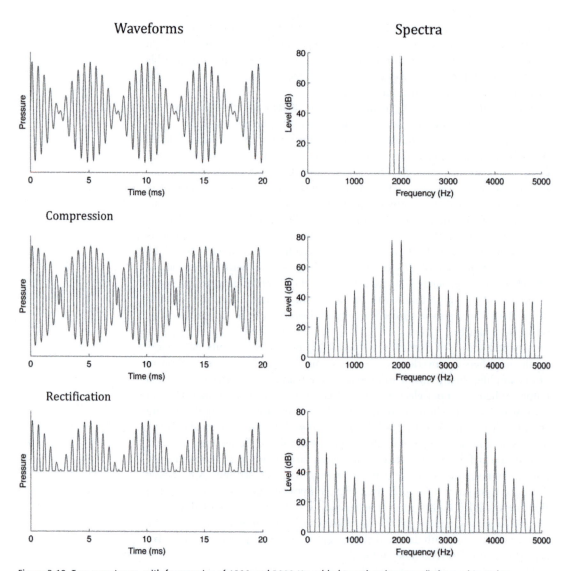

Figure 3.19 Two pure tones, with frequencies of 1800 and 2000 Hz, added together (top panel) then subjected to a square-root compressive nonlinearity (middle panel) or half-wave rectification (bottom panel).

little distortion will be produced, because the fine structure of the sound will be almost unaffected.

3.4 DIGITAL SIGNALS

With the advent of cheap, high-quality equipment for recording and manipulating sounds using computers and other digital devices, background knowledge of the nature of digital recordings is extremely useful. Anyone considering a career in auditory science should at least familiarize themselves with the basics of digital techniques. All the sounds that I use in my experiments are generated on my computer. Because of this, I have almost unlimited control over the characteristics of the sounds that I present to my grateful participants.

3.4.1 Waves to numbers

When an analog recording of a sound is made, the pressure of the sound wave is converted into electric potential by means of a microphone. This electric potential is then converted into a magnetic field on a tape. There is a one-to-one relation between the pressure of the sound wave, the electric potential coming out of the microphone, and the magnetic field on the tape. A continuously changing pressure will be represented as a continuously changing magnetic field. In a digital recording, the electric potential at the output of the microphone is recorded by converting the voltage into a series of numbers. These numbers are stored in the form of a binary digital code: a sequence of ones and zeros. The continuously varying pressure of the sound wave has been translated into a recording that effectively consists of a sequence with only two values: one and zero. A single one or zero is called a *bit*: The smallest unit of memory on a computer.

The device that produces the digital code that corresponds to the voltage is called an *analog to digital converter* (ADC). If the *sampling rate* is 44100 Hz – the standard for compact disc recordings – then the ADC converts the voltage into a number 44,100 times every second. For a stereo recording, 88,200 numbers need to be generated every second. In a 16-bit recording, again, the accepted standard for compact discs, each number is stored in the form of a digital code that consists of 16 ones and zeros (a "16-bit code"). Figure 3.20 shows how a

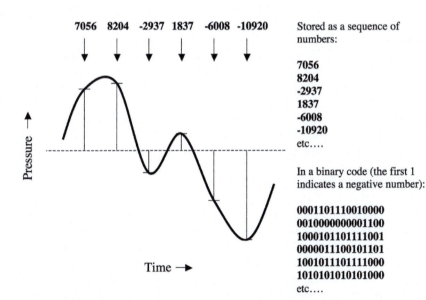

Figure 3.20 An illustration of a how a sound wave can be converted into a sequence of numbers and represented in a binary code.

sound wave can be converted into a series of numbers, represented at the output of the ADC as a 16-bit binary code (bottom right of the figure).

3.4.2   The limits of digital information

Each bit in the 16-bit code can take two possible values (one or zero). One bit can store two different values; two bits can store two times two – that is, four different values (00, 01, 10, 11 gives four possibilities). Sixteen bits can store $2 \times 2 \times 2 \times 2 \times 2 \times 2 \times 2 \times 2 \times 2 \times 2 \times 2 \times 2 \times 2 \times 2 \times 2 \times 2$ ($= 2^{16}$) – that is, 65,536 different values. In practical terms, this code can represent any integer between $-32,767$ and $32,768$ (65,536 different numbers altogether, including zero). The largest rms pressure possible to record with this code is 65,536 times greater than the smallest rms pressure possible to record. The span is called the *dynamic range* of the recording. The dynamic range corresponds to a factor of $65,536 \times 65,536 = 4.29$ billion in units of intensity. The dynamic range is 96 dB for a 16-bit code in units of level. A useful trick when converting from resolution (in bits) to dynamic range (in decibels) is to remember that each extra bit corresponds to a doubling in the range of pressure or electric potential values that can be represented by the digital code. A doubling in pressure corresponds to approximately a 6-dB increase. So we can get the dynamic range of a recording (in decibels) simply by multiplying the number of bits by 6 (e.g., $16 \times 6 = 96$).

Using a 16-bit code for sound pressure, or electric potential, is adequate for most purposes (even though 24-bit resolution is now common in hearing laboratories). Although humans can hear over a dynamic range of 120 dB, a 96-dB range is more than sufficient to give a realistic reproduction. A sound 96 dB above the threshold of hearing is quite loud. The range of intensities in an analog recording is usually much less than 96 dB, because low-intensity inputs are obscured by the tape, or record, hiss. Furthermore, despite the fact that the signal has been chopped up by the sampling process, digital recordings are virtually indistinguishable from the source and are generally more realistic than analog recordings. Why is this? It is because a digital recording can represent *any* frequency component between 0 Hz and half the sampling rate (also called the *nyquist* frequency). You only need two readings (e.g., one in a peak, one in a trough) to specify the frequency of a pure tone. Hence, an ADC with a 44100-Hz sampling rate can record any frequency between 0 and 22050 Hz, which is greater than the highest frequency that humans can perceive.

3.4.3   The benefits of digital processing

Storing information about sound in the digital domain means that almost anything can be done to a recording without adding noise, because the sound is simply a set of numbers. Digital delays, filters, modulation, reverberation, and more can be produced by mathematical manipulation of these numbers. Furthermore, it is possible to *synthesize* highly specific sounds on a computer very easily. First, apply an equation (e.g., the waveform equations in Chapter 2) to a set of time values and generate a set of numbers to represent the pressure variations of the sound wave over time. Second, convert these numbers into *electric potential variations* using the opposite of an ADC, a digital to analog converter

(DAC). Finally, use the electric potential variations to produce sound waves from a loudspeaker or a pair of headphones. Many of the waveforms presented in this book were generated digitally, and the spectra were all determined using a digital analysis. The possibilities are limitless.

3.5 SUMMARY

This chapter addresses a number of different topics that complete a brief introduction to physical acoustics. The discussions serve to emphasize the importance of the spectrum in understanding the ways that sounds are produced, propagated, and modified. Sound sources have particular spectral characteristics determined by their resonant properties; the spectra of sounds can be altered by interactions with objects in the environment; and sounds and their representations can be modified using filters and nonlinear devices that alter their spectra in sometimes dramatic ways. Spectral analysis is vital both for an understanding of the sound waves that reach our ears, and for an understanding of how our ears perceive these sound waves.

1   A sound source is an object or event that produces pressure fluctuations. Many objects have a natural *resonant frequency* and, when struck, will produce sound waves at that frequency. The frequency of vibration is determined by the mass and stiffness of the material. Some sound sources are highly tuned and vibrate for a considerable time after being struck, whereas other sound sources are *damped* and produce brief oscillations.

2   The resonant properties of an object may be quite complex. The properties determine not only the characteristic sound of an object when it is struck but also the way an object reacts to different frequencies of excitation. An object will produce the largest vibration in response to excitation at its resonant frequency.

3   Resonance can also occur in an enclosed volume of air, as a result of reflections within the space. Excitation at a resonant frequency will set up a *standing wave* with places of minimum pressure variation (*nodes*) and places of maximum pressure variation (*antinodes*).

4   The human vocal apparatus and tonal musical instruments contain vibrating sources that produce complex tones. The spectrum of the tone is modified by resonant structures in the vocal tract and in the body of the instrument, respectively.

5   Sound waves propagate through air in three dimensions. Sound intensity decreases with the *square* of the distance from the sound source.

6   When a sound wave meets an object, it may be *reflected* back from the object, be *transmitted* through the object, *diffract* around the object, or be *absorbed* by it (in which case the sound energy is dissipated as frictional heat). The greater the mismatch between the *impedance* of the material and the impedance of

the air, the more sound energy is reflected. The complex combination of reflections in a closed space is called *reverberation*. Low-frequency components diffract farther around objects and are often less easily absorbed by objects.

7   Filters modify the spectrum of a sound or other signal. A low-pass filter allows low frequencies through and reduces or *attenuates* high frequencies. A high-pass filter allows high frequencies through and attenuates low frequencies. Band-pass filters only allow a limited range of frequency components through and attenuate frequencies below and above this range.

8   Modifying the spectrum of a sound modifies the temporal waveform of the sound, and each filter has an associated *impulse response* (the output of the filter in response to an instantaneous click or impulse) that describes these effects. The spectrum of the impulse response is the same as the attenuation characteristics of the filter.

9   In a *linear* system, the output pressure or electric potential is a constant multiple of the input pressure or electric potential (for a given waveform shape). The output only contains frequency components that were present in the input. In a *nonlinear* system, the output pressure or electric potential is not a constant multiple of the input pressure or electric potential. Frequency components are present in the output which were not present in the input. These components are called *distortion products*.

10 A continuous waveform can be converted into a series of binary numbers, which represent pressure or electric potential at discrete points in time. The resulting *digital signal* can represent any component in the original waveform with a frequency up to half the rate at which the readings were taken (the *sampling rate*). Once information about a sound wave is on a computer, just about any manipulation of the information is possible. The digital revolution has vastly enhanced our ability to synthesize and manipulate sounds.

3.6   READING

Good introductions to these topics can be found in:

Everest, F. A., & Pohlmann, K. C. (2014). *The master handbook of acoustics* (6th ed.). New York: McGraw-Hill.
Rossing, T. D., Moore, F. R., & Wheeler, P. A. (2002). *The science of sound* (3rd ed.). San Francisco: Addison-Wesley.

Hartmann provides a detailed analysis of filters, nonlinearity, and digital signals:

Hartmann, W. M. (1998). *Signals, sound, and sensation*. New York: Springer-Verlag.

4 A JOURNEY THROUGH THE AUDITORY SYSTEM

The main function of sensory systems is to get information about the outside world to the brain, where it can be used to build representations of the environment and to help plan future behavior. In hearing, that information is carried by pressure variations in the air (sound waves). In this chapter, we explore how the information in the sound waves is converted (or *transduced*) into a form that can be used by the brain, specifically in the form of electrical activity in nerve cells or *neurons*. Later in the book, we look at how our perceptions relate to the physiological mechanisms. First, however, we must learn something about the biological hardware involved: Where it is, what it looks like, and what it does. Because the left and right ears are roughly mirror images of one another, I will focus on the anatomy of the right ear. It should be remembered that everything is duplicated on the opposite side of the head to produce a pleasing symmetry. Please also note that when specific numbers and dimensions are given, they refer to the *human* auditory system unless otherwise stated.

The human ear is an exquisitely sensitive organ. A low-level 1000-Hz pure tone is audible even when it produces displacements of the eardrum of less than one tenth the width of a hydrogen atom.[1] Natural selection has managed to engineer an instrument of such elegance and sophistication that our best efforts at sound recording and processing seem hopelessly crude in comparison. In the classic film *Fantastic Voyage*, an intrepid group of scientists travels around the blood vessels of a dying man in a miniaturized submarine, passing various organs and sites of interest as they go. In our version of the journey, we will follow a sound wave into the ear where transduction into electrical signals occurs and continue, after transduction, up to the brain. Be prepared, for we shall behold many strange and wondrous things. . . .

4.1 FROM AIR TO EAR

The main anatomical features of the peripheral auditory system are shown in Figure 4.1. The peripheral auditory system is divided into the *outer ear*, *middle ear*, and *inner ear*.

4.1.1 Outer ear

The *pinna* is the external part of the ear – that strangely shaped cartilaginous flap that you hook your sunglasses on. The pinna is the bit that gets cut off when

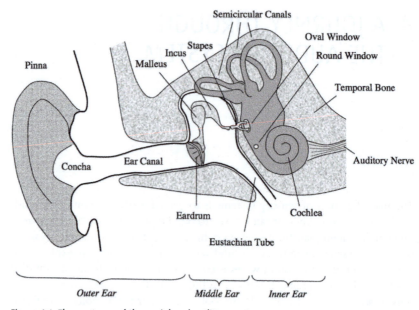

Figure 4.1 The anatomy of the peripheral auditory system.

someone has his or her ear cut off, although the hearing sense is not greatly affected by this amputation. Van Gogh did not make himself deaf in his left ear when he attacked his pinna with a razor in 1888. The pinnae are more important in other animals (bats, dogs, etc.) than they are in humans. Our pinnae are too small and inflexible to be very useful for collecting sound from a particular direction, for example. They do, however, cause spectral modifications (i.e., filtering) to the sound as it enters the ear, and these modifications vary depending on the direction the sound is coming from. The spectral modifications help the auditory system determine the location of a sound source (see Section 9.2.2).

The opening in the pinna, the *concha*, leads to the *ear canal (external auditory meatus)* that is a short and crooked tube ending at the *eardrum (tympanic membrane)*. The tube is about 2.5 cm long and has resonant properties like an organ pipe that is open at one end (see Section 3.1.3). Another way of thinking about this is that the ear canal acts like a broadly tuned band-pass filter. Because of the resonance of the ear canal and the concha, we are more sensitive to sound frequencies between about 1000 and 6000 Hz. The pinna, concha, and ear canal together make up the *outer ear*. The propagation of sound down the ear canal is the last stage in hearing in which sound waves are carried by the air.

4.1.2   Middle ear

The eardrum is a thin, taut, and easily punctured membrane that vibrates in response to pressure changes in the ear canal. On the other side of the eardrum from the ear canal is the *middle ear*. The middle ear is filled with air and is connected to the back of the throat by the *Eustachian tube*. Swallowing or yawning opens this tube to allow the pressure in the middle ear to equalize with the external air pressure. The pressure changes we experience as we climb rapidly in an aircraft, for instance, can create an imbalance between the air pressures on the two sides of the eardrum, causing our ears to "pop." Swallowing helps alleviate this problem.

Although the middle ear is filled with air, the acoustic vibrations are carried from the eardrum to the cochlea (where transduction takes place) by three tiny bones – the smallest in the body – called the *malleus, incus,* and *stapes* (literally, "hammer," "anvil," and "stirrup"). These bones are called, collectively, the *ossicles*. Their job is to transmit the pressure variations in an air-filled compartment (the ear canal) into pressure variations in a water-filled compartment (the *cochlea*) as efficiently as possible. The transmission is not as trivial as it might seem. If you shout from the side of a swimming pool at someone swimming underwater in the pool they will find it hard to hear you. Most of the sound energy will be reflected back from the surface of the pool, because water has a much higher *impedance* than air (see Section 3.2.2). For the same reason, music from your radio sounds much quieter if you dip your head below the surface when you are having a bath. A similar situation would occur if the eardrum were required to transmit vibration directly to the water-filled cochlea. Most of the sound energy would bounce straight back out of the ear, and our hearing sensitivity would be greatly impaired. The bones in the middle ear solve this problem by concentrating the forces produced by the sound waves at the eardrum onto a smaller area (the *oval window* in the cochlea). Because pressure equals force divided by area, the effect of this transformation is to increase the pressure by a factor of about 20. The ossicles also act as a lever system so that large, weak vibrations at the eardrum are converted into smaller, stronger vibrations at the oval window. Finally, the eardrum itself performs a buckling motion that increases the force of the vibrations and decreases the displacement and velocity. The overall effect of all these components is to increase the pressure at the oval window to around 20–30 times that at the eardrum (see Rosowski & Relkin, 2001). The middle ear as a whole acts as an *impedance-matching transformer*.

Attached to the malleus and stapes are small muscles that contract reflexively at high sound levels (above about 75 dB SPL). This increases the stiffness of the chain of ossicles and reduces the magnitude of the vibrations transmitted to the cochlea. The mechanism is most effective at reducing the level of low-frequency sounds (below about 1000 Hz), and hence acts like a high-pass filter. The reflex does not do much to protect the ear against high-frequency sounds, which are often the most damaging. Because the reflex involves neural circuits in the brainstem, the mechanism is also too slow (latency of 60–120 ms) to protect our ears against impulsive sounds, such as gunshots. Instead, the reflex may be useful in reducing the interference produced by intense low-frequency sounds or in reducing the audibility of our own vocalizations (e.g., speech), which mostly reach our ears via the bones in our head.

4.2 THE COCHLEA

So far we have followed the sound waves down the ear canal to the eardrum and through the delicate structures of the middle ear. We now arrive at the cochlea in the inner ear. The cochlea is the most important part of the story because this is where *transduction* occurs. It is here that acoustic vibrations are converted into electrical neural activity. However, the cochlea is much more than a simple microphone that transforms sounds into electrical signals. Structures within the cochlea perform processing on the sound waveform that is of great significance to the way we perceive sounds.

4.2.1   Anatomy

The cochlea is a fluid-filled cavity that is within the same compartment as the semicircular canals that are involved in balance. ("Fluid" here means water with various biologically important chemicals dissolved in it.) The cochlea is a thin tube, about 3.5 cm long, with an average diameter of about 2 mm, although the diameter varies along the length of the cochlea, being greatest at the *base* (near the oval window) and least at the *apex* (the other end of the tube). The cochlea, however, is not a straight tube. The tube has been coiled up to save space. The whole structure forms a spiral, similar to a snail shell, with about two and a half turns from the base to the apex (see Figure 4.1). The cochlea has rigid bony walls. I heard a story of a student who was under the impression that as sound enters the ear, the cochlea stretches out by uncoiling the spiral like the "blow out" horns you find at parties. Note: This does *not* happen.

A cross-section through the middle of the cochlea reveals the structures within the spiral (see Figure 4.2). Notice that the tube is divided along its length by two membranes, *Reissner's membrane* and the *basilar membrane*. This creates three fluid-filled compartments: the *scala vestibuli*, the *scala media*, and the *scala tympani*. The scala vestibuli and the scala tympani are connected by a small opening (the *helicotrema*) between the basilar membrane and the cochlea wall at the apex (see Figure 4.3). The scala media, however, is an entirely separate compartment that contains a different fluid composition (*endolymph*) from that in the other two scalae (*perilymph*). Endolymph has a positive electric potential of about 80 mV, called the *endocochlear potential*, due to a high concentration of positively charged potassium ions. The *stria vascularis* is a structure on the lateral wall of the cochlea

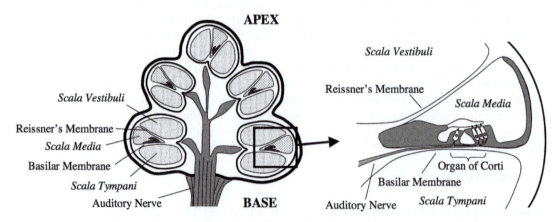

Figure 4.2 Two magnifications of a cross-section of the cochlea. The spiral is viewed from the side, in contrast to the view from above in Figure 4.1.

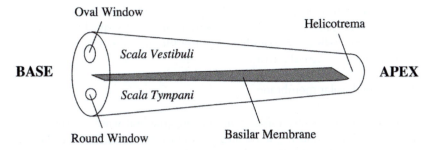

Oval Window

Helicotrema

Scala Vestibuli

BASE **APEX**

Scala Tympani

Round Window Basilar Membrane

Figure 4.3 A highly schematic illustration of the cochlea as it might appear if the spiral were unwound. The vertical dimension is exaggerated relative to the horizontal. Reissner's membrane and the scala media are not illustrated.

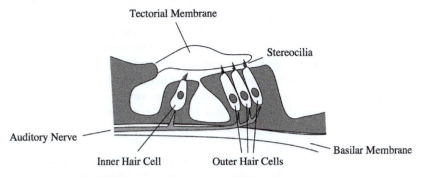

Tectorial Membrane

Stereocilia

Auditory Nerve

Basilar Membrane

Inner Hair Cell Outer Hair Cells

Figure 4.4 The tectorial membrane and the organ of Corti.

that pumps potassium ions into the scala media to maintain the concentration of potassium and hence the positive electric potential. The potassium concentration and endocochlear potential are necessary for the function of the auditory hair cells, as we will discover later.

Figure 4.4 shows a further magnification of a part of the cochlear cross-section shown in Figure 4.2. Above the basilar membrane is a gelatinous structure called the *tectorial membrane*. Just below this, and sitting on top of the basilar membrane, is the *organ of Corti*, which contains rows of *hair cells* and various supporting cells and nerve endings. Cells are the tiny little bags of biochemical machinery, held together by a membrane, that make up most of the human body. Hair cells vary in size, but like most other cells are much too small to see without a microscope, having lengths of about 20 *millionths* of a meter. Hair cells are very specialized types of cells. As their name suggests, they look like they have rows of minute hairs, or more correctly *stereocilia*, sticking out of their tops. However, stereocilia have very little in common with the hairs on our heads. Rather than being protein filaments, stereocilia are extrusions of the cell membrane, rather like the fingers on a rubber glove. In each human cochlea there is one row of *inner hair cells* (closest to the inside of the cochlear spiral) and up to five rows of *outer hair cells*. Along the length of the cochlea there are thought to be about 3,500 inner hair cells and about 12,000 outer hair cells (Møller, 2013). The tallest tips of the stereocilia of the outer hair cells are embedded in the tectorial membrane, whereas the stereocilia of the inner hair cells are not. The outer hair cells change the mechanical properties of the basilar membrane, as described in Chapter 5. The inner hair cells are responsible for converting the vibration of the basilar membrane into electrical activity.

4.2.2   The basilar membrane

Sound enters the cochlea through an opening (the oval window) covered by a membrane. The fluid in the cochlea is almost incompressible, so if the oval window moves in suddenly, due to pressure from the stapes, Reissner's membrane and the basilar membrane are pushed down, and the round window (a second membrane-covered opening at the other side of the base) moves out. It follows that vibration of the stapes leads to vibration of the basilar membrane.

The basilar membrane is very important to mammalian hearing. The basilar membrane *separates out the frequency components* of a sound. At the base of the cochlea, near the oval window, the basilar membrane is narrow and stiff. This area is most sensitive to high frequencies. The other end of the membrane, at the tip or apex of the cochlea, is wide and loose and is most sensitive to low frequencies. (Note that the basilar membrane becomes *wider* as the cochlea becomes *narrower*; see Figure 4.3.) The properties of the membrane vary continuously between these extremes along its length so that each place on the basilar membrane has a particular frequency of sound, or *characteristic frequency*, to which it is most sensitive.

You can understand how this works if you are familiar with stringed musical instruments. The higher the tension in the string, the higher the frequency of the note that is produced: Stiff strings have higher *resonant frequencies* than do loose ones (see Section 3.1.4). Another simple way to understand this mechanism is to imagine a long series of springs, hanging alongside each other from a horizontal wooden rod. Each spring has a mass attached to it. (The basilar membrane is not actually composed of a series of coiled springs: This is just an analogy.) The springs at the left end (corresponding to the base of the cochlea) are very stiff. As we move along, toward the right end of the rod, the springs get looser until, at the end of the rod (corresponding to the apex of the cochlea), the springs are very loose.

If you have played with a spring, you understand some of the properties of these systems. If you attach a mass to the end of a spring, pull it down, and release it, the mass will move up and down at a particular rate, the oscillations slowly dying out over time. The rate of oscillation is the resonant frequency of the system (see Section 3.1.2). If the spring is very stiff, the mass will move up and down rapidly – that is, at a high frequency. If the spring is very loose, the mass will move up and down slowly – that is, at a low frequency. As described in Section 3.1.2, if you hold the end of the spring and move your hand up and down at a rate higher than the resonant frequency, the mass and spring may vibrate a little but not much movement will be obtained. If you move your hand up and down at the resonant frequency, however, then the oscillations will build and build and become much more intense.

Now imagine that the whole rod of masses and springs is moved up and down at a particular rate (this corresponds to stimulating the basilar membrane with a pure tone at a particular frequency). To be accurate, the movement should be sinusoidal. What you would see is that a small group of masses and springs vibrate very strongly over large distances. For these masses and springs, the motion of the rod is close to their resonant frequencies. If the rod is moved up and down at a slower rate, this group of springs would be located nearer to the right (apex) of the rod. If a higher rate is used, springs near the left (base) of the rod would be excited. If you could move the rod up and down at two rates at once (impose lots of high frequency wiggles on a low-frequency up and down movement), a group of springs to the left would respond to the high-frequency movement and a group of springs to the right would respond to the low-frequency movement. We would have effectively *separated out* the two different frequencies.

Unfortunately for us, the basilar membrane and the cochlea as a whole are much more complex than this simple model might suggest. The motion of the membrane is affected by the inertia of the surrounding fluids, resonance in the tectorial membrane, and the stereocilia of the outer hair cells (see Møller, 2013, p. 52). The motion is also affected, crucially, by the mechanical action of the outer hair cells. The outer hair cells enhance the tuning of the basilar membrane by actively influencing the motion of the membrane. We look at this important mechanism in Chapter 5.

Despite the complications, it is fair to say that the basilar membrane behaves like a continuous array of tuned resonators, and this means that it behaves as a *bank of overlapping band-pass filters* (see Figure 4.5). These filters are often called *auditory filters*. Each place on the basilar membrane has a particular characteristic frequency, a bandwidth, and an impulse response. When a complex sound enters the ear, the higher frequency components of the sound excite the basilar membrane toward the base and the lower frequency components excite the basilar membrane toward the apex (Figure 4.6). The mechanical separation of the individual frequency components depends on their frequency separation. In this way, the basilar membrane performs a *spectral analysis* of the incoming sound (see Figure 4.7).

Figure 4.5 A popular model of the cochlea, in which the frequency selectivity of the basilar membrane is represented by an array of overlapping band-pass filters. Each curve shows the relative attenuation characteristics of one auditory filter. The curves to the left show the responses of places near the apex of the cochlea, whereas those to the right show the responses of places near the base. The basilar membrane is effectively a *continuous* array of filters: Many more filters, which are much more tightly spaced, than those in the figure.

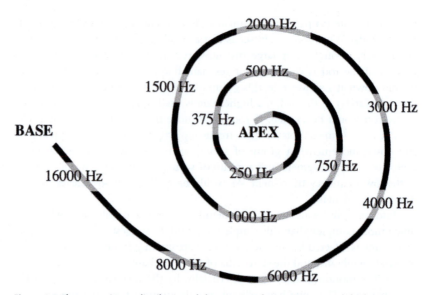

Figure 4.6 The approximate distribution of characteristic frequencies around the human cochlea, with a viewpoint above the spiral.

Figure 4.7 A schematic illustration of how a complex sound waveform (left) is decomposed into its constituent frequency components (right) by the basilar membrane. The approximate locations on the basilar membrane that are vibrating with these patterns are shown in the center.

4.2.2.1 The traveling wave

The basilar membrane in humans and other mammals is a tiny delicate structure (only 0.45 mm at its widest point) hidden within the bony walls of the cochlea. Nevertheless, by careful surgery, physiologists have been able to make direct observations of the motion of the basilar membrane in response to sound. Georg von Békésy was the pioneer of this line of research, observing the motion of the basilar membrane in cochleae isolated from human and animal cadavers. Actually, he observed the motion of silver particles scattered on Reissner's membrane,

but since Reissner's membrane moves with the whole *cochlear partition* (the structures around the scala media, including the basilar membrane and the organ of
Corti), the responses he measured apply to the basilar membrane as well.

Békésy observed that if a pure tone is played to the ear, a characteristic pattern
of vibration is produced on the basilar membrane. If we imagine the cochlea is
stretched out to form a thin, straight tube, the motion of the basilar membrane
looks a bit like a water wave traveling from the base to the apex of the cochlea.
This pattern of vibration is called a *traveling wave*, as illustrated in Figure 4.8. If we
follow the wave from the base to the apex, we can see that it builds up gradually
until it reaches a maximum (at the place on the basilar membrane that resonates
at the frequency of the tone) before diminishing rapidly. Similar to a water wave
on a pond, the traveling wave does not correspond to any movement of material
from base to apex. Rather, the wave is a consequence of each place on the basilar
membrane moving up and down in response to the pure-tone stimulation. It
is important to remember that the frequency of vibration at each place on the
basilar membrane is equal to the frequency of the pure tone.

A common misconception is that the motion of the traveling wave from base
to apex is a result of the pressure variations entering the cochlea at the oval
window (i.e., at the base). This is *not* the case. Sound travels very quickly in the
cochlear fluids, and thus all places on the basilar membrane are stimulated virtually instantaneously when there is a pressure variation at the oval window. The
traveling wave would look the same if sound entered near the apex rather than
the base. The characteristic motion of the traveling wave arises because there is a
progressive *phase delay* from base to apex. That is, the vibration of the membrane
at the apex lags behind that at the base, so that the wave appears to travel from
base to apex.

The peak of the traveling wave traces an outline, or envelope, which shows
the overall region of response on the basilar membrane. Although there is a
peak at one place on the basilar membrane, the region of response covers a fair

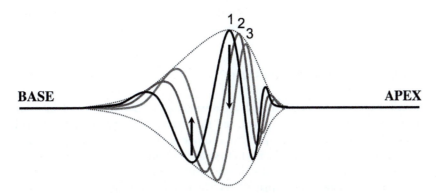

Figure 4.8 Three time frames in the motion of the basilar membrane in response to a pure
tone. The arrows show the direction of motion of the basilar membrane at two places along
its length. The dotted lines show the envelope traced out by the traveling wave (i.e., the
maximum displacement at each place). Compared to the real thing, these plots have been
hugely exaggerated in the vertical direction.

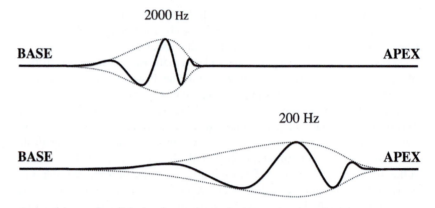

Figure 4.9 A snapshot of the basilar membrane displacement at a single instant, in response to pure tones with two different frequencies. Based on measurements by Békésy (see Békésy, 1960).

proportion of the total length, especially for low-frequency sounds (see Figure 4.9). This is because each place acts as a band-pass filter and responds to a range of frequencies. It is clearly not the case that each place on the basilar membrane responds to one frequency and one frequency only (although the response will be maximal for stimulation at the characteristic frequency). Indeed, in response to very intense low-frequency sounds, every place on the membrane produces a significant vibration, irrespective of characteristic frequency.

4.3 TRANSDUCTION

We have seen that the sound waves entering the ear produce vibrations on the basilar membrane. The different frequencies in the sound wave are separated onto different places on the basilar membrane. This is all a pointless exercise if the ear cannot now tell the brain which parts of the membrane are vibrating and by how much. The ear must convert the mechanical vibrations of the basilar membrane into electrical activity in the auditory nerve. This task is accomplished by the inner hair cells.

4.3.1 How do inner hair cells work?

Recall that on top of each hair cell are rows of stereocilia, which look like tiny hairs. When the basilar membrane and the tectorial membrane move up and down, they also move sideways relative to one another. This "shearing" motion causes the stereocilia on the hair cells to sway from side to side (see Figure 4.10). The movement of the stereocilia is very small (the figures in this section show huge exaggerations of the actual effect). For a sound near the threshold of audibility, the displacement is only 0.3 billionths of a meter. If the stereocilia were the size of the Sears Tower in Chicago, then this would be equivalent to a displacement of the top of the tower by just 5 cm (Dallos, 1996).

The stereocilia are connected to one another by protein filaments called tip links. When the stereocilia are bent toward the scala media (i.e., toward the

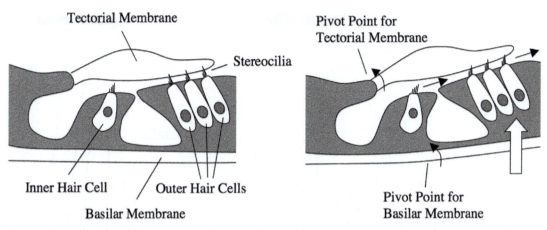

Figure 4.10 An illustration of how displacement of the basilar membrane toward the scala vestibuli (curved arrows) produces a shearing force between the basilar membrane and the tectorial membrane, causing the stereocilia on the hair cells to be bent to the right (straight arrows). Both the basilar membrane and the tectorial membrane pivot about the points shown on the figure. Displacement of the basilar membrane toward the scala tympani produces the opposite effect, causing the stereocilia to be bent to the left (not shown).

outside of the cochlea), the tip links are stretched. The stretching causes them to pull on tiny molecular "trapdoors." These trapdoors block channels in the membranes of the stereocilia (see Figure 4.11). Recall that the endolymph fluid in the scala media is at a positive electric potential of about 80 mV and contains a high concentration of positively charged potassium ions. The inside of the hair cell contains a lower concentration of potassium ions and also has a negative "resting" potential of about −45 mV. Hence, if the channels in the stereocilia are opened up, positively charged potassium ions flow from the endolymph into the hair cell, following both the electrical gradient (positive charge is attracted by negative charge) and the chemical gradient (molecules tend to flow from regions of high concentration to regions of low concentration). This influx of positive charge produces an increase in the electric potential of the cell (the inside of the cell becomes more positively charged). Because the resting electric potential of the inner hair cell is negative relative to the potential of the scala media, the increase in the electric potential of the inner hair cell is called depolarization (the potential between the inner hair cell and the scala media becomes smaller and hence less polarized). Depolarization causes a chemical neurotransmitter (glutamate) to be released into the tiny gap (or synaptic cleft) between the hair cell and the neuron in the auditory nerve (see Figure 4.12). When the neurotransmitter arrives at the neuron, it causes electrical activity in the neuron (neural spikes, see Section 4.4.1). When the stereocilia are bent in the opposite direction (i.e., toward the center of the cochlea), the tip links slacken, the trapdoors in the channels close, fewer potassium ions enter the hair cell, the electric potential of the cell decreases, and the release of neurotransmitter is reduced. Hence, the response differs depending on the time point in each cycle of basilar membrane vibration.

It is important to note that this mechanism is not like an on-off switch; it is sensitive to the intensity of the sound waves entering the ear. The larger the

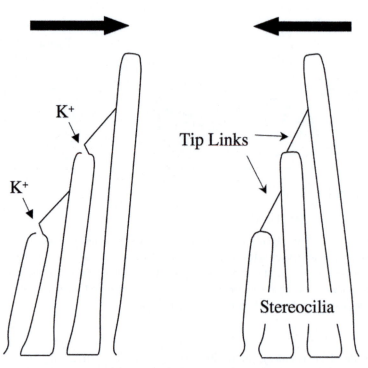

Figure 4.11 How movement of the stereocilia causes an electrical change in the hair cell. When the stereocilia are bent to the right (toward the scala media), the tip links are stretched and ion channels are opened. Positively charged potassium ions (K+) enter the cell, causing the interior of the cell to become more positive (depolarization). When the stereocilia are bent in the opposite direction, the tip links slacken and the channels close.

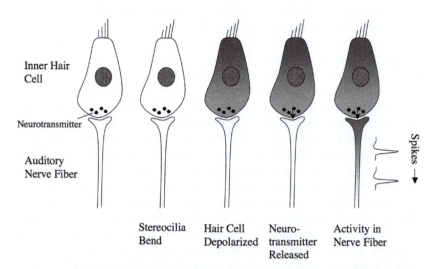

Figure 4.12 The main stages in the transduction process. Time proceeds from left to right.

movement of the basilar membrane, the greater the deflection of the stereocilia, the more channels are open, the greater the electrical change in the hair cell, the more neurotransmitter is released, and the greater is the resulting activity in the auditory nerve. Also, because each inner hair cell is at a particular place along the basilar membrane, it shares the frequency tuning characteristics of that place. So hair cells near the base respond best to high frequencies and hair cells near the apex respond best to low frequencies.

The outer hair cells are activated in the same way as the inner hair cells – by the bending of the stereocilia and the opening of ion channels. However, it is thought that the resulting changes in the electric potential of the cell produce changes in the *cell length*, thus allowing the outer hair cell to affect the motion of the basilar membrane (see Section 5.2.5). Outer hair cells are *not* thought to be involved, to any significant extent, in the transmission of information about basilar membrane motion to the auditory nerve and to the brain.

4.4 THE AUDITORY NERVE

4.4.1 Neurons

One problem with being a large organism is the difficulty of passing messages between different parts of the body. The solution for all large animals is a nervous system. A nervous system is composed of cells called *neurons*. Neurons are responsible for rapid communication between sensory cells, muscle cells, and the brain. The human brain contains over a hundred billion neurons, each of which has hundreds of connections to other neurons. The neurons and connections form a processing network of enormous complexity and power that enables us to think, feel, and interact with the environment.

A neuron is composed of four main structures: the *dendrites*, the *soma* (or cell body), the *axon*, and the *terminal buttons*. Figure 4.13 shows the structures of two typical neurons. Broadly speaking, the dendrites *receive* information (from sensory cells like the inner hair cells or from other neurons), the soma *integrates* the information, the axon *carries* the information, and the terminal buttons *pass the information on*, usually to the dendrites of another neuron. A connection between a terminal button and a dendrite, or between a sensory cell and a dendrite, is called a *synapse*. In the brain, the dendrites of a single neuron usually form synapses with the terminal buttons of hundreds of other neurons.

Axons can be quite long (almost a *meter* in length for some "motor" neurons involved in the control of muscles). They carry information in the form of electrical impulses called *action potentials* or *spikes*. The magnitude of every spike is the same (about 100 mV) so that information is carried by the *firing rate* (number of spikes per second) or *pattern* of spikes, not by variations in the magnitude of the electric potential for each spike. Spikes travel along the axon at speeds of up to 120 m/s. The change in electric potential caused by the arrival of a spike at the terminal button triggers the release of neurotransmitter that diffuses across the synaptic cleft between the two cells. The more spikes that arrive, the more neurotransmitter is released. If neurotransmitter is detected by the receiving neuron, then this may trigger – or inhibit – the production of spikes in that neuron. In other words, the connection between two neurons can be *excitatory* or *inhibitory*.

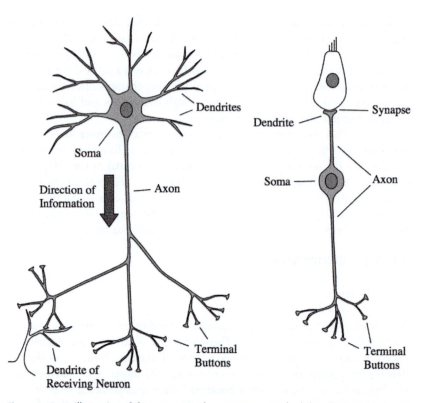

Figure 4.13 An illustration of the structures of two neurons. On the left is the type of neuron one might find in the brain, with many dendrites and terminal buttons. At the bottom left, the terminal buttons of the neuron are shown forming synapses with the dendrites of another neuron. On the right is a sensory neuron with one dendrite (in this case, one of the neurons from the auditory nerve). The lengths of the axons, and the complexity of the branching dendrites and axons, have been reduced for illustrative purposes.

Hence, neural communication is *electrochemical* in nature: Electrical impulses in one neuron lead to the release of a chemical that influences the production of electrical impulses in another neuron. The complex interplay between excitation and inhibition, multiplied several hundred billion times, is how your brain works.

4.4.2   Activity in the auditory nerve

The *auditory*, or *cochlear*, *nerve* is a bundle of axons or nerve fibers that are connected to (*synapse with*) the hair cells. The auditory nerve and the vestibular nerve (which carries information about balance from the vestibular system) together constitute the eighth cranial nerve (also called the *vestibulocochlear* nerve). In total, there are about 30,000 neurons in the human auditory nerve. The majority of nerve fibers connect to the inner hair cells. Each inner hair cell is contacted by the dendrites of approximately 10–20 auditory nerve fibers. Because each inner hair cell is attached to a specific place on the basilar membrane, information about the vibration of the basilar membrane at *each place* in the cochlea is carried by 10–20 neurons in the auditory nerve. In addition, because each place in the cochlea is most sensitive to a particular characteristic frequency, each neuron in the auditory nerve is also most sensitive to a particular characteristic frequency. Figure 4.14 shows the tuning properties of neurons with a range of character- istic frequencies. The figure shows that each neuron becomes progressively less sensitive as the frequency of stimulation is moved away from the characteristic frequency, as does the place on the basilar membrane to which the neuron is connected. Tuning curves are essentially inverted versions of the filter shapes we discussed in this chapter (compare with Figure 4.5).

In terms of spatial layout, the characteristic frequencies of the nerve fibers increase from the center to the periphery of the auditory nerve. Those fibers near the center of the auditory nerve bundle originate in the apex of the cochlea and have low characteristic frequencies, and those fibers near the periphery of the auditory nerve originate in the base of the cochlea and have high character- istic frequencies (Figure 4.2 illustrates the pattern of innervation). The spatial frequency map in the cochlea is preserved as a spatial frequency map in the auditory nerve. The organization of frequency in terms of place is called *tonotopic*

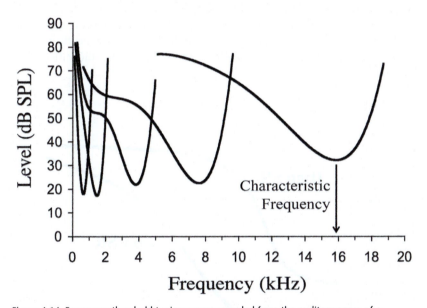

Figure 4.14 Frequency threshold tuning curves recorded from the auditory nerve of a chinchilla. Each curve shows the level of a pure tone required to produce a just measur- able increase in the firing rate of a neuron, as a function of the frequency of the tone. Low levels on each curve indicate that the neuron is sensitive to that frequency, and high levels indicate that the neuron is insensitive to that frequency (since the level has to be high to cause the neuron to respond). The tip of the curve (highest sensitivity) indicates the char- acteristic frequency of the neuron. Five curves are shown, illustrating the tuning properties of five neurons with characteristic frequencies ranging from about 500 Hz to about 16 kHz. The curves are smoothed representations of recordings made by Ruggero and Semple (see Ruggero, 1992).

organization and is preserved right up to the primary auditory cortex, part of the cerebral cortex of the brain. There are cross-connections between neurons in the brain with different characteristic frequencies. However, to a first approximation, the place on the basilar membrane that is excited determines the place in the auditory nerve that is excited, which (via several other staging posts in the neural auditory pathway) determines the places on the auditory cortex that are excited.

In quiet, most fibers in the auditory nerve show a background level of firing called *spontaneous activity*. Most fibers (perhaps 90%) have high spontaneous rates, producing about 60 spikes per second when no sound is present. These fibers tend to be quite sensitive and show an increase in firing rate in response to a low stimulus level. The remaining fibers have low spontaneous rates of less than about 10 spikes per second. These fibers tend to be less sensitive. The difference in sensitivity may be related to the location of the synapse with the inner hair cell. High spontaneous rate fibers synapse on the side of the cell closest to the outer hair cells. Low spontaneous rate fibers synapse on the opposite side of the cell (see Sewell, 1996). When stimulated with a pure tone at its character-istic frequency, a neuron will increase its firing rate as the level of the tone is increased, up to a certain maximum firing rate, at which point the response is *saturated*: Further increases in level will have no effect on the firing rate. A plot of firing rate against sound level is called a *rate-level function*. In general, high sponta-neous rate fibers have steeper rate-level functions that saturate at a much lower level (no more than about 60 dB SPL in the mid-frequency region) than do low spontaneous rate fibers (see Figure 4.15). An explanation for this difference is provided in Section 5.3.2.

Figure 4.15 An illustration of the relation between the level of a tone at characteristic frequency and firing rate (in spikes per second), for auditory nerve fibers with high (high SR) and low (low SR) spontaneous firing rates. Based (loosely) on recordings from the cat by Sachs and Abbas (1974).

Figure 4.16 A simulation of the activity over time of a high spontaneous rate auditory nerve fiber in response to a 100-ms pure tone (the time course of the tone is indicated by the thick black line above the plot). The vertical scale represents the mean firing rate over 1,500 repetitions of the stimulus.

Auditory nerve fibers also show a characteristic change in firing rate with time from the onset of a sound. When a sound is turned on, the fibers produce a peak of activity (the onset response) that declines with time. In addition, when the sound is turned off, the activity in a neuron falls below its spontaneous activity for 100 milliseconds or so (see Figure 4.16). The neuron is said to be *adapted*. Adaptation may be the result of the depletion of neurotransmitter from the inner hair cell. When a sound is first turned on, the inner hair cell releases a lot of neurotransmitter and produces a large response in the auditory nerve fiber. However, the hair cell then has to replenish its supply of neurotransmitter, and until it has a chance to do so (when the sound is turned off), it cannot respond as strongly as it did at the sound's onset.

4.4.3 Place coding

The firing rate of a neuron in the auditory nerve is determined by the magnitude of basilar membrane vibration at the place to which it is connected. In addition, increases in sound level increase the firing rate of the neuron (up to the saturation level). Therefore, one way in which the auditory system represents the spectrum of a sound is in terms of the firing rates of different neurons in the auditory nerve. If a sound with low-frequency components is presented, then neurons with low characteristic frequencies (near the center of the auditory nerve bundle) will increase their firing rates. If a sound with high-frequency components is presented, then neurons with high characteristic frequencies (near the periphery of the auditory nerve bundle) will increase their firing rates. Representation of spectral information in this way is called a *place* code or a *rate-place* code, because the spectral information is represented by the pattern of activity across the array of neurons.

4.4.4 Phase locking and temporal coding

Place coding is not the only way in which the characteristics of sounds are represented. An electrical change in the inner hair cells occurs only when their stereocilia are bent toward the outside of the cochlea (see Section 4.3.1). If the basilar membrane is vibrating happily up and down in response to a low-frequency pure tone, the stereocilia will bend from side to side, but the hair cells will only depolarize when the stereocilia are bent in one direction – that is, at a particular *phase* of the vibration. Hence, the electric potential of the hair cell fluctuates up and down in synchrony with the vibration of the basilar membrane. This, in turn, means that neurons in the auditory nerve will tend to produce most spikes at a particular phase of the waveform. This property is called *phase locking*, because the response of the neuron is locked to a particular phase of the stimulation, or more accurately, a particular phase in the *vibration of the basilar membrane*. The mechanism of phase locking is illustrated in Figure 4.17.

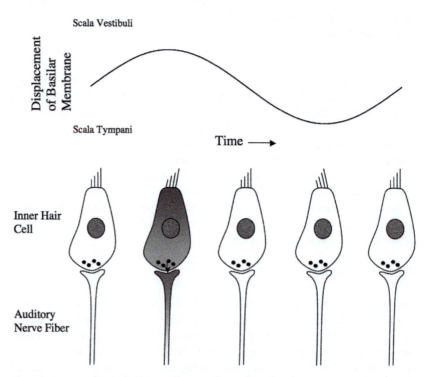

Figure 4.17 How electrical activity in the inner hair cells and in the auditory nerve is related to the motion of the basilar membrane. Activity is greatest at a particular phase during each cycle of basilar membrane vibration (indicated by the second time point from the left).

The existence of phase locking immediately suggests another way in which frequency can be represented in the auditory nerve, specifically in terms of the timing or synchrony of the activity in the auditory nerve. Although an individual neuron may not produce a spike on every cycle of the waveform, when it does respond, it will do so at the same phase in the cycle. This means that if a pure tone is presented, each neuron will tend to produce spikes that are spaced at integer (whole number) multiples of the period of the waveform (although there will be some variability in the timing of individual spikes). For example, if a 100-Hz pure tone is presented, the time intervals between successive spikes will tend to be either 10, 20, or 30 ms and so on. Neurons cannot fire at rates greater than about 200 spikes per second, and this would seem to limit the usefulness of phase locking to a frequency of around 200 Hz. However, even if an individual fiber cannot respond at a sufficiently high rate to represent every cycle of the incoming waveform, information may be combined across neurons to represent the frequency of a high-frequency tone. If one neuron produces spikes on the first, third, fifth, and so on cycle of the incoming pure tone, another might produce spikes on the second, fourth, sixth, and so on cycle of the tone. The combined firing patterns of the two neurons reflect each cycle of the pure tone. In reality, neurons are not nearly as regular as this simplistic example might suggest, but the principle holds. Figure 4.18 illustrates typical patterns of phase-locked spikes for three individual fibers and the pattern of activity averaged across many fibers. Remember that each neuron is responding to the temporal pattern of vibration of the place on the basilar membrane to which it is connected. If pure tones with frequencies of 100 and 500 Hz are presented, some neurons will phase lock to 100 Hz and some neurons will phase lock to 500 Hz, reflecting the separation of these components on the basilar membrane.

There is a limit to how rapidly the electric potential can fluctuate in an inner hair cell, and at high stimulation frequencies the potential does not vary up and down with every period of the waveform. Consequently, auditory nerve fibers show a tendency to produce spikes at a particular phase of the sound waveform up to a maximum frequency of about 5000 Hz (Johnson, 1980). Up to this frequency, therefore, spectral information may be represented partly by a temporal code (the time between consecutive spikes). Above about 5000 Hz, the spikes are not related to a particular phase in the temporal fine structure of the waveform (in other words, the timing of spikes is not related to the individual fluctuations in pressure). However, neurons also tend to phase lock to the envelope of a sound, the slower variations in the peak amplitude of the waveform (see Section 2.5.1). So neurons will tend to produce spikes at a particular phase of amplitude modulation, even if the carrier frequency is greater than 5000 Hz (Joris & Yin, 1992). For example, if an 8000-Hz pure tone is amplitude modulated at 100 Hz (see Section 2.5.1), neurons with characteristic frequencies close to 8000 Hz will phase lock to the 100-Hz envelope. Therefore, phase locking may be a general way of representing the periodicity of waveforms such as complex tones. We see in Chapter 7 how phase locking may be the basis for pitch perception and in Chapter 9 why phase locking is necessary for the precise localization of sounds.

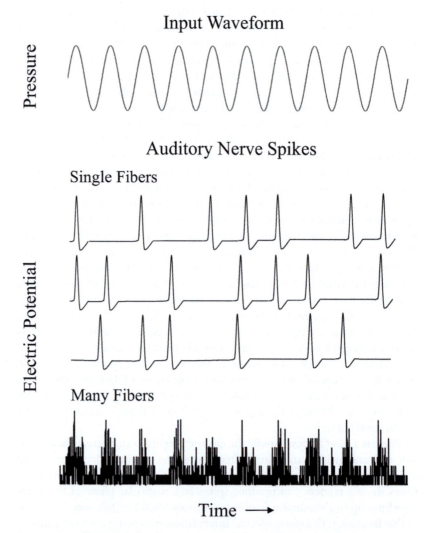

Figure 4.18 An illustration of auditory nerve activity in response to a 250-Hz pure tone (top panel). The middle panels show the patterns of spikes that may be produced by three individual auditory nerve fibers. The bottom panel represents the combined spikes produced by 500 nerve fibers. Notice that, although there is some variability in the phase at which a single neuron fires from cycle to cycle, the periodicity of the waveform is well represented across the array of fibers.

4.5   FROM EAR TO BRAIN (AND BACK)

Let's recap what we have found out in our journey so far. Sound enters the ear canal and causes the eardrum to vibrate. These vibrations are transmitted to the oval window in the cochlea by the bones in the middle ear. Vibrations of the oval window cause pressure changes in the cochlea that cause the basilar membrane to vibrate, with different places on the basilar membrane responding best to different frequencies. Vibrations on the basilar membrane are detected by the inner hair cells, which cause electrical activity (spikes) in the auditory nerve. From here on in the journey we are following *electrical signals* through the auditory nervous system. Now that the acoustic information has been represented in terms of neural activity, the hard part can begin. The task of analyzing the information and separating and identifying the different signals is performed by the brain.

4.5.1 Ascending auditory pathways

The auditory nerve carries the information about incoming sound from the cochlea to the *cochlear nucleus*, a collection of neurons in the *brainstem*. The brainstem is the part of the brain on top of the spinal cord. The auditory centers in the brainstem and cerebral cortex are called the *central auditory system*. The information from the cochlear nucleus is passed (via synapses) to a number of other nuclei that are arranged in pairs, one on each side of the brainstem: the *superior olive* (or *superior olivary complex*), the *nuclei of the lateral lemniscus*, and the *inferior colliculus* (see Figure 4.19). At the superior olive, neural signals from the ear on the opposite side of the head (the *contralateral* ear) are combined with those from the ear on the same side of the head (the *ipsilateral* ear). Although the neural pathways from each ear travel on both sides of the brain, above the level of the cochlear nucleus the main pathways are *contralateral*. That is, the right ear mainly activates the left side of the brain, and vice versa. It is also important to remember that, at all stages in the ascending pathways, neurons are *tonotopically arranged*. Neurons in each nucleus are arranged in arrays covering a range of characteristic frequencies.

Brainstem nuclei analyze and decode the auditory signal using different types of neurons, with varying properties. Although many of the properties of

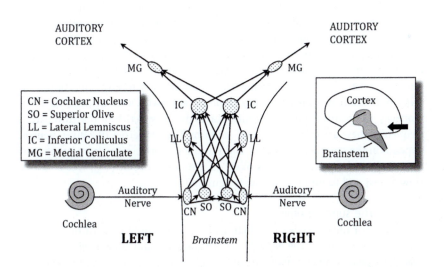

Figure 4.19 A highly simplified map of the ascending auditory pathways, showing the main neural connections in the brainstem. The viewpoint is toward the back of the brain, as indicated by the arrow on the illustration to the right (cerebellum removed).

these neural populations are well documented, to understand their functions with respect to our perceptual abilities is a difficult task. It is difficult to relate the properties of individual neurons to an ability that may depend on many thousands or millions of neurons working together. Because many of the suggested functions are quite controversial (and depend on detailed analyses that are beyond the scope of this chapter), I do not dwell on what functions particular neurons may or may not be involved in here, although I mention some of the less speculative proposals, which are elaborated further in later chapters. The following sections provide just a brief summary of the characteristics and connections of the auditory nuclei.

4.5.1.1 The cochlear nucleus

Auditory nerve fibers synapse with neurons in the cochlear nucleus, and hence the cochlear nucleus is the first port of call, and first processing center, for neural signals from the cochlea. The signal from the ear is divided at the cochlear nucleus into two "streams" (Pickles, 2013). The more *ventral* part of the nucleus at the front of the brainstem (ventral means toward the belly, which is the underside for quadrupeds such as guinea pigs, but toward the front for humans as we stand upright) contains neurons whose axons project mainly to the superior olivary complexes on *both sides of the head*, and this *ventral stream* carries the information (time of arrival and intensity) that is used for sound localization. The more *dorsal* part of the cochlear nucleus toward the back of the brainstem (dorsal means toward the back; think dorsal fin) contains neurons whose axons project mainly to the nuclei of the lateral lemniscus and the inferior colliculus on the *opposite side of the head* (contralateral to the cochlear nucleus from which they originate). This pathway may be involved in sound identification.

Although auditory nerve fibers are relatively uniform in their properties, cochlear nucleus neurons exhibit a wide variety of different properties and are responsible for the initial processing of features in the sound stimulus. Some neurons are similar to auditory nerve fibers (Figure 4.16), whereas others fire at the onset of a continuous stimulus and then produce little response. These onset neurons receive input from neurons with a wide range of characteristic frequencies (hence they have broad tuning curves). Some neurons have a response that builds up relatively slowly over time: These neurons may receive inhibition from other neurons that suppresses their response at onset. Other neurons have the tendency to produce spikes at regular intervals, irrespective of the stimulation frequency. These are called "chopper" neurons. The properties of a given neuron depend on the complex excitatory and inhibitory connections from other neurons, and on the particular physiology of the neuron itself (e.g., if it is fast or slow to respond to inputs from other neurons).

4.5.1.2 The superior olive

Each superior olive receives connections from the ventral parts of the cochlear nuclei on both sides of the head (i.e., both *ipsilaterally* and *contralaterally*). It is here that the signals from the two ears are combined and neurons in the superior olive respond to sounds presented to either ear. The superior olive is divided into two main parts: the *medial superior olive* (toward the midline of the brainstem) and the *lateral superior olive* (toward the sides of the brainstem). The superior olive is thought to use the information from the two ears to determine the direction of sound sources. Neurons in the medial superior olive are sensitive to differences in the time of arrival of a sound between the two ears, and neurons in the lateral superior olive are sensitive to differences in the sound intensity between the two ears (most neurons in the lateral superior olive receive excitatory input from the ipsilateral ear and inhibitory input from the contralateral ear). Both of these cues, time differences and intensity differences, are used for sound localization (see Chapter 9). Neurons in the superior olive project to the nuclei of the lateral lemniscus and to the inferior colliculus on both sides of the head.

4.5.1.3 The nuclei of the lateral lemniscus

The lateral lemniscus is a tract of nerve fibers running from the cochlear nucleus and superior olive to the inferior colliculus. However, some neurons synapse with nuclei that are located in this region. The ventral nucleus of the lateral lemniscus receives input from the contralateral cochlear nucleus and may be part of the "sound identification" stream. Neurons from the ventral nucleus of the lateral lemniscus project to the ipsilateral inferior colliculus. The dorsal nucleus of the lateral lemniscus receives input from the ipsilateral medial superior olive, the ipsilateral and contralateral lateral superior olive, and the contralateral cochlear nucleus. The dorsal nucleus of the lateral lemniscus is thought to be part of the "sound localization" stream (Pickles, 2013). Neurons from the dorsal nucleus form inhibitory connections with the ipsilateral and contralateral inferior colliculus.

4.5.1.4 The inferior colliculus

The inferior colliculus is a vital processing stage in the auditory pathway, and almost all ascending nerve fibers synapse here. The information streams concerning sound localization and sound identity converge at this nucleus. Neurons in the central nucleus of the inferior colliculus are *tonotopically arranged* in layers, each layer containing neurons with the same characteristic frequency. Nerve fibers from different nuclei, but with the same characteristic frequency, converge on the same *isofrequency* layer in the inferior colliculus. Some neurons in the inferior colliculus may be involved in the processing of amplitude modulation and in the extraction of pitch information (see Chapter 7). They may also be involved in the further processing of information from the superior olive that is used in sound localization. However, it may be misleading to suggest that the inferior colliculus is concerned with just a few specialized tasks. It is likely that a wide range of auditory processing occurs at this stage.

4.5.2 The auditory cortex

Nerve fibers from the inferior colliculus synapse with the *medial geniculate body*, which is part of the *thalamus* in the *midbrain* (just about in the center of the head). The thalamus acts as a sort of relay station for sensory information. Nerve fibers from the medial geniculate body project to the *auditory cortex*, which is part of the *cerebral cortex*. The cerebral cortex is the convoluted or crinkly bit you see when you look at a brain. It covers most of the surface of the brain and is involved in high-level cognitive processes, as well as basic sensory and motor functions. The convolutions are present because the cortex is a relatively thin sheet of neurons (only 3 mm thick) that is greatly folded and creased so that the total area is large. Some regions of the cerebral cortex (the primary visual, auditory, and somatosensory areas) receive input from the sensory systems. The primary motor cortex projects (relatively) directly to the muscles. Regions adjacent to the primary areas (association cortex) carry out further processing on the sensory input and integrate information between the senses. Broadly speaking, the farther the region is from the primary area, the more holistically it processes information (e.g., identifying a sentence as opposed to identifying a spectral feature).

The auditory cortex is located at the top of the temporal lobe, hidden in a crease (or *fissure*) in the cerebral cortex called the *Sylvian fissure* (see Figure 4.20). The auditory cortex consists of a primary field (called "AI") and several adjacent fields. The primary field is located on a "bump" in the folds of the cortex called *Heschl's gyrus*. The primary field contains a *tonotopic* representation, in which neurons with similar characteristic frequencies are arranged in strips. The same may be true of the adjacent fields so that there are multiple representations of the cochlea. However, the properties of cortical neurons are much more complex than this description suggests. Cortical neurons perform a detailed analysis of the individual *features* in the auditory signal. The response is often brief and synchronized with envelope peaks in the sound waveform. Some cortical neurons are most sensitive to a particular range of sound levels, and their activity actually reduces as level is increased (or decreased) beyond this range. Many cortical neurons have complex binaural properties (reflecting input from the two ears that has been processed in the brainstem). Some cortical neurons have complex spectral properties with "multipeaked" tuning curves. Some cortical neurons show a preference for particular *changes* in frequency over time (e.g., an increase in frequency produces a higher response than a decrease in frequency). The selectivity of cortical neurons for specific acoustic features may reflect stages in sound identification. Of course, much of our knowledge of the auditory cortex has been derived from neurophysiological experiments on nonhuman mammals. At this relatively high-level stage in processing, there may be considerable differences in processing between species that reflect the species-specific importance of sounds and sound features.

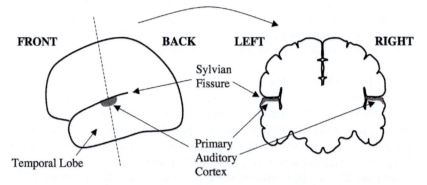

Figure 4.20 The location of the primary auditory cortex on the cerebral cortex, shown from the side (left), and in a cross-section taken along the dashed line (right)

Somewhere away from the auditory cortex, probably in the temporal and parietal lobes, the signals from the auditory system are finally identified as a specific word, melody, object, and so on, and the information is linked to that from other sensory systems to provide a coherent impression of the environment.

4.5.3 Descending auditory pathways

Information flows through the auditory system in not just one way from the ear to the brain. There are also *descending* auditory pathways carrying information from higher auditory centers to lower auditory centers, even as far as the cochlea itself. The *olivocochlear bundle* contains fibers that originate in the ispilateral (same side) and contralateral (opposite side) superior olives. These *efferent* (i.e., from the brain) fibers travel down the auditory nerve and synapse in the cochlea. Some synapse on the axons of the *afferent* (i.e., to the brain) fibers innervating the inner hair cells, and others synapse directly on the outer hair cells. Those that synapse on the outer hair cells can control the motion of the basilar membrane, to some extent. Stimulation of the olivocochlear bundle has been shown to suppress the motion of the membrane. Efferent activity is triggered automatically by moderate-to-high sound levels, in a reflex neural pathway from the cochlea to the cochlear nucleus to the contralateral superior olive and back to the cochlea. This effect is called the *medial olivocochlear reflex* (see Guinan, 1996, and Section 5.2.5.1, for a discussion of the role of the olivocochlear efferents).

There are also descending pathways to the cochlear nucleus, which originate mainly from the superior olive and from the lateral lemniscus and inferior colliculus. In addition, there are descending pathways from the auditory cortex to the medial geniculate body and to the inferior colliculus. A complete chain of connections may exist from the auditory cortex, through the brainstem nuclei, to the cochlea itself (Pickles, 2013, Chapter 8). It seems that the auditory system is designed so that higher auditory, and perhaps cognitive, centers can exert control on the activity of lower auditory centers, and thus influence the processing of sound. In particular, these descending neural pathways may be involved in *perceptual learning*. Signals from higher centers may cause changes in the ways neurons in the brainstem process sounds, to enhance their ability to extract relevant stimulus characteristics and to adapt to changing conditions. For example, it has been shown that destroying one of the major descending connections from the cortex to the inferior colliculus impairs the ability of ferrets to relearn sound localization cues after one ear is blocked (Bajo, Nodal, Moore, & King, 2010).

4.6 SUMMARY

This chapter covers the main stages in the process by which pressure variations in the air (sound waves) are converted into electrical activity in neurons in the auditory system and how these electrical signals are transmitted through the auditory nervous system. On a basic level, this is how your ears work. The role of the cochlea in performing a spectral analysis of the sound has been described, but such is the importance of this mechanism that we return to it in the next chapter.

1   Sound enters the ear through an opening in the pinna leading to the ear canal, which ends with the eardrum. Vibrations at the eardrum are transformed into pressure variations in the cochlear fluids by three tiny bones: the malleus, incus, and stapes.

2   The cochlea is a tube coiled up into a spiral, divided along its length by two membranes: Reissner's membrane and the basilar membrane. Pressure variations in the cochlear fluids cause the basilar membrane to vibrate in a wavelike motion traveling from base to apex (the traveling wave).

3   The mechanical properties of the basilar membrane vary along its length so that the different frequency components of a sound cause different parts of the basilar membrane to vibrate, with high frequencies toward the base and low frequencies toward the apex. Each place on the basilar membrane is tuned to a particular characteristic frequency. The basilar membrane as a whole behaves as a bank of overlapping band-pass filters (auditory filters). In this way, the basilar membrane extracts the spectrum of a sound.

4   Vibration of the basilar membrane causes a shearing force between the basilar membrane and the overlying tectorial membrane. This causes the stereocilia on the tops of the hair cells to sway from side to side at the same rate as the basilar membrane vibration. Motion of the stereocilia of the inner hair cells produces an electrical change in the cell (depolarization), leading to the release of a chemical neurotransmitter that induces electrical impulses (spikes) in the auditory nerve fibers connected to the cell.

5   Each auditory nerve fiber is connected to a particular place in the cochlea and represents the activity at that place. Because each place in the cochlea is most sensitive to a single characteristic frequency, each neuron in the auditory nerve is also most sensitive to a single characteristic frequency.

6   Neural firing rates increase as sound level increases, until they saturate at a firing rate of about 200 spikes per second. High spontaneous rate fibers start to increase their firing at low sound levels (they have low thresholds), but they also saturate at fairly low levels (less than about 60 dB SPL). Low spontaneous rate fibers have higher thresholds and much higher saturation levels (maybe 100 dB SPL or more).

7   Because the inner hair cells depolarize when their stereocilia are bent in one direction (away from the center of the cochlea), nerve fibers tend to fire at a particular phase of the basilar membrane vibration for frequencies up to about 5000 Hz. This is called phase locking.

8   Information about a sound is represented in the auditory nerve in two ways: in terms of firing rate (nerve fibers represent the magnitude of vibration at different places on the basilar membrane) and in terms of phase locking or firing synchrony (nerve fibers represent the temporal pattern of vibration at different places on the basilar membrane).

9   Information travels up the auditory nerve, through a chain of nuclei in the brainstem (the information receives processing at each stage), before being passed on to the auditory cortex. There also are descending neural pathways that allow higher centers to control lower centers, and even the basilar membrane itself through efferent neural connections to the outer hair cells.

4.7   READING

Pickles's book provides an excellent introduction to auditory physiology:

Pickles, J. O. (2013). *An introduction to the physiology of hearing* (4th ed.). Leiden: Brill.

I also found the following book very useful:

Møller, A. R. (2013). *Hearing: Anatomy, physiology, and disorders of the auditory system* (3rd ed.). San Diego: Plural Publishing.

Yost provides a good overview of the central auditory system:

Yost, W.A. (2006). *Fundamentals of hearing: An introduction* (5th ed.). New York: Academic Press.

For a detailed account of auditory neurophysiology:

Rees, A., & Palmer, A. R. (2010). *The auditory brain.* Oxford: Oxford University Press.

NOTE

[1] Since the eardrum response is linear, the tiny displacements of the eardrum near the hearing threshold ($< 10^{-11}$ m) can be inferred from the displacements in response to higher level sounds, such as those reported by Huber et al. (2001).

5 FREQUENCY SELECTIVITY

The term *frequency selectivity* is used to refer to the ability of the ear to separate out the different frequency components of a sound. This spectral analysis is absolutely crucial for mammalian hearing. Chapter 4 describes the basic mechanisms underlying this ability. Chapter 5 goes into much more depth about the nature of frequency selectivity in the cochlea, including the role of the outer hair cells, and describes measurements of tuning at higher centers in the auditory system. It concludes with a discussion of behavioral measures in human listeners.

5.1 THE IMPORTANCE OF FREQUENCY SELECTIVITY

The first thing the visual system does is focus the light coming from each point in space onto a particular place on the retina, so that a spatial arrangement of light sources and reflective surfaces in the world around us is mapped onto a spatial arrangement of photoreceptors. The visual system performs a *place-to-place* mapping of the visual world. One of the first things the auditory system does is separate out the different frequency components of the incoming sound on the basilar membrane. The basilar membrane performs a partial spectral (or Fourier) analysis of the sound, with each place on the basilar membrane being most sensitive to a different frequency component. In other words, the auditory system performs a *frequency-to-place* mapping of the acoustic world.

The visual system has only three different patterns of sensitivity to the spectral information in light, and the patterns correspond to the spectral sensitivities of the three different color receptor cells in the retina (the three types of *cone* cells). These cells behave like band-pass filters for light, but there are effectively only three different center frequencies; our rich color perception depends on the balance of activity across just three different types of receptor. It follows that any color that humans can perceive can be produced by mixing together just three different wavelengths of light (for example, from the red, green, and blue parts of the visible spectrum). Despite our seemingly vivid perception of color, we actually only get a very limited picture of the variety of wavelengths of light that are reflected, or produced, by objects. In contrast, the auditory system has, arguably, several hundred different spectral sensitivities. The auditory system extracts quite detailed information about the spectral composition of sounds. It is impossible to recreate the full perceptual experience produced by sounds like speech with just three different pure tones. We would need many more components to simulate the spectral complexity that the auditory system is able to perceive.

There is a good reason for this difference between the senses, of course. Visual objects are characterized mainly by their shapes, and so spatial visual information is very important to us. Auditory objects are characterized mainly by their spectra and by the way their spectra change over time. For instance, different vowel sounds in speech can be identified by the positions of their spectral peaks (formants). The way in which the frequencies of the formants change over time helps identify preceding consonants. Similarly, different musical instruments can be identified by the spectral distribution of their harmonics. Indeed, the sound quality, or *timbre*, that characterizes most sounds we hear is largely dependent on spectral information.

In addition to being important for sound identification, frequency selectivity enables us to *separate out* sounds that occur together. To offer a crude example, we can easily "hear out" a double bass in the presence of a piccolo. Most of the energy of the double bass is concentrated in low-frequency regions. Most of the energy of the piccolo is concentrated in high-frequency regions. When the two instruments are playing simultaneously, the sound waves are mixed together in the air to produce a sound wave that is a combination of the waves from the two sources. However, because they cover different frequency ranges, the basilar membrane can separate out the sounds originating from each instrument. As we see in Chapter 10, we can even separate two complex tones with harmonics distributed over the *same* frequency region, as long as the fundamental frequencies of the tones, and hence the frequencies of the individual harmonics, are different. Without acute frequency selectivity, we would find it very hard to separate simultaneous sounds, and this is a common problem experienced by listeners with hearing impairment (see Chapter 13).

In short, frequency selectivity can be considered just as important to hearing as spatial sensitivity is to vision. Frequency selectivity is *fundamental* to the way in which we perceive sounds, and that is why the topic is given an entire chapter in this book.

5.2 FREQUENCY SELECTIVITY ON THE BASILAR MEMBRANE

5.2.1 Recent measurements

Békésy (1960) reported fairly broad tuning in the cochlea, what we now think of as the "passive" response of the basilar membrane (Section 4.2.2). The bandwidths of the filters, and consequently, the spatial spread of the traveling wave, were much greater than they would be in a healthy ear at moderate sound levels. (Békésy used levels as high as 140 dB SPL!) It is now known that cochlear tuning is highly dependent on the physiological state of an animal. Even a slight deterioration in the condition of an animal can have large effects on tuning and therefore on the ability of the ear to separate out different frequency components. More recent experiments have been conducted on anaesthetized chinchillas or guinea pigs. The cochlea is opened up, usually near the base, so that the basilar membrane can be observed. The motion of the membrane can be measured by bouncing laser light off a reflective surface (e.g., a tiny glass bead) that has been placed on the membrane (see Appendix). This technique is usually used to measure the response (velocity or displacement) of a single place on the basilar membrane rather than the entire traveling wave.

The left panel of Figure 5.1 contains a set of *iso-level* curves, each of which shows the velocity of a *single place* on the basilar membrane (with a characteristic frequency of 10 kHz) as a function of the frequency of a pure tone of a particular level. Basilar membrane velocity is expressed in decibels relative to 1 μm/s: A velocity of one millionth of a meter per second would be represented by 0 dB on this scale. The plots use data from a widely cited article by Ruggero, Rich, Recio, Narayan, and Robles (1997) and show measurements from a chinchilla. Think of these curves as representing filter shapes. The closer the frequency of the tone is to the best frequency of a place on the basilar membrane, the higher is the velocity of that place. Conversely, the more remote the frequency from the best frequency, the lower is the response. Each place on the basilar membrane behaves like a band-pass filter that attenuates frequency components remote from its best frequency. The curves in Figure 5.1 show that the basilar membrane displays a high degree of tuning at low levels (good ability to separate out different frequency components). At high levels, the width of the iso-level curve (or auditory filter) at each place on the basilar membrane is broad, so each place will respond to a wide range of frequency components, and a single pure tone will stimulate a wide region of the basilar membrane (i.e., the traveling wave will cover a wide region of the basilar membrane).

Note also in Figure 5.1 that the best frequency of this place on the basilar membrane *decreases* as level is increased, from 10 kHz at low levels to 7 kHz at high levels. Because of this, the term *characteristic frequency* is usually used to refer to the best frequency in response to a *low-level* sound. A consequence of the reduction in the best frequency with increasing level is that the peak of the traveling wave moves toward the base of the cochlea as level is increased. This is called the *basalward shift* of the traveling wave. Think about it in this way: For a pure tone at a low level, the place that responds best to the tone has a characteristic frequency equal to the frequency of the tone (by definition). A more basal place

Figure 5.1 Iso-level curves (left panel) and tuning curves (right panel) for a single place at the base of the basilar membrane of a chinchilla. The iso-level curves show basilar membrane velocity (in decibels relative to 1 μm/s) as a function of the frequency of a pure tone for various levels of the tone. The tuning curves show the level of a pure tone needed to produce a criterion velocity of the basilar membrane (shown in the legend in decibels relative to 1 μm/s) as a function of frequency. The plots are based on data from Ruggero et al. (1997).

with a slightly higher characteristic frequency does not respond as vigorously. At a higher level, however, the best frequency of the original place is now lower than the frequency of the tone, and the best frequency of a more basal place may have moved down so that it is now *equal to* the frequency of the tone. The result is that the vibration of the membrane will be stronger at a more basal place than it was at low levels.

The frequency selectivity of a place on the basilar membrane can also be measured by playing a tone at a particular frequency to the ear of an animal and finding the sound level needed to produce a criterion velocity or displacement of the membrane. When the frequency of the tone is close to the best frequency of the place being measured, the level needed will be low. When the frequency of the tone is remote from the best frequency of the place, the level needed will be high. A plot of the level required against the frequency of the tone describes a *tuning curve* for that place on the basilar membrane.

The right panel of Figure 5.1 shows tuning curves for a place on the basilar membrane with a characteristic frequency of 10 kHz. (These data are actually interpolated from the same set of data that are used to construct the iso-level curves on the left.) Note that at low levels, the tuning curves have very steep high-frequency sides and shallower low-frequency sides. A tuning curve can be regarded as an inverted filter shape. If the tuning curve were flipped upside down, the plot would represent the attenuation of different frequencies relative to the best frequency. If a high level is needed to produce the criterion response, then it is implied that the frequency component in question is being *attenuated* by the filter. Any pure-tone level and frequency within the V of the tuning curve will produce *at least* the criterion velocity, although the higher the level and the closer the frequency to the best frequency, the greater the response.

Figure 5.2 shows iso-level curves and tuning curves measured at an apical site (from the tectorial membrane rather than from the basilar membrane, but this shouldn't make much difference), with a characteristic frequency of about 300 Hz. The absolute bandwidths of the filters (in hertz) are less at the apex than they are at the base. However, measured as a *proportion* of characteristic frequency, the bandwidths *decrease* from apex to base. The Q_{10}s of the filters (a measure of the sharpness of tuning; see Section 3.3.2) increase as the characteristic frequency increases, from about 2 at 300 Hz to about 5 at 10 kHz. Note also that the downward shift in the peak of tuning with increasing level does not occur in the apex: The maximum response in the left panel of Figure 5.2 is at 300 Hz at all levels.

5.2.2   Ringing

In Section 3.3.3, it is shown how the response of a filter to an impulse depends on the *absolute* bandwidth of the filter. If the filter is very narrow, then the filter will ring for a long time after the impulse. If the filter is broadly tuned, the ringing will be brief. The same is true for the basilar membrane. If a click is played to the ear, places near the apex with low characteristic frequencies and narrow bandwidths may vibrate for several tens of milliseconds, whereas places near the base with high characteristic frequencies and wider bandwidths may only vibrate for a millisecond or so. Figure 5.3 shows a simulation of the pattern of vibration at three different places on the basilar membrane in response to a click.

Figure 5.2 Iso-level curves (left panel) and tuning curves (right panel) for a single place at the apex of the basilar membrane of a chinchilla. The iso-level curves show basilar displacement (in decibels relative to 1 nm) as a function of the frequency of a pure tone for various levels of the tone. The tuning curves show the level of a pure tone needed to produce a criterion displacement of the basilar membrane (shown in the legend in decibels relative to 1 nm) as a function of frequency. The plots are based on data from Rhode and Cooper (1996).

Figure 5.3 A simulation of the pattern of vibration at three places on the basilar membrane in response to a brief impulse (an almost instantaneous rise and fall in pressure). These curves represent the *impulse responses* of three places on the membrane. The characteristic frequency of each place is indicated on the right. Notice that the period of vibration of the basilar membrane is equal to the period of a pure tone at the characteristic frequency (i.e., one divided by the characteristic frequency).

5.2.3   Nonlinearity

A quick observation of the iso-level curves and the tuning curves in Figure 5.1 is enough to tell us one crucial thing about the response of the base of the basilar membrane: It is highly *nonlinear* (see Section 3.3.4). In a linear system, the output amplitude should be a constant multiple of the input amplitude, irrespective of the level of the input. On a decibel scale, this means that the output level should be a constant number of decibels greater or smaller than the input level. If the system is a filter, then the filter attenuation characteristics should not change with level. The tuning curves in Figure 5.1 tell us that this is not the case for a healthy cochlea. The filters become *broader* as the criterion (and, therefore, the overall level) is increased. Furthermore, in the base of the cochlea the frequency to which the place on the basilar membrane is most sensitive (effectively, the center frequency of the filter) shifts *downward* as level is increased.

The nonlinearity is made even more apparent when we look at the growth in the response of the basilar membrane as input level is increased. The data in Figure 5.4 are a subset of those that were used to derive the iso-level curves and tuning curves in Figure 5.1. The data show the basilar membrane response expressed in decibels as a function of the sound pressure level of a stimulating tone at different frequencies. As described in Section 3.3.4, a linear system should show a straight line, with a slope of 1, on these coordinates. Note that for input frequencies lower than the characteristic frequency of 10 kHz, the basilar

Figure 5.4 The velocity of vibration as a function of input level for a single place on the basilar membrane of a chinchilla in response to pure tones of various frequencies. The characteristic frequency of the place was 10 kHz. Notice that the response to the tone at characteristic frequency is highly *compressive* at moderate to high input levels (linear growth has a slope of 1 on these coordinates, as exemplified by the response curves for 3-kHz and 17-kHz pure tones). The data are selected from a study by Ruggero et al. (1997).

membrane response is roughly linear. However, the slope of the response function is very different for a tone close to characteristic frequency. At low levels, the
response is almost linear, but at medium-to-high levels, the slope is very shallow.
This is indicative of a very *compressive* system: A 10-dB increase in input level
may produce only a 2-dB increase in the output level. This compression is very
important because it enables us to use acoustic information over a wide range of
sound levels (see Chapter 6).

Like the frequency selectivity of the basilar membrane, the nonlinear properties of the basilar membrane are dependent on the physiological condition of
an animal. This is illustrated in Figure 5.5, also from the article by Ruggero et al.
(1997). The curve on the right shows the characteristic frequency response of
the basilar membrane after the animal had died. Note that the response now is
nearly linear and that the basilar membrane is much less sensitive than it was
before death (i.e., a much higher input level is needed to produce the same
output level).

Most direct measurements of basilar membrane tuning have been made in
the base of the cochlea, near the oval window, mainly because the surgical procedure is more difficult in the apex. Those measurements that have been taken
near the apex suggest that the basilar membrane is much more linear here than it
is near the base. As shown in Figure 5.2, the auditory filters with low characteristic frequencies have a low Q and do not change their shape or best frequencies
substantially as the input level is increased (Rhode & Cooper, 1996). While there
may be some compression, the measurements suggest that it is less than at high
characteristic frequencies, with a maximum value of about 2:1 (a 10-dB increase

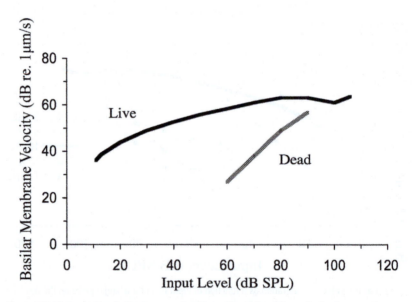

Figure 5.5 The velocity of vibration as a function of input level for a single place on the
basilar membrane of a chinchilla in response to a pure tone at the characteristic frequency of
the place (10 kHz). The curves show the response function before and after the death of the
animal. In the latter case, the response is almost linear (slope equal to 1). Data are from a
study by Ruggero et al. (1997).

in input level produces a 5-dB increase in basilar membrane displacement). In addition, compression at a place in the apex does not just affect stimulus frequencies close to the characteristic frequency of the place (as in the base) but affects a wide range of input frequencies (which is why the filter shapes do not change with level).

5.2.4 Suppression and distortion

There are two other consequences of cochlear nonlinearity that are worth mentioning here. The first is *suppression*. Suppression refers to the reduction in the response to one frequency component when another frequency component is added. If I am playing to my ear a 1000-Hz tone at 40 dB SPL, for example, the response of the place on the basilar membrane tuned to that tone may actually *decrease* when I add a 1300-Hz tone at 60 dB SPL. This is clearly very nonlinear behavior: In a linear system, adding an extra component that on its own is excitatory will *never* cause a decrease in the output of the system. We look at measurements of two-tone suppression in the auditory nerve in Section 5.3.3.

A second consequence of nonlinearity is distortion. Recall that a nonlinear system produces frequency components that were not present in the input (Section 3.3.5). The healthy ear is very nonlinear and produces loads of distortion, particularly intermodulation distortion when two or more components interact at a particular place on the basilar membrane. The components have to be fairly close together so that they both fall within the range of frequencies that are compressed by a single place on the basilar membrane. When they do, however, distortion products called *combination tones* are produced. These distortion products may include the difference tone and other intermodulation products with frequencies *lower* than the frequencies of the original components. Combination tones propagate from the place of generation to excite the places on the basilar membrane tuned to the frequencies of the combination tones. They can be clearly audible in some situations.

Suppression and distortion are characteristic of ears in good condition and are absent when the cochlea is severely damaged. Somewhat ironically, a healthy ear distorts much more than an unhealthy one.

5.2.5 The "active" mechanism

We have seen that, for an ear in poor condition, the response of the basilar membrane is linear and the tuning curves are broad: The frequency selectivity of an unhealthy ear is similar to that of a healthy ear at high levels. In a *healthy* ear, the tuning curves at low-to-medium levels are sharp, and the response to a tone with a frequency near the characteristic frequency is almost linear at low levels but highly compressive at higher levels. Furthermore, the tuning of a place near the base of the basilar membrane has a higher best frequency (i.e., higher resonant frequency) at low levels than it does at high levels.

How do we make sense of all this? It seems that the response of the unhealthy ear reflects the passive response of the basilar membrane, as measured by Békésy (1960). You cannot get much more unhealthy than a cadaver. These broad tuning characteristics are the result of the basic mechanical properties of the cochlea, particularly the variation in stiffness along the length of the basilar membrane. In the healthy ear, however, something else seems to be contributing to the motion of the basilar membrane in the base. That "something else" seems to provide the equivalent of a *level- and frequency-dependent amplification* of the basilar membrane response. Low-level sounds are amplified, but high-level sounds are not, and this amplification, or *gain*, only takes place for frequencies close to the characteristic frequency of each place on the basilar membrane. In the basal region of the cochlea, the characteristic frequency is *higher* than the best frequency of the passive response so that, as the amplification goes away at high levels, the tip of the tuning curve shifts to lower frequencies.

I will try to explain this more clearly: Imagine that you have a broad filter and you want to make it sharper so that it is better at separating frequency components close to the center frequency of the filter from frequency components remote from the center frequency of the filter. One of the ways to do this is to increase the attenuation of the remote components so that less energy from these components is passed by the filter. Another way, however, is to *amplify* frequency components close to the center of the filter so that the relative output from these components is greater. The second method is the one used by the cochlea. However, the frequencies that are amplified are higher (by perhaps half an octave) than the center frequency of the original broad filter (the passive basilar membrane), so as the amplification goes away at high levels, the center frequency of the auditory filter decreases as it returns to its passive state. Figure 5.6 shows how the amplification enhances frequency selectivity (and sensitivity) to low-level tones and how the reduction in amplification at high levels leads to compression.

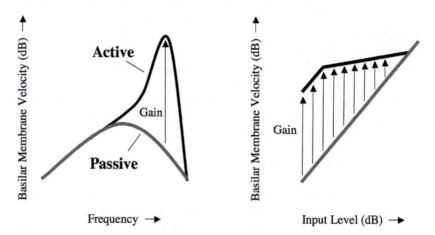

Figure 5.6 An illustration of how activity by the outer hair cells may change the basilar membrane filtering characteristics (left panel) and the response to a tone at characteristic frequency (right panel). The gray lines show the passive response of the basilar membrane (unhealthy ear or healthy ear at high-stimulation levels); the thick black lines show the healthy, active, response of the basilar membrane. Arrows indicate amplification or gain. The left panel shows how gain over a limited range of frequencies can sharpen the frequency selectivity of the membrane. The right panel shows how gain at low levels increases the sensitivity to a tone at characteristic frequency (a low-level tone now produces a larger response). Notice that as level increases, the gain decreases. The result is a shallow response function (compression).

It is thought that the *outer hair cells* are involved in this active amplification process. The dominant theory, at present, is that outer hairs respond to vibration of the basilar membrane by stretching and contracting at a rate equal to the stimulating frequency (see Møller, 2013, p. 55). Like pushing on a swing at the right time to make it go higher, this motion may amplify the vibration of the basilar membrane in response to a tone near the characteristic frequency. The maximum gain may be about 50 dB, but it is not the same for all input levels (i.e., it is not linear). At higher levels, the outer hair cells cannot respond sufficiently and the gain decreases. The result is a compressive response to a tone at characteristic frequency and a broadening in the tuning curve at high levels. The very molecule responsible for the length changes in outer hair cells has been identified (Zheng et al., 2000). The protein *prestin* is found in the membrane of outer hair cells, and it changes its shape in response to changes in the electric potential across the cell membrane. The electric potential changes are caused by the influx of positively charged potassium ions when the stereocilia are bent by the motion of the basilar membrane (see Section 4.3.1). Shape changes in the prestin molecules result in length changes in the outer hair cell, and hence a greater deflection of the basilar membrane. The motion of the basilar membrane may be amplified by a "positive feedback" loop in this way.

The outer hair cells are very sensitive to physiological trauma, which is why experimental animals need to be in good condition to show the healthy cochlear response. Even mild drugs, like aspirin, can temporarily impair outer hair cell function. Outer hair cells are also susceptible to damage by loud sounds, and when they are lost, they do not grow back. As we get older, we tend to lose outer hair cell function. Dysfunction of the outer hair cells results in a loss of sensitivity *and* a reduction in frequency selectivity and is believed to be the main cause of hearing impairment in humans (see Chapter 13).

5.2.5.1   Effects of efferents

The action of the outer hair cells is also influenced by activity in the *olivocochlear efferent fibers* from the brainstem, as described in Section 4.5.3. Activity in the efferents *reduces the gain* of the outer hair cells, resulting in a more linear basilar membrane response (Cooper & Guinan, 2006). Efferent activity is triggered automatically by moderate-to-high sound levels, in a reflex neural pathway. This effect is called the *medial olivocochlear reflex*. Efferent activity may also be under "top-down" control from the brain. The purpose of this mechanism is not fully understood, but it may protect the ear from overstimulation and may also help increase the detection of sounds in background noise in some circumstances (Guinan, 1996). A compressive response is good for increasing the range of sound levels to which we are sensitive, but it may not be so good for signal detection in background noise because it reduces the level difference between the signal and the noise. A linear response results in a greater difference in basilar membrane vibration between the signal and the noise, improving the *signal-to-noise ratio*.

5.2.6   Magical sounds from your ear

Before we leave the discussion of basilar membrane physiology, a quick word about *otoacoustic emissions*. At the end of the 1970s, David Kemp (1978) made the remarkable discovery that the ear can actually *emit* sounds. Virtually no one believed him at the time, but now it is a well-documented phenomenon. For instance, if an impulse or click is played to the ear, the ear may emit a sound containing certain frequency components. These otoacoustic emissions are also called "cochlear echoes," and they originate from the activity of the outer hair cells described in the previous section. If more than one pure-tone component is present in the input, the emission may contain combination tone distortion products called *distortion product* otoacoustic emissions. The energy emitted may even exceed that of the original stimulus, which provides evidence that some sort of amplification is happening. Indeed, sometimes ears can produce pure tones without any input at all. These sounds are called *spontaneous* otoacoustic emissions and may result from spontaneous activity of the outer hair cells at a particular place on the basilar membrane. Strong otoacoustic emissions are a characteristic of a healthy ear with functioning outer hair cells, and the emissions are now used to screen babies for hearing loss (see Section 13.5.3).

5.3   NEURAL FREQUENCY SELECTIVITY

5.3.1   Tuning in the auditory nerve

A physiologist can insert a microelectrode (a very thin electrode) into the auditory nerve of, say, an anaesthetized guinea pig or a chinchilla and record the activity of a single auditory nerve fiber. Each fiber shows tuning properties very similar to those of the place on the basilar membrane to which it is attached. In other words, the fiber will respond with a high rate of firing to a pure tone at its characteristic frequency and at a lower rate of firing to a pure tone with a frequency higher or lower than its characteristic frequency.

Frequency threshold tuning curves can be obtained by finding the level of a pure tone required to produce a just-measurable increase in the firing rate of a neuron as a function of the frequency of the pure tone. These curves are equivalent to the tuning curves on the basilar membrane described earlier: The closer the frequency of the tone to the characteristic frequency of the neuron, the lower is the level required. Figure 5.7 shows tuning curves for five neurons from the auditory nerve of the chinchilla, representing a range of characteristic frequencies. The curves are plotted on a linear axis (left panel) and on a logarithmic axis in which equal distances along the axis correspond to equal *frequency ratios* (right panel). The graphs illustrate that although the *absolute* bandwidths of the filters increase with characteristic frequency (left panel), the bandwidths *relative* to the characteristic frequency *decrease* with characteristic frequency (right panel).

The most important point in this section is this: Because each auditory nerve fiber innervates a single inner hair cell, the frequency selectivity in the auditory nerve is very similar to that of the basilar membrane. Because of the difficulties involved in measuring the vibration of the basilar membrane directly, much of what we know about frequency selectivity has been derived from auditory nerve recordings.

5.3.2   The effects of cochlear nonlinearity on rate-level functions

I mentioned in Section 4.4.2 that, in response to a pure tone at characteristic frequency, high spontaneous rate fibers have steeper rate-level functions, which

Figure 5.7 Frequency threshold tuning curves recorded from the auditory nerve of a chinchilla. Each curve shows the level of a pure tone required to produce a just-detectable increase in the firing rate of a neuron as a function of the frequency of the tone. Five curves are shown, illustrating the tuning properties of five neurons with characteristic frequencies ranging from about 500 Hz to about 16 kHz. The curves are plotted on a linear frequency axis (left panel) and on a logarithmic frequency axis (right panel). The curves are smoothed representations of recordings made by Ruggero and Semple (see Ruggero, 1992).

saturate at much lower levels, than do low spontaneous rate fibers. I promised that I would explain this in Chapter 5. The important difference between the fiber groups is that the high spontaneous rate fibers are more sensitive than the low spontaneous rate fibers and, thus, they respond to the motion of the basilar membrane at levels for which the response function of the basilar membrane is nearly linear (i.e., the *steep* low-level portion of the function). In the low-level region, the vibration of the basilar membrane grows rapidly with input level; hence, the *firing rate* of the fiber grows rapidly with input level. Because of this, the firing rate at which the neuron saturates is reached at a *low stimulus level*.

The low spontaneous rate fibers are less sensitive than the high spontaneous rate fibers. This means that the range of levels to which a low spontaneous rate fiber is sensitive falls within the *compressive* region of the basilar membrane response function. For these fibers, a given change in input level will result in a much smaller change in the vibration of the basilar membrane, and hence a smaller change in the firing rate of the fiber. The result is a shallow rate-level function that saturates at a *high stimulus level*.

If the shapes of the rate-level functions for low spontaneous rate neurons are dependent on cochlear nonlinearity, then we should expect that the functions would be steeper for tones below characteristic frequency, because the basilar membrane response to a tone below characteristic frequency is roughly linear (see Figure 5.4). This is, indeed, the case. Figure 5.8 shows recordings from a guinea pig auditory nerve fiber with a characteristic frequency of 20 kHz. The rate-level function for the pure tone at the characteristic frequency is quite shallow, because of the shallow slope of the basilar membrane response. The rate-level function for the tone below the characteristic frequency is much steeper, because the basilar membrane response to this tone, at the place tuned to 20 kHz, is much steeper. By assuming that the response to a tone below characteristic frequency is linear, Yates, Winter, and Robertson (1990) were able to

Figure 5.8 Firing rate as a function of stimulus level for a low spontaneous rate auditory nerve fiber with a characteristic frequency of 20 kHz. The frequency of the pure-tone stimulus was either 20 kHz (at the characteristic frequency) or 17 kHz (below the characteristic frequency). The curves are based on guinea pig recordings reported by Yates et al. (1990).

derive the basilar membrane response to a tone at characteristic frequency from a comparison of the auditory nerve rate-level functions in response to tones at and below the characteristic frequency of the fiber. Without delving into the details of their procedure, the important general point is that *the rate-level functions of auditory nerve fibers reflect the response function of the basilar membrane.* This has to be the case, because the firing rate of an auditory nerve fiber is determined by the magnitude of vibration of the basilar membrane at the place in the cochlea where the dendrite of the nerve fiber synapses with an inner hair cell.

5.3.3   Suppression in the auditory nerve

As I describe in Section 5.2.4, one of the consequences of the nonlinear response of the basilar membrane is suppression. Suppression can be measured in the response of the auditory nerve. For instance, the firing rate of an auditory nerve fiber can be measured in response to a low-level pure tone at the characteristic frequency of the fiber. A second tone is then added. When the second tone falls well within the tuning curve of the fiber, the firing rate will increase. However, for certain levels and frequencies of the second tone outside the tuning curve, the firing rate in the fiber will *decrease* when the second tone is added. These suppression regions are shown in Figure 5.9. What this figure does not show is that, for a given increase in the level of the second tone, the reduction in firing rate is greater for a low-frequency second tone than for a high-frequency second tone (see Delgutte, 1990).

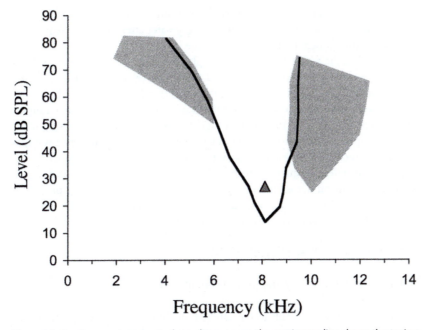

Figure 5.9 Two-tone suppression in the auditory nerve. The continuous line shows the tuning curve of an auditory nerve fiber, with a characteristic frequency of 8000 Hz. The triangle indicates the level and frequency of a probe tone. When a second (suppressor) tone was added, with a level and frequency within the shaded regions, the firing rate of the fiber was *reduced* by at least 20%. Data are from Arthur, Pfeiffer, and Suga (1971).

5.3.4 Tuning in the central auditory system

The tonotopic organization seen on the basilar membrane and in the auditory nerve, with different neurons tuned to different frequencies, continues up to higher auditory centers. In the cochlear nucleus, for instance, there are three separate regions, each with its own tonotopic map. Think of the information being passed up the auditory system in an array of parallel *frequency channels*, each containing information from a narrow range of frequencies around the characteristic frequency of the channel. Neurons in the brainstem nuclei show frequency selectivity, but the tuning properties are not always the same as those seen in the auditory nerve (see Møller, 2013, Chapter 6). The diversity of tuning curve shapes seems to increase with distance up the ascending auditory pathways and reflects the convergence of excitatory and inhibitory inputs from several neurons at a lower level in the pathway. Some neurons have very broad tuning properties, which perhaps reflect the convergence of excitatory inputs from several neurons with a range of different characteristic frequencies. Tuning curves with multiple peaks are also observed, which again reflects input from neurons with different characteristic frequencies. Some neurons may even exhibit *sharper* tuning than neurons in the auditory nerve. This can arise because excitatory input from one neuron is accompanied by inhibitory input from neurons with characteristic frequencies on either side, effectively adding greater attenuation to frequencies away from the characteristic frequency of the neuron.

Neurons in the auditory cortex also display a diversity of tuning shapes. Most have sharp tuning, but some have broad tuning curves or multipeaked tuning curves, and many display patterns of inhibition (see Pickles, 2013, Chapter 7). These diverse response patterns reflect the ways in which different neural inputs are combined to process the auditory signal. It would be very surprising if the tuning properties of neurons did not change along the ascending pathways, as it would suggest that the auditory system is not interested in comparing the activity in different frequency channels. Because sound segregation and identification depend on across-frequency comparisons, complex tuning properties are expected, even if it is not obvious exactly what an individual neuron may be contributing to hearing as a whole.

5.4   PSYCHOPHYSICAL MEASUREMENTS

5.4.1   Masking and psychophysical tuning curves

The basilar membrane is able to separate out the different frequency components of sounds, and this frequency selectivity is preserved throughout the auditory system. What are the consequences of this for our *perceptions?* One of the things it enables us to do is to "hear out" one frequency component in the presence of other frequency components. Imagine that I play to you a noise that has been band-pass filtered to contain frequency components only between 1000 and 1200 Hz (a *narrowband* noise). I now add a pure tone with a frequency of 2000 Hz and a level 20 dB below that of the noise. If you have normal hearing you will easily be able to hear the tone, because it is separated from the noise on the basilar membrane: The two sounds excite different *places* on the basilar membrane. If I now change the frequency of the tone to 1100 Hz, however, you will not be able to hear the tone. The tone is said to be *masked* by the noise, because the noise is effectively obscuring the tone. Masking occurs whenever the activity produced on the basilar membrane by one sound (the *masker*) obscures the activity produced by the sound you are trying to hear (the *signal*). If the masker and the signal are far apart in frequency, then the masker will have to be much more intense than the signal to mask it. If the masker and the signal are close together in frequency, then the masker may have to be only a few decibels more intense than the signal to mask it.

Physiological techniques can be used to measure frequency selectivity in nonhuman mammals. *Psychophysical* techniques, such as masking experiments, can be used to measure the frequency selectivity of the *human* auditory system. In one technique, the pure-tone signal is fixed at a fairly low level, say, 10 dB above the level at which it is just audible in quiet (the *absolute threshold*). This is sometimes called 10-dB *sensation level*. A narrowband noise or pure-tone masker is presented at one frequency, and its level increased until the listener can no longer detect the signal. The procedure is then repeated for a number of different masker frequencies. The results can be used to produce a *psychophysical tuning curve,* which is a plot of the level of a masker needed to mask a signal as a function of the frequency of the masker.

A psychophysical tuning curve describes the shape of a band-pass filter (auditory filter) that has a center frequency equal to the frequency of the pure-tone signal. The technique of measuring psychophysical tuning curves assumes that we have the ability to "listen" selectively to the output of a single auditory filter – that is, to a single place on the basilar membrane. When the masker is remote in frequency from the center of the filter, it receives a lot of attenuation. To overcome this, the masker level has to be high to mask the signal. When the masker is close to the center of the filter, it receives less attenuation and the level required to mask the signal is lower. The psychophysical tuning curve is therefore directly comparable to the basilar membrane tuning curve and neural (frequency threshold) tuning curve described earlier.

Figure 5.10 shows psychophysical tuning curves measured in my labora-tory. In this experiment, the masker was presented before the signal in a design known as *forward masking*. We will discuss forward masking in more detail in

Figure 5.10 Psychophysical tuning curves at 4000 Hz. The curves show the level of a pure-tone masker needed to mask a 4000-Hz pure-tone signal as a function of masker frequency. The signal was fixed at 10 dB above absolute threshold and was presented after the masker (forward masking). The masker-signal interval was varied to produce a set of psychophysical tuning curves covering a range of masker levels. As level increases (filled diamonds to open squares), the tuning curve becomes broader (less frequency selectivity, larger equivalent rectangular bandwidth) and the tip of the tuning curve shifts down in frequency. This implies that the place on the basilar membrane tuned to 4000 Hz at low levels is tuned to *lower* frequencies at high levels. Data are from Yasin and Plack (2003).

Section 8.1.3. For the moment, all we need to know is that as the gap between the masker and the signal was increased, the masker level needed to make the signal undetectable also increased. Because the signal was fixed at a low level, a family of psychophysical tuning curves, corresponding to different levels, was produced by simply varying the masker-to-signal gap. Note that as the level increases, the tuning curves broaden (less frequency selectivity) and the tip of the tuning curve (i.e., the best frequency) shifts downward in frequency. Notice the similarity with the basilar membrane tuning curves in the right panel of Figure 5.1.

5.4.2   The notched-noise technique

The tuning curve experiment described in the previous section is only one of many different psychophysical procedures that have been used to measure the frequency selectivity of the human auditory system (see Moore, 1995, for a review). Thousands of masking experiments have been tried (tones on tones, noise on tones, etc.). Although some techniques may be more reliable than others, the overall conclusions regarding frequency selectivity are consistent with what I report here. However, a popular way of estimating the shape of the auditory filter, worth mentioning in this section, is the notched-noise technique developed by Patterson (1976). In his technique, a pure-tone signal is presented with two bands of noise, one above and one below the signal frequency, that act as maskers. The signal is in a *spectral notch* between the noise bands (Figure 5.11).

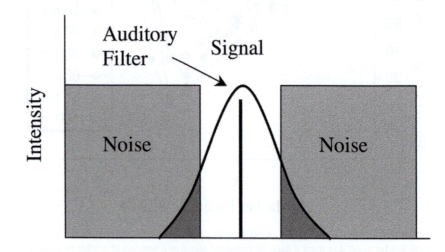

Figure 5.11 A schematic illustration of the spectrum of the stimulus used by Patterson (1976). A pure tone signal (vertical line) is masked by two noise bands (light shaded rectangles). The area of the dark shading is proportional to the noise energy passed by the auditory filter centered on the signal frequency. As the width of the spectral notch between the noise bands is increased, the noise passed decreases and the signal becomes easier to detect (hence, threshold decreases). Based on Moore (2012).

The signal is usually presented simultaneously with the noise bands, but the signal can be presented after the noise in a forward-masking design. The lowest detectable level of the signal (the signal threshold) is determined as a function of the spectral gap between the signal and the edge of each of the noise bands. If the noise bands are close to the signal, then a large amount of noise energy will be passed by the filter centered on the signal, and the signal threshold will be high. As the width of the spectral notch is increased, threshold decreases. By measuring the way in which signal threshold changes as the spectral notch is changed, it is possible to estimate the shape of the auditory filter.

One of the advantages of presenting the signal between two noise bands is that this limits the effectiveness of off-frequency listening. Off-frequency listening describes a situation in which the listener detects the signal by using an auditory filter tuned lower or higher than the frequency of the signal. For example, if only the lower frequency band of noise were used, the listener might detect the signal through an auditory filter tuned slightly higher than the signal frequency (equivalent to listening to vibration of the basilar membrane at a more basal location). Because the auditory filter has a slightly flat tip, the reduction in signal level at the output of the filter may be less than the reduction in masker level, and so the signal may be easier to detect. Off-frequency listening can lead to overestimates of the sharpness of tuning. Adding a noise above the signal frequency means that such a listening strategy is much less beneficial because a shift in center frequency away from one noise band will be a shift toward the other noise band.

5.4.3 Variation with center frequency

As I describe in Section 3.3.2, the equivalent rectangular bandwidth (ERB) of a filter is the bandwidth of a rectangular filter, with the same peak output and the same area under the curve (in units of intensity) as that filter. Based on notched-noise-masking experiments with human listeners, Glasberg and Moore (1990) estimated that the ERB for the auditory filter (in hertz) follows the relation

$$\text{ERB} = 24.7(0.00437f_c + 1), \tag{5.1}$$

where f_c is the center frequency of the filter in hertz. According to this equation, for frequencies above about 1000 Hz, the ERB is approximately proportional to the center frequency (constant Q) and has a value of about 11% of the center frequency at high frequencies (Q_{10} of about 5). At high levels, this equation is not valid – we know that the filters broaden considerably. In addition, more recent evidence has suggested that the filters may be sharper than previously thought at high frequencies and at low levels. The ERB equation of Glasberg and Moore was based on measurements using simultaneous masking (i.e., the masker and the signal were presented at the same time). In simultaneous masking, part of the masking may be caused by the masker suppressing the signal, and this may broaden the apparent tuning curve. As shown in Figure 5.9, the suppression tuning curve (the frequency regions for which one tone will suppress a tone at the characteristic frequency) is broader than the excitation tuning curve (the frequency regions that cause excitation at the same place). In short, when tuning is measured using forward masking and the masker cannot suppress the signal because the two are not physically present on the basilar membrane at the same time, you get sharper tuning curves at low levels, with ERBs that may be as little as 5% of the center frequency at 8000 Hz (Shera, Guinan, & Oxenham, 2002).

Of course, the million-dollar question is whether the tuning properties of the basilar membrane are similar to the tuning properties measured psychophysically. The answer is a qualified yes. The similarity between the psychophysical tuning curves in Figure 5.10 and the basilar membrane tuning curves in Figure 5.1 is obvious. The degree of frequency selectivity observed in the masking experiments is roughly the same as that observed by direct measurements of the basilar membrane response in other mammals. This has to be qualified somewhat, because the measurements of Shera et al. (2002) described previously suggest that humans may have better frequency selectivity than chinchillas or guinea pigs, and so a direct comparison between species may be problematic. In addition, it is possible that the human cochlea is more compressive at low characteristic frequencies, compared to some other mammals (Plack & Drga, 2003). Nevertheless, the correspondence between species is close enough to suggest that the frequency selectivity of the auditory system is determined by the tuning properties of the basilar membrane. This is a very important point, so it is worth repeating: The frequency selectivity of the *entire auditory system* is determined by the tuning properties of the *basilar membrane*. What happens on the basilar membrane is the limiting factor for our ability to separate sounds on the basis of frequency.

5.4.4   Excitation patterns

As mentioned earlier, it is common to regard the cochlea as a bank of overlapping band-pass filters. Because we have a reasonable understanding of the characteristics of these filters and how these characteristics change with frequency and level, we can produce an estimate of how an arbitrary sound is represented in the cochlea by plotting the output of each auditory filter as a function of its center frequency (equivalent to the characteristic frequency of each place on the basilar membrane). This plot is called an *excitation pattern*, and it is very useful for visualizing the effects of peripheral frequency selectivity on the representation of sounds in the auditory system. The excitation pattern is the auditory system's version of the *spectrum*: It shows the degree to which the different frequency components in complex sounds are resolved by the cochlea.

The top panel of Figure 5.12 shows excitation patterns for a 1000-Hz pure tone as a function of the level of the tone. These plots were derived using a sophisticated model of the basilar membrane that takes into account the non-linear characteristics described in Section 5.2.3. Let us try to understand the basic shape of the excitation pattern of a pure tone. If the center frequency of the auditory filter matches the frequency of the tone, then the auditory filter output has a high value and there is a peak in the excitation pattern at that frequency. For center frequencies higher or lower than the frequency of the tone, the output of the auditory filter is less (the tone is attenuated), and hence the excitation level is not as high. Because the filters are broader at high frequencies and have steeper high-frequency slopes than low-frequency slopes, a filter that

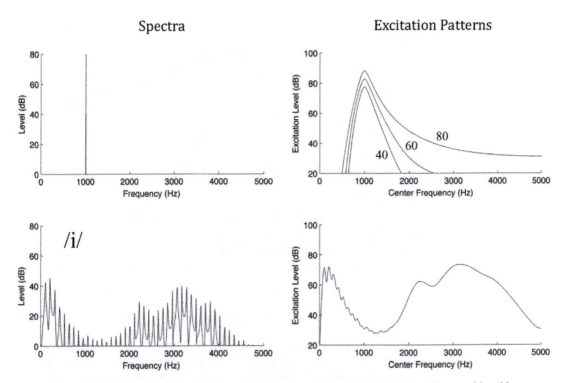

Figure 5.12 Spectra (left panels) and excitation patterns (right panels) for a 1000-Hz pure tone (top panels) and for the vowel /i/ (bottom panels). Excitation patterns for the pure tone were calculated at three levels: 40, 60, and 80 dB SPL. Only the 80-dB tone is shown in the spectrum.

has a center frequency *below* the frequency of the tone will let less energy through than a filter with a center frequency the same deviation *above* the frequency of the tone. Therefore, on a linear center frequency axis such as this, the excitation pattern has a shallower high-frequency slope than low-frequency slope.

Note also that the peak of the excitation pattern does not increase by as much as the level of the input tone. This is because, for a characteristic frequency equal to the frequency of the tone, the tone is *compressed* by the basilar membrane. For a characteristic frequency above the frequency of the tone, however, we know that the response of the basilar membrane is roughly linear (see Figure 5.4). At center frequencies higher than the frequency of the tone, therefore, the excitation pattern grows *linearly* (a 20-dB increase in the level of the pure tone produces a 20-dB increase in excitation level). The overall effect is that the high-frequency side of the excitation pattern becomes broader as level is increased, as we would expect from the fact that the individual auditory filters are getting broader on the low-frequency side (see Figure 5.1 and Figure 5.10).

The characteristics of the excitation pattern are reflected in the effects of a masker with a limited bandwidth, for instance, a pure tone or a narrowband noise (see Figure 5.13). For a signal frequency equal to the masker frequency, the growth of signal threshold with masker level is roughly linear so that a 10-dB increase in masker level produces about a 10-dB increase in the lowest detectable

Figure 5.13 An illustration of the upward spread of masking. The curves show the threshold level of a pure-tone signal in the presence of a 2.4-kHz pure-tone masker as a function of signal frequency. Thresholds are shown for two levels of the masker (see legend). Threshold is highest (masking is greatest) when the signal frequency is equal to the masker frequency. As the masker level increases, the signal threshold increases, although the increase is greatest on the high-frequency side of the masking pattern. Data are from an unpublished study by Oxenham, reported by Oxenham and Bacon (2004).

level of the signal. However, more rapid growth of excitation on the high-frequency side of the excitation pattern contributes to a phenomenon called the *upward spread of masking* (the other contributor, at low signal levels, is suppression of the signal by the masker). Simply put, maskers lower in frequency than the signal become *relatively* more effective as level is increased. For an 80-dB SPL masker at 2000 Hz, the lowest detectable signal level at 4000 Hz might be about 30 dB SPL. For a 90-dB SPL masker at 2000 Hz, the lowest detectable signal level at 4000 Hz might be as much as 70 dB SPL.

The effect can be explained as follows. When someone is listening to the place on the basilar membrane tuned to the signal, the signal is compressed. If the masker has the *same* frequency as the signal, then the masker is also compressed at that place and the growth of excitation level with physical level for the two is the same (hence, a roughly linear growth in signal threshold with masker level). When the masker frequency is *below* the signal frequency, however, the excitation produced by the masker grows linearly, and hence more rapidly with level than the excitation produced by the signal. If the masker level is increased by 10 dB, then the signal level may have to be increased by 40 dB to produce the same 10-dB increase in excitation level.

The bottom panels of Figure 5.12 show the spectrum and excitation pattern for the vowel /i/ ("ee"). Notice that only the first few harmonics of the vowel form separate peaks or bumps in the excitation pattern. This is because the spacing between the harmonics is constant, but the auditory filters become broader (in terms of absolute bandwidth) as frequency is increased. At low center frequencies, the output of an auditory filter centered on a harmonic is dominated by that harmonic. An auditory filter centered *between* two harmonics has a lower output because the harmonics are attenuated by the filter. The result is a succession of bumps in the excitation pattern. At high center frequencies, several harmonics fall within each auditory filter, and variations in center frequency have little effect on the excitation level. The higher formants appear in the excitation pattern as broad peaks rather than as a succession of bumps. The auditory system can *separate out* the lower harmonics in a complex tone but not the higher harmonics. This is of great significance for pitch perception (see Chapter 7).

In addition to being a representation of the pattern of activity on the basilar membrane, the excitation pattern can also be considered a representation of the pattern of activity in the *auditory nerve*. Center frequency in that case would refer to the characteristic frequency of an auditory nerve fiber. Neural activity should really be measured in terms of firing rate rather than as a level in decibels, and it is common to plot excitation patterns in terms of neural firing rate as a function of characteristic frequency. However, the firing rate at each neural characteristic frequency is related to the basilar membrane vibration at that characteristic frequency. The *information* in the auditory nerve is broadly equivalent to that described by the excitation pattern expressed as excitation level.

We come across more excitation patterns like this over the course of this book, so it is worth taking some time to be certain you understand how they are produced and what they signify.

5.5   SUMMARY

Frequency selectivity is one of the most important topics in hearing, because the nature of auditory perception is largely determined by the ear's ability to separate out the different frequency components of sounds. Frequency selectivity can be measured at all stages of the auditory system, from the basilar membrane to the auditory cortex, as well as in our perceptions. Arguably, more is known about frequency selectivity than about any other aspect of auditory processing.

1   The tuning properties of the basilar membrane can be measured directly in nonhuman mammals. At the base of the cochlea (high characteristic frequencies), a single place on the basilar membrane shows a high degree of tuning at low levels (narrow bandwidth) but broader tuning at high levels (particularly on the low-frequency side). In addition, the best frequency of each place on the basilar membrane shifts downward by about half an octave from low levels to high levels.

2   In the apex of the cochlea (low characteristic frequencies), the tuning curves are narrower than in the base, when measured in terms of absolute bandwidth in hertz, but broader as a proportion of characteristic frequency (i.e., the Q_{10}s are smaller in the apex).

3   Frequency selectivity in the base is enhanced by an *active mechanism*, dependent on the motion of the outer hair cells, which effectively amplifies the response to low- and medium-level frequency components close to the characteristic frequency. The active mechanism sharpens the tuning at low-to-medium levels and, because the gain is greatest at low levels and absent at high levels, leads to a shallow growth of basilar membrane velocity with input level (compression).

4   Two side effects of the nonlinearity are *suppression* and *distortion*. Suppression refers to the situation in which one tone *reduces* the response to another tone at its best place on the basilar membrane. Distortion is observed when two or more frequency components interact at a place on the basilar membrane, creating lower frequency intermodulation products called *combination tones*.

5   The tuning properties of the basilar membrane are reflected in the tuning properties in the auditory nerve and at higher centers in the auditory system. At higher centers, the outputs of neurons with different characteristic frequencies can converge and produce neurons with complex tuning curves.

6   Frequency selectivity in *humans* can be measured using masking experiments: Our ability to detect a signal in the presence of a masker depends on how close the two sounds are in frequency. The tuning properties are consistent with those seen on the basilar membrane and in the auditory nerve, which suggests that the frequency selectivity of the entire auditory system is determined by the properties of the basilar membrane.

7   An *excitation pattern* is a plot of the outputs of the auditory filters as a function of center frequency in response to a given sound. An excitation pattern is a representation of the overall activity of the basilar membrane as a function of characteristic frequency, or of the overall activity in the auditory nerve as a function of characteristic frequency. The excitation pattern is the auditory system's version of the spectrum.

5.6   READING

Pickles and Møller provide good introductions to the physiology of frequency selectivity:

Pickles, J. O. (2013). *An introduction to the physiology of hearing* (4th ed.). Leiden: Brill.
Møller, A. R. (2011). *Hearing: Anatomy, physiology, and disorders of the auditory system* (3rd ed.). San Diego: Plural Publishing.

Details of cochlear frequency selectivity can be found in:

Robles, L., & Ruggero, M. A. (2001). Mechanics of the mammalian cochlea. *Psychological Review*, 81, 1305–1352.

For an introduction to the psychophysics of frequency selectivity:

Moore, B. C. J. (2012). *An Introduction to the psychology of hearing* (6th ed.). London: Emerald. Chapter 3.

Oxenham, A. J., & Wojtczak, M. (2010). Frequency selectivity and masking. In C. J. Plack (Ed.), *Hearing* (pp. 5–44). Oxford: Oxford University Press.

For an excellent overview of auditory compression from physiological and psychophysical perspectives:

Bacon, S. P., Fay, R. R., & Popper, A. N. (Eds.) (2004). *Compression: From cochlea to cochlear implants.* New York: Springer-Verlag.

6 LOUDNESS AND INTENSITY CODING

Loudness, the perceptual correlate of sound intensity, is one of the main components of auditory sensation. However, the perception of sound intensity is not just a matter of determining how loud a sound is or whether one sound is louder than another. Sounds are largely characterized by variations in intensity across frequency and across time. To use speech as an example, vowel sounds are characterized by variations in intensity across frequency (e.g., formant peaks), and consonants are characterized (in part) by variations in intensity across time (e.g., the sudden drop in intensity that may signify a stop consonant, such as /p/). To identify these sounds, the auditory system must have a way of *representing* sound intensity in terms of the activity of nerve fibers and a way of making *comparisons* of intensity across frequency and across time. The purpose of this chapter is to show how information regarding sound intensity is analyzed by the auditory system. The chapter examines how we perceive sound intensity and discusses the ways in which sound intensity may be represented by neurons in the auditory system.

6.1 THE DYNAMIC RANGE OF HEARING

To begin, let us consider the range of sound levels that the auditory system can analyze. The *dynamic range* of a system is the range of levels over which the system operates to a certain standard of performance. To determine the dynamic range of human hearing, we need to know the lower and upper level limits of our ability to process sounds effectively.

6.1.1 Absolute threshold

Absolute threshold refers to the lowest sound level a listener can perceive in the absence of other sounds. This is usually measured for pure tones at specific frequencies – to find, for example, a listener's absolute threshold at 1000 Hz. If you have had a hearing test, the audiologist may have measured an *audiogram* for each of your ears. The audiogram is a plot of absolute threshold as a function of the frequency of a pure tone. In a clinical setting, audiograms are often plotted in terms of hearing loss (the lower the point on the graph, the greater the hearing loss) relative to the normal for young listeners (see Chapter 13).

The lower curve in Figure 6.1 shows a typical plot of absolute threshold as a function of frequency for young listeners with normal hearing, measured by

Figure 6.1 Equal loudness contours. Each curve represents the levels and frequencies of pure tones of equal loudness, measured relative to a 1000-Hz pure tone. A pure tone corresponding to a point on a given curve will sound as loud as a pure tone at any other point on the same curve. The level of the 1000-Hz tone for each curve (in dB SPL) is shown on the figure above each loudness contour. Also shown is the lowest detectable level (absolute threshold) at each frequency. Stimuli were presented in the "free field," with a sound source directly in front of the listener. Hence the absolute threshold curve is labeled "MAF" for "minimum audible field." The data are replotted from the latest ISO standard (ISO/DIS 226).

presenting pure tones from a loudspeaker in front of the head. Note that sensitivity is greatest (threshold is lowest) for sound frequencies between about 1000 and 6000 Hz and declines for frequencies above and below this region. The region of high sensitivity corresponds to resonances in the outer and middle ear, as sounds in this frequency range are transmitted to the cochlea more efficiently than sounds of other frequencies (see Section 4.1.1). The frequency range of normal hearing is about 20 Hz to 20 kHz in humans (the range often extends to higher frequencies in other mammals). Near the extremes of this range, absolute threshold is very high (80 dB SPL or more): Although not shown in Figure 6.1, thresholds increase rapidly for sound frequencies above 15 kHz or so.

6.1.2 The upper limit

How loud is too loud? The sound level at which we start to feel uncomfortable varies between individuals, and some people with a condition called *hyperacusis* have an abnormally low tolerance to sounds even at moderate levels (see

Section 13.4.2). However, 110 dB SPL would be quite uncomfortable for most people, and if the level were raised much above 120 dB SPL, most of us would experience something akin to physical pain, almost irrespective of the frequency of the sound. Exposure to these high sound levels for only a short time may cause permanent damage to the ear.

Another way of approaching this problem is to ask over what range of sound levels can we make use of differences in level to distinguish sounds. Although we may be able to hear a sound at 140 dB SPL, we may not be able to distinguish it from a sound at 130 dB SPL by using the auditory system. Not many experiments have been conducted at very high levels on humans for obvious ethical reasons, but it appears that our ability to detect differences between the levels of two sounds begins to deteriorate for sound levels above about 100 dB SPL, although discrimination is still possible for levels as high as 120 dB SPL (Viemeister & Bacon, 1988). These results are discussed in more detail in Section 6.3.2.

In summary, the lower and upper limits of hearing suggest that the dynamic range of hearing (the range of levels over which the ear operates effectively) is about 120 dB in the mid-frequency region (1000–6000 Hz) and decreases at low and high frequencies. 120 dB corresponds to an increase in pressure by a factor of one million and an increase in intensity by a factor of one million million. In other words, the quietest sounds we can hear are about *one million million* times less intense than sounds near pain threshold.

6.2 LOUDNESS

6.2.1 What is loudness?

Loudness can be defined as the perceptual quantity most related to sound intensity. We use words like "quiet" and "loud" to refer to sounds that we hear in our daily lives ("turn down the TV, it's too loud"). Strictly speaking, however, loudness refers to the *subjective* magnitude of a sound, as opposed to terms such as pressure, intensity, power, or level, which refer to the *physical* magnitude of a sound. If I turn up the amplifier so that the intensity of a sound is increased, you *perceive* this as a change in loudness. It is *not* accurate to say, "This sound has a loudness of 50 dB SPL." Decibels are units of *physical* magnitude, not subjective magnitude.

6.2.2 Loudness matching: effects of frequency, bandwidth, and duration

Because loudness is a subjective variable, does this mean that it cannot be measured? Fortunately, the answer is no. One of the obvious things we can do is ask listeners to vary the level of one sound until it seems as loud as another sound. In this way, we can compare the loudness of sounds with different spectral or temporal characteristics. An example is shown in Figure 6.1. The figure shows *equal loudness contours*, which are curves connecting pure tones of equal loudness, all matched to a 1000-Hz pure tone. Note that, like the absolute threshold curve, the equal loudness curves dip in the middle, indicating a region of high sensitivity around 1000–6000 Hz. The loudness curves flatten off slightly at high levels: Loudness does not vary as much with frequency at high levels. It follows that the growth of loudness with level is greater at low frequencies than at high frequencies.

The *loudness level* (in units called *phons*) of a tone at any frequency is taken as the level (in dB SPL) of the 1000-Hz tone to which it is equal in loudness. From Figure 6.1 we can see that a 100-Hz pure tone at 40 dB SPL is about as loud as a 1000-Hz pure tone at 10 dB SPL. So a 100-Hz tone at 40 dB SPL has a loudness level of about 10 phons. Similarly, any sound that is as loud as a 1000-Hz tone at 60 dB SPL has a loudness level of 60 phons.

Loudness matching can also be used to measure the effects of bandwidth on loudness, by varying the level of a sound of fixed bandwidth until it matches the loudness of a sound with a variable bandwidth. Experiments like these have shown that increasing the bandwidth of a noise with a *fixed overall level* (so that the spectrum level, or spectral density, decreases as bandwidth is increased) results in an *increase* in loudness, if the noise is wider than the auditory filter bandwidth and presented at moderate levels (see Figure 6.2). If the noise is narrower than the auditory filter bandwidth, then variations in bandwidth have little effect on the loudness of a sound with a fixed overall level. To look at this in another way, if the power of a sound is distributed over a wider region of the cochlea, then

Figure 6.2 Variations in loudness with bandwidth for a noise band geometrically centered on 1420 Hz. The three curves show the level of a comparison stimulus judged to be as loud as the noise band for different overall levels of the noise band (30, 50, or 80 dB SPL). For a given overall level, the overall level does not change as bandwidth is increased (hence the *spectrum level* decreases with increases in bandwidth). The comparison stimulus was a noise band geometrically centered on 1420 Hz with a bandwidth of 2300 Hz. Based on Zwicker, Flottorp, and Stevens (1957).

the loudness may increase (Section 6.2.4 provides an explanation for this effect). This is an important point. Loudness is not determined simply by the level of a sound; it also depends on the spectral distribution.

Finally, loudness matching can be used to measure the effects of duration on loudness by varying the level of a sound of fixed duration until it matches the loudness of a sound with a different duration. Up to a few hundred milliseconds, the longer the sound, the louder it appears. At midlevels, a short-duration pure tone has to be much higher in level than a long-duration tone to be judged equally loud (Buus, Florentine, & Poulsen, 1997). The difference is less at low and high levels. The midlevel effect is probably related to midlevel compression on the basilar membrane (see Section 5.2.3). Compression means that a given change in input level produces a much smaller change in the level of basilar membrane vibration. Hence, at midlevels, a greater increase in the level of the tone is necessary to produce the increase in basilar membrane vibration (or increase in excitation level) required to compensate for the decrease in duration. For long-duration sounds, it is hard to judge the "overall" loudness as opposed to the loudness at a particular instant or over a short time period, and loudness matches may become very variable.

6.2.3   Loudness scales

Loudness matching can provide important information about how loudness is influenced by some stimulus characteristics (e.g., frequency, bandwidth, and duration), but it cannot tell us directly how loudness changes with sound level. Loudness matching cannot provide a number that corresponds directly to the magnitude of our sensation. If we had such a set of numbers for different sound levels, we would be able to construct a *loudness scale* describing the variation in subjective magnitude with physical magnitude.

One of the ways we can measure the variation in loudness with level is to simply present two sounds and ask a listener to give a number corresponding to how much louder one sound seems than the other. Alternatively, we can ask a listener to adjust the level of one sound until it seems, say, twice as loud as another sound. These two techniques are called *magnitude estimation* and *magnitude production*, respectively, and have been used with some success to quantify the subjective experience of loudness. Stevens's power law (Stevens, 1957, 1972) is based on the observation that for many sensory quantities, the subjective magnitude of a quantity scales with the *power* of the physical magnitude of that quantity. For loudness,

$$L = kI^{\alpha}, \tag{6.1}$$

where L is loudness, I is sound intensity, and k is a constant. Loudness quantified in this way is expressed in units called *sones*, where one sone is defined as the loudness of a 1000-Hz pure tone with a level of 40 dB SPL. A sound that appears to be four times as loud as this reference tone has a loudness of 4 sones, and so on. The exponent, α, is usually between 0.2 and 0.3 for sound levels above about 40 dB SPL and for frequencies above about 200 Hz. For sound levels below 40 dB SPL and for frequencies less than 200 Hz, loudness grows more rapidly with intensity (the exponent is greater). Figure 6.3 illustrates the growth of loudness with sound level for a 1000-Hz pure tone.

To give a clearer idea of the loudness scale, imagine that you want to increase the level of a sound so that it seems twice as loud as it did before. What increase in level (in decibels) would you need? If we assume, for the sake of argument, that the exponent is 0.3, then the sound level would have to increase by 10 dB. This corresponds to an increase in intensity by a factor of 10. Loudness is a *compressed* version of sound intensity: A tenfold increase in intensity produces a doubling in loudness. If you want your new guitar amplifier to sound four times as loud as your old one, you have to increase the power rating (in watts) by a factor of 100!

It is important to note that the function relating sound level to loudness is similar to the function relating sound level to the velocity of basilar membrane motion. Both the basilar membrane response function and the loudness growth function are steeper at low levels than they are at higher levels when plotted on logarithmic axes as in Figure 5.4 and Figure 6.3. Indeed, loudness may be roughly proportional to the *square* of basilar membrane velocity (Schlauch, DiGiovanni, & Reis, 1998). This is not a coincidence, of course. Sounds are detected by virtue of the vibrations that they elicit on the basilar membrane. Hence, basilar membrane compression determines the growth of loudness. It is interesting, however, that the relation is so direct. This suggests that whatever processing occurs in the central auditory nervous system, in terms of our perceptions the net effect is largely to maintain the representation of sound intensity that exists on the basilar membrane.

6.2.4 Models of loudness

The effects of sound level and bandwidth can be explained by models of loudness based on the excitation pattern (Moore, Glasberg, & Baer, 1997; Zwicker &

Figure 6.3 The relation between loudness (plotted in sones on a *logarithmic* scale) and sound level for a 1000-Hz pure tone. The curve is based on magnitude estimation and magnitude production data collected by Hellman (1976).

Scharf, 1965). These models calculate the *specific loudness* at the output of each auditory filter. Specific loudness is a compressed version of stimulus intensity in each frequency region, reflecting the compression of the basilar membrane. You can think of the specific loudness at a particular center frequency as being the loudness at the corresponding place on the basilar membrane. The final loudness of the sound is taken as the sum of the specific loudness across center frequency, with the frequencies spaced at intervals proportional to the equivalent rectangular bandwidth (ERB) at each frequency (higher center frequencies are spaced farther apart than lower center frequencies). Because this spacing of frequencies corresponds to a roughly constant spacing in terms of distance along the basilar membrane (see Figure 4.6), the process is broadly equivalent to a summation of specific loudness along the length of the basilar membrane. In other words, loudness is related to the total activity of the basilar membrane.

Consider the effect of bandwidth on loudness described in Section 6.2.2. If the bandwidth is doubled, then the excitation spreads to cover a wider region of the cochlea. If the overall intensity is held constant, then the intensity per unit frequency will be halved. However, the reduction in the specific loudness at each center frequency will be much less than one half because of the compression (Figure 6.4): The input-output function of the basilar membrane has a shallow slope, so any change in physical intensity will result in a much smaller change in the intensity of basilar membrane vibration. The modest reduction in specific

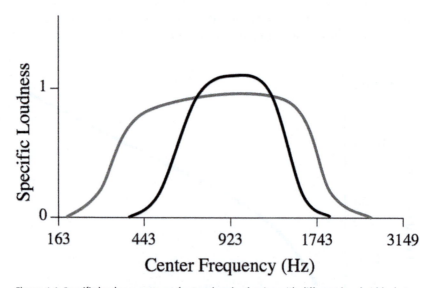

Figure 6.4 Specific loudness patterns for two bands of noise with different bandwidths but with the *same overall level*. In models of loudness, the loudness of a sound is assumed to be equal to the area under the specific loudness pattern, so the narrow band of noise (black line) has a lower loudness than the wide band of noise (gray line). The bandwidth of the noise has doubled, so the spectral density of the noise has been halved. However, the specific loudness at each center frequency reduces by much less than this because of cochlear compression. Note that the center frequencies are spaced according to an ERB scale (equal distance corresponds to equal number of ERBs). Based on Moore (2012).

loudness at each center frequency is more than compensated for by the increase in bandwidth, because doubling bandwidth with a constant spectral density can produce a large increase in the overall loudness (the output from the different center frequencies are added linearly). It follows that spreading the stimulus energy across a wider frequency range, or across a wider region of the cochlea, can increase the loudness.

Loudness models can be used to estimate the loudness of an arbitrary sound. Their success suggests that our sensation of loudness is derived from a combination of neural activity across the whole range of characteristic frequencies in the auditory system.

6.3 HOW IS SOUND INTENSITY REPRESENTED IN THE AUDITORY NERVOUS SYSTEM?

One of the basic properties of auditory nerve fibers is that increases in sound level are associated with increases in firing rate, the number of spikes the fiber produces every second (see Section 4.4.2). Therefore, the answer to the question in the heading seems obvious: Information about the intensity of sounds is represented in terms of the *firing rates of auditory neurons*. If only it were that simple. . . .

6.3.1 Measuring intensity discrimination

Intensity discrimination refers to our ability to detect a difference between the intensities of two sounds. In a typical experiment (see Figure 6.5), the two sounds to be compared are presented one after the other, with a delay between the two *observation intervals* (the times during which the stimuli are presented) of half a second or so. The listener is then required to pick the most intense sound. Over the course of several such trials, the intensity difference between the two sounds is reduced until the listener can no longer perform the task above a certain criterion of correct responses (e.g., 71% correct). This determines the *just-noticeable difference* (jnd) in intensity.

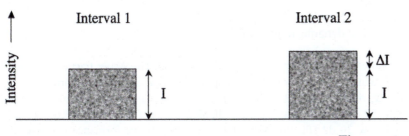

Figure 6.5 The stimuli for a typical intensity discrimination experiment. The listener's task is to pick the observation interval that contains the most intense sound (interval 2 in this case). The interval containing the most intense sound would be randomized from trial to trial. The sound in interval 1 is called the *pedestal*, because it can be regarded as a baseline sound to which the increment (of intensity Δ*I*) is added.

The jnd in intensity can be expressed in many ways. Two of the most popular are the *Weber fraction* (expressed in decibels) and ΔL. The Weber fraction is generally used in perception research to refer to the ratio of the smallest detectable change in some quantity to the magnitude of that quantity. For auditory intensity discrimination,

Weber fraction = $\Delta I / I$,   (6.2)

where I is the baseline (or *pedestal*) sound intensity and ΔI is the smallest detectable change in that intensity (the difference between the intensity of the higher level sound and the intensity of the lower level sound, or pedestal, when the listener can just detect a difference between them). Expressed in decibels, the equation becomes

Weber fraction $(\text{in dB}) = 10 \times \log_{10} (\Delta I / I)$.   (6.3)

It follows from Equation 6.3 that if you need to double the intensity of one sound to detect that its intensity has changed (i.e., if ΔI is equal to I), then the Weber fraction is 0 dB [$10 \times \log_{10} (1) = 0$]. If the jnd corresponds to an increase in intensity that is less than a doubling (i.e., if ΔI is less than I), then the Weber fraction in decibels is *negative* (the logarithm of a number between zero and one is negative).

ΔL is the jnd expressed as the ratio of the intensity of the higher level sound to the intensity of the lower level sound when the listener can just detect a difference between them:

$$\Delta L = 10 \times \log_{10} \{(I + \Delta I) / I\}.$$ (6.4)

Note the distinction between ΔL and the Weber fraction. If you need to double the intensity of one sound to detect that its intensity has changed, then ΔL is about 3 dB [$10 \times \log_{10} (2) \approx 3$]. Unlike the Weber fraction in decibels, ΔL can never be negative, because $(I + \Delta I)/I$ is always greater than 1. If the jnd is very large (ΔI is much greater than I), then the Weber fraction in decibels and ΔL are almost the same.

6.3.2   The dynamic range problem

Just how good are we at intensity discrimination? The Weber fraction for wide-band white noise (noise with a flat spectrum) is about −10 dB (corresponding to a ΔL of about 0.4 dB) and is roughly *constant* as a function of level for levels from 30 dB SPL up to at least 110 dB SPL (Miller, 1947)(Figure 6.6). For levels below 30 dB SPL, the Weber fraction is higher (performance is worse). In Miller's experiment, these levels refer to the *overall* level of a noise that has a flat spectrum between 150 and 7000 Hz. A constant Weber fraction implies that the smallest detectable increment in intensity is proportional to the pedestal intensity, a property called *Weber's law* that is common across sensory systems. A Weber fraction of −10 dB means that we can just detect a 10% difference between the intensities of two wideband noises.

Figure 6.6 Intensity discrimination performance (expressed as the Weber fraction in decibels) for a wideband noise and for a 1000-Hz pure tone as a function of level. In both experiments, listeners were required to detect a brief increment in a continuous sound. Data are from Miller (1947) and Viemeister and Bacon (1988).

For pure tones, however, it has been found that the Weber fraction *decreases* with increasing level (performance improves) for levels up to about 100 dB SPL. This has been called the "near miss" to Weber's law (McGill & Goldberg, 1968). Figure 6.6 shows data from Viemeister and Bacon (1988). Although the Weber fraction increases again for levels above 100 dB SPL, performance is still good for these very high levels: In the same study, Viemeister and Bacon measured a Weber fraction of −6 dB for a pure-tone pedestal with a level of 120 dB SPL.

This is where we have a problem. Human listeners can discriminate intensities at levels as high as 120 dB SPL for pure tones. However, most auditory nerve fibers – the high spontaneous rate fibers – are saturated by 60 dB SPL (see Section 4.4.2). That is, if you increase the level of a 60 dB SPL pure tone with a frequency equal to the characteristic frequency of a high spontaneous rate fiber, the neuron will not increase its firing rate significantly. Most neurons cannot *represent* sound levels above 60 dB SPL in terms of their firing rates alone and cannot provide any information about changes in level above 60 dB SPL. Furthermore, the minority of fibers that do have wide dynamic ranges, the low spontaneous rate fibers, have shallow rate-level functions compared to the high spontaneous rate fibers. A shallow rate-level function means that changes in level have only a small effect on firing rate, and so these fibers should not be very sensitive to differences in intensity. How can we possibly be so good at intensity discrimination at high levels?

6.3.3 Coding by spread of excitation

One explanation for the small Weber fraction at high levels for pure tones (and other stimuli with restricted bandwidths) is that listeners are able to use information from the whole excitation pattern. At low levels, only a small region of the basilar membrane is stimulated (the region surrounding the place tuned to the pure tone's frequency), but as the level is increased, a wider area is stimulated. The extra information traveling up the auditory nerve may benefit intensity discrimination at high levels for two reasons. First, although most nerve fibers with characteristic frequencies close to the frequency of the pure tone may be saturated at high levels, neurons with characteristic frequencies remote from the frequency of the tone (representing the skirts of the excitation pattern, or regions of the basilar membrane remote from the place of maximum vibration) will receive less stimulation and may not be saturated. These neurons will be able to represent the change in level with a change in firing rate.

Figure 6.7 shows a simulation of the activity of high spontaneous rate (left panel) and low spontaneous rate (right panel) fibers as a function of characteristic frequency, in response to a 1000-Hz pure tone presented at different levels. These plots can be regarded as neural excitation patterns (see Section 5.4.4). The peak of the excitation pattern is saturated for the high spontaneous rate fibers at high levels because those neurons with characteristic frequencies close to the frequency of the tone are saturated. For example, a high spontaneous rate fiber with a characteristic frequency of 1000 Hz (equal to the pure-tone frequency) does not change its firing rate as the level is increased from 80 to 100 dB SPL. However, fibers tuned significantly lower or higher than the stimulation frequency are not saturated. These fibers can represent the change in level (e.g., observe the change in firing rate of the 2000-Hz fiber in the left-hand panel as level is increased from 80 to 100 dB SPL).

A second possible reason for the benefit of spread of excitation is that listeners may combine information from across the excitation pattern to improve performance (Florentine & Buus, 1981). The more neurons that are utilized, the more accurate is the representation of intensity. Information from the high-frequency side

Figure 6.7 A simulation of firing rate as a function of characteristic frequency for representative high spontaneous rate (left panel) and low spontaneous rate (right panel) auditory nerve fibers in response to a 1000-Hz pure tone presented at different levels. The rate-level functions of the two fibers in response to a tone at characteristic frequency are illustrated to the right of the figure.

of the excitation pattern may be particularly useful, as this region grows more rapidly with stimulus level than the center of the excitation pattern. This arises from the compressive growth of the central region of the excitation pattern compared to the linear growth of the high-frequency side (see Section 5.4.4 and Figure 5.12, upper right panel). Note in Figure 6.7 that the change in firing rate with level is greatest on the high-frequency side for the high spontaneous rate fibers.

Some researchers have tested the hypothesis that information from the skirts of the excitation pattern is used to detect intensity differences by masking these regions with noise. Figure 6.8 shows the results of such an experiment (Moore & Raab, 1974), in which intensity discrimination for a 1000-Hz pure tone was measured with and without the presence of a band-stop masking noise (noise that has a notch in the spectrum). The noise would have masked information from the skirts of the excitation pattern, yet addition of the noise resulted in only a small deterioration of performance at high levels, removing the near miss and resulting in Weber's law behavior (as also observed for wideband noise).

Hence, the pattern of firing rates across the auditory nerve may provide more information about the level of a pure tone than is present in a single nerve fiber or in a group of nerve fibers with similar characteristic frequencies. The use of this extra information may explain the reduction in the Weber fraction with level for pure tones, referred to as the near miss to Weber's law. However, even if the use of the excitation pattern is restricted by the addition of masking noise, performance at high levels is still very good. It seems that the auditory system can represent high sound levels using neurons with only a narrow range of characteristic frequencies, many of which must be saturated.

6.3.4 Coding by phase locking

In some circumstances, intensity may be coded by the pattern of phase locking in auditory neurons. Recall that nerve fibers will tend to fire at a particular phase of the fine structure of the sound waveform (see Section 4.4.4). For a pure tone in

Figure 6.8 Intensity discrimination for a 1000-Hz pure tone, with and without a band-stop noise. The noise had cutoff frequencies of 500 and 2000 Hz (see schematic spectrum on the right). The data are those of one listener (BM) from Moore and Raab (1974).

the presence of noise, for example, the auditory system may be able to detect the tone by detecting regularity in the otherwise irregular firing pattern (noise produces irregular patterns of phase locking). Furthermore, increasing the intensity of a pure tone in the presence of a noise can increase the degree of regular, synchronized firing to the tone, even when the nerve fiber is saturated and cannot change its firing rate. The *pattern* of activity in auditory neurons can change with level, even if the spikes per second do not. This may help the auditory system to represent complex sounds at high levels, since each nerve fiber will tend to phase lock to the dominant spectral feature close to its characteristic frequency, for instance, a formant peak (Sachs & Young, 1980). The spectral profile can be represented by the changing pattern of phase locking with characteristic frequency rather than by changes in firing rate with characteristic frequency.

In situations in which intensity discrimination for a pure tone is measured in a noise, such as the band-stop noise experiment illustrated in Figure 6.8, nerve fibers may represent changes in level by changes in the degree of *synchronization* of spikes to the pure tone. The band-stop noise that was used to prevent the use of the skirts of the excitation pattern may incidentally have increased the effective dynamic range of the fibers! However, intensity discrimination in band-stop noise is still possible at high levels and at high frequencies (Carlyon & Moore, 1984) above the frequency at which phase locking to fine structure is thought to break down. Although phase locking may contribute to intensity discrimination in some situations, it does not look like the whole story. Despite this, the hypothesis that intensity is represented, and stimuli are detected, by virtue of changes in the pattern of firing rather than in the overall firing rate, has some support in the literature (Carney, Heinz, Evilsizer, Gilkey, & Colburn, 2002).

6.3.5   The dynamic range solution?

The psychophysical data described in Section 6.3.3 suggest that Weber's law is the characteristic of intensity discrimination when a relatively small number of auditory nerve fibers responding to a restricted region of the cochlea are used, even for stimulation at high levels. Given that only a small number of auditory nerve fibers have large dynamic ranges, and that these fibers have shallow rate-level functions, we would expect intensity discrimination to be much better at low levels than at high levels (in contrast to the psychophysical findings). An analysis of auditory nerve activity by Viemeister (1988) confirms this interpretation. Viemeister took a representative range of rate-level functions based on physiological data. He also took into account the *variability* in firing rate for each neuron (the amount the firing rate varies over the course of several identical stimulus presentations). The shallower the rate-level function or the greater the variability, the less the sensitivity of the fiber to changes in level. The overall variability in the representation can be reduced by *combining information* across a number of fibers (assumed to have similar characteristic frequencies). In this way, Viemeister was able to predict Weber fractions as a function of level.

The results of Viemeister's analysis are shown in Figure 6.9. The figure shows the best possible intensity-discrimination performances that could be achieved based on the firing rates of a group of 10 neurons and a group of 50 neurons.

Figure 6.9 Weber fractions predicted by the optimum use of information from a sample of 10 or 50 auditory nerve fibers. The curves are replotted from Viemeister (1988).

The curves show that there is much more firing-rate information at low levels (around 30 dB SPL) than at high levels, as expected from the characteristics and relative numbers of the high and low spontaneous rate fibers. The distribution of firing-rate information in the auditory nerve as a function of level does not correspond to human performance. However, a comparison of these curves with the human data in Figure 6.8 shows that only 50 neurons are needed to account for discrimination performance for pure tones in band-stop noise over a fairly wide range of levels. Even if the number of usable fibers is restricted by the band-stop noise, we might still expect several hundred, perhaps even several thousand, to provide useful information about the vibration of a small region of the basilar membrane. According to Viemeister's analysis, this would decrease the predicted Weber fractions even further.

It is probable, therefore, that there is enough firing-rate information in the auditory nerve to account for human performance across the entire dynamic range of hearing. Despite the low numbers and shallow rate-level functions of the low spontaneous rate fibers, these neurons seem to be sensitive enough to take over the responsibility for intensity coding at levels above the saturation point of the high spontaneous rate fibers (see Figure 6.7). The pertinent question may not be why we are so good at intensity discrimination at high levels but why we are so bad at intensity discrimination at low levels. It appears that intensity discrimination is limited by processes central to the auditory nerve (in the brainstem or cortex) that do not make optimum use of the information from the peripheral auditory system.

Consider this final point: The remarkable dynamic range of human hearing is dependent on the compression of the basilar membrane. The compression is a consequence of the level-dependent action of the outer hair cells, which effectively amplify low-level sounds but not high-level sounds (see Section 5.2.5). The shallow growth in basilar membrane velocity with level means that the low spontaneous rate fibers have shallow rate-level functions and therefore wide dynamic ranges (see Section 5.3.2). The auditory system uses compression to map a large range of physical intensities onto a small range of firing rates.

6.4   COMPARISONS ACROSS FREQUENCY AND ACROSS TIME

6.4.1   Absolute and relative intensity

The *loudness* of a sound is related to the *absolute* intensity of the sound: The higher the sound pressure level, the louder the sound appears. Absolute intensity may be a useful measure in some situations, when estimating the proximity of a familiar sound source, for example. When we are *identifying* sounds, however, absolute intensity is not very important. The identity of the vowel /i/ is the same whether the vowel sound is played at an overall level of 50 or 100 dB SPL. To identify sounds, it is much more important for us to be sensitive to the *relative* intensities of features within the sound (see Figure 6.10), for instance, the spectral peaks and dips that characterize a vowel. The overall level may vary between presentations, but as long as the spectral shape stays the same, so will the identity of the vowel.

6.4.2   Profile analysis

A comparison across the spectrum is sometimes called *profile analysis*, because the auditory system must perform an analysis of the spectral envelope, or profile. Many of the important early experiments were conducted by Green and colleagues (see Green, 1988). In a typical profile analysis experiment, a listener is presented with a complex spectrum consisting of a number of pure tones of different frequencies. In one observation interval, the tones all have the same level. In the other interval, the level of one of the tones (the "target") is higher than that of the other tones. The listener's task is to pick the interval containing the incremented tone, equivalent to picking the spectrum with the "bump." To prevent listeners from just listening to the target in isolation, the overall level

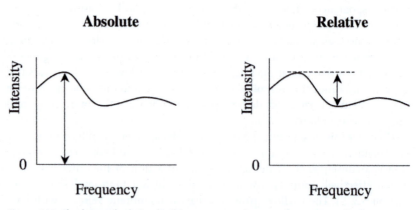

Figure 6.10 Absolute and relative (in this case, across-frequency) measures of intensity.

of the stimulus is randomly varied between observation intervals (Figure 6.11) so that the level of the target in the incorrect interval is higher than that in the correct interval on almost half the trials. To perform well on this task, the listener must be able to compare the level of the target to the level of the other frequency components. In other words, the listener is forced to make *relative* comparisons of level across frequency.

Green's experiments showed that listeners are able to make comparisons of spectral shape, detecting bumps of only a few decibels, even when absolute level is not a useful cue. That is not particularly surprising, since if we couldn't do that, we wouldn't be able to detect formants in vowels. Of greater interest, perhaps, is the finding that performance was almost independent of the time delay between the two observation intervals (at least, up to 8 seconds: Green, Kidd, & Picardi, 1983). If level is randomized between *trials* (so that listeners cannot build up a long-term memory representation of the pedestal), pure-tone intensity discrimination performance drops off as the time interval between the two tones to be compared is increased. It appears that we have difficulty holding a detailed representation of absolute intensity in our memories over several seconds. That performance is much less affected by the time interval for comparisons between two spectral shapes suggests that relative intensity is stored in a more robust way, perhaps because we can simply categorize a particular spectrum as "bumped" or "flat," for example. That information is much easier to remember than a detailed representation of the target.

Within-Trial Level Variation:

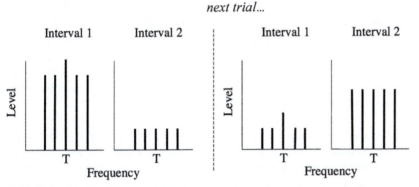

Figure 6.11 A schematic illustration of the spectra of the stimuli in two trials of a typical profile analysis task. The target component is denoted by the "T." The listener's task is to pick the observation interval containing the incremented target (interval 1 in both trials here, or it could equally well be interval 2, determined at random). The overall level of the components has been randomized between each interval so that the listener is forced to compare the target level to the level of the other components across frequency. If the listener just chose the interval containing the most intense target, then the listener would pick interval 1 on the first trial (correct) but interval 2 on the second trial (incorrect). Based on a similar figure in Green et al. (1983).

6.4.3 Comparisons across time

A static image can provide a great deal of visual information. Think about the amount of information contained on the front page of a newspaper, for example. However, a static, or constant, sound provides comparatively little auditory information. I can say "eeee" for as long as I like, but you wouldn't learn very much from it, except perhaps about the state of my mental health. When there is a bit of variability in the sounds I am producing, for example, "evacuate the building," you have been given much more information. We must be able to make intensity comparisons across time, as well as across frequency, so that we can determine how the spectrum is changing. We see in Chapter 11 that this is very important for speech perception.

Most auditory intensity discrimination experiments measure comparisons across time, because listeners are required to compare the levels of two sounds presented one after the other. However, the time intervals between observation intervals (see Figure 6.5) are often much larger than those that usually occur between the temporal features that help identify sounds. *Increment detection* experiments, on the other hand, measure listeners' ability to detect a brief intensity "bump" on an otherwise continuous pedestal. It has been shown that listeners can detect smaller increments in these cases than when discriminating the levels of two tones separated by several hundred milliseconds (Viemeister & Bacon, 1988). It would appear, therefore, that comparisons of intensity over short time intervals are highly accurate. The temporal resolution experiments described in Chapter 8 also demonstrate that the auditory system is very sensitive to brief fluctuations in intensity.

6.5 SUMMARY

The ability to represent sound intensity and to make comparisons of intensity across frequency and time is crucial if the auditory system is to identify sounds. It seems likely that sound intensity is represented in terms of the firing rates of auditory nerve fibers. Because these fibers respond to the vibration of the basilar membrane, the loudness of sounds is dependent on the characteristics of the basilar membrane, in particular, *compression*.

1   We are most sensitive to sounds in the mid-frequency region (1000–6000 Hz). In this region, the absolute threshold for normally hearing listeners is about 0 dB SPL. The *dynamic range* of hearing (the range of levels over which we can use the ear to obtain information about sounds) is about 120 dB in the mid-frequency region and decreases at low and high frequencies.

2   *Loudness* is the sensation most closely associated with sound intensity. Increases in intensity increase the loudness of a sound, as do increases in bandwidth and duration. Increases in bandwidth can increase loudness even when the overall level of the sound is kept constant.

3   Loudness scales show that subjective magnitude is a power function (exponent 0.2–0.3) of intensity over most levels. The shape of the loudness

function suggests that, at a given frequency, loudness is roughly proportional to the square of basilar membrane velocity. The auditory system may effectively sum this quantity across characteristic frequency to produce the loudness of a complex sound.

4   There seems to be enough information in the auditory nerve to represent the intensity of sounds over the entire dynamic range of hearing in terms of firing rate alone, despite the fact that most auditory nerve fibers are saturated at 60 dB SPL. The wide dynamic range is dependent on the low spontaneous rate fibers, whose shallow rate-level functions are a consequence of basilar membrane compression. In other words, basilar membrane compression is the basis for the wide dynamic range of human hearing.

5   Intensity is also represented by the spread of excitation across characteristic frequency as level is increased, for a sound with a narrow bandwidth, and possibly by the increased *synchronization* of spikes (phase locking) to a sound as its level is increased in a background sound.

6   Intensity comparisons across frequency and across time are needed to identify sounds. It appears that these *relative* measures of intensity may be more robust than the absolute measures of intensity we experience as loudness.

6.6   READING

The following chapters are useful introductions:

Epstein, M., & Marozeau, J. (2010). Loudness and intensity coding. In C. J. Plack (Ed.), *Hearing* (pp. 45–70). Oxford: Oxford University Press.

Moore, B. C. J. (2012). *An introduction to the psychology of hearing* (6th ed.). London: Emerald. Chapter 4.

Plack, C. J., & Carlyon, R. P. (1995). Loudness perception and intensity coding. In B. C. J. Moore (Ed.), *Hearing* (pp. 123–160). New York: Academic Press.

Green provides an excellent account of intensity discrimination, including profile analysis:

Green, D. M. (1993). Auditory intensity discrimination. In W. A. Yost, A. N. Popper, & R. R. Fay (Eds.), *Human psychophysics* (pp. 13–55). New York: Springer-Verlag.

7 PITCH AND PERIODICITY CODING

Most sound sources involve a vibrating object of some kind. Regular vibration produces sound waves that *repeat over time*, such as the pure and complex tones described in Chapters 2 and 3. Within a certain range of repetition rates, we perceive the periodic sound wave as being associated with a *pitch*. It is important for us to be able to identify the repetition rate or fundamental frequency of sounds. The variation in the fundamental frequency of vowel sounds in speech can be used to convey prosodic information, and pitch perception is central to the enjoyment of most forms of music: Many musical instruments produce complex tones, and the fundamental frequencies of these tones can be varied to produce different melodies and chords. Less obviously, differences in fundamental frequency are very important in allowing us to *separate out* different sounds that occur at the same time and *group together* those frequency components that originate from the same sound source. These aspects are discussed in Chapter 10.

This chapter will concentrate on how the auditory system represents – and then extracts – information about the periodicity of a sound waveform. The discussion will begin with our perceptions and go on to describe the auditory mechanisms that may form the basis for these perceptions.

7.1 PITCH

7.1.1 What is pitch?

In auditory science, pitch is considered, as is loudness, to be an attribute of our *sensations*: The word should not be used to refer to a *physical* attribute of a sound (although it often is). So you should not say that a tone has a "pitch" of 100 Hz, for example. When we hear a sound with a particular fundamental frequency, we may have a sensation of pitch that is related to that fundamental frequency. When the fundamental frequency increases, we experience an increase in pitch, just as an increase in sound intensity is experienced as an increase in the sensation of loudness.

The American National Standards Institute's latest definition of pitch reads as follows:

> That attribute of auditory sensation by which sounds are ordered on the scale used for melody in music.
>
> (American National Standards Institute, 2015)

In other words, if a sound produces a sensation of pitch, then it can be used to produce recognizable melodies by varying the repetition rate of the sound. Conversely, if a sound does not produce a sensation of pitch, then it cannot be used to produce melodies. This definition is consistent with what some researchers regard as an empirical test of the presence of pitch: If you can show that a sound can produce melodies, then you can be sure that it has a pitch (e.g., Burns & Viemeister, 1976).

7.1.2 Pure tones and complex tones

In Chapter 2, I introduce the sinusoidal pure tone as the fundamental building block of sounds and, from the point of view of acoustics, the simplest periodic waveform. Broadly speaking, a complex tone is "anything else" that is associated with a pitch or has a periodic waveform, and usually consists of a set of pure-tone components (harmonics) with frequencies that are integer multiples of the fundamental frequency of the waveform (see Section 2.4.1). Within certain parameters, both pure and complex tones can be used to produce clear melodies by varying frequency or fundamental frequency, and hence they qualify as pitch evokers according to the ANSI definition. Furthermore, if the fundamental frequency of a complex tone is equal to the frequency of a pure tone, then the two stimuli usually have the same pitch, even though the *spectra* of these sounds might be very different. What seems to be important for producing the same pitch is that the *repetition rate* of the waveform is the same (see Figure 7.1). In a sense, pitch is the *perceptual correlate* of waveform repetition rate.

Research on pitch perception has tended to be divided into research on pure tones and research on complex tones, and I am going to keep this distinction. I am not saying that the pitch of pure tones is in some way a dramatically different percept to the pitch of complex tones. After all, a pure tone is a complex tone containing just the first harmonic. Because of their simplicity, however, pure tones have a special place in the heart of an auditory scientist and have been given much attention. Understanding how simple sounds are perceived can help our understanding of the perception of more complex stimuli, and in many cases, it is possible to extrapolate findings from pure tones to complex tones.

7.1.3 The existence region for pitch

What are the lowest and highest frequencies, or fundamental frequencies, that can be used to produce a pitch? Put another way, what is the frequency range, or *existence region*, for pitch? In regard to pure tones, there is a reasonable consensus on the upper limit. Studies have indicated that, for frequencies above about 5000 Hz, the perception of musical melody breaks down (Attneave & Olson, 1971). This is similar to the highest *fundamental* frequency of a complex tone that can be used to produce a pitch, as long as it has a strong first harmonic. Effectively, the pitch percept is dominated by the first harmonic at these high rates, and because the frequency of the first harmonic is equal to the fundamental frequency, the upper limit is similar. It can surely be no coincidence that the highest note on an orchestral instrument (the piccolo) is around 4500 Hz. Melodies played using frequencies above 5000 Hz sound rather peculiar. You can tell that something is changing, but it doesn't sound musical in any way.

Figure 7.1 The waveforms (left panels) and spectra (right panels) of three sounds, one pure tone and two complex tones, that have the same pitch. Notice that the similarity between the sounds is in the waveform repetition rate (200 Hz) and not in the overall spectrum.

Complex tones, however, can produce a pitch even if the first harmonic is not present (see Section 7.3.1). In these situations, the range of fundamental frequencies that produce a pitch depends on the harmonics that are present. Using a complex tone consisting of only three consecutive harmonics, Ritsma (1962) reported that, for a fundamental frequency of 100 Hz, a pitch could not be heard when harmonics higher than about the 25th were used. For a 500-Hz fundamental, the upper limit was only about the 10th harmonic. It appears that the higher the fundamental, the lower the harmonic numbers need to be (not to be confused with a low number of harmonics!).

At the other end of the scale, for broadband complex tones containing harmonics from the first upward, melodies can be played with fundamental frequencies as low as 30 Hz (Pressnitzer, Patterson, & Krumbholz, 2001). This value is close to the frequency of the lowest note on the grand piano (27.5 Hz). In summary, therefore, the range of repetition rates that evoke a pitch extends from about 30 Hz to about 5000 Hz.

7.2   HOW IS PERIODICITY REPRESENTED?

The first stage of neural representation occurs in the auditory nerve. Any information about a sound that is not present in the auditory nerve is lost forever as far as the auditory system is concerned. This section will focus on the aspects of auditory nerve activity that convey information about the periodicity of sounds.

7.2.1 Pure tones

In Chapters 4 and 5, it is described how different neurons in the auditory nerve respond to activity at different places in the cochlea (*tonotopic* organization). In response to a pure tone, the firing rate of a neuron depends on the level of the pure tone (the higher the level, the higher the firing rate) and the frequency of the pure tone (the closer the frequency to the characteristic frequency of the neuron, the higher the firing rate). It follows that the firing rates of neurons in the auditory nerve provide information about the frequency of the pure tone. The characteristic frequency of the neuron that produces the most spikes should be *equal* to the frequency of the tone (for low levels at least). More generally, however, frequency may be represented in terms of the *pattern* of activity across neurons with different characteristic frequencies.

The *rate-place* coding of frequency is illustrated by the excitation pattern representation, introduced in Sections 5.4.4 and 6.3.3. The left panel of Figure 7.2 shows neural excitation patterns (expressed in terms of the simulated firing rates of high spontaneous rate nerve fibers) for two pure tones whose frequencies differ by 10%. The difference between these sounds is represented not only by the locations of the peaks of the excitation patterns but also by the difference in firing rate at any characteristic frequency for which a response is detectable. Zwicker (1970) suggested that we might detect pure-tone frequency *modulation* by detecting changes in excitation level at the point on the pattern where the level changes most (usually somewhere on the steeply sloping low-frequency side).

Figure 7.2 Rate-place and temporal representations of pure-tone frequency. The figure shows simulated neural excitation patterns (left panel) and temporal spike patterns (right panel) for 500-Hz and 550-Hz pure tones. Both tones were presented at 60 dB SPL. The excitation pattern shows the firing rates of high spontaneous rate fibers as a function of characteristic frequency. The temporal spike patterns show the response of a single auditory nerve fiber.

We are neglecting the other type of information in the auditory nerve, however – the information provided by the propensity of neurons to *phase lock* to the vibration of the basilar membrane. When a low-frequency pure tone is played to the ear, neurons tend to fire at a particular phase of the waveform, so the intervals between neural spikes (*interspike intervals*) are close to *integer multiples* of the period of the pure tone (see Section 4.4.4). Different frequencies produce *different patterns* of spikes across time. For example, a 500-Hz pure tone (2-ms period) will tend to produce spikes separated by 2, 4, 6, . . . ms. A 550-Hz pure tone (1.8-ms period) will tend to produce spikes separated by 1.8, 3.6, 5.5, . . . ms (Figure 7.2, right panel). Any neuron that can respond to the tone tends to phase lock to it, and neurons will continue to phase lock even when they are saturated (see Section 6.3.4). Hence, the same temporal regularity will be present across a wide array of neurons.

So, the information about the frequency of a pure tone is represented by the pattern of neural activity across characteristic frequency and by the pattern of neural activity across time. But which type of information is used by the brain to produce the sensation of pitch? There is a certain amount of disagreement about that, but a couple of facts help sway the balance for many researchers. The first is that our ability to discriminate between the frequencies of two pure tones, below 4000 Hz or so, may be too fine to be explicable in terms of changes in the excitation pattern. Figure 7.3 shows the smallest detectable difference in frequency between two pure tones as a function of frequency. The data show that we can just about detect the difference between a 1000-Hz pure tone and a 1002-Hz pure tone. My own modeling results suggest that the maximum

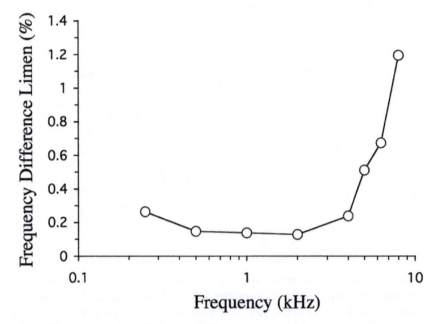

Figure 7.3 Frequency discrimination as a function of frequency for a 200-ms pure tone. The smallest detectable increase in frequency, or frequency difference limen, is expressed as a percentage of the baseline frequency. Data are from Moore (1973).

difference in excitation level across the excitation pattern is only about 0.1 dB for these stimuli. Given that the smallest detectable change in pure-tone level is about 1 dB, we may be asking too much of the auditory system to detect such small frequency differences by changes in excitation level (or equivalently, neural firing rate) alone. We are much worse at frequency discrimination at higher frequencies (Figure 7.3), above the limit of phase locking, where pure-tone frequency is presumably represented by a rate-place code. The other salient fact is that the breakdown of phase locking at about 5000 Hz (see Section 4.4.4) seems to coincide neatly with the loss of the sensation of pitch (in terms of melody recognition) at around the same frequency. The implication is that phase locking, or temporal coding, may be *necessary* for the sensation of pitch.

My own view is that while it remains possible that the *frequency* of pure tones may be represented in part by firing rate across characteristic frequency (especially at high frequencies), the sensation of *pitch* is probably derived mainly from the temporal pattern of firing, or perhaps from a combination of place and temporal cues. After all, if both sets of information are available to the auditory system, why not use both?

7.2.2 Complex tones

Figure 7.4 shows the excitation pattern of a complex tone with a number of equal-amplitude harmonics. In the region of the excitation pattern corresponding to the low harmonic numbers, there is a sequence of peaks and dips in excitation level. Each peak corresponds to a single harmonic, so the center frequency of the auditory filter giving a peak output is equal to the frequency of the harmonic. An auditory filter (or a place on the basilar membrane) tuned to a low harmonic responds mostly to that harmonic only; the other harmonics are attenuated by the filter. In a filter with a center frequency between two harmonics, both harmonics may receive substantial attenuation and the result is a dip in the excitation pattern. The first few harmonics are effectively *separated out* or *resolved* by the frequency selectivity of the basilar membrane. Each resolved harmonic has a separate representation in the cochlea. Furthermore, the representation in the cochlea is reflected in our perceptions. With practice, or an appropriate cue, such as a pure tone with the frequency of one of the harmonics presented separately, it is possible for listeners to "hear out" the first five or so harmonics of a complex tone as separate pure tones (Plomp & Mimpen, 1968).

As we go to the right of the excitation pattern, toward higher harmonic numbers and higher center frequencies, the difference between the peaks and dips decreases. Above about the tenth harmonic, the pattern is almost smooth. Why is this? The spacing between harmonics is constant, 100 Hz in this example. However, the auditory filters get broader (in terms of the bandwidth in hertz) as center frequency increases (Section 5.4.3). A filter centered on a high harmonic may pass *several* harmonics with very little attenuation, and variations in center frequency will have little effect on filter output. These higher harmonics are not separated out on the basilar membrane and are said to be *unresolved*.

The resolution of harmonics depends more on harmonic number than on spectral frequency or fundamental frequency. If the fundamental frequency is doubled, the spacing between the harmonics doubles. However, the frequency

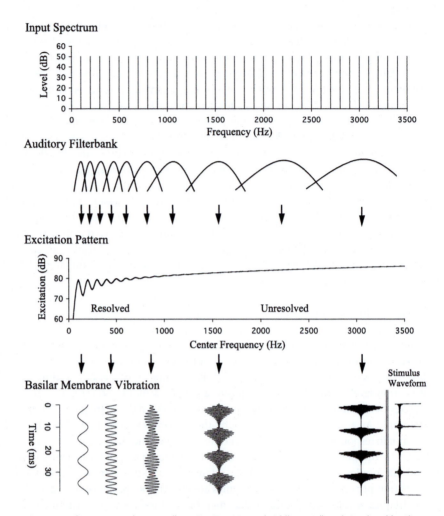

Figure 7.4 The spectrum (top panel), excitation pattern (middle panel) and simulated basilar membrane vibration (bottom panel) for a complex tone consisting of a number of equal-amplitude harmonics with a fundamental frequency of 100 Hz. The auditory filters become broader as center frequency increases, hence the high-frequency harmonics are not resolved in the excitation pattern. The basilar membrane vibration is simulated for five different center, or characteristic, frequencies (indicated by the origins of the downward-pointing arrows). The original waveform of the complex tone is also shown for reference (bottom right).

of each harmonic also doubles. Because the bandwidth of the auditory filter is approximately proportional to center frequency, the doubling in spacing is accompanied by a doubling in the bandwidth of the corresponding auditory filter. The result is that the resolvability of the harmonic does not change significantly. Almost irrespective of fundamental frequency, about the first eight harmonics are resolved by the cochlea (see Plack & Oxenham, 2005, for a discussion of this issue). The number of the highest resolvable harmonic does decrease somewhat at low fundamental frequencies (below 100 Hz or so), because the Q of the auditory filters is less at low center frequencies (i.e., the bandwidth as a proportion of center frequency is greater).

Information about the individual resolved harmonics is preserved in the auditory nerve both by the pattern of firing rates across frequency (rate-place, as illustrated by the excitation pattern) and by the phase-locked response of the nerve fibers. At the bottom of Figure 7.4 is a simulation of the vibration of the basilar membrane at different characteristic frequencies in response to the complex tone. A fiber connected to the place in the cochlea responding to a low harmonic will produce a pattern of firing synchronized to the vibration on the basilar membrane at that place, which is similar to the sinusoidal waveform of the harmonic. The time intervals between spikes will tend to be integer multiples of the period of the harmonic. The *individual frequencies* of the first few harmonics are represented by different patterns of firing in the auditory nerve.

The pattern of basilar membrane vibration for the unresolved harmonics is very different. Because several harmonics are stimulating the same region of the basilar membrane, the pattern of vibration is the complex waveform produced by the addition of the harmonics. The spacing between the harmonics is the same as the fundamental frequency; hence, the resulting vibration has a periodicity equal to that of the original complex tone. (The harmonics are *beating together* to produce amplitude modulation with a rate equal to the frequency difference between them; see Section 2.5.1.) The pattern of vibration at a place tuned to high harmonic numbers is effectively the waveform of a complex tone that has been *band-pass filtered* by the auditory filter for that place.

There is little information about fundamental frequency in terms of the distribution of firing rates across nerve fibers for complex tones consisting entirely of unresolved harmonics. Firing *rate* does not substantially change as a function of characteristic frequency. There is still information, however, in the temporal pattern of firing. Neurons will tend to phase lock to the *envelope* of the basilar membrane vibration (Joris & Yin, 1992), so the time intervals between spikes will tend to be integer multiples of the period of the complex tone. That the auditory nerve can phase lock to the envelope means that the modulation rate of stimuli, such as amplitude-modulated noise, is also represented in terms of the pattern of firing. It has been shown that sinusoidally amplitude-modulated noise (a noise whose envelope varies sinusoidally over time, produced by multiplying a noise with a pure-tone modulator) can elicit a weak, but demonstrably musical, pitch sensation, which corresponds to the frequency of the modulation (Burns & Viemeister, 1976).

Figure 7.5 illustrates the temporal pattern of firing that might be expected from nerve fibers tuned to a resolved harmonic (bottom left panel) and those responding to several higher unresolved harmonics (bottom right panel). Time intervals between spikes reflect the periodicity of the harmonic for low harmonic numbers. Time intervals between spikes reflect the periodicity of the original waveform (equal to the envelope repetition rate) for high harmonic numbers (and for amplitude-modulated noise).

It is clear from the bumps in the excitation pattern in Figure 7.4 that there will be information about the resolved harmonics in the pattern of firing rates across characteristic frequency. As is the case for pure tones, however, it is thought by many researchers that the *temporal* code illustrated in Figure 7.5 is

Basilar Membrane Vibration

Auditory Nerve Spikes

Time ⟶

Figure 7.5 Basilar membrane vibration and spike patterns in response to a resolved harmonic (the second harmonic, left panel) and in response to several unresolved harmonics (right panel) of the same fundamental frequency. The nerve fiber tuned to the resolved harmonic phase locks to the fine structure. The nerve fiber tuned to the unresolved harmonics phase locks to the envelope.

more important for carrying information about the fundamental frequencies of complex tones to the brain. Our sensitivity to differences in fundamental frequency (less than 1% for resolved harmonics) suggests that we do not rely on rate-place information for resolved harmonics. Furthermore, unresolved harmonics and modulated noise simply do not produce any rate-place information in the auditory nerve concerning repetition rate, but they can still evoke a (weak) pitch. This pitch is presumably coded temporally.

However, some findings have called into question the view that temporal coding is *necessary* for pitch perception. Andrew Oxenham and colleagues showed that listeners could hear a clear pitch produced by tones with harmonic frequencies well above the supposed neural limit of phase locking (Oxenham, Micheyl, Keebler, Loper, & Santurette, 2011). These authors confirmed that a fundamental frequency less than 5000 Hz is necessary for a clear pitch. However, they also showed that as long as the fundamental frequency is below 5000 Hz, the harmonic frequency components need not be. For example, listeners could hear a clear pitch corresponding to 1200 Hz when the tone only contained harmonics of 7200 Hz and above (i.e., harmonics of 7200, 8400, 9600, . . . Hz; see Figure 7.6). Listeners could recognize melodies created with tones containing just these high-frequency resolved harmonics, hence satisfying my definition for pitch. Oxenham and colleagues were careful to control for potential confounds produced by interactions between the harmonics on the basilar membrane that might provide temporal envelope information.

Why is this bad news for the temporal account of pitch coding? Well, if all the harmonics are above the upper frequency limit of phase locking, then their frequencies cannot be represented by phase locking in the auditory nerve. The alternative is that, for these high frequencies at least, harmonics are represented by the *place* of activation on the basilar membrane and in the neural array. The results of Oxenham and colleagues seem to imply that temporal information is

Figure 7.6 The spectrum of one of the complex tones used in the experiment of Oxenham et al. (2011). The fundamental frequency is 1200 Hz, but the lowest harmonic is 7200 Hz, which is above the supposed upper limit of phase locking (dashed line). However, listeners could still hear a pitch corresponding to 1200 Hz (dotted line).

not necessary for pitch, although of course temporal information may still be used when the harmonics are within the phase locking range.

7.2.3 Pitch representations in the human brainstem and the role of experience

When a large number of neurons phase lock together, they produce an electric potential that is large enough to be measured by attaching electrodes to the head. This is the basis for the *frequency-following response*, an electrophysiological recording that can be made, from humans, using electrodes placed on the scalp (see Section A.3.2). In response to a regular stimulus such as a pure or a complex tone, a repetitive pattern can be observed in the electrophysiological recording, after combining over many repeats to improve the strength of the response. Because the response is generated by neural phase locking to the stimulus, the frequencies present in the frequency-following response usually correspond to the frequency components present in the stimulus, including the stimulus envelope, and the fundamental frequencies of complex tones. The frequency-following response is thought to reflect mainly phase-locked activity in the region of the inferior colliculus (Krishnan, 2006), although there may be contributions from earlier and later generators in the auditory pathway, including the auditory cortex (Coffey, Herholz, Chepesiuk, Baillet, & Zatorre, 2016).

The frequency-following response provides important information about temporal representations in the brainstem. Because the response often includes a representation of the fundamental frequency, it has been suggested that the response may reflect the encoding of pitch in the brainstem. Supporting this view, it has been reported that musicians (Wong, Skoe, Russo, Dees, & Kraus, 2007), and speakers of "tone languages" such as Chinese (Krishnan, Xu,

Gandour, & Cariani, 2005), have stronger frequency-following responses to some stimuli. In addition, there is evidence that the response strengthens in response to the trained stimuli when people are given a few hours training on a pitch discrimination task (Carcagno & Plack, 2011). These findings suggest that extensive experience with pitch discrimination may increase the precision of brainstem neural phase locking in some way, and that this enhanced representation of periodicity might underlie the improved pitch discrimination abilities demonstrated by these individuals.

However, the frequency-following response may only reflect the basic temporal representations of pitch in the brainstem, not too dissimilar from the representation seen in the auditory nerve. The periodicity in the frequency-following response does not always reflect that pitch that is heard, and it doesn't seem that the response reflects the output of a "higher level" pitch extraction process (Gockel, Carlyon, Mehta, & Plack, 2011).

7.3 HOW IS PERIODICITY EXTRACTED?

The repetition rate of the waveform of a pure tone is equal to the spectral frequency. All other periodic waveforms (complex tones) consist of a number of frequency components, each of which contains information about the fundamental frequency of the waveform. In fact, the fundamental frequency is defined unambiguously by the frequencies of any two successive harmonics. We know that the cochlea separates out these components to some extent and that phase locking in the auditory nerve provides a temporal code for the frequencies of the resolved harmonics and a temporal code for the envelope repetition rate for the unresolved harmonics. How is the information in the auditory nerve used by the auditory system to derive periodicity and to give us the sensation of pitch?

7.3.1 The missing fundamental and the dominant region

Early luminaries of acoustics such as Ohm (1843) and Helmholtz (1863) thought that the pitch of a complex tone was determined by the frequency of the first harmonic, or fundamental component. The idea is that, if you hear a series of frequency components, you just extract the frequency of the lowest component and that gives you the fundamental frequency and the periodicity. This method works well for most complex tones we encounter outside psychoacoustic laboratories. The fundamental frequency is equal to the frequency of the first harmonic, which is usually present in the spectra of sounds such as vowels and musical tones. However, Licklider (1956) showed that the pitch of a complex tone is unaffected by the addition of low-pass noise designed to mask the frequency region of the fundamental. Even if the fundamental component is inaudible or missing, we still hear a pitch corresponding to the basic periodicity of the complex. (Recall that the repetition rate of the waveform of a complex tone does not change when the fundamental component is removed; see Section 2.4.1 and Figure 7.1.) The auditory system must be able to extract information about the fundamental frequency from the higher harmonics.

In fact, research has shown that the first harmonic may not even be the most important for determining the pitch of some complex tones. There is a region of low-numbered harmonics that tends to "dominate" the percept, so frequency variations in these harmonics have a substantial effect on the pitch. For example, Moore, Glasberg, and Peters (1985) varied the frequency of one component in a complex tone so that the component was "mistuned" from the harmonic relation. For small mistunings, changes in the frequency of the harmonic produced small changes in the pitch of the complex tone as a whole. The results for one listener are shown in Figure 7.7. Note that the greater the mistuning of the harmonic, the greater the shift in pitch. This occurs for mistunings up to about 3%, after which the magnitude of the pitch shift *decreases* as the frequency of the harmonic is increased (see Section 10.2.2 for an explanation). Although there was some variability between individuals in the experiment of Moore et al., variations in the second, third, and fourth harmonics produced the largest effects for fundamental frequencies from 100 to 400 Hz.

Dai (2000) used a slightly different technique, in which the frequencies of all the harmonics were jittered randomly (i.e., randomly displaced from their

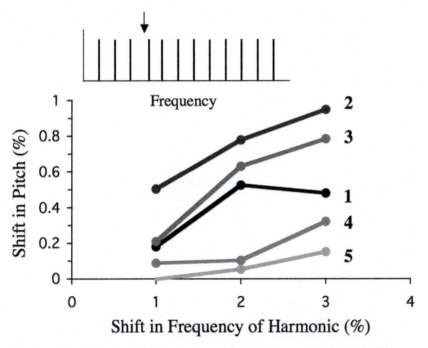

Figure 7.7 The effects of a shift in the frequency of a single harmonic on the pitch of the whole complex tone. The harmonic number of the shifted harmonic is shown to the right. A schematic spectrum for the stimulus with a shifted fourth harmonic is shown above the graph (the arrow indicates the usual location of the fourth harmonic). The pitch shift was determined by changing the fundamental frequency of a complex tone with regular harmonic spacing until its pitch matched that of the complex tone with the shifted harmonic. The results are those of listener BG, for a fundamental frequency of 200 Hz, from the study by Moore et al. (1985). For this listener, the second harmonic was the most dominant, followed by the third, first, fourth, and fifth.

strict harmonic values). The contribution of each harmonic to the pitch of the complex as a whole was determined by the extent to which a large jitter in that harmonic was associated with a large change in pitch. For a range of fundamental frequencies, Dai found that harmonics with frequencies around 600 Hz were the most dominant. The dominant harmonic *numbers* were therefore dependent on the fundamental frequency. For a fundamental frequency of 100 Hz, the sixth harmonic was the most dominant, and for a fundamental frequency of 200 Hz, the third harmonic was the most dominant. For fundamental frequencies above 600 Hz, the first harmonic (the fundamental component) was the most dominant.

Whatever the precise harmonic numbers involved, it is clear from all the research on this topic that the *resolved* harmonics are the most important in pitch perception. For the complex tones that we hear in our everyday environment (e.g., vowel sounds), which usually have strong low harmonics, pitch is determined mainly by a combination of the frequency information from the resolved harmonics. Although they can be used for melody production, complex tones consisting entirely of unresolved harmonics have a weak pitch (i.e., the pitch is not very clear or salient). In addition, we are much better at detecting a difference between the fundamental frequencies of two complex tones if they contain resolved harmonics than if they are entirely composed of unresolved harmonics (Figure 7.8).

Just a note here, in case you ever end up doing research on pitch perception. It is *very* important to include low-pass masking noise in experiments than involve removing low harmonics from a complex tone. If the fundamental component,

Figure 7.8 The smallest detectable difference in fundamental frequency (the fundamental frequency difference limen, or FODL, expressed as a percentage) as a function of the lowest harmonic number in a group of 11 successive harmonics with a fundamental frequency of 200 Hz. When all the harmonics are unresolved (lowest harmonic numbers of 11 and above), performance is worse than when there are some resolved harmonics (lowest harmonic number of 7). Data are from Houtsma and Smurzynski (1990).

or any low harmonics, are simply removed from the waveform entering the ear, they can be *reintroduced* as combination tone distortion products on the basilar membrane (see Section 5.2.4 and Pressnitzer & Patterson, 2001). Although you may think that you are presenting a stimulus that only contains unresolved harmonics, thanks to nonlinearities on the basilar membrane, the input to the auditory nervous system may well contain resolved harmonics. Unless you mask these components with noise, as Licklider did in the missing fundamental experiment, you cannot be sure that you are just measuring the response to the unresolved harmonics. Many experiments (including my own) have left themselves open to criticism by not taking this precaution.

7.3.2 Pattern recognition

The low-numbered harmonics in a complex tone are resolved in terms of the pattern of excitation on the basilar membrane and in terms of the firing rates of auditory nerve fibers as a function of characteristic frequency. Because of this resolution, a neuron tuned to an individual low-numbered harmonic will tend to phase lock only to that harmonic. Information about the individual frequencies of resolved harmonics is present in the auditory nerve, and indeed, we can be cued to "hear out" and make frequency matches to individual resolved harmonics. Because the individual frequencies of the low-numbered harmonics are available, it has been suggested that the auditory system could use the *pattern* of harmonic frequencies to estimate the fundamental frequency (Goldstein, 1973; Terhardt, 1974). For instance, if harmonics with frequencies of 400, 600, and 800 Hz are present, then the fundamental frequency is 200 Hz. If harmonics with frequencies of 750, 1250, and 1500 Hz are present, then the fundamental frequency is 250 Hz. Since the spacing between successive harmonics is equal to the fundamental frequency, any two successive resolved harmonics should be enough, and we can, indeed, get a sense of musical pitch corresponding to the fundamental frequency of just two successive resolved harmonics (Houtsma & Goldstein, 1972).

Pattern recognition may be implemented as a form of *harmonic template*. For example, the auditory system may contain a template for a 100-Hz fundamental frequency that has slots at frequencies of 100, 200, 300, 400, 500, 600, . . . Hz (Figure 7.9). When a group of harmonics is presented to the ear, the auditory system may simply find the best matching template from its store in memory. A complex tone that has frequency components close to the slots on a template (e.g., 99.5, 201, and 299.5 Hz) is heard as having the best matching fundamental frequency (e.g., 100 Hz), even though the sound may not be strictly harmonic. That is how pattern recognition models can predict the pitch shift produced by mistuning a single harmonic — the best matching fundamental frequency is also shifted slightly in this case.

Note that, in general terms, the pattern recognition approach does not rely on any specific mechanism for deriving the frequencies of the individual harmonics. The frequencies may be derived from the rate-place representation, from the temporal representation, or from a combination of the two. The distinctive feature of pattern recognition models is that the individual frequencies of the resolved harmonics must be extracted before the fundamental frequency

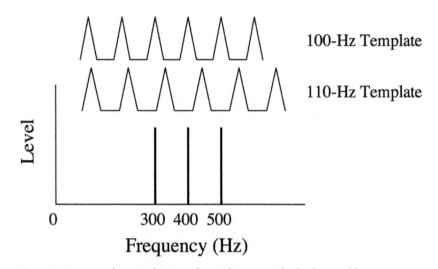

Figure 7.9 How template matching may be used to extract the fundamental frequency of resolved harmonics. Harmonics of 300, 400, and 500 Hz produce a strong match to the 100-Hz template but a weak match to the 110-Hz template.

can be derived. Pattern recognition models cannot account for the pitches of stimuli that do not contain resolved harmonics. However, a weak, but clearly musical, pitch can be evoked when only unresolved harmonics are present. Furthermore, musical melodies can be played by varying the modulation rate of amplitude-modulated noise (Burns & Viemeister, 1976). Neither of these stimuli contains resolved harmonics. The only information about periodicity available to the auditory system in these cases is in the temporal pattern of basilar membrane vibration, as represented by the phase-locked response of auditory nerve fibers. Although pattern recognition can account for the pitch of stimuli containing resolved harmonics, it is unlikely to be an explanation for all pitch phenomena.

7.3.3 Temporal models

Schouten (1940, 1970) proposed a purely temporal mechanism for the extraction of fundamental frequency. The unresolved harmonics interact on the basilar membrane to produce a waveform that repeats at the frequency of the fundamental (see Figure 7.4). Schouten suggested that we derive the fundamental frequency by measuring the periodicity of the interaction of the unresolved harmonics. However, we know that the resolved harmonics are much more dominant, and important to the pitch of naturalistic stimuli, than the unresolved harmonics. In the absence of resolved harmonics, unresolved harmonics evoke only a weak pitch. The pattern recognition approach fails because we don't need resolved harmonics for pitch, and Schouten's approach fails because we don't need unresolved harmonics for pitch. Is there a way of using the information from both types of harmonics?

Researchers are still looking for ways in which the phase-locked activity in auditory nerve fibers may be decoded by the auditory system. Some temporal theories of pitch perception suggest that there is a single mechanism that combines the information from the resolved and unresolved harmonics. As described in Section 7.2.2, neurons that have low characteristic frequencies will tend to phase lock to the individual resolved harmonics, whereas neurons with higher characteristic frequencies will tend to phase lock to the envelope produced by the interacting unresolved harmonics. In both cases, there will be interspike intervals that correspond to the period of the original waveform. For example, a neuron tuned to the second harmonic of a 100-Hz fundamental frequency may produce spikes separated by 5 ms (1/200 seconds), but the 10-ms interval corresponding to the period of the complex (1/100 seconds) will also be present. A neuron tuned to the unresolved harmonics will also produce a proportion of intervals corresponding to the period of the fundamental frequency, because the neuron will phase lock to the envelope that repeats at the fundamental frequency. By picking the most prominent interspike interval (or perhaps the shortest common interspike interval) across frequency channels, an estimate of fundamental frequency (or indeed, the frequency of a pure tone) may be obtained (Moore, 2012). Figure 7.10 illustrates the idea in a schematic way: Neurons at each characteristic frequency contain a representation of the period of the fundamental, even though many other interspike intervals may be present.

An effective way of extracting periodicity in this manner is by a computation of the *autocorrelation function* (Licklider, 1951). An autocorrelation function is computed by correlating a signal with a delayed representation of itself

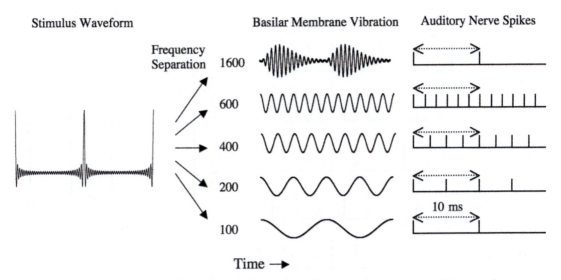

Figure 7.10 Basilar membrane vibration and phase locking in the auditory nerve in response to a 100-Hz complex tone. The responses to the first, second, fourth, and sixth harmonics are shown, along with the response to a group of interacting unresolved harmonics. The characteristic frequencies of each place on the basilar membrane (in hertz) are shown to the left of the vibration plots. The temporal patterns of spikes are unrealistic for individual fibers (e.g., individual neurons would not phase lock to every cycle of the sixth harmonic) but can be taken as representative of the combined responses of several fibers. The important point is that the interspike interval corresponding to the period of the fundamental frequency (illustrated by the arrows) is present at each characteristic frequency.

(see Figure 7.11). At time delays equal to integer multiples of the repetition rate of a waveform, the correlation will be strong. Similarly, if there are common time intervals between waveform features, then this delay will show up strongly in the autocorrelation function. For instance, a pulse train is a complex tone with a regular sequence of pressure pulses (see Figure 2.13, top panel): If there is an interval of 10 ms between successive pulses, a delay of 10 ms will match each pulse to the subsequent pulse. A simple addition of the autocorrelation functions of auditory nerve spikes across characteristic frequencies produces a summary function that takes into account the information from both the resolved and unresolved harmonics. Any common periodicity (e.g., the 10-ms interval in Figure 7.10) will show up strongly in the summary function. The delay of the first main peak in the summary function provides a good account of the pitch heard for many complex stimuli (Meddis & Hewitt, 1991).

Although modern autocorrelation models do a reasonable job, there are still some niggling doubts. In particular, many autocorrelation models do not provide a satisfactory explanation of why we are so much better at fundamental frequency discrimination, and why pitch is so much stronger, for resolved harmonics than for unresolved harmonics (Carlyon, 1998). This is true even when the fundamental frequencies are chosen so that the harmonics are in the same spectral region (Shackleton & Carlyon, 1994). One possible explanation for this is that the temporal mechanism only works well when the frequency represented by phase locking is close to the characteristic frequency of the neuron

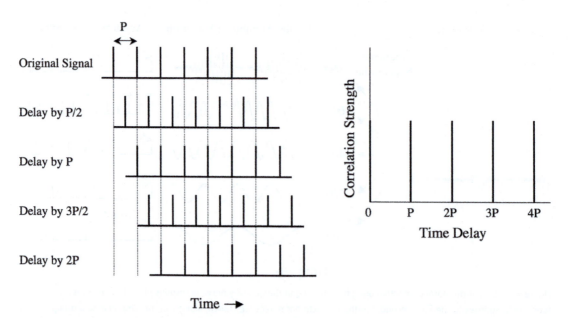

Figure 7.11 How autocorrelation extracts the periodicity of a waveform. A pulse train, or set of neural spikes (top left panel), is subject to different delays. When the delay is an integer multiple of the period of the pulse train (P), the delayed version of the waveform is strongly correlated with the original (the timings of the original pulses are indicated by the dotted lines). Correlation strength (right panel) is measured by *multiplying* the delayed version with the original version and summing the result across time.

concerned – in other words, when the *temporal* representation of frequency is consistent with the *tonotopic* or *place* representation (Oxenham, Bernstein, & Penagos, 2004). This could be because the mechanism that extracts pitch information from temporal firing patterns is tuned only to analyze periodicities in neural firing that are close to the characteristic frequency (Srulovicz & Goldstein, 1983). This would be the case for phase locking to the frequencies of the resolved harmonics. However, for phase locking to the envelope produced by the interactions of unresolved harmonics, the frequency represented in the neural spike patterns will tend to be much lower than the characteristic frequency (see Figure 7.10). Hence, the temporal spike patterns produced by the unresolved harmonics may simply not be processed efficiently. Note that this type of model depends on a *combination* of both temporal and place information.

7.3.4 Neural mechanisms

We are unclear, therefore, about the precise nature of the algorithm that is used to extract the repetition rate of a periodic stimulus from the peripheral neural code. We are also unclear about *where* in the auditory system such an algorithm might be implemented. It is likely that the processing occurs after the inputs from the two ears are combined, because a pitch can be derived from just two harmonics presented to *opposite ears* (Houtsma & Goldstein, 1972). That could be almost anywhere in the ascending auditory pathways but probably after the cochlear nucleus.

The maximum repetition rate to which a neuron will phase lock decreases as the signal is transmitted up the ascending pathways. In the medial geniculate body, the upper limit may be about 800 Hz (Møller, 2013), compared to about 5000 Hz in the auditory nerve. Some investigators think that, at some stage before the medial geniculate body in the ascending auditory pathways, a representation of pitch by the temporal pattern of neural spikes is converted into a representation by firing *rate*, with different neurons tuned to different periodicities/fundamental frequencies. Just as the spectrum of a sound is encoded by the distribution of firing rates across characteristic frequency (tonotopic organization), the fundamental frequencies of sounds may be encoded by the pattern of activity across neurons with different characteristic (or "best") periodicities (*periodotopic* organization). It would be particularly nice to find a neuron that responds with a high firing rate to complex tones with a particular fundamental frequency, irrespective of the spectrum of the complex tone (e.g., regardless of whether it contains only low harmonics or only high harmonics). Unfortunately, the evidence for such neurons in the brainstem is not conclusive. There was some excitement about neurons in the inferior colliculus that show tuning to periodicity, with different neurons being sensitive to different modulation rates (Langner & Schreiner, 1988). However, the tuning may be too broad to provide the accurate representation of periodicity required for pitch.

When we move up to the auditory cortex, the evidence is more compelling. Neurons have been found in the auditory cortex of marmoset monkeys that each respond selectively to a complex tone with a specific fundamental frequency, irrespective of the spectral distribution of harmonics (Bendor & Wang, 2005). In the experimental recordings, such a neuron would respond to a pure tone at its characteristic frequency, and also to a missing fundamental complex tone as long as the fundamental frequency was equal to the neuron's characteristic frequency. For example, if the fundamental frequency was right, complex tones containing harmonics 4, 5, and 6, or 8, 9, and 10 would both excite the neuron. However, except for the first harmonic (which has a frequency equal to the fundamental frequency), such a neuron would not respond to each harmonic component when presented individually; it would only respond strongly when its best fundamental frequency was present in a pattern of several harmonics, not just to a single component such as the fifth or sixth harmonic presented on its own. Neurons with different best fundamental frequencies, covering a range from about 100 to 800 Hz, were reported. These neurons, located near the border of primary auditory cortex, might function as "pitch-selective neurons" (Bendor & Wang, 2005).

Some brain imaging studies suggest that an analogous brain region in humans, the lateral portion of Heschl's gyrus, is more sensitive to sounds that evoke a pitch than to sounds with a similar spectrum that do not evoke a pitch. However, when a wide range of pitch-evoking stimuli was tested using functional magnetic resonance imaging (see Section A.4), the main consistent pitch-related response was posterior to Heschl's gyrus, in a region called *planum temporale* (Hall & Plack, 2009). Of course, these cortical areas might be receiving signals from a pitch-extracting region of the brainstem and may not be directly involved in pitch extraction itself.

A pitch template that forms the basis of a pattern recognition mechanism could be produced by combining the activity of neurons with different characteristic frequencies, spaced at integer multiples of a particular fundamental frequency, or possibly by combining the outputs of neurons that are sensitive to the different patterns of phase locking in response to the resolved harmonics. Intriguingly, there are neurons in the marmoset auditory cortex that show several peaks in their tuning curves to pure tones, positioned at harmonically related frequencies (Bendor, Osmanski, & Wang, 2012). These neurons respond even more strongly to combinations of harmonics of a particular fundamental frequency. There are other neurons that respond very strongly to particular combinations of harmonics, but only weakly or not at all to individual pure tones (Feng & Wang, 2017). The responses to both types of neurons may occur due to input from several neurons with characteristic frequencies spaced at harmonic intervals. Neurons sensitive to combinations of components may function as harmonic templates that feed into pitch-selective neurons such as those identified by Bendor and Wang (2005).

There is little direct evidence for a neural network that can perform autocorrelation as described in Section 7.3.3. These networks require a set of delay lines so that the neural firing pattern can be delayed then combined (theoretically multiplied) with the original version. A large set of delays is needed, from 0.2 ms to extract the periodicity of a 5000-Hz stimulus to 33 ms to extract the periodicity of a 30-Hz stimulus. Delays may be implemented by using neurons with long axons (spikes take longer to travel down long axons) or by increasing the number of synapses (i.e., number of successive neurons) in a pathway, since transmission across a synapse imposes a delay. A "pitch neuron" could then combine the activity from a fast path and from a delayed path in order to perform the autocorrelation. If the delays were different for different pitch neurons, each neuron would respond to a different periodicity. Langner and Schreiner (1988) have found some evidence for neural delay lines in the inferior colliculus of the cat, but again the evidence is inconclusive.

Overall, then, the picture from the neurophysiology is still a little unclear. Although researchers may have found pitch-selective neurons and harmonic templates in auditory cortex, we are unsure how these responses might arise from earlier neural mechanisms. Researchers have some idea what they are looking for in terms of the neural basis of pitch extraction, but finding it is a different matter altogether.

7.4 SUMMARY

We are at the stage in the book where facts begin to be replaced by conjecture. We know quite a lot about the representation of periodicity in the auditory nerve, but how that information is used to produce a neural signal that corresponds to our sensation of pitch is still a matter for investigation. The perceptual experiments on human listeners help guide the search for pitch neurons. We need to know what the perceptions are before we can identify the neural mechanisms that may underlie these perceptions.

1   Sounds that repeat over time (*periodic* sounds) are often associated with a distinct pitch that corresponds to the repetition rate. The range of repetition rates that evoke a musical pitch extends from about 30 Hz to about 5000 Hz.

2   The frequency of pure tones is represented in the auditory nerve by the pattern of firing rates across characteristic frequency (*rate-place* code) and by the pattern of phase-locked activity across time (*temporal* code). It is probable that the temporal code, or perhaps some combination of the temporal and rate-place code, is used to produce the sensation of pitch.

3   The low harmonics of complex tones are *resolved* on the basilar membrane and produce separate patterns of near-sinusoidal vibration at different places along the membrane. The higher harmonics are *unresolved* and interact on the basilar membrane to produce complex waveforms that repeat at the fundamental frequency. Neurons phase lock to the individual frequencies of the resolved harmonics and to the envelope that results from the interaction of the unresolved harmonics.

4   Complex tones produce a clear pitch even if the first harmonic (the fundamental component) is absent. However, the resolved harmonics are dominant and produce a clearer pitch than the unresolved harmonics. In the case of most complex tones that we encounter in the environment, pitch is mainly determined by a *combination* of the information from the individual resolved harmonics.

5   Pattern recognition models suggest that the auditory system extracts the frequencies of the resolved harmonics and uses the patterning of these

harmonics to estimate the fundamental frequency. However, these models cannot account for the pitch of unresolved harmonics.

6   The period of a complex tone is reflected in the time intervals between spikes of nerve fibers responding to both resolved *and* unresolved harmonics. Some temporal models assume that activity is combined across fibers with different characteristic frequencies to estimate this period (and, hence, to provide the sensation of pitch).

7   The neural basis of pitch extraction is unclear. Somewhere in the brainstem, temporal patterns of firing may be converted into a code based on firing rate, with different neurons tuned to different periodicities. Neurons have been identified in primate auditory cortex that respond selectively to a particular fundamental frequency, irrespective of the complex tone's spectral characteristics. These neurons might be "pitch selective."

7.5   READING

Brian Moore and Alain de Cheveigné provide excellent introductions:

de Cheveigné, A. (2010). Pitch perception. In C. J. Plack (Ed.), *Hearing* (pp. 71–104). Oxford: Oxford University Press.

Moore, B. C. J. (2012). *An introduction to the psychology of hearing* (6th ed.). London: Emerald. Chapter 6.

For a broad account of pitch perception, I recommend:

Plack, C. J., Oxenham, A. J., Fay, R. R., & Popper, A. N. (Eds.) (2005). *Pitch: Neural coding and perception*. New York: Springer-Verlag.

For those interested in learning more about the frequency-following response, this volume provides a comprehensive overview:

Kraus, N., Anderson, S., White-Schwoch, T., Fay, R. R., & Popper, A. N. (Eds.) (2017). *The frequency-following response: A window into human communication*. New York: Springer.

8 HEARING OVER TIME

Information in the auditory domain is carried mainly by *changes* in the characteristics of sounds over time. This is true on a small time scale, when interpreting individual speech sounds, and on a larger time scale, when hearing the engine of a car become gradually louder as it approaches. However, it is the speed at which the auditory system can process sounds that is truly remarkable. In free-flowing speech, consonants and vowels may be produced at rates of 30 per second (see Section 11.2.1). In order to process such fast-changing stimuli, the auditory system has to have good *temporal resolution*.

This chapter examines two aspects of hearing over time: First, our ability to follow rapid changes in a sound over time, and second, our ability to combine information about sounds over much longer durations to improve detection and discrimination performance.

8.1 TEMPORAL RESOLUTION

8.1.1 Temporal fine structure and envelope

In general, temporal resolution refers to the resolution or separation of events in time. In Section 2.5.1, I explain how the temporal variations in the amplitude of a sound wave can be described in terms of the rapid individual pressure variations, known as the *temporal fine structure*, and the slower changes in the peak amplitude of these variations, known as the *envelope* (see Figure 2.17). For frequencies up to about 5000 Hz, auditory nerve fibers will tend to phase lock to the fine structure of the basilar membrane vibration at each place in the cochlea (Section 4.4.4). Hence, the auditory nerve contains a rich representation of the temporal fine structure of sounds. In other chapters of the book, I describe why it is thought that fine structure information is important for pitch perception (Chapter 7) and for spatial hearing (Chapter 9). Additionally, fine structure information may be important in speech perception and for detecting sounds in amplitude-modulated maskers (see Moore, 2008, for a review). However, we do not perceive these rapid pressure variations as fluctuations in magnitude. When a continuous pure tone is played, we hear a continuous stable sound. Our perception of the magnitude of a sound is more closely linked to the *envelope*. Hence, in auditory science, the term "temporal resolution" is usually used to refer to our ability to respond to rapid fluctuations in the envelope. If the response is sluggish, then the auditory system will not be able to track rapid envelope fluctuations. The internal representation of the sound will be blurred in time, just as an out-of-focus visual image is blurred in space (and just as the excitation pattern in the cochlea is a blurred representation of the spectrum of a sound).

8.1.2   Measures of temporal resolution

Most of the early experiments on temporal resolution tried to measure a single duration that described the briefest change in a stimulus that can be perceived. The design of these experiments was complicated by the fact that any change in the *temporal* characteristics of a stimulus automatically produces changes in the *spectral* characteristics of the stimulus. We encountered this in Section 2.3.2 as spectral splatter. For example, one of the most popular temporal resolution experiments is the gap detection experiment. In this experiment, the listener is required to discriminate between a stimulus that is uninterrupted and a stimulus that is the same in all respects except that it contains a brief silent interval or gap, usually in the temporal center of the stimulus (see Figure 8.1). By varying the gap duration, it is possible to find the smallest detectable gap (the gap threshold). Unfortunately, introducing a sudden gap in a pure tone or other narrowband stimulus will cause a spread of energy to lower and higher frequencies. Hence, the gap may be detected by the auditory system as a change in the *spectrum* rather than as a temporal event per se. Leshowitz (1971) showed that the minimum detectable gap between two clicks is only 6 microseconds. However, this task was almost certainly performed using differences in the spectral energy at high frequencies associated with the introduction of the gap.

To avoid this confound, some researchers have measured gap detection for white noise (Figure 2.16, top panel). The spectrum of white noise is not affected by an abrupt discontinuity, because it already contains components covering the whole range of frequencies. The gap threshold for white noise is about 3 ms (Penner, 1977). Another way to avoid spectral cues is to mask the spectral splatter with noise. Shailer and Moore (1987) measured gap detection for pure tones presented in a band-stop noise to mask the spectral splatter. They measured thresholds of about 4–5 ms that were roughly independent of the frequency of the tone, at least for frequencies above 400 Hz.

The magnitude spectrum of a sound is the same whether a sound is played forward or backward. Taking advantage of this property, Ronken (1970) presented listeners with two pairs of clicks. In one pair, the first click was higher in

Figure 8.1 The stimuli for a typical gap detection experiment. The listener's task is to pick the observation interval that contains the sound with the temporal gap (in this case, interval 2). The location of the gap (interval 1 or interval 2) would be randomized from trial to trial.

amplitude than the second, and in the other pair, the second click was higher in amplitude than the first. The stimuli were therefore mirror images of each other in the time domain. Ronken found that listeners could discriminate between these stimuli when the gap between the clicks was just 2 ms.

Putting the results together, it appears that we can detect a change in level lasting only about 2–5 ms (less than a hundredth of a second). As described in Section 8.2.1, our sensitivity to *repetitive* envelope fluctuations in sounds is even greater than that suggested by the results in this section.

8.1.3   Forward and backward masking

We have seen that when two sounds of similar frequency are presented together, the more intense sound may mask or obscure the less intense sound so that the less intense sound is inaudible (Section 5.4). The masking effect extends *over time*, so masking may be caused by a masker presented just before the signal (*forward masking*) or just after the signal (*backward masking*). Forward and backward masking are also called *nonsimultaneous* masking, because the masker and the signal do not overlap in time. Backward masking is a weak effect in trained listeners and only causes an increase in the lowest detectable level of the signal when the signal is within 20 ms or so of the onset of the masker (Oxenham & Moore, 1994). Forward masking, however, can persist for over 100 ms after the offset of the masker (Jesteadt, Bacon, & Lehman, 1982). These effects can be regarded as aspects of temporal resolution, because they reflect our limited ability to "hear out" sounds presented at different times.

Figure 8.2 shows the smallest detectable level of a signal presented after a forward masker. The data are plotted as a function of the masker level (left panel) and as a function of the gap or silent interval between the masker and the signal

Figure 8.2 The just-detectable level of a signal presented after a masker (i.e., a *forward* masker) as a function of the masker level and as a function of the gap between the masker and the signal. The masker and the signal were both 6000-Hz pure tones. Data are from Plack and Oxenham (1998).

(right panel). As the masker level is increased, the level of the signal at threshold also increases. As the gap is increased, the masking decays so that lower level signals can be detected. Looking at the left panel, note that for low signal levels (below about 30 dB SPL), the growth of masking is shallow, so a large change in masker level produces only a small change in the level of the signal at threshold. At higher levels, the growth of masking is roughly linear (1:1). These effects are reflected in the decay of forward masking with time. At high levels, the decay is faster than at low levels (right panel).

To summarize, the amount of forward masking increases with an increase in the level of the masker and with a reduction in the gap between the masker and the signal. However, the relations between these variables are not straightforward. It is thought that forward and backward masking are strongly influenced by the nonlinearities in the cochlea discussed in Section 5.2.3. Recall that the response of the basilar membrane to a tone at characteristic frequency is roughly linear at low levels but compressive (shallow growth) at higher levels (see Figure 8.3). For the conditions in Figure 8.2, the masker falls within the

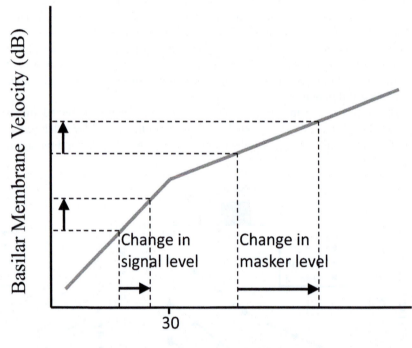

Figure 8.3 An illustration of why the growth of forward-masking functions in the left panel of Figure 8.2 are shallow for the 20- and 40-ms gap conditions. The masker is in the compressive region of the basilar membrane response function (illustrated by the shallow gray line), and the signal is in the linear region of the basilar membrane response function (illustrated by the steeper gray line for input levels below 30 dB SPL). To produce the *same change* in basilar membrane velocity (in decibels, the vertical arrows to the right of the *y*-axis), the change in signal level is less than the change in masker level (the horizontal arrows above the *x*-axis).

compressive region of the response function: A 10-dB increase in masker level may produce only a 2-dB increase in the vibration of the basilar membrane. If the signal level is below about 30 dB SPL, it falls within the steeper, linear region of the response function, so a 2-dB increase in the vibration of the basilar membrane may require only a 2-dB increase in the signal level. It follows that the signal level needs to be increased by much less than the masker level to remain detectable, and the masking function (Figure 8.2, left panel) has a shallow slope. When the signal level is above 30 dB SPL, both the signal and the masker are compressed so that the effects cancel out and the result is linear growth in the masking function.

The apparent rapid decay of masking at high signal levels (Figure 8.2, right panel) is a result of the same mechanism. Suppose that a given increase in gap results in a constant reduction in the level of basilar membrane vibration required for the signal to be detected. When the signal is at high levels, in the compressive region of the response, a given reduction in basilar membrane vibration will be associated with a much larger reduction in the signal level. The result is a steep reduction in signal threshold with time.

The response of the basilar membrane to a tone well below characteristic frequency is roughly linear. One might expect, therefore, the growth of forward masking with masker level to look very different when the masker frequency is below the signal frequency, and indeed it does. When the masker is below the signal frequency and the signal level is within the compressive region, the growth of masking is very steep (an example of the *upward spread of masking*, see Section 5.4.4). A given change in masker level requires a much larger change in signal level, because the signal is compressed and the masker is not. Based on this reasoning, forward masking can be used to estimate the response of the human basilar membrane (Nelson, Schroder, & Wojtczak, 2001; Oxenham & Plack, 1997).

8.1.4   What limits temporal resolution?

The auditory system is very good at representing the temporal characteristics of sounds. But it is not perfect. What aspects of auditory processing limit temporal resolution, and is there a reason why resolution should be limited?

The temporal response of the auditory filter (*ringing*; see Section 5.2.2) is a potential limitation on temporal resolution. The basilar membrane continues to vibrate for a few milliseconds after the stimulus has ceased, effectively extending the stimulus representation in time and smoothing temporal features such as gaps. Because the auditory filters are narrower at low center frequencies, the temporal response is longer at low frequencies than at high (see Figure 5.3). If temporal resolution were limited by filter ringing, then we would expect resolution to be much worse at low frequencies than at high frequencies. However, the gap detection threshold for pure tones is roughly constant as a function of frequency, except perhaps at very low frequencies. Similarly, the decay of forward masking does not vary greatly with frequency. We do not have the hyperacuity at high frequencies that may be suggested by the brief impulse response at 4000 Hz in Figure 5.3. It is unlikely, therefore, that the temporal response of the basilar membrane contributes to the temporal resolution limitation for most frequencies.

It has been suggested that forward masking is a consequence of neural adaptation. Indeed, some physiologists make the implicit assumption that this is the case and regard "adaptation" and "forward masking" as synonymous (much to my annoyance!). In Section 4.4.2, I describe how the firing rate in an auditory nerve fiber decreases with time after the onset of a sound. After the sound is turned off, the spontaneous firing rate is reduced below normal levels for 100 ms or so. The fiber is also less sensitive during this period of adaptation. The firing rate in response to a second sound will be *reduced* if it is presented during this time period. If adaptation is strong enough to push the representation of the second sound below its effective absolute threshold, then this could provide an explanation for forward masking. Although adaptation in the auditory nerve does not seem to be strong enough to account for the psychophysical thresholds (Relkin & Turner, 1988), adaptation at some other stage in the auditory system may be sufficient. For example, for neurons in the inferior colliculus of the marmoset monkey, the reduction in the response to a signal produced by a preceding stimulus seems to be sufficient to account for human forward masking (Nelson, Smith, & Young, 2009).

So forward masking may, at least in part, be a consequence of neural adaptation. However, adaptation cannot account for backward masking, in which the signal precedes the masker, and it cannot readily account for gap detection: An overall reduction in firing rate may have little effect on the internal representation of a 5-ms gap. The temporal resolution limitation in these cases may be better explained by an *integration* mechanism that combines or sums neural activity over a certain period of time. Such a mechanism would necessarily produce a limitation in temporal resolution, because rapid fluctuations would effectively be "averaged out" as they are combined over time. The integration mechanism would also result in a *persistence* of neural activity, because after the stimulus had been turned off, the mechanism would still be responding to activity that had occurred earlier. An analogy is the electric hob on a cooker. The hob takes time to warm up after the electricity has been switched on and time to cool down after the electricity has been switched off. The temperature at a given time is dependent on a weighted integration of the electric power that has been delivered previously.

Some neurons in the auditory cortex have sluggish responses that may provide the neural substrate for such an integration device. In general, however, the integration time may arise from the processing of information in the central auditory system. Neural spikes are "all or nothing" in that each spike has the same magnitude. Information is carried, not by the *magnitude* of each spike, but by the number of spikes per second, or by the temporal regularity of firing in the case of phase-locking information. To measure intensity or periodicity, it is necessary to *combine* information over time: To count the number of spikes in a given time period or perhaps to compute an autocorrelation function over a number of delays. Both these processes imply an integration time that will necessarily limit temporal resolution. A model of the integration process is described in the next section.

8.1.5   The temporal window

The temporal window model is a model of temporal resolution that is designed to accommodate the results from most temporal resolution experiments, although the model parameters are based on forward- and backward-masking results (Moore, Glasberg, Plack, & Biswas, 1988; Plack, Oxenham, & Drga, 2002). The stages of the model are shown in Figure 8.4. The first stage of the model is a simulation of the auditory filter, which includes the nonlinear properties discussed in Chapter 5. This stage provides a simulation of the vibration of a single place on the basilar membrane. The second stage is a device that simply squares the simulated velocity of vibration. Squaring has the benefit of making all the values positive, but it may also reflect processes in the auditory pathway. Finally, the representation of the stimulus is smoothed by the *temporal window*, a sliding temporal integrator.

The temporal window is a function that *weights* and *sums* the square of basilar membrane velocity over a short time period and is assumed to reflect processes in the central auditory system. The temporal window has a center time, and times close to the center of the window receive more weight than times remote from the center of the window, just like the auditory filter in the frequency domain. (Indeed, there is a temporal equivalent of the equivalent rectangular bandwidth called the *equivalent rectangular duration*, or ERD, of the window. The ERD is around 8 ms and is assumed not to vary with frequency, because measures of temporal resolution such as forward masking and gap detection do not vary with frequency.) Times before the center of the window are given more weight than times after the center of the window, to reflect the greater effectiveness of forward compared to backward masking. Thus, at any instant, the output of the temporal window is a *weighted average* or *integration* of the intensity of basilar membrane vibration for times *before* and *after* the center of the window. A smoothed representation of the stimulus is derived by calculating the output of the temporal window as a function of center time. This is called the *temporal excitation pattern* (TEP) and is analogous to the excitation pattern in the frequency domain. The TEP is a description of how variations in level are represented in the central auditory system.

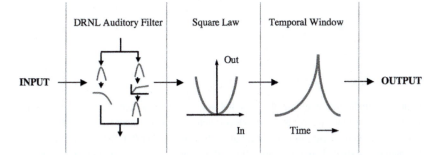

Figure 8.4 The latest version of the temporal window model, comprising a simulation of the auditory filter (i.e., the response of a single place on the basilar membrane), a device that squares the output of the filter, and the temporal window itself, which smooths the output of the cochlear simulation. The output of the model represents the internal representation of the input for a single frequency channel. The figure is redrawn from Plack et al. (2002). The auditory filter design (the dual-resonance nonlinear, or "DRNL," auditory filter) is based on Meddis, O'Mard, and Lopez-Poveda (2001).

Figure 8.5 shows how the temporal window model predicts the decay of neural activity after the offset of a forward masker. The shallow skirts of the temporal window for times before the center mean that the abrupt offset of the physical masker is represented internally as a shallow decay of excitation. The model suggests that the neural activity produced by the masker *persists* after the masker has been turned off. If the masker has not decayed fully by the time the signal is presented, then, effectively, the signal is masked *simultaneously* by the residual masker excitation. It is assumed that the listener only has access to the TEP produced by the signal and the masker combined, and so the signal may be detected by virtue of the bump on the combined TEP.

The single-value measures of temporal resolution described in Section 8.1.2 may not appear at first glance to be consistent with the much longer time scale

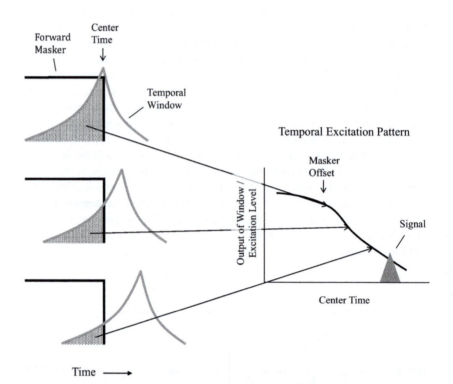

Figure 8.5 An illustration of how the temporal window model accounts for forward masking. The masker excitation passed by the window is indicated by the shaded areas in the left panel. As time progresses from the offset of the forward masker (top to bottom plots in the left panel), the shaded area decreases. This is shown by the temporal excitation pattern in the right panel that is a plot of the masker excitation passed by the temporal window (the gray shaded area) as a function of the center time of the window. The temporal excitation pattern can be regarded as a representation of activity in the central auditory nervous system. Notice that the masker excitation at the output of the window gradually decays after masker offset. For a signal presented shortly after the masker (gray triangle), the persistence of masker excitation acts to mask the signal just as if the masker and signal were simultaneous.

associated with the interactions between the masker and the signal in forward masking. However, the temporal window model shows us that there are two components limiting performance on the standard temporal resolution task. The first is the degree to which the representation of the stimulus is smoothed by the sluggish response of the system, as modeled by the temporal window. This is illustrated in Figure 8.6 for a stimulus with a temporal gap. The second is our ability to detect the fluctuation in level in the smoothed representation (i.e., at the output of the temporal window). These tasks involve an *intensity discrimination* component, as well as the "pure" temporal resolution component. Because the signal level at threshold in a forward-masking task is usually much less than the masker level, it has the effect of producing only a small bump in the otherwise smooth decay of masker excitation, even though the gap between the masker and the signal may be several tens of milliseconds. On the other hand, in a typical gap detection experiment, the change of level that produces the gap is very great, and so it can be detected at shorter time intervals. The temporal window model predicts that the bump in the TEP corresponding to the signal in forward masking (see Figure 8.5), and the dip in the TEP corresponding to the gap in the gap detection task (see Figure 8.6) should be roughly the same size at threshold.

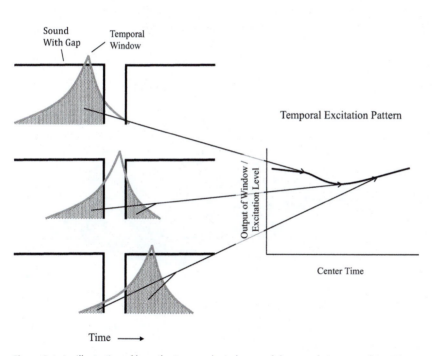

Figure 8.6 An illustration of how the temporal window model responds to a sound containing a temporal gap, using the same description as in Figure 8.5. As in Figure. 8.5, the shaded areas show the excitation passed by the window. Notice that the temporal window centered in the gap integrates energy from before and after the gap, so the period of absolute silence in the original stimulus (left panel) is replaced by a shallow dip in excitation level in the central neural representation (right panel).

Because the first stage in the simulation is an auditory filter with a center frequency that can be allowed to vary, the temporal window model illustrated in Figure 8.4 represents the output of just a single frequency channel. However, if the TEP is calculated for a number of center frequencies, a description of the internal representation of a stimulus across both frequency and time can be obtained. This is a three-dimensional plot called a *spectro-temporal excitation pattern* (STEP). Figure 8.7 shows the STEP for the utterance "bat." A cross-section across frequency at a given time provides an excitation pattern and shows the blurring in the frequency domain produced by the auditory filters. A cross-section across time at a given frequency provides a temporal excitation pattern and shows the blurring in the time domain produced by the temporal window. The STEP is, therefore, an estimate of the resolution of the auditory system with respect to variations in level across both frequency and time. As a rule of thumb, if a stimulus feature can be seen in the STEP, then we can probably hear it – if not, then we probably can't hear it.

Now, before we (or perhaps I) get too carried away, the temporal window model does come with a health warning. Although the model provides a reasonable account of some temporal resolution phenomena and is a useful tool for predicting human performance on a range of discrimination tasks, there is as yet no direct physiological evidence that neural activity in the central auditory system behaves in the way described by the model. It is quite possible that

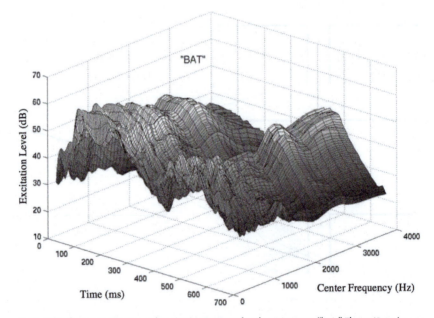

Figure 8.7 The spectro-temporal excitation pattern for the utterance "bat." The pattern is a simulation of the central neural representation of the utterance across time and center (or characteristic) frequency. The low frequency resolved harmonics and the upper formant peaks (composed of unresolved harmonics) can be seen for times up to around 300 ms after the start. The "t" sound produces excitation at high center frequencies around 500 ms after the start.

forward masking is largely determined by neural adaptation rather than neural persistence (Nelson et al., 2009). If this is so, then the model still works as a useful tool for predicting thresholds in forward-masking experiments but should not be taken as a description of physiological reality.

8.1.6 Across-frequency temporal resolution

It is important that we are able to track rapid changes occurring at a particular frequency. It is also important that we are sensitive to the timing of events *across* frequency. We need the latter ability to detect frequency sweeps such as formant transitions in speech (see Section 11.1.1) and to segregate sounds on the basis of differing onset or offset times (see Section 10.2.1). Pisoni (1977) reported that we are capable of detecting a difference between the onset times of a 500-Hz pure tone and a 1500-Hz pure tone of just 20 ms. With evidence of even greater resolution, Green (1973) reported that listeners could discriminate delays in a limited spectral region of a wideband click down to 2 ms. On the other hand, our ability to detect a temporal gap between two pure tones separated in frequency is very poor, with gap thresholds of the order of 100 ms (Formby & Forrest, 1991). In this latter case, however, listeners are required to judge the time interval between an offset and an onset (rather than between two onsets). It could be that the auditory system has no particular ecological reason to be good at this, and hence has not evolved or developed the appropriate neural connections.

A difficulty with some of these experiments is avoiding "within-channel" cues. For example, in an across-frequency gap detection experiment, the output of an auditory filter with a center frequency *between* the two tones may show a response to both tones so that the representation is not dissimilar to the standard gap-detection task in which both tones have the same frequency. Although it is perfectly valid for the auditory system to detect across-frequency temporal features by the activity in a single frequency channel, it does mean that the experiments may not be measuring across-*place* (or across-characteristic-frequency) processes in every case.

8.2 THE PERCEPTION OF MODULATION

Our ability to detect a sequence of rapid fluctuations in the envelope of a stimulus can also be regarded as a measure of temporal resolution. However, I have given modulation a separate section, because there are some phenomena associated with modulation perception that go beyond the question of how rapidly the system can react to changing stimuli.

8.2.1 The modulation transfer function

In a typical modulation detection task, the listener is required to discriminate a noise or tone that is sinusoidally amplitude modulated (see Section 2.5.1) from one that has a flat envelope (see Figure 8.8). A plot of the smallest detectable depth of modulation against the *frequency* of modulation describes a *modulation transfer function* for the auditory system. The choice of carrier (the sound that is

Figure 8.8 The stimuli for a typical modulation detection experiment. The listener's task is to pick the observation interval that contains the sound with the modulated envelope (in this case, interval 2). The location of the modulation (interval 1 or interval 2) would be randomized from trial to trial.

being modulated) is very important. If a pure-tone carrier is used, then care must be taken to ensure that the spectral sidebands – the two frequency components on either side of the carrier frequency (see Figure 2.18, top right panel) – are not separated out (resolved) on the basilar membrane. If they are resolved and hence can be "heard out", then listeners may perform the modulation detection task using features in the excitation pattern rather than by a temporal analysis of the envelope: Since an unmodulated pure-tone carrier does not have sidebands, detecting the presence of the sidebands is equivalent to detecting that the stimulus is modulated. Because the frequency difference between the carrier and each side band is equal to the modulation rate, the use of pure-tone carriers is limited to relatively low modulation rates to prevent resolution of the sidebands. The highest modulation frequency that can be used depends on the carrier frequency, because the bandwidth of the auditory filter increases (and, hence, the resolving power of the basilar membrane decreases) as center frequency is increased. Thus higher modulation frequencies can be used with higher frequency carriers.

When the carrier is a white noise, there are no long-term spectral cues to the presence of the modulation. In this case, listeners show roughly equal sensitivity to amplitude modulation for frequencies of up to about 50 Hz, and then sensitivity falls off (see Figure 8.9). The modulation transfer function has a low-pass characteristic and behaves like a low-pass filter in the envelope or modulation domain. As expected from the temporal resolution results in Section 8.1, the auditory system cannot follow fluctuations that are too fast. However, when the modulation depth is 100% (i.e., the envelope goes right down to zero in the valleys), we are able to detect modulation frequencies as high as 1000 Hz! The auditory system is much faster than the visual system in this respect. The maximum rate of flicker detectable by the visual system is only about 50 Hz. The highest detectable modulation frequency for a sound (corresponding to a period of only 1 ms) is higher than would be expected from the gap detection data and suggests that the auditory system is more sensitive to repeated envelope fluctuations (as in the modulation detection task) than to a single envelope fluctuation (as in the gap detection task).

A problem with using noise as a carrier is that it contains "inherent" envelope fluctuations: The envelope of noise fluctuates randomly in addition to any modulation added by the experimenter. These inherent fluctuations may obscure

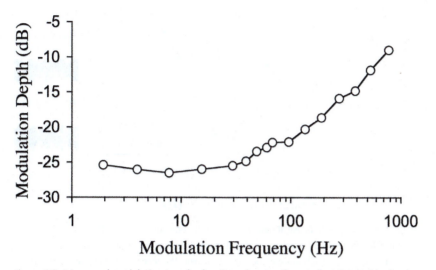

Figure 8.9 A temporal modulation transfer function, showing the smallest detectable depth of sinusoidal amplitude modulation, imposed on a white noise carrier, as a function of the frequency of modulation. The lower the modulation depth at threshold, the greater the sensitivity to that frequency of modulation. Modulation depth is expressed as $20 \log_{10} (m)$, where m is the modulation index (see Section 2.5.1). On this scale, 0 dB represents 100% modulation (envelope amplitude falls to zero in the valleys). Data are from Bacon and Viemeister (1985).

high-frequency modulation that is imposed on the carrier. If sinusoidal carriers, which have flat envelopes, are used instead, then the high-sensitivity portion of the modulation transfer function extends up to about 150 Hz rather than just 50 Hz (Kohlrausch, Fassel, & Dau, 2000).

8.2.2 Modulation interference and the modulation filterbank

The idea that modulation processing can be characterized by a low-pass filter in the envelope domain, with low modulation frequencies passed and high modulation frequencies attenuated, may be too simplistic. The implication is that all envelope fluctuations are processed together. However, our ability to hear one pattern of modulation in the presence of another pattern of modulation depends on the frequency separation of the different modulation frequencies. If they are far removed in modulation frequency, then the task is easy. If they are close in modulation frequency, then the task is hard (Figure 8.10). The auditory system exhibits *frequency selectivity* in the envelope domain, just as it does in the fine-structure domain. Indeed, the two types of analysis may be independent to some extent: Interference between nearby modulation frequencies occurs even if the *carrier* frequencies are very different (Yost, Sheft, & Opie, 1989).

Dau, Kollmeier, and Kohlrausch (1997) argue that the auditory system contains a bank of overlapping "modulation filters" (analogous to the auditory filters) each tuned to a different modulation frequency. Just as we can listen to the auditory filter centered on the signal frequency, thus attenuating maskers of

Figure 8.10 Two psychophysical tuning curves in the envelope domain. The curves show the modulation depth of "masker" modulation required to mask "signal" modulation as a function of the modulation frequency of the masker. The legend shows the modulation frequency of the signal. Both masker and signal modulation were imposed on the *same* noise carrier (see schematic on the right). The modulation depth of the signal was fixed at –15 dB for the 16-Hz signal modulation and at –17 dB for the 64-Hz signal modulation. The curves show tuning in the envelope domain. When the masker modulation frequency is remote from the signal modulation frequency, then the auditory system can separate the two modulation patterns, and a high modulation depth is required to mask the signal. Data are from Ewert and Dau (2000).

different frequencies, we also may be able to listen to the *modulation* filter centered on the *modulation* frequency we are trying to detect, and masker modulation frequencies remote from this may be attenuated. It has been estimated that the bandwidth of the modulation filters is roughly equal to the center modulation frequency, so a modulation filter tuned to 20-Hz modulation has a bandwidth of about 20 Hz (Ewert & Dau, 2000). There is evidence that some neurons in the inferior colliculus are sensitive to different modulation frequencies (Langner & Schreiner, 1988), and these neurons may be the physiological substrate for the modulation filterbank.

Although there is controversy over the main premise, the modulation filterbank can account for many aspects of modulation perception, including the interference between different modulation frequencies described previously. Looking at the broader picture, it seems plausible that the auditory system may decompose a complex sound in terms of modulation frequency as a source of information for determining sound identity. Furthermore, the modulation filterbank may help the auditory system to separate out sounds originating from different sources, which often contain different rates of envelope fluctuations (see Section 10.2.1).

8.2.3 Comodulation masking release

When we are trying to detect a pure-tone signal in the presence of a *modulated* masker, it helps if there are additional frequency components in a different part of the spectrum that have the *same pattern of envelope fluctuations* as the masker (Hall, Haggard, & Fernandes, 1984). These additional components are said to be *comodulated* with the masker, and the reduction in threshold when they are added is called *comodulation masking release*. Many experiments use a modulated noise band or pure tone centered on the signal as the on-frequency masker. Additional "flanking" noise bands or pure tones, with frequencies removed from the masker but with coherent modulation, can then be added to produce the masking release (see Figure 8.11). Although some of the performance improvements may be the result of interactions between the flankers and the masker at a single place on the basilar membrane (*within-channel* cues), a comodulation masking release of around 7 dB can be produced when the flankers are far removed in frequency from the masker and the signal, and even when the flankers are presented in the *opposite ear* to the masker and the signal (Schooneveldt & Moore, 1987).

It appears that the auditory system has the ability to make comparisons of envelope fluctuations across frequency and across ears. When the signal is added to the masker, the pattern of envelope fluctuations will change slightly, and the signal may be detected by a disparity between the fluctuations produced by the masker and signal and the fluctuations of the flanking bands (Richards, 1987). Alternatively, the auditory system may use a dip in the envelope of the flankers as a cue to the best time to listen for the signal (Buus, 1985): In the case of

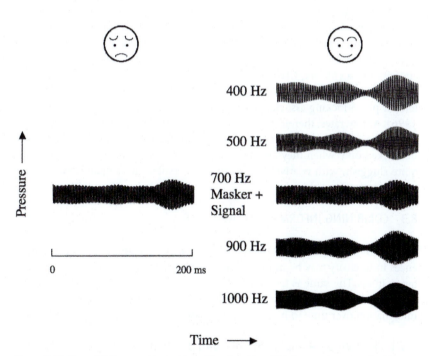

Figure 8.11 Comodulation masking release. The signal is a 700-Hz pure tone, masked by a modulated 700-Hz pure tone. Signal detection is hard when the masker and the signal are presented on their own (left panel) but is easier with the addition of flanking tones with frequencies of 400, 500, 900, and 1000 Hz, comodulated with the masker (right panel). Notice the distinct envelope of the 700-Hz band, caused by the presence of the signal.

comodulated flankers, dips in the flanker envelope correspond to dips in the masker envelope, which is when the masker intensity is least. Like the modulation interference experiments, these experiments may be illustrating ways in which the auditory system uses envelope fluctuations to separate sounds from different sources. Sound components from a single source tend to have coherent envelope fluctuations across frequency, just like the comodulated flankers.

8.2.4 Frequency modulation

Amplitude modulation and frequency modulation may seem to be very different aspects of dynamic stimuli. In the former, the amplitude is varying, and in the latter, the frequency is varying. However, the distinction may not be so obvious to the auditory system. Consider the response of an auditory filter (or the response of a place on the basilar membrane) with a center frequency close to the frequency of a pure tone that is frequency modulated. As the frequency of the pure tone moves *toward* the center of the filter, the filter output will *increase*. As the frequency of the pure tone moves *away from* the center of the filter, the filter output will *decrease*. In other words, the output of the auditory filter will be *amplitude* modulated. Considering the whole excitation pattern, as the frequency moves up, the excitation level will decrease on the low-frequency side and increase on the high-frequency side, and conversely as the frequency moves down.

It is thought that for modulation frequencies of greater than about 10 Hz, frequency modulation and amplitude modulation are detected by the *same mechanism*, based on envelope fluctuations on the basilar membrane. At these rates, frequency modulation can interfere with the detection of amplitude modulation, and vice versa (Moore, Glasberg, Gaunt, & Child, 1991). For lower modulation frequencies, the auditory system may be able to track the change in the pattern of phase locking associated with the variation in frequency (Moore & Sek, 1996). At low rates, therefore, detection of frequency modulation may be based more on *pitch* cues than on envelope cues. The fact that variations in pitch can be tracked only when they are fairly slow suggests that the pitch mechanism is quite sluggish, with relatively poor temporal resolution compared to temporal resolution for level changes.

8.3 COMBINING INFORMATION OVER TIME

In Section 6.3.5, I describe how the sensitivity of the auditory system to differences in intensity may be improved by combining the information from several nerve fibers. The same is true (at least theoretically) of combining information over time. In this section, we explore how the auditory system may integrate information over time to improve performance on a number of auditory tasks.

8.3.1 Performance improvements with duration

For many of the mindless experiments that we pay people to endure, performance improves as the duration of the stimuli is increased. Figure 8.12 shows the effect of duration on our ability to detect a pure tone, to discriminate between the intensities of two pure tones, to discriminate between the frequencies of two

Figure 8.12 Performance improvements with stimulus duration for four different auditory tasks: (A) detection of a 1000 Hz pure tone (Florentine, Fastl, & Buus, 1988); (B) intensity discrimination for a 1000-Hz pure tone (Florentine, 1986); (C) frequency discrimination for 250- and 1000-Hz pure tones (Moore, 1973); and (D) fundamental frequency discrimination for complex tones consisting of resolved or unresolved harmonics, both with a fundamental frequency of 250 Hz (Plack & Carlyon, 1995). FDL and FODL refer to frequency difference limen and fundamental frequency difference limen, respectively.

pure tones, and to discriminate between the fundamental frequencies of two complex tones. In each task, performance improves rapidly over short durations, but after a certain "critical" duration, there is little additional improvement as the stimulus duration is increased.

The range of durations over which performance improves differs between tasks. The critical duration can be as much as 2 seconds at 8000 Hz for intensity discrimination (Florentine, 1986). The duration effect depends on frequency for frequency discrimination: Low-frequency tones show a greater improvement with duration than high-frequency tones (Moore, 1973). Similarly, the duration effect increases as fundamental frequency decreases for fundamental frequency discrimination with unresolved harmonics (Plack & Carlyon, 1995). In addition, unresolved harmonics show a greater improvement with duration than do resolved harmonics, even when the fundamental frequency is the same (White & Plack, 1998). The following sections examine ways in which the auditory system may combine information over time in order to improve performance.

8.3.2   Multiple looks

Imagine that you are given a big bucket of mud containing a large number of marbles, and you are asked to decide whether there are more blue marbles or more red marbles in the bucket. You are allowed a certain number of opportunities to select marbles from the mud at random, and you can select four marbles each time, although you have to replace them in the bucket after you have counted them. Let's say, on your first try, you pick out three blue marbles and one red. On your second try, you pick out four blue marbles and no red. On your third try, you pick out two blue marbles and two red. On your fourth try, you pick out three blue marbles and one red. Note that the more picks you have, the more confident you are that there are more blue marbles than red marbles. If you simply add up the total numbers of blue marbles and red marbles that you have removed, you can make your decision based on whichever color is most numerous. The more chances to pick you have, the greater the accuracy of this final measure.

If you replace "decide whether there are more blue marbles or more red marbles" with "make a correct discrimination between sounds," you have the basis for the multiple-looks idea. The more often you sample, or take a "look" at, a stimulus, the more likely you are to make a correct discrimination or to decide, for example, whether one sound is higher or lower in intensity than another sound. Discrimination performance is usually limited by the *variability* of our internal representation of the stimulus (see Appendix). The variability might be due to variations in the firing rates of neurons or in the precision of phase locking, or it might be due to some variation in the stimulus itself (e.g., in the level of a noise). If we only sample a short time interval, we might make a mistake because, just by chance, the number of neural spikes in the sample in response to one sound may be greater than the spikes in response to a slightly more intense sound. If we could add up the neural spikes from several samples over a longer time interval, we would be much more likely to make an accurate judgment. Figure 8.13 shows how a long stimulus might be broken down into a number of discrete samples.

The multiple-looks method will only work if the samples are *independent* of each other. It would be no use taking just one sample of marbles and multiplying the numbers of each color in that sample by 10. You would be just as likely to make a mistake as if you had stuck with the original numbers. Similarly, if you take two counts of the number of spikes over intervals that overlap in time, you will be counting the same spikes twice, and they won't help you any further. Sometimes, there is a problem even if the samples don't overlap. Imagine that you have a noise stimulus whose amplitude is modulated randomly – but slowly – up and down. If you take two samples close together in time, then they will not be independent. They might both fall on the same peak, for example. Your estimate of the *overall* level of the noise will not benefit greatly from the second sample in this case.

The mathematics of combining information in this way was sorted out a while ago (see McNicol, 2004). The ability to make a discrimination between two stimuli can be expressed not only in terms of percentage correct responses

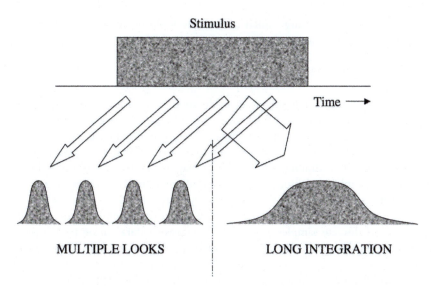

Stimulus

Time ⟶

MULTIPLE LOOKS   LONG INTEGRATION

Figure 8.13 A highly schematic illustration of how the information in a sound may be analyzed using several short-duration samples (left panel) or one long-duration sample (right panel).

but also in terms of the discrimination index, d' ("d-prime"). Thus, d' is a measure of a listener's ability to discriminate between two stimuli (see Section A.2), where d' is equal to the difference between the internal representations of the stimuli, divided by the standard deviation of the representations. If two independent samples of the difference are simply added, then the difference increases by a factor of two, but the standard deviation increases only by the square root of two. It follows that d' increases by $\sqrt{2}$ (1.414). In general, d' increases in proportion to the *square root* of the number of samples. Hence, if the duration of a stimulus is increased, which allows more independent samples, then performance should improve. Crucially, performance should not depend on *when* the samples are taken, so long as a memory representation of the earlier samples can be held until they are combined with the later ones.

Evidence for the use of multiple looks by the auditory system can be found in several tasks. Viemeister and Wakefield (1991) demonstrated that the detectability of a pair of short pure-tone bursts is greater than that for a single short-tone burst, even when there is a noise between the bursts. Furthermore, performance is *independent* of the level of the noise. It appears that the auditory system can sample and combine the information from the two bursts, without including the intervening noise that would have acted as a powerful masker had it been integrated with the tones. White and Plack (1998) found that fundamental frequency discrimination performance for two 20-ms complex-tone bursts separated by a brief gap (5–80 ms) is almost exactly that predicted by the multiple-looks hypothesis, when compared to performance for one tone burst. Performance is independent of the gap between the bursts, again consistent with the multiple-looks hypothesis. There is good evidence, therefore, that something similar to multiple-looks processing is used by the auditory system in some circumstances.

8.3.3   Long integration

An alternative to taking several short-duration samples is to take one long-duration sample. Figure 8.13 illustrates the distinction between multiple looks and long integration in the processing of a long stimulus. In some situations, it may be beneficial for the auditory system to perform an analysis on a long contin-uous chunk of the stimulus. Alternatively, it may be problematic for the auditory system to combine multiple samples from different times in an optimal way.

There is some evidence that the auditory system is able to obtain a benefit from continuous long integration that it would not get from combining a succession of discrete samples. The effect of increasing duration on performance is often much greater than would be predicted by the multiple-looks model, particularly over short durations (note the rapid improvements in performance over short durations in Figure 8.12). For instance, a doubling in the duration of an unresolved complex tone from 20 to 40 ms results in a threefold increase in d' for fundamental frequency discrimination (White & Plack, 1998). This is much larger than the factor of $\sqrt{2}$ predicted by a doubling in the number of independent samples.

In Section 6.2.2, it is described how loudness increases with duration, for durations up to several hundred milliseconds. When we are judging the absolute magnitude of sounds, we seem to be able to combine level information over quite a long period, and this may involve some sort of long integration mechanism. Long integration may be useful to us when trying to determine, for example, whether a sound is getting closer. We need to be able to detect changes in the long-term magnitude of the sound, not in the rapid fluctuations in level that are characteristic of the particular sound that is being produced.

8.3.4   Flexible integration

Viemeister and Wakefield (1991) reported that when two pure-tone bursts are separated by a gap of 5 ms or more, detection performance for the two tone bursts, compared to one tone burst, is consistent with multiple looks. However, when the bursts are less than 5 ms apart, performance is improved further. Sim-ilarly, White and Plack (1998) found that fundamental frequency discrimination for a pair of complex-tone bursts is better when the tone bursts are continuous rather than when there is a gap between the bursts. It is possible that the auditory system uses a long integration window for continuous stimuli, benefiting from the performance advantages, but resets the integration time when there is a discontinuity. In these situations, the two bursts may be integrated separately and the information combined (when necessary) using a multiple-looks mechanism.

It makes sense that the auditory system should be flexible in this way. A discontinuity is often indicative of the end of one sound feature and the beginning of another. These separate features may require separate analysis. It may not be optimal, for example, to average the pitches of two consecutive tones, when identification of the sound may depend on detecting a difference between them.

Furthermore, temporal resolution tasks, such as gap detection (or the detection of a stop consonant), require that a short integration time, possibly something similar to the temporal window, be used. An integration time of several hundred milliseconds would not be able to track a discontinuity of only 3 ms: Any brief dips or bumps would be smoothed out in the internal representation. If true long integration does exist, then shorter integration times must also exist. It is possible (and I am speculating freely here!) that the different integration times may be implemented by auditory neurons with different temporal responses. Sluggish neurons could provide long integration; relatively fast neurons could provide short integration.

8.4 SUMMARY

In addition to being able to detect very rapid changes in a stimulus, the auditory system is capable of combining information over much longer times to improve performance. The neural mechanisms underlying these abilities may represent a flexible response to the different temporal distributions of information in sounds.

1   Variations in the amplitude of a sound wave over time can be described in terms of the individual pressure fluctuations (*temporal fine structure*), and the variations in the peak amplitude of these fluctuations (*envelope*). Temporal resolution usually refers to our ability to resolve rapid changes in the *envelope* of a sound over time.

2   Auditory temporal resolution is very acute. We can detect level changes lasting less than 5 ms.

3   Forward and backward masking show that the influence of a stimulus is *extended over time*, affecting the detection of stimuli presented after or before. This influence may reflect a persistence of neural activity after stimulus offset (and a build-up in response after onset), which can be modeled using a sliding temporal integrator or *temporal window*. Alternatively, forward masking may be a consequence of the post-stimulus reduction in sensitivity associated with neural adaptation.

4   We are extremely sensitive to repetitive fluctuations. We can detect amplitude modulation at rates up to 1000 Hz.

5   One pattern of modulation may interfere with the detection of another pattern of modulation but not when the modulation frequencies are very different. We may have specific neural channels that are tuned to different rates of modulation and behave like a *modulation filterbank*.

6   The addition of frequency components in different regions of the spectrum, but with the *same pattern of modulation* as a masker, can improve our ability to detect a signal at the masker frequency. This is known as *comodulation masking release*. This finding may reflect a general ability to use coherent patterns of modulation across frequency to separate out simultaneous sounds.

7   Frequency modulation may be detected by the induced amplitude modulation in the excitation pattern for modulation frequencies above about 10 Hz. At lower rates, the frequency excursions may be tracked by a (sluggish) mechanism based on phase locking.

8   Performance improves in many hearing tasks as the duration of the stimulus is increased. These improvements may result from a multiple-looks mechanism that combines several short samples of the stimulus or from a long integration mechanism, which analyzes a continuous chunk of the stimulus. Flexible integration times may allow the auditory system to respond to rapid changes in a stimulus and to integrate over longer durations when necessary.

8.5   READING

The ideas expressed in this chapter are developed further in:

Eddins, D. A., & Green, D. M. (1995). Temporal integration and temporal resolution. In B. C. J. Moore (Ed.), Hearing (pp. 207–242). New York: Academic Press.

Verhey, J. L. (2010). Temporal resolution and temporal integration. In C. J. Plack (Ed.), Hearing (pp. 105–121). Oxford: Oxford University Press.

Viemeister, N. F., & Plack, C. J. (1993). Time analysis. In W. A. Yost, A. N. Popper, & R. R. Fay (Eds.), Human psychophysics (pp. 116–154). New York: Springer-Verlag.

9 SPATIAL HEARING

"Where is that sound coming from?" is an important question for the auditory system. Most sounds originate from a particular place because the *source* of most sounds is a vibrating object with a limited spatial extent. There are several reasons why we might like to locate the source of a sound. First, the location of the sound source may be important information in itself. For example, did the sound of distant gunfire come from in front or behind? Second, the location of the sound source may be used to orient visual attention: If someone calls your name, you can turn to see who it is. Finally, sound source location can be used to separate out sequences of sounds arising from different locations and to help us attend to the sequence of sounds originating from a particular location (see Chapter 10). Location cues can help us to "hear out" the person we are talking to in a room full of competing conversations. Similarly, location cues help us to hear out different instruments in an orchestra or in a stereo musical recording, adding to the clarity of the performance.

I must admit that the visual system is about a hundred times more sensitive to differences in source location than is the auditory system, and the visual system can accurately determine the shapes of objects, which is largely impossible for the human auditory system. However, our eyes are limited in their field of view, whereas our ears are sensitive to sounds from any direction and from sound sources that may be hidden behind other objects. Much information about approaching danger comes from sound, not light. This chapter describes how the auditory system localizes sounds and how it deals with the problems of sound reflection in which the direction of a sound waveform does not correspond to the location of the original source. We also consider how sound reproduction can be made more realistic by incorporating spatial cues.

9.1 USING TWO EARS

Binaural means listening with two ears, as compared to *monaural*, which means listening with one ear. The visual system contains many millions of receptors, each responding to light from a particular location in the visual field. In comparison, the auditory system has just two peripheral spatial channels – the two ears. However, just as we get a complex sensation of color from just three different cone types in the retina of the eye, so our two ears can give us quite accurate information about sound location.

Figure 9.1 shows the coordinate system for sound direction, in which any direction relative to the head can be specified in terms of *azimuth* and *elevation*. Figure 9.2 illustrates the smallest detectable difference between the directions of sound sources in the horizontal plane (differences in *azimuth*). These thresholds are plotted as *minimum audible angles*, where 1 degree represents one 360th of a complete revolution around the head. For example, if the minimum audible angle is 5 degrees, then we can just discriminate sounds played from two loud-speakers whose direction differs by an angle of 5 degrees with respect to the head. Note that our ability to discriminate pure tones originating from different directions depends on the frequency of the tones, with best performance at low frequencies. Note also that we have better spatial resolution if the sound source is straight ahead (0 degrees azimuth) than if the sound source is to the side of the head (e.g., 30 degrees azimuth, as shown in Figure 9.2). The minimum audible angle increases from about 1 degree for a sound straight ahead to perhaps 20 degrees or more for a sound directly to the right (90 degrees azimuth) or directly to the left (−90 degrees azimuth).

There are two cues to sound source location that depend on us having two ears. Both involve a comparison of the sound waves arriving at the two ears. The first is the *time* difference between the arrival of the sound at the two ears, and the second is the difference in sound *level* between the two ears. We consider each of these cues in turn.

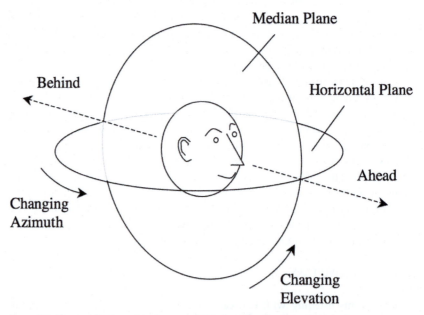

Figure 9.1 The coordinate system for sound direction. The direction of a sound source relative to the head can be specified in terms of azimuth (the angle of direction on the horizontal plane; increasing clockwise) and elevation (the angle of direction on the median plane; positive for upward directions and negative for downward directions). A sound with 0 degrees azimuth and 0 degrees elevation comes from straight ahead. A sound with 90 degrees azimuth and 45 degrees elevation comes from the upper right, and so on. Adapted from Blauert (1997) and Moore (2012).

Figure 9.2 The smallest detectable change in the direction of a pure-tone sound source in the horizontal plane, plotted as a function of frequency. The listener was presented with a sound coming from a reference location (labeled "REF" in the diagram to the right) and was then played a second sound from a loudspeaker slightly to the right or to the left. The listener had to indicate if the second sound was to the right or left of the reference. The *minimum audible angle* was defined as the angle between the reference sound and the second sound at which the listener chose the correct direction 75% of the time. The minimum audible angle was measured at two reference locations, straight ahead (0° azimuth) and to the side (30° azimuth). Data are from Mills (1958) cited by Grantham (1995).

9.1.1   Time differences

Imagine that you are listening to a sound that is coming from your right. Sound travels at a finite speed (about 340 meters per second in air at room temperature), so the sound waves will arrive at your right ear before they arrive at your left ear (see Figure 9.3). A sound from the right will arrive at your right ear directly, but to reach your left ear, it will have to diffract around your head (see Section 3.2.4). The time of arrival will depend on the path length, which includes the distance the sound wave has to travel as it bends around your head (see Figure 9.4). Differences in arrival time between the two ears are called *interaural time differences*. When low-frequency components are present (in other words, for most natural sounds), interaural time differences are the most important cues to sound source location (Wightman & Kistler, 1992).

For a sound source directly in front, directly behind, or anywhere in the vertical plane going through the center of the head (the *median* plane; see Figure 9.1), the interaural time difference will be zero. The *maximum* interaural time difference will occur when the sound source is either directly to the left or directly to the right of the head. The maximum time difference is only about 0.65 ms for adult humans, which is the distance between the ears divided by the speed of sound. (The maximum difference depends on the size of the head and is less for infants and much less for guinea pigs.) While 0.65 ms is a very short time, it is much greater than the smallest *detectable* interaural time difference, which is an amazing 10 µs (10 microseconds, or 10 millionths of a second), for wideband noise in the horizontal plane (Klump & Eady, 1956). A shift between

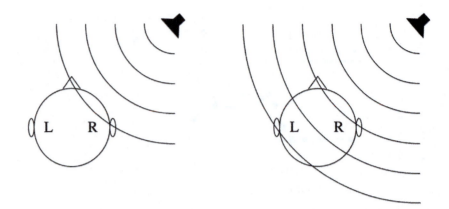

Time 1   Time 2

Figure 9.3 A bird's-eye view of the head with a sound source to the right. The curved lines show the peaks in the sound waveform at two consecutive instants. The sound waves arrive at the right ear before the left ear. This figure is a little misleading, because in the real world the sound would diffract *around* the head (taking a curved path), further delaying the arrival time for the left ear (see Figure 9.4).

an interaural time difference of zero and an interaural time difference of 10 µs corresponds to a shift in sound source location by about 1 degree in azimuth relative to straight ahead, which coincides with the smallest detectable direction difference (see Figure 9.2). This remarkable resolution suggests that highly accurate information about the *time of occurrence* of sounds is maintained in the auditory system up to at least the stage in the ascending auditory pathways where the inputs from the two ears are combined (the superior olive; see Section 4.5.1.2).

Interaural time differences may lead to ambiguity regarding location for some continuous sounds. Consider a continuous pure tone that is originating from a sound source directly to the right of the head. If the frequency of the tone is greater than about 750 Hz, the interaural time difference (0.65 ms) will be greater than half a cycle of the pure tone. For a frequency a little above 750 Hz, a waveform peak at the left ear will be followed closely by a waveform peak at the right ear. Although the sound originates from the right, it may appear to the listener as if the sound waves are arriving at the *left* ear first (see Figure 9.5). Fortunately, most natural sounds contain a wide range of frequency components, and they also contain *envelope* fluctuations. Envelope fluctuations are usually much slower than fluctuations in fine structure, so the arrival times of envelope features can be used to resolve the ambiguity, even if the carrier frequency is above 750 Hz (see Figure 9.5). Some measurements have used "transposed" stimuli (van de Par & Kohlrausch, 1997), in which the *envelope* of a high-frequency carrier is designed to provide similar information to the *fine structure* of a low-frequency pure tone (including matching the modulation rate to the pure-tone frequency). The smallest detectable interaural time difference for a transposed stimulus with a slowly varying envelope is similar to that of the equivalent low-frequency pure

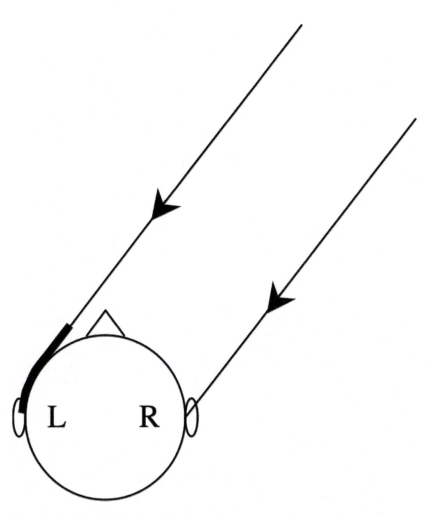

Figure 9.4 The lines indicate the paths of sound waves arriving from a sound source far away and to the right. The thick line shows the path difference (the difference in the distance covered) between the sound waves arriving at the left ear and the sound waves arriving at the right ear. Based on Blauert (1997).

tone, even when the carrier frequency of the transposed stimulus is as high as 10000 Hz (Bernstein & Trahiotis, 2002). This suggests that the mechanisms that process interaural time differences are similar (and equally efficient) at low and high frequencies. The single abrupt increase in envelope amplitude at the onset of a sound is also a useful cue (Rakerd & Hartmann, 1986), as the time of arrival of this feature can be compared easily between the ears, with no ambiguity.

Although the auditory system can discriminate stable interaural time differences with a high resolution, the system is relatively poor at tracking *changes* in the interaural time difference over time (which are associated with changes in the direction of a sound source). So, for instance, if the interaural time difference is varied sinusoidally (corresponding to a to-and-fro movement of the sound source in azimuth), then we can track these changes only if the rate of

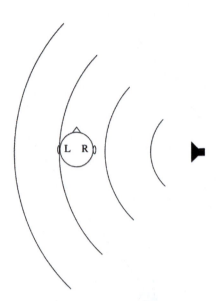

a) Pure Tone

LEFT

RIGHT

b) Modulated Pure Tone

LEFT

RIGHT

Time ⟶

Figure 9.5 A schematic illustration of the pressure peaks in space of a sound wave at an instant (left panel, ignoring diffraction effects) and the pressure variations at each ear as a function of time (right panel). In this illustration, the sound originates from the right, but waveform (fine-structure) peaks appear to occur at the left ear before the right ear (a). The ambiguity is resolved if the waveform is modulated, in which case it is clear that the sound waves arrive at the right ear before the left ear (b).

oscillation is less than about 2.4 Hz (Blauert, 1972). Because we can follow only slow changes in location, the binaural system is said to be "sluggish," especially in comparison with our ability to follow monaural variations in sound level up to modulation rates of 1000 Hz (see Section 8.2.1).

9.1.2   Level differences

The other binaural cue to sound source location is the difference in the *level* of a sound at the two ears. A sound from the right will be more intense at the right ear than at the left ear. *Interaural level differences* arise for two reasons. First, as described in Section 3.2.1, sound intensity decreases as the distance from the source increases. If the left ear is farther away from the source than the right ear, the level at the left ear will be less. In most circumstances, the width of the head is small compared to the distance between the head and the sound source, so the effect of distance is a very minor factor. Second, and of much more significance, the head has a "shadowing" effect on the sound, so the head will prevent some of the energy from a sound source on the right from reaching the left ear (and vice versa). Low frequencies diffract more than high frequencies (see Section 3.2.4), so the low-frequency components of a sound will tend to *bend around the head* (see Figure 9.4), minimizing the level difference. It follows that, for a sound source in a given location, the level difference between the ears will be greater for a sound containing mostly high-frequency components than for a sound containing mostly low-frequency components. For example, the interaural level difference for pure tones played from a loudspeaker directly to the side of the head may be less than 1 dB for a 200-Hz tone but as much as 20 dB for a 6000-Hz tone (see Moore, 2012, p. 248). The smallest *detectable* interaural level difference is about 1–2 dB (Grantham, 1984).

Interaural time differences work better for low-frequency pure tones (because of the phase ambiguity with high-frequency tones) and interaural level differences are greater for high-frequency tones (because there is less diffraction and therefore a greater head-shadow effect). It follows that these two sources of information can be combined to produce reasonable spatial resolution across a range of pure-tone frequencies (this is the "duplex" theory of Rayleigh, 1907). As we have seen, for more complex stimuli that contain envelope fluctuations, interaural time differences may provide useful information across the entire frequency range. In addition, it is probable that interaural time differences are dominant in most listening situations, since most sounds in the environment contain low-frequency components.

9.1.3 Binaural cues and release from masking

In addition to the obvious benefits of binaural information to sound localization, we can also use binaural information to help us detect sounds in the presence of other sounds. As described in Section 9.1.2, if a high-frequency sound is coming from the right, then it may be much more intense in the right ear than in the left ear, and conversely if the sound is coming from the left. This means that if one sound is to the right and another sound is to the left, the right-side sound will be most detectable in the right ear and the left-side sound will be most detectable in the left ear. In some situations, we seem to be able to selectively listen to either ear (with little interference between them), so if sounds are separated in space, any level differences can be used to help hear them out separately.

More interesting perhaps is the use of interaural time differences to reduce the masking effect of one sound on another. Suppose that the same noise and the same pure tone are presented to both a listener's ears over headphones so that the noise acts to mask the tone. In that situation, the smallest detectable level of the tone is little different to that detectable when the noise and tone are presented to one ear only. Now, keeping everything else the same, suppose that the phase of the tone is changed in one ear so that it is "inverted": A peak becomes a trough and a trough becomes a peak. In this situation, the tone is much more detectable (see Figure 9.6). The smallest detectable level of the tone drops by as much as 15 dB for low-frequency tones, although the effect is negligible for frequencies of the tone above 2000 Hz or so. The difference between the threshold measured when the stimuli are identical in the two ears and the reduced threshold measured when the tone is inverted in one ear is called a *binaural masking level difference*. Similar effects are obtained if the tone is delayed in one ear relative to the other, if the noise is delayed in one ear relative to the other, or if the tone is removed entirely from one ear (see Figure 9.6). With the exception of the last example, the level and magnitude spectrum are the same in the two ears in each case, but the small differences in interaural delay help the auditory system separate the two sounds.

RIGHT EAR   **LEFT EAR**

Same noise and same pure tone to both ears. Tone detection poor.

Pure tone *inverted* in one ear. Tone detection good.

Pure tone *removed* from one ear. Tone detection good.

Figure 9.6 Examples of listening situations in which a binaural masking level difference can be observed. Based on Moore (2012).

The effect also works for more complex stimuli, such as speech. If you are listening to someone speaking in an environment with competing sound sources, it is often easier to understand what the person is saying with two ears than with one ear (Bronkhurst & Plomp, 1988). However, interaural time or level differences can separate two simultaneous speech sounds only when they also differ along some other dimension, such as fundamental frequency (Shackleton, Meddis, & Hewitt, 1994). When the two competing sounds are similar in all respects except location, the tendency is to *group them together* so that the sound heard is a fusion of the two (see Section 10.2.3).

It is possible that the use of interaural time differences for masking release is not directly related to their use in sound localization. Although in many cases the combination of interaural time differences in the masking release situation is similar to that which occurs when the two sounds originate from different locations in space, in some cases it is not. The largest masking release occurs when the signal is inverted in one ear with respect to the other. However, this occurs only in natural listening conditions for high frequencies (above 750 Hz; see Section 9.1.1), whereas the phase-inversion masking release effect (Figure 9.6, middle panel) is greatest for frequencies around 200 Hz (Blauert, 1997, p. 259). The results of masking release experiments suggest that time differences *per se* are aiding detection, not the fact that they may lead to the subjective impression that the masker and the signal come from different directions.

9.1.4   Neural mechanisms

9.1.4.1   Time differences
Lloyd Jeffress (1948, 1972) suggested that interaural time differences are extracted by a *coincidence detector* that uses delay lines to compare the times of

arrival at each ear. The Jeffress model has become a standard explanation for
how the ear processes time differences. A simplified version of the Jeffress model
is illustrated in Figure 9.7. The model consists of an array of neurons, each of
which responds strongly when the two inputs to the neuron are coincident.
The clever bit is that each neuron receives inputs from the two ears that have
been *delayed by different amounts* using neural delay lines (which might be axons of
different lengths). For example, one neuron may receive an input from the right
that is delayed by 100 μs relative to the input from the left. This neuron will

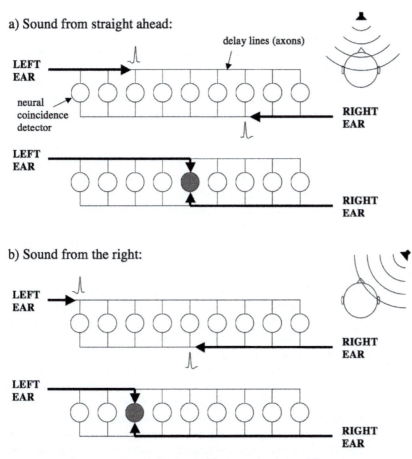

Figure 9.7 An illustration of a popular theory of how interaural time differences are
extracted by the auditory system (the Jeffress model). The circles represent neurons tuned to
different interaural time differences (equivalent to different locations in the horizontal plane;
neurons to the left of the array respond best to sounds from the right, and vice versa).
The thin lines represent the axons of neurons innervating the binaural neurons. Each panel
shows two successive time frames: (a) a sound from straight ahead arrives at the two ears
at the same time, and the neural spikes from the two ears coincide to excite a neuron in the
center of the array; (b) a sound from the right arrives at the right ear first, and the spikes
from the two ears coincide at a different neuron in the array.

respond best when the sound arrives in the right ear 100 μs before it arrives in the left ear (corresponding to a sound located about 10 degrees azimuth, to the right of straight ahead). For this neuron, the interaural time difference and the effect of the delay line cancel out, so the two inputs to the neuron are coincident. Over an array of neurons sensitive to different disparities, the processing in the Jeffress model is equivalent to *cross-correlation*, in that the inputs to the two ears are compared at different relative time delays. You may have noticed the similarity between this processing and the hypothetical *autocorrelation* mechanism for pitch extraction, in which a single input signal is compared with a copy of itself, delayed by various amounts (see Section 7.3.3). The arrival times at the two ears have to be specified very exactly by precise *phase locking* of neural spikes to peaks in the waveform (see Section 4.4.4) for the mechanism to work for an interaural time difference of just 10 μs.

It is surmised that there is a separate neural array for each characteristic frequency. The locations of the different frequency components entering the ears can be determined independently by finding out which neuron in the array is most active at each characteristic frequency. The way in which the location information from the different frequency channels may be combined is discussed in Section 10.2.3.

Is there any evidence that the Jeffress model is a physiological reality? There are certainly examples of neurons in the medial superior olive and in the inferior colliculus that are tuned to different interaural time differences. An array of these neurons could form the basis of the cross-correlator suggested by the Jeffress model, and indeed, there is good evidence for such an array of delay lines and coincidence detectors in the brainstem of the barn owl (Carr & Konishi, 1990). However, the story seems to be very different in mammals. Recordings from the medial superior olive of the gerbil have cast doubt on the claim that there is a whole array of neurons at each characteristic frequency, each tuned to a different interaural time difference. Instead, it has been suggested that there is broad sensitivity to just two different interaural time differences at each characteristic frequency (McAlpine & Grothe, 2003). The binaural neurons in the left medial superior olive have a peak in tuning corresponding to an arrival at the right ear first, and the binaural neurons in the right medial superior olive have a peak in tuning corresponding to an arrival at the left ear first (see Figure 9.8). Furthermore, the interaural time difference that produces the strongest response decreases with increasing characteristic frequency (Grothe, Pecka, & McAlpine, 2010). Although these response peaks are at time differences outside the range that occur naturally for the gerbil, any real location may be derived from the relative firing rates of the two types of neuron. For example, if binaural neurons in the right hemisphere fire more than those in the left hemisphere, then the sound is coming from the left. This type of computation is called "opponent process" analysis, because location is determined by the balance of activity from two opponent channels (left and right). Incidentally, this is similar to the way in which the visual system represents color. Our ability to distinguish many thousands of different colors is based on the relative responses of just three different color-sensitive receptors (three different cone types) in the retina, compared by different color-opponent combinations.

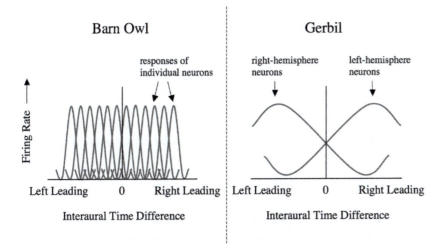

Figure 9.8 How interaural time differences may be represented in the brainstem of birds and mammals. In the barn owl (left panel) at each characteristic frequency in each hemisphere of the brain, there is an array of neurons tuned to different interaural time differences: Each neuron produces a maximal response when the sound arrives from a particular location. This is the array of coincidence detectors proposed by Jeffress (Figure 9.7). In the gerbil, however, neurons in each hemisphere have a single broad tuning, responding maximally to a sound leading in the opposite ear (right panel). Location may be derived by comparing the firing rates of the neurons in the two hemispheres. Based on McAlpine and Grothe (2003).

The fact that human direction discrimination is best for sounds directly in front of the head, rather than to either side (Figure 9.2), is also consistent with this two-channel account. Notice that the tuning curves for the left and right hemisphere channels in Figure 9.8 (right panel) are steepest when there is no difference in arrival time between the ears (e.g., for a sound directly in front of the head). This means that, for a given change in time difference, the change in firing rate will be greatest for sounds straight ahead, which should result in greater discrimination performance. A model based on a two-channel opponent process analysis produces good predictions of human direction discrimination performance as a function of azimuth (Briley, Kitterick, & Summerfield, 2012). In summary, the recent data suggest that the Jeffress model does not reflect the processing of time differences in humans and that instead a two-channel mechanism is involved.

9.1.4.2 Level differences

With regard to interaural level differences, a different type of processing is involved, in which the relative levels at the two ears are compared. The interaural level difference produced by a sound source at a particular location varies with frequency (see Section 9.1.2), and this variation must be taken into account by the nervous system. Neurons that receive an excitatory input from the *ipsilateral* ear and an inhibitory input from the *contralateral* ear have been identified in the lateral superior olive, in the dorsal nucleus of the lateral lemniscus, and in the central nucleus of the inferior colliculus (see Møller, 2013, p. 176), although the initial site of level difference processing is generally accepted to be the lateral superior olive (Grothe et al., 2010). A neuron in the right lateral superior olive, receiving excitatory input from the right ear and inhibitory input from the left ear, responds most to sounds from the right. Similarly, a neuron in the left lateral superior olive, receiving excitatory input from the left ear and inhibitory input from the right ear, responds most to sounds from the left. In this way, these neurons in the lateral superior olive may be responsible for extracting location by comparing the sound levels in the two ears.

9.2   ESCAPE FROM THE CONE OF CONFUSION

Interaural time differences and interaural level differences are important cues for sound source location in the horizontal plane, but they do not specify precisely the direction of the sound source (unless the sound is coming directly from the side, i.e., ±90 degrees azimuth in the horizontal plane). For example, any sound source on the median plane (see Figure 9.1) will produce an interaural time difference of zero and an interaural level difference of zero! We cannot use either of these cues to tell us whether a sound source is directly in front, directly behind, or directly above. More generally, for each interaural time difference, there is a cone of possible sound source locations (extending from the side of the head) that will produce that time difference (see Figure 9.9). Locations on such a "cone of confusion" may produce similar interaural level differences as well. There must be some additional cues that enable us to resolve these ambiguities and to locate sound sources accurately.

9.2.1   Head movements

Much of the ambiguity about sound location can be resolved by moving the head. If a sound source is directly in front, then turning the head to the right

Figure 9.9 Two cones of confusion. For a given cone, a sound source located at any point on the surface of the cone will produce the same interaural time difference. The cone on the left is for a greater time difference between the ears than the cone on the right. You should think of these cones as extending indefinitely, or at least until the air runs out. . . .

will decrease the level in the right ear and cause the sound to arrive at the left ear before the right ear (see Figure 9.10). Conversely, if the sound source is directly behind, then the same head movement will decrease the level in the left ear and cause the sound to arrive at the right ear first. If the head rotation has no effect, then the sound source is either directly above or (less likely) directly below. By measuring carefully the effects of known head rotations on time and level differences, it should be possible (theoretically) for the auditory system to specify the location of any sound source, with the only ambiguity remaining that of whether the source elevation is up or down. If head rotations in the median plane are also involved (tipping or nodding of the head), then the location may be specified without any ambiguity.

It seems to be the case that listeners make use of head rotations and tipping to help them locate a sound source (Thurlow, Mangels, & Runge, 1967). However, these movements are useful only if the sound occurs for long enough to give

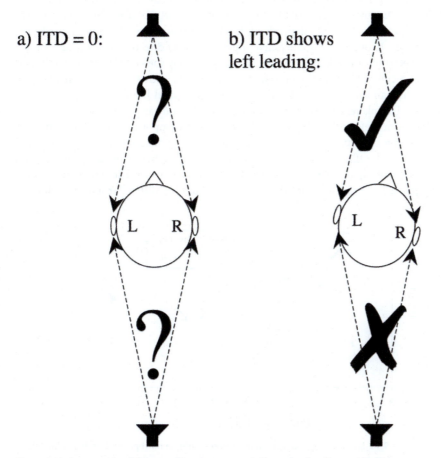

Figure 9.10 An example of the use of head movements to resolve location ambiguities. A sound directly in front of the listener (a) produces the same interaural time difference (ITD) and interaural level difference as a sound directly behind. The effect of turning the head on the interaural time difference (b) reveals the true situation.

the listener time to respond in this way. Brief sounds (e.g., the crack of a twig in a dark forest!) may be over before the listener has had a chance to make the head movement.

9.2.2   Monaural cues

Although we have two ears, a great deal of information about sound source location can be obtained by listening through just one ear. *Monaural* cues to sound source location arise because the incoming sound waves are modified by the head and upper body and, especially, by the *pinna*. These modifications depend on the *direction* of the sound source.

If you look carefully at a pinna, you will see that it contains ridges and cavities. These structures modify the incoming sound by processes including *resonance* within the cavities (Blauert, 1997, p. 67). Because the cavities are small, the resonances affect only high-frequency components with short wavelengths (see Section 3.1.3). The resonances introduce a set of spectral peaks and notches in the high-frequency region of the spectrum, above 4000 Hz or so. The precise pattern of peaks and notches depends on the *angle* at which the sound waves strike the pinna. In other words, the pinna imposes a sort of directional "signature" on the spectrum of the sound that can be recognized by the auditory system and used as a cue to location. As an example, Figure 9.11 shows recordings, made from a human ear canal, of a broadband noise presented from two elevations in the median plane. The effects of variations in elevation can be seen in the spectra.

Pinna effects are thought to be particularly important for determining the *elevation* of sound sources. If the cavities of the pinnae are filled in with a soft rubber, localization performance for sound sources in the median plane declines dramatically (Gardner & Gardner, 1973). There is also a shadowing effect of the pinna for sounds behind the head, which have to diffract around the pinna to

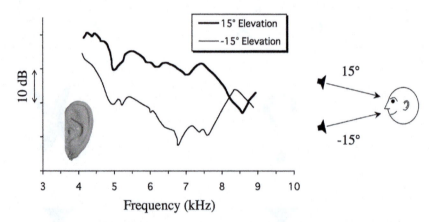

Figure 9.11 Spectra of a broadband noise recorded from a microphone inserted in the left ear canal of a single listener. The noise was presented from a loudspeaker at an elevation of either –15° or 15° relative to the head. The spectra demonstrate the direction-specific filtering properties of the pinna. From Butler and Belendiuk (1977).

reach the ear canal. The shadowing will tend to *attenuate* high-frequency sound components coming from the rear (remember that low frequencies diffract more than high frequencies, and so can bend round the obstruction) and may help us to resolve front–back ambiguities.

9.3   JUDGING DISTANCE

Thus far, we have focused on our ability to determine the *direction* of a sound source. It is also important in some situations to determine the *distance* of a sound source (is the sound of screaming coming from the next room or the next house?). Overall sound level provides a cue to distance for familiar sounds. In an open space, every doubling in distance produces a 6-dB reduction in sound level (see Section 3.2.1). If the sound of a car is very faint, then it is more likely to be 2 miles away than 2 feet away. However, when listeners are required to estimate the distance of a familiar sound based on level cues, then the response tends to be an *underestimate* of the true distance, so a 20-dB reduction in sound level is required to produce a *perceived* doubling in distance (see Blauert, 1997, pp. 122–123). The use of the level cue depends on our experience of sounds and sound sources. If a completely alien sound is heard, we cannot know without additional information whether it is quiet because the sound source is far away or because the sound source is very weak. Generally, however, loud sounds are perceived as being close, and quiet sounds are perceived as being far away, even though these perceptions may at times be misleading.

Another cue to distance in rooms with reflective walls or in other reverberant environments is the ratio of direct to reverberant sound. The greater the distance of the source, the greater is the proportion of reflected sound. This cue can be used by listeners to estimate distance, even if the sound is unfamiliar. However, our limited ability to detect changes in the direct-to-reverberant ratio implies that we can only detect changes in distance greater than about a *factor of two* using this cue alone. In other words, we may not be able to tell the difference between a sound source 10 meters away and a sound source 20 meters away using this cue alone. The direct-to-reverberant ratio provides only coarse information about the distance of a sound source (Zahorik, 2002b). In any natural listening environment, the auditory system will tend to *combine* the level information and the direct-to-reverberant ratio information to estimate distance. It is still the case, however, that for distances greater than a meter or so, we seem to consistently underestimate the true distance of a sound source when we rely on acoustic information alone (Zahorik, 2002a).

Finally, large changes in distance tend to change the *spectral balance* of the sound reaching the ears. The air absorbs more high-frequency energy than low-frequency energy, so the spectral balance of the sound from a source far away is biased toward low frequencies as compared to the sound from a source close by. Consider, for example, the deep sound produced by a distant roll of thunder compared to the brighter sound of a nearby lightning strike. However, the change in spectral balance with distance is fairly slight. The relative attenuation is only about 3–4 dB per 100 meters at 4000 Hz (Ingard, 1953). Spectral balance is not a particularly salient cue and is useless for small distances.

9.4   REFLECTIONS AND THE PERCEPTION OF SPACE

9.4.1   The precedence effect

When we listen to a sound source in an environment in which there are reflective surfaces (e.g., a room), the sound waves arriving at our ears are a complex
combination of the sound that comes directly from the sound source and the
sound that is reflected, perhaps many times, by nearby surfaces. The problem
with reflections, in terms of localizing sound sources, is that the reflected sound
provides directional information that conflicts with that from the direct sound. If
heard in isolation, reflected sound waves would appear to come from the direction of the reflective surface rather than from the direction of the sound source
(just as the direction of an image in a mirror is different from the direction of
the original object). This problem is illustrated in Figure 9.12. How does the
auditory system know that the sound waves come from the sound source (A)
and not from the direction of one of the numerous sites of reflection (e.g., B and
C)? The task appears difficult, yet human listeners are very good at localizing
sounds in reverberant environments.

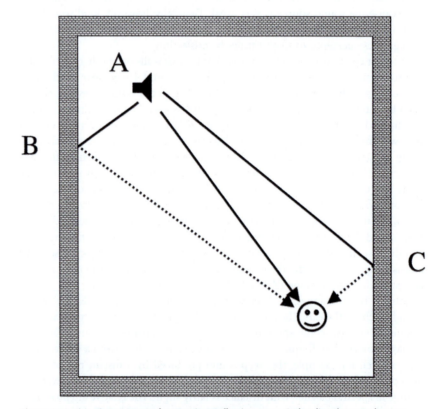

Figure 9.12 Listening to a sound source in a reflective room. To localize the sound source
correctly (A), the listener must ignore sound waves that appear to originate from the
direction of the points of reflection (e.g., B and C).

To avoid the ambiguity, the auditory system uses the principle that the direct sound will always arrive at the ears *before* the reflected sound. This is simply because the path length for the reflected sound is always longer than the path length for the direct sound. The *precedence effect* refers to our ability to localize on the basis of information from the leading sound only. The precedence effect has been demonstrated using sounds presented over headphones and from loud-speakers (see Litovsky, Colburn, Yost, & Guzman, 1999, for a review). In the latter case, the listener may be facing two loudspeakers at different locations in the horizontal plane but equidistant from the head. One loudspeaker acts as the source of the direct sound, and the other loudspeaker is used to simulate a reflection (see Figure 9.13). If identical sounds are played through the two loudspeakers without any delay, then the sounds are *fused* perceptually, and the location of the sound source appears to be midway between the two loudspeakers. If the sound from the second loudspeaker is delayed by up to about a millisecond, then the sound source appears to move toward the first loudspeaker, because the interaural time differences between the ears suggest that the sound is arriving at the ear closest to the first loudspeaker before it arrives at the ear closest to the second loudspeaker. If, however, the sound from the second loudspeaker is delayed by between about 1 and 30 ms (these times are for complex sounds such as speech; for clicks, the upper limit is about 5 ms), then the sound appears localized *almost entirely* to the first loudspeaker. The simulated echo from the second loudspeaker is effectively ignored for the purposes of localization. For larger delays, the percept breaks down into two sound sources located at the two loudspeakers, each of which can be localized independently. In other words, the precedence effect works only for fairly short reflections (corresponding to path length differences of about 10 meters). The precedence effect also works best when the sound contains large envelope fluctuations, or transients such as clicks, so that there are clear time markers to compare between the direct and reflected sounds. Stable tones with slow onsets are localized very poorly in a reverberant room (Rakerd & Hartmann, 1986).

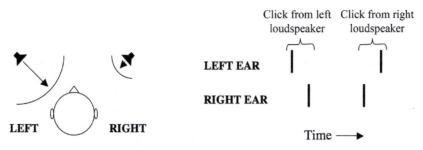

Figure 9.13 A typical experimental configuration for observing the precedence effect. A click from the left loudspeaker arrives at the left ear before the right ear. Subsequently, a click is played from the right loudspeaker and arrives at the right ear before the left ear. If the click from the right loudspeaker is delayed by 1–5 ms, then a single sound source is heard, located in the direction of the left loudspeaker. The auditory system treats the click from the right loudspeaker as a reflection (echo) of the click from the left loudspeaker, and the location information from the second click is suppressed. Based on Litovsky et al. (1999).

Moore (2012, p. 270) describes how the precedence effect can be a nuisance when listening to stereo recordings over loudspeakers. The stereo location of an instrument in a recording is usually simulated by adjusting the relative levels in the left and right channels during mixing (i.e., by using a cue based on interaural *level* differences). If the guitar is more intense in the left loudspeaker than in the right loudspeaker, then it sounds as if it is located toward the left. However, the music is being played out of the two loudspeakers *simultaneously*. This means that the relative time of arrival of the sounds from the two loudspeakers depends on the listener's location in the room. If the listener is too close to one loudspeaker such that the sound from that loudspeaker arrives more than about 1 ms before the sound from the other loudspeaker, the precedence effect operates and all the music appears to come from the closer loudspeaker alone! Moore suggests that if you venture more than 60 cm either side of the central position between the two loudspeakers, then the stereo image begins to break down.

Although the precedence effect shows that we can largely ignore short-delay reflected sound for the purposes of *localization*, when we are in an environment we are well aware of its reverberation characteristics. We can usually tell whether we are in the bathroom or the bedroom by the quality of the reflected sound alone. The smaller bathroom, with highly reflective walls and surfaces, usually has a higher level of reverberation at shorter delays than the bedroom. Furthermore, we see in Section 9.3 that the level of reverberation compared to the level of direct sound can be used to estimate the distance of the sound source. It follows that the information about reflected sounds is not erased; it is just not used for determining the direction of sound sources.

9.4.2   Auditory virtual space

The two main cues to sound location are interaural time differences and interaural level differences. By manipulating these cues in the sounds presented to each ear, it is possible to produce a "virtual" source location. As noted, most stereophonic music is mixed using interaural level differences to separate the individual instruments. Realistic interaural time differences cannot be easily implemented for sounds played over loudspeakers, because each ear receives sound from *both* loudspeakers. Realistic time and level differences can be introduced into sounds presented over *headphones*, because the input to each ear can be controlled independently. However, the sounds often appear as if they originate from within the head, either closer to the left ear or closer to the right ear. Sounds played over headphones are usually heard as *lateralized* within the head rather than *localized* outside the head. This is because the modifications associated with the head and pinnae are not present in the sound entering the ear canal. It seems that we need to hear these modifications to get a strong sense that a sound is external.

It is possible to make stereo recordings by positioning two microphones in the ear canals of an artificial "dummy head" that includes model pinnae. In this case, the spectral modifications of the head and pinnae are included in the recordings. When these recordings are played over headphones, listeners experience a strong sense of the sound source being localized *outside* the head. Alternatively, *head-related transfer functions*, which mimic the modifications of the pinna and can also include interaural time and interaural level differences, can be used to process a sound recording so that it elicits a realistic external spatial image when played over headphones. Since pinnae vary from one individual to the next, it is perhaps unsurprising to discover that head-related transfer functions work best when they are derived from the ears of the person being tested (Wenzel, Arruda, Kistler, & Wightman, 1993).

Although you may not be aware of it at all times, your brain processes the reverberation characteristics of the space you are in and uses this information to obtain an appreciation of the dimensions and reflectivity of that space. It follows that for sounds presented over headphones or loudspeakers, reverberation is also important for the simulation of a natural listening environment. Recordings made in an anechoic (nonreverberant) room sound unnatural and give a strange sensation of the acoustic space. Such a recording may be processed to simulate the delayed reflections that might occur in a more natural space. By progressively increasing the delays of the simulated reflections, it is possible to make someone sound as if he or she is singing in a bathroom, in a cathedral, or in the Grand Canyon. While not all of these scenarios may be appropriate, a considered use of reverberation can benefit a recording greatly. Sophisticated "reverb" devices are considered vital tools for sound engineers and music producers.

9.5 SUMMARY

There are several different types of information about sound source location available to the auditory system, and it appears that our brains combine these different cues. Interaural time and level differences provide detailed information about the direction of a sound source, but this information is ambiguous and accurate localization depends on the use of other types of information, such as the effects of head movements and the location-dependent modifications of the pinna. Our appreciation of the acoustic space around us is dependent on information about source location and the information about reflective surfaces from the characteristics of reverberation.

1 Having two ears helps us determine the direction of a sound source. There are two such binaural cues: *interaural time differences* (a sound from the right arrives at the right ear first) and *interaural level differences* (a sound from the right is more intense in the right ear). Interaural time differences are dominant for most natural sounds.

2 Interaural time differences are most useful for the localization of low-frequency components. If the wavelength of a continuous pure tone is less than twice the distance between the ears, ambiguity arises as to whether the sound is leading to the left or right ear. However, time differences between peaks in the (slowly varying) envelope can be used at these higher frequencies.

3 Interaural level differences arise mainly because of the shadowing effect of the head. Low frequencies diffract more than high frequencies, so the level cue is most salient at high frequencies.

4   Binaural cues can help us to separate perceptually sounds that arise from different locations. However, the use of interaural time differences for masking release may be independent from their use in localization.

5   Our remarkable sensitivity to interaural time differences (minimum threshold of 10 μs) implies very accurate phase-locked encoding of the time of arrival at the two ears. The information is extracted by neurons in the brainstem that receive input from both ears and are sensitive to differences between the arrival times at each ear.

6   Interaural time and level differences do not unambiguously specify the location of the sound source. The "cone of confusion" can be resolved by head movements and by the use of monaural information based on the effects of the *pinna*, which imposes a direction-specific signature on the spectrum of sounds arriving at the ear. The pinna is particularly important for determining the elevation of a sound source.

7   The most salient cues to the distance of a sound source are *level* (because quiet sounds are usually from sound sources that are farther away than the sources of loud sounds) and the *ratio of direct to reflected sound* (which decreases with increasing distance). The auditory system combines these cues but tends to underestimate.

8   In a reverberant environment, the ear is able to identify the direction of a sound source by using the location information in the direct sound and suppressing the delayed (and misleading) location information in the reflected sound. This is called the precedence effect. We still perceive the reverberation, however, and this provides information regarding the dimensions and reflective properties of the walls and surfaces in the space around us.

9   Sounds presented over headphones can be made to sound external and more realistic by simulating the filtering characteristics of the pinnae. Similarly, the addition of appropriate reverberation helps produce the impression of a natural space.

9.6 READING

You may have noticed that I found Jens Blauert's book very helpful for this chapter:

Blauert, J. (1996). *Spatial hearing: The psychophysics of human sound localization*. Cambridge, MA: MIT Press.

I also recommend:

Culling, J. F., & Akeroyd, M. A. (2010). Spatial hearing. In C. J. Plack (Ed.), *Hearing* (pp. 123–144). Oxford: Oxford University Press.

Gilkey, R. H., & Anderson, T. A. (Eds.). (1997). *Binaural and spatial hearing in real and virtual environments.* Mahwah, NJ: Lawrence Erlbaum.

Grantham, D. W. (1995). Spatial hearing and related phenomena. In B. C. J. Moore (Ed.), *Hearing* (pp. 297–345). New York: Academic Press.

For an excellent review of the neurophysiology of sound localization:

Grothe, B., Pecka, M., & McAlpine, D. (2010). Mechanisms of sound localization in mammals. *Physiological Reviews, 90,* 383–1012.

10 THE AUDITORY SCENE

Professor Chris Darwin once wrote, "How often do you hear a single sound by itself? Only when doing psychoacoustic experiments in a sound-proof booth!" (Darwin, 2005, p. 278). Unless you are reading this in a very quiet place, the chances are that you will be able to identify sounds from several sources in the space around you. As I write these words in a study in my house, I can hear the singing of birds in the garden, the rustling of trees in the wind, and (somewhat less idyllically) the whirr of the fan in my laptop computer. Our ears receive a mixture of all the sounds in the environment at a given time: The sound waves simply add together when they meet (Figure 10.1). As you might imagine, in a noisy environment such as a party or a busy street, the result can be very messy indeed! To make sense of all this, the auditory system requires mechanisms that can *separate out* the sound components that originate from different sound sources and *group together* the sound components that originate from the same sound source. Bregman (1990) has termed the whole process *auditory scene analysis*.

It is arguable that scene analysis is the hardest task accomplished by the auditory system, and artificial devices are nowhere near human performance in this respect. To explain why, I'll resort to a common analogy. Imagine that you are paddling on the shore of a lake. Three people are swimming on the lake, producing ripples that combine to form a complex pattern of tiny waves arriving at your feet. By looking only at the pattern of waves below you, you have to determine how many swimmers there are, where they are, and which stroke each one is using. If you think that would be hard, imagine doing the same thing with a speedboat on the water, producing large waves that crash over your legs. Although the computation seems impossible, the auditory system can manage tasks of even greater complexity involving sound waves. Perhaps the most remarkable aspect is that the sound from a single source generally sounds the same when it is presented with other sounds as when it is presented in isolation. We are blissfully unaware of the complexity of the processing that underlies this perception.

One of the tricks the auditory system employs, of course, is to break down the sound waves into different *frequency components* using the spectral analysis powers of the cochlea. After the sound has been separated out in this way, the auditory system can assign the different frequency components to different sound sources. Without spectral analysis, the auditory system would be lost when it comes to separating out simultaneous sounds. One of the main problems experienced by listeners with hearing impairment is in sound segregation: Listening to

Figure 10.1 Our ears receive a mixture of the sounds from all the sources in the environment. The figure shows the waveforms of music from a loudspeaker, speech, and the sound of a car engine. The sound waves add together in the air to produce a combined waveform. To attend to one of the three sound sources, the ear has to *separate out* the relevant components from the combined waveform.

a conversation in a noisy room, for example. The problem arises because hearing impairment is usually associated with a reduction in frequency selectivity (see Section 13.3.2.3).

In this chapter, we consider both *simultaneous* grouping (organizing sounds that occur at the same time) and *sequential* grouping (organizing sound sequences). First, however, we look at the principles that the auditory system uses to interpret the complex information arriving at our ears.

10.1   PRINCIPLES OF PERCEPTUAL ORGANIZATION

Without some implicit knowledge about the nature of sounds in the environment, the auditory system cannot know whether the sound waves arriving at the ear come from one sound source, two sound sources, or a thousand sound sources. (Indeed, for a monophonic musical recording played through a single loudspeaker, we may hear several sound sources, corresponding to the different instruments, whereas in reality there is just one sound source – the loudspeaker.)

How does the auditory system know that the sound waves arriving at the ear do not all come from the same source? The answer is that the auditory system contains a set of "rules of thumb": Principles, or heuristics, that describe the expected characteristics of sounds in the environment. These principles are based on constraints in the production of sounds by vibrating objects. The auditory system, by applying these principles (using complex neural processing), can not only determine whether there is one sound source or several but can also assign sound components to the appropriate sound sources. Once sounds have been grouped by source, we can attend to the sound source that we are interested in (e.g., the person speaking to us in a crowded bar) and ignore the sound sources that we are not interested in (the other people in the bar, the music coming from a jukebox, etc.).

In the 1930s, the gestalt psychologists proposed a list of the principles of organization that apply to sensory stimuli (Koffka, 1935). The most important of these principles for hearing are as follows:

Similarity: Sound components that come from the same source are likely to be similar.

Good continuation: Sound components that come from the same source are likely to flow naturally over time from one to the other (without any abrupt discontinuities).

Common fate: Sound components that come from the same source are likely to vary together (e.g., they will be turned on and off at the same times).

Belongingness: A single sound component is usually associated with a single source: It is unlikely that a single sound component originates from two (or more) different sources simultaneously.

Closure: A continuous sound obscured briefly by a second sound (e.g., speech interrupted by a door slam) is likely to be continuous during the interruption unless there is evidence to the contrary.

These principles ensure that our perceptions are organized into the simplest pattern consistent with the sensory information and with our implicit knowledge of the nature of sound production in the environment. Although they work for most "natural" sound sources, it is, of course, possible to violate these principles using artificial sound sources, and many researchers make a (modest) living by doing just that.

10.2   SIMULTANEOUS GROUPING

As described at the beginning of the chapter, simultaneous grouping involves the allocation of frequency components to the appropriate sound sources. Simultaneous grouping is dependent on the spectral analysis of the cochlea. Without spectral analysis, the auditory system would have to deal with the single complex waveform that is a sum of the sound waves from all the sound sources in the environment. By separating the different frequency components (into separate waveforms at different places on the basilar membrane), the auditory system can separate those components that come from the sound source of interest from those that come from other sources. Simultaneous grouping, therefore, is all about the correct allocation of the different frequency components provided by the cochlea.

For example, Figure 10.2 shows spectra and excitation patterns (effectively, cochlear representations) for vowel sounds produced by a man (top panel) and by a woman (middle panel). The low-numbered harmonics are resolved by the ear and produce separate peaks in the excitation patterns. When the vowels are presented together, the spectra are combined (bottom panel). The question is, how does the auditory system determine which harmonic, or which peak in the excitation pattern, belongs to which vowel?

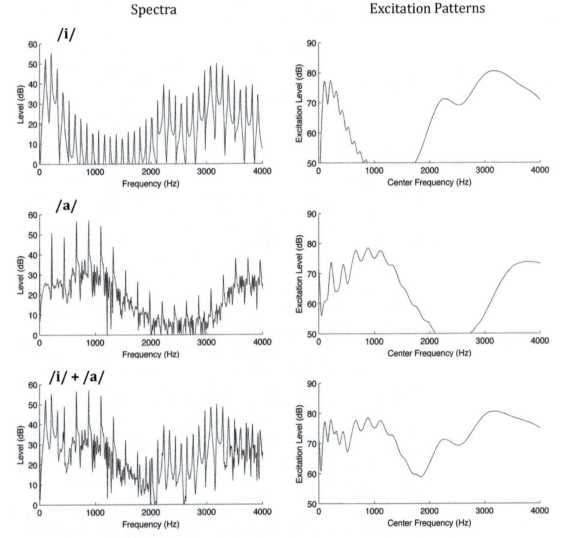

Figure 10.2 The spectra and excitation patterns of vowel sounds from two different speakers: A man saying "ee" (/i/) and a woman saying "ah" (/a/). Notice that the harmonics in the first formant region (the first broad spectral peak) are resolved (they produce separate peaks in the excitation pattern). The bottom panel shows the spectrum and excitation pattern produced when the two vowels are spoken together. To separate the sounds from the two speakers, the auditory system has to determine which harmonic belongs to which vowel.

10.2.1   Temporal cues

Perhaps the strongest cue that enables us to separate out simultaneous sounds is related to the gestalt principle of *common fate*. The frequency components from a single sound source will tend to start together and stop together. For example, as you speak, your mouth opens and closes, and this imposes a temporal envelope on all the sounds you are making. Similarly, if your vocal folds start vibrating to produce a vowel sound, all the harmonics of the vowel will start at (roughly) the same time. The auditory system is aware of this correlation and will tend to *group together* frequency components that start together and to *segregate* frequency components that start at different times.

There are many examples of this phenomenon in the literature. If a single harmonic in a vowel is started at least 32 ms before the rest of the vowel, then this can reduce the effect of the harmonic on the overall quality of the vowel, suggesting that the harmonic is segregated perceptually (Darwin & Sutherland, 1984). Similarly, it is described in Section 7.3.1 that a shift in the frequency of a single low harmonic can cause the pitch of a complex tone to change. Positive shifts cause the pitch to increase slightly, while negative shifts cause the pitch to decrease slightly. It is as if the auditory system is combining the frequency information from the individual resolved harmonics and having a best guess at what the pitch should be, even though the stimulus is not strictly harmonic. This effect is dependent on the mistuned harmonic being grouped with the rest of the complex. If the harmonic starts 160 ms *before* the rest of the complex, then the effect of the mistuning is reduced (Darwin & Ciocca, 1992; see Figure 10.3). Onset disparities can also be used by a musician to help emphasize the part the musician is playing in relation to the rest of the orchestra. By departing slightly from the notated metric positions, the notes are heard to stand out perceptually (Rasch, 1979). *Offset* asynchronies can also cause sound components to be segregated (although this appears to be a weaker effect, especially for long sounds).

Onset synchrony is regarded as a specific instance of the more general property that frequency components from a single source tend to vary in level together (i.e., they vary *coherently*). There is some evidence that sound components that are amplitude modulated with the same modulator, so that their temporal envelopes vary up and down together, tend to be grouped together by the auditory system. We see in Section 8.2.2 that the auditory system can hear out one frequency of modulation in the presence of another, although this does not imply that the *carriers* are segregated. The cross-frequency grouping of coherently modulated components may be the basis for comodulation masking release (see Section 8.2.3). Frequency components that are amplitude modulated can be "heard out" from components that are not modulated (Moore & Bacon, 1993), and modulation of the fundamental frequency, so that all the harmonics are frequency modulated together, helps to group harmonics (Chowning, 1980, cited in Bregman, 1990, p. 252). Although harmonics can be grouped together based on coherent modulation, it is less clear whether components can be *segregated* on the basis of *incoherent* amplitude modulation, in which different components have *different patterns* of modulation, and there seems to be little evidence that frequency modulation incoherence can be used to segregate components (Carlyon, 1994;

Figure 10.3 An illustration of some of the stimuli used in experiments investigating the influence of grouping mechanisms on the pitch shifts produced by harmonic mistuning. The thick horizontal lines show the individual harmonics. Panel (a) shows a harmonic complex tone. The arrow shows the location of the fourth harmonic. In panel (b), the fourth harmonic has been mistuned slightly. In panel (c), the fourth harmonic has been mistuned and started before the rest of the complex. In panel (d), the fourth harmonic has been mistuned and preceded by a sequence of four pure tones at the harmonic frequency. Only in condition (b) is the pitch substantially higher than that for the reference. In conditions (c) and (d), the harmonic forms a separate perceptual stream from the rest of the complex (illustrated by gray ovals). In these cases, the harmonic does not contribute to the pitch of the complex, and hence there is no effect of mistuning.

Summerfield & Culling, 1992). This latter finding may not be too surprising, since the frequency locations of the formants in the vowel sounds produced by a single speaker can vary differently (incoherent frequency modulation) as the shape of the vocal tract is changed to produce different vowels (see Section 11.1.1). In this case, at least, incoherent frequency modulation does not imply the presence of more than one sound source.

The segregation of simultaneous components is also facilitated if those components can be grouped into separate *sequential streams*. For instance, a sequence of pure tones at a harmonic frequency can act to segregate the harmonic from a subsequently presented complex tone (Figure 10.3) so that the effects on pitch of mistuning the harmonic disappear (Darwin, Hukin, & al-Khatib, 1995). It appears that the auditory system assumes the harmonic is a part of a temporal sequence of pure tones from a distinct source, and the gestalt principle of belongingness prevents it from also contributing to the pitch of the complex (assumed to originate from a separate source). The result is particularly interesting, because it suggests that grouping mechanisms operating over a long time period (and therefore almost certainly involving processing in the cerebral cortex) can affect the way the pitch mechanism combines the information from the individual harmonics. The effect of grouping on pitch may be an example of *top-down* processing, in that a higher level of the auditory system interacts with a lower level.

10.2.2   Harmonicity cues

As described in Chapters 2 and 3, many sound sources vibrate repetitively to generate periodic waveforms whose spectra can be described by harmonic series, the frequency of each harmonic being an integer multiple of the repetition rate (or fundamental frequency) of the waveform. Based on the principle of similarity, pure-tone frequency components that are *harmonically related* are likely to come from the same sound source, whereas components that do not fit into the harmonic series may be assumed to come from a different sound source. The auditory system appears to use harmonicity in this way to group individual frequency components. For example, a vowel sound produced by a single speaker is normally heard as *fused* in that all the components appear to come from the same sound source. This percept can be disrupted by separating the harmonics into two groups, say, into first and second formants (the regions around the first and second broad peaks in the spectrum), and by giving each group a different fundamental frequency (Broadbent & Ladefoged, 1957). Because the harmonics have different fundamental frequencies, the auditory system assumes that they come from different sound sources, and two voices are heard.

Returning once again to the phenomenon of the mistuned harmonic, we see that if a low harmonic in a complex tone is shifted slightly in frequency, it can affect the overall pitch of the complex tone. For frequency shifts greater than about 3%, however, the effect of the mistuning on pitch *decreases* with increasing mistuning (see Figure 10.4). For a harmonic mistuning of 8% or more, the pitch shift is negligible. As the mistuning is increased, the auditory system begins to regard the mistuned harmonic as belonging to a separate sound source from the rest of the complex, and hence reduces the contribution of the harmonic to its estimate of pitch.

Outside the walls of soundproof booths in hearing laboratories, we often encounter complex tones from different sources that occur simultaneously. For instance, we may be listening to one speaker in the presence of other speakers at a party, and the vowel sounds from the different speakers may overlap in time. Differences in fundamental frequency between the vowel sounds (and the associated differences in the harmonic frequencies) help us to segregate the vowels and to "hear out" the speaker of interest. A fundamental frequency difference of only a quarter of one semitone (1.5%) is sufficient to improve the identification of two simultaneously presented vowels, and performance improves up to one semitone (6%) difference (Culling & Darwin, 1993). The improvement in identification for small differences in fundamental frequency is based on the resolved harmonics in the first formant region (see Figure 10.2). Only at much larger

Figure 10.4 The continuous line shows the changes in the pitch of a complex tone produced by varying the frequency of the fourth harmonic. The fundamental frequency was 155 Hz. A schematic spectrum for the stimulus with a (positively) shifted fourth harmonic is shown above the graph (the arrow indicates the usual location of the fourth harmonic). Based on the results of Darwin and Ciocca (1992; see Darwin, 2005).

fundamental frequency differences (2–4 semitones) is there a contribution from the unresolved harmonics in the higher formant regions.

Figure 10.5 illustrates the use of onset time and harmonicity to separate a mixture of harmonics into the components arising from each of two separate sound sources.

10.2.3 Spatial cues

A single sound source usually occupies a single location in space, and different sound sources usually occupy different locations in space. As an example of the gestalt principle of similarity, we might expect sound components that come from the same location to be grouped together and sound components that come from different locations to be separated. It may be somewhat surprising to

Figure 10.5 The use of onset time and harmonicity to segregate a mixture of harmonics from two sound sources.

discover, therefore, that sound location does not seem to be very important for simultaneous grouping (although it is important for sequential grouping; see Section 10.3.3).

Some experiments have shown that the segregation of components that have harmonicity or onset-time differences can be *enhanced* by presenting them at different apparent locations. For example, the identification of two simultaneous vowels whose fundamental frequencies differ by one semitone improves when the vowels are presented with different interaural time differences or different interaural level differences, so the two vowels appear to come from distinct locations (Shackleton, Meddis, & Hewitt, 1994). Section 9.1.3 describes binaural listening advantages for the detection of tones or speech in noise when there is a clear spectral and periodic difference between the signal and the masker. However, if there is no other basis for segregation, the tendency seems to be to group together components from different apparent sound locations that occur at the same time. For example, a resolved harmonic with a slight mistuning contributes to the pitch of a complex tone even if it is presented to the *opposite ear* to the other harmonics in the complex. The pitch shift produced by the mistuning is only slightly less than that obtained when all the harmonics are presented to the same ear (Darwin & Ciocca, 1992). Furthermore, our ability to identify two simultaneous vowels with the *same* fundamental frequency does *not* improve when the vowels are given different interaural time or level differences (Shackleton et al., 1994).

Darwin (2005) argues that localization is not an important cue for simultaneous grouping because in noisy or reverberant environments, where reflections of the sound from a single source may arrive from different directions (see Section 9.4.1), the location cues in just one frequency channel (i.e., for one characteristic frequency in both ears) are rather weak. These cues may not be robust enough to allow the frequency component in that channel to be assigned reliably to a specific group. Rather, the "low-level" grouping cues of onset time and harmonicity determine the group, and this group is then assigned to a specific spatial location by combining the location information across the grouped frequency components (as suggested by Woods & Colburn, 1992). Simultaneous grouping may occur before the location of the sound source is determined.

10.3 SEQUENTIAL GROUPING

Sequential grouping refers to the organization of a sequence of sounds from a single source into a perceptual stream, such as a speech utterance or a musical melody. When we are listening to one speaker in the presence of others, we want to be able to follow the sequence of sounds from the speaker of interest while ignoring the interfering sounds. If one speaker says, "I love you" at the same time as another speaker is saying, "I hate ants," you do not want to hear this as "I hate you" or "I love ants." Similarly, we also need to be able to follow the sounds produced by a single instrument in an orchestra or ensemble so that we may appreciate the melody that the instrument is playing, in isolation from the melodies played by the other instruments. We are much better at identifying the temporal order of a sequence of sounds when the sounds are grouped perceptually into a single stream than when they are grouped into several streams (Bregman & Campbell, 1971). Sequential grouping is a precursor to the identification of temporal patterns, such as sentences in speech, and we are only usually interested in the temporal order of sounds from the attended source.

10.3.1 Periodicity cues

A sequence of tones that are similar in periodicity and, hence, similar in pitch (e.g., pure tones with similar frequencies or complex tones with similar fundamental frequencies) tends to form a single stream. Indeed, one of the main functions of pitch processing in the auditory system may be to facilitate such streaming. If two melodies are interleaved (i.e., notes from one melody are alternated with notes from another melody), then it is much easier to hear the two melodies separately if they occupy different frequency ranges (Dowling, 1973) (see Figure 10.6). Two melodies close in frequency tend to sound "fused" together, forming a single melody perceptually. The effect is also illustrated by a stimulus developed by van Noorden (1975). Two 40-ms pure tones A and B (where A and B have different frequencies) are played in the following sequence: ABA ABA ABA. . . . When the tones are close together in frequency, a single galloping rhythm is heard. When the tones differ sufficiently in frequency (e.g., by 30%), the tones tend to be perceived as two separate streams, A A A A A A . . . and B B B. . . . Figure 10.7 illustrates these two percepts. For a given frequency difference, the tendency to hear two streams increases as the rate at which the tones are presented is increased.

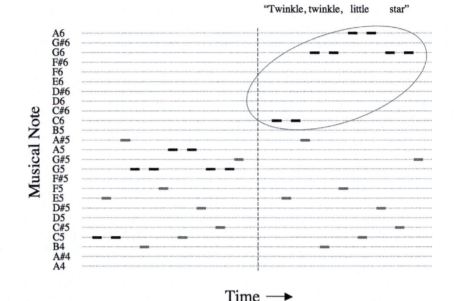

Figure 10.6 The segregation of interleaved musical melodies by differences in fundamental frequency. The target melody (short black lines) is alternated with an interfering melody (short gray lines). When the two melodies occupy a similar range of notes (left panel), a single sequence is heard and the target melody cannot be recognized. When the target melody is shifted in fundamental frequency by an octave (right panel), identification is possible. The vertical scale is in units of musical interval. Each division represents a change of 6% in fundamental frequency.

In the case of a pure tone, and in the case of the low-numbered (resolved) harmonics of a complex tone, the differences in periodicity are reflected by spectral differences that can be resolved by the cochlea. Two pure tones with different frequencies excite different places in the cochlea, and two complex tones with different fundamental frequencies have resolved harmonics that excite different places in the cochlea. A crucial question is whether it is *necessary* for the tones to be differentiated spectrally before they can be grouped into separate streams on the basis of periodicity. The answer appears to be no. It has been shown that sequences of complex tones containing only unresolved harmonics can form two separate streams based on differences in fundamental frequency, even when the harmonics are filtered so that they occupy the *same spectral region* (Vliegen & Oxenham, 1999). In other words, even when there is no difference between stimuli in terms of the spatial pattern of activity in the cochlea, sequential grouping is still possible based on periodicity cues, presumably mediated by a temporal pitch mechanism (see Section 7.3.3).

Fundamental frequency differences are also important for the separation of voices in speech. It is much easier to separate the sounds from two people speaking together, and hence to identify the words they are saying, when there is a difference between the fundamental frequencies of their voices (i.e., when one

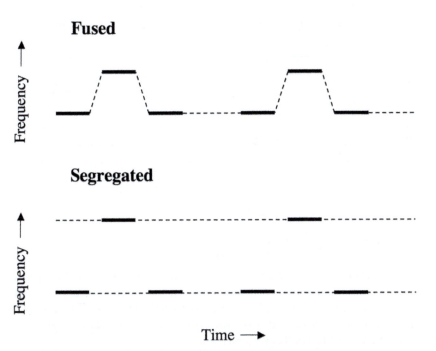

Fused

Frequency →

Segregated

Frequency →

Time →

Figure 10.7 The thick lines show the stimuli used by van Noorden (1975) to study stream segregation. The dotted lines illustrate the two possible perceptions of fusion (galloping rhythm) and segregation (two separate pulsing rhythms).

speaker has a higher fundamental frequency than the other, such as a woman and a man; see Brokx & Nooteboom, 1982). Some of the segregation may be due to simultaneous grouping cues based on harmonicity (see Section 10.2.2), but the grouping of sequences of speech sounds over time is also dependent on fundamental frequency similarity, or at least on a smooth variation in fundamental frequency (see Section 10.3.4).

10.3.2   Spectral and level cues

As described in Section 10.3.1, sound sequences can be segregated in the absence of spectral cues. Spectral differentiation is not a *necessary* condition for the segregation of streams. However, it does appear to be a *sufficient* condition in some cases. *Spectral balance* refers to the overall distribution of frequency components across low and high frequencies. Differences in spectral balance, which are associated with differences in the sensation of *timbre*, can be used to segregate sequences of sounds even in the absence of differences in periodicity or pitch. This is another example of the principle of similarity, in that a single sound source tends to produce sounds with similar spectra, or at least sounds with spectra that change smoothly over time.

Complex tones with similar fundamental frequencies but with different patterns of harmonics tend to form separate perceptual streams. Van Noorden (1975) synthesized a sequence of complex tones with a constant fundamental

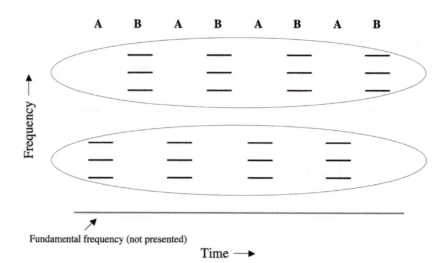

Figure 10.8 Stream segregation by spectral balance. Alternating complex tones A and B have the same fundamental frequency (indicated by the continuous gray line). However, they are grouped into two sequential streams (gray ovals) on the basis of the different harmonics that are present in each tone. Tone A contains harmonics 3, 4, and 5, and tone B contains harmonics 8, 9, and 10. Based on Bregman (1990).

frequency (140 Hz). Alternating tones had different harmonics, either the third, fourth, and fifth or the eighth, ninth, and tenth (see Figure 10.8). This sequence was heard as two sequential streams, one containing the lower harmonics and one containing the higher harmonics. In music, segregation by spectral balance means that melodies played by different instruments (with characteristic spectra) will tend to segregate, even if they occupy a similar range of fundamental frequencies.

Level differences can also be used to segregate tone sequences. Van Noorden (1975) showed that two sequences of tones with the same frequency but differing in level by 3 dB or more could be heard as two separate streams. Although ambiguous in some cases, level differences are often associated with differences in sound source (e.g., two people at different distances). However, the level cue does not seem to be as powerful as periodicity or timbre (see Bregman, 1990, pp. 126–127).

10.3.3   Spatial cues

Despite being relatively unimportant for simultaneous grouping, location is a strong cue for sequential grouping. A sequence of sounds that comes from – or appears to come from – a single location in space is more likely to form a perceptual stream than a sequence whose individual components come from different spatial locations. Similarly, it is easier to segregate two sequences if each sequence has a different real or virtual location. Different sound sources generally occupy distinct locations in space, so it is not surprising that location cues are used by the auditory system to group sounds from a single source. Block one ear at a noisy party, and it is much harder to follow a conversation.

If two interleaved melodies are presented so that each melody appears to come from a different location in space, then the melodies are more likely to be segregated and form separate perceptual streams (Dowling, 1968). If speech is alternated between the two ears at a rate of three alternations per second (left, then right, then left, then right, etc.), producing extreme switches in location based on interaural level cues, then the intelligibility of the speech is reduced and listeners find it hard to repeat back the sequence of words they hear (Cherry & Taylor, 1954). Conversely, Darwin and Hukin (1999) showed that listeners are able to selectively attend to a sequence of words with a particular interaural time difference in the presence of a second sequence of words with a different interaural time difference. In this experiment, both sentences were presented to both ears, but there were slight differences (tens of microseconds) in the relative arrival times at the two ears: One sentence led to the left ear, and the other sentence led to the right ear. The resulting difference in apparent location allowed segregation. Indeed, a target word tended to group with the sentence with the same interaural time difference, even if its fundamental frequency better matched the other sentence.

Darwin and Hukin (1999) suggest that, while spatial location is not used to attend to individual frequency components (and is not a major factor in simultaneous grouping), location is used to direct attention to a previously grouped *auditory object* (see Figure 10.9). In other words, we can attend to the location of a simultaneous group and treat the sequence of sounds that arises from that location as one stream. That all these cues – periodicity, spectral balance, level, and location – can be used as a basis for forming a perceptual stream suggests that sequential grouping is based on *similarity* in a fairly broad sense.

10.3.4 Good continuation

The gestalt principle of good continuation is apparent in sequential streaming. Variations in the characteristics of a sound that comes from a single source are often smooth, as the acoustic properties of a sound source usually change smoothly rather than abruptly. The auditory system uses good continuation to group sounds sequentially. It is more likely that a sequence will appear fused if the transitions between successive elements are smooth and natural. A sequence of pure tones with different frequencies groups together more easily if there are frequency *glides* between the tones (Bregman & Dannenbring, 1973; see Figure 10.10).

The fundamental frequency contour of the human voice is usually smooth (see Section 11.1.3): Large jumps in fundamental frequency are rare, even in singing. If rapid alternations between a low and high fundamental frequency are introduced artificially into an otherwise natural voice, then listeners tend to report that there are two speakers, one on the low fundamental frequency and one on the high fundamental frequency (Darwin & Bethell-Fox, 1977). Because one speaker is heard as suddenly starting to produce sound as the fundamental frequency changes, the (illusory) abrupt onset of the speech is perceived

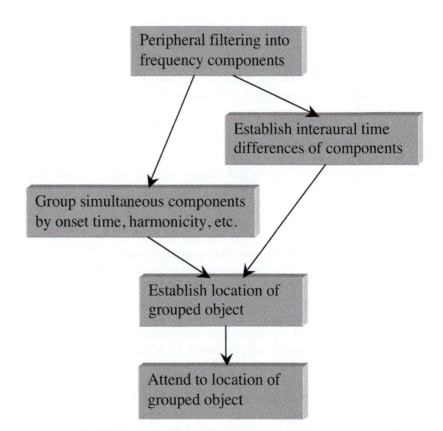

Figure 10.9 Sequential streaming by spatial location, as suggested by Darwin and Hukin (1999). According to this model, interaural time differences are not used to group together individual frequency components, but are used to assign a location to a grouped auditory object. Attention is then directed toward that location, and sounds from that location form a perceptual stream. Based on Darwin and Hukin (1999).

incorrectly as a stop consonant (stop consonants, such as /t/ and /p/, are produced by complete constrictions of the vocal tract, resulting in a period of silence between the vowel sounds before and after; see Section 11.1.2).

Spectral peaks or formants in natural speech tend to glide between the different frequency locations, as the articulators in the vocal tract move smoothly between one position and another (see Section 11.1.1). These smooth formant transitions help group sequences of vowels. Vowel sequences in which the formants change abruptly from one frequency to another tend not to fuse into a single stream, whereas those with smooth transitions do fuse (Dorman, Cutting, & Raphael, 1975). Good continuation applies to both periodicity and spectral balance. Abrupt changes in these quantities are associated with two or more sound sources (based on the principle of similarity). Smooth changes suggest that there is one sound source that is smoothly changing its acoustic properties, and the auditory system forms a perceptual stream accordingly.

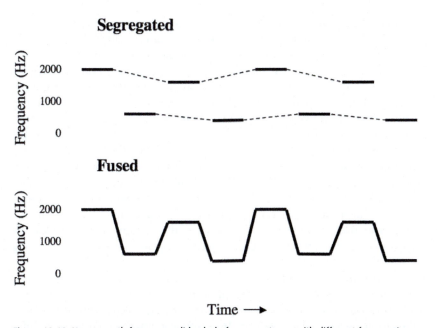

Figure 10.10 How smooth frequency glides help fuse pure tones with different frequencies into a single perceptual stream. The top panel shows how alternating high and low tones (thick lines) form two perceptual streams (the perception is indicated by the dotted lines). When smooth frequency transitions (sloping thick lines in the bottom panel) connect the tones, they are combined by the auditory system into a single perceptual stream. Based on Bregman and Dannenbring (1973).

10.3.5 Perceptual restoration

If we hear a sound interrupted by a second sound so that the first sound is briefly obscured, then we perceive the first sound to continue during the interruption even though we could not detect it during this time. This effect is an example of the gestalt principle of *closure* applied to hearing. The phenomenon has also been described as *perceptual restoration* (Warren, 1970), because the auditory system is making an attempt to restore the parts of the first sound that were obscured by the second sound. Examples from everyday life include speech interrupted by a door slam, the sound of a car engine interrupted by a horn beep, a musical melody interrupted by a drum beat, and so on. Whenever there is more than one sound source, there is a good chance that an intense portion of one stream of sound will obscure a less intense portion of another stream. We do not notice these interruptions because the auditory system is so good at restoration. (There are visual examples as well; e.g., when looking at a dog behind a series of fence posts, we perceive the dog to be whole, even though the image on the retina is broken up by the fence posts.)

Perceptual restoration can lead to the *continuity illusion*. If a brief gap in a sound is filled with a more intense second sound, the first sound may appear to continue during the gap (see Figure 10.11), even though it is really discontinuous. The first condition necessary for this illusion to occur is that the second sound would have masked the first sound in the gap, had the first sound actually been continuous. If the first sound is a pure tone, then the evidence suggests that the neural activity must not drop perceptibly at any characteristic frequency during the interruption for the illusion of continuity to occur. For example, consider the case in which a gap in a pure tone is filled with a second pure tone with a different frequency. The greater the frequency difference between the tones, the higher in level the second tone needs to be for the first tone to appear continuous. Due to the frequency selectivity of the cochlea, the masking effect of one sound on another decreases with increasing frequency separation (see Section 5.4.1). Indeed, it is possible to use the level at which the second tone causes the first tone to appear continuous rather than pulsing on and off (the *pulsation threshold*) as a measure of the overlap of the two tones in the cochlea. The pulsation threshold technique can be used to measure psychophysical tuning curves (see Houtgast, 1973).

The second condition that must apply for the continuity illusion to occur is that the sounds before and after the interruption must appear to come from the *same sound source* (by virtue of the sequential grouping mechanisms described in this chapter; see Bregman, 1990, pp. 361–369). For instance, there will be no illusion of continuity if the frequency of the tone before the interruption is 1000 Hz and the frequency after the interruption is 2000 Hz. If these two conditions

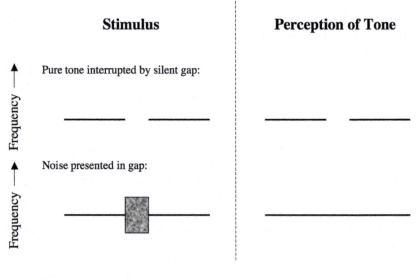

Figure 10.11 The continuity illusion. If a gap in a stimulus (e.g., a pure tone) is filled with another, more intense, stimulus (e.g., a band of noise) that would have masked the tone in the gap if the tone really had been continuous, then the tone is *perceived* as being continuous.

(masking and grouping) are met, then the auditory system has no way of knowing whether the interrupted sound was continuous during the interruption. As a best guess, it *assumes* that it was continuous and restores it perceptually (as best it can) so that we have the sensation of continuity.

The restoration process can be more involved than simply deciding that a pure tone is continuous. If a glide in the frequency of a pure tone is interrupted by a gap, then presenting a noise in the gap restores the glide perceptually. If the interrupted stimulus is frequency modulated, then the modulation is heard to continue during the interruption (see Figure 10.12). Speech, which involves formant transitions and fundamental frequency variations, is also restored after interruption by other sounds. Speech that is broken up regularly (say 10 times a second) by periods of silence sounds unnatural and harsh. When a more intense white noise is presented during the periods of silence, the speech sounds more natural (Miller & Licklider, 1950). The auditory system assumes that the speech is continuous behind the noise, and this is the sensation that is passed on to the rest of the brain. It must be emphasized, however, that the *information* conveyed by the sound is limited by what enters the ear. The auditory system cannot magically generate more information than it receives: If a part of the speech is obscured by another sound, we can only make a guess as to what was obscured based on the speech before and after. For example, if the sentence was "it was found that the *eel was on the shoe" (where * represents a portion of the speech replaced

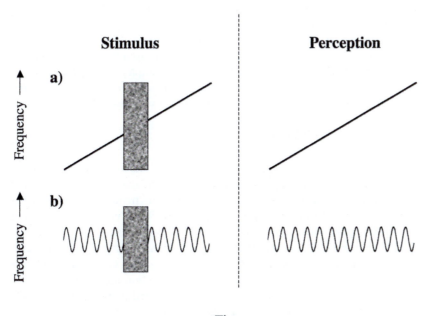

Figure 10.12 Two more examples of the continuity illusion. The illustrations show the restoration of a frequency glide (a), and of a frequency-modulated tone (b), when the silent gap between the two segments is filled with noise. Based on illustrations in Warren (2008) and Bregman (1990).

by a cough), then the word heard is "heel." If the sentence was "it was found that the *eel was on the table," then the word heard is "meal" (Warren, 1970). Perceptual restoration cannot restore the information that is obscured, but it can use the information that is not obscured to extrapolate across the interruption so that the sensation is one of continuity.

10.3.6   Effects of attention

There is some evidence that our ability to form a perceptual stream from a sequence of sounds is not an automatic response, but depends on whether we are paying attention to the sounds. In the experiment of van Noorden (1975; see Figure. 10.7) the streaming effect can take some time to build up, so the ABA sequence can sound fused initially. After listening for several seconds, the percept changes to one of segregation (separate sequences of A tones and B tones), and the galloping rhythm is lost. Carlyon, Cusack, Foxton, and Robertson (2001) found that this build-up of streaming did not occur when participants were asked to perform a discrimination on sounds presented to the ear opposite to the tone sequence, so their attention was directed away from the ear containing the tones. In one condition, they asked listeners to attend to this opposite-ear task for the first 10 seconds of the tone sequence, and then to start making segregation judgments. The listeners mostly responded that the sequence was fused (galloping rhythm), indicating that the build-up of streaming had not occurred while the listeners were not attending to the tones. It is possible that in the absence of attention the sequences of sounds from different sources tend to stay fused into one perceptual stream.

This finding is consistent with the gestalt principle that perceptual stimuli from several sources are divided in two: the stimuli from the source of interest (the "figure") and the rest (the "ground"). For example, we may attend to the stream of sounds from one speaker at a party, whereas the sounds from all the other speakers are perceived as an undifferentiated aural background.

10.3.7   Neural mechanisms

Beauvois and Meddis (1996) produced a computational model, based on "low-level" neural mechanisms in the brainstem, that can account for some aspects of sequential stream segregation. The model uses the frequency analysis of the peripheral auditory system, preserved in the auditory nerve and brainstem nuclei, to separate tone sequences such as the ABA sequence of van Noorden (1975). However, the model cannot account for stream segregation in which there is no frequency separation (for example, Vliegen & Oxenham, 1999; see Section 10.3.1). Furthermore, the finding that attention may be necessary for this type of stream segregation suggests that sequential grouping is a relatively "high-level" process. Because conscious attention is thought to be the result of mechanisms in the cerebral cortex, this could put the sequential grouping mechanism above the level of the brainstem. Another possibility, however, is that some aspects of grouping are low level (perhaps in the brainstem) but that they may receive some control from executive processes in the cortex (top-down processing).

Neural activity in the human auditory cortex consistent with some aspects of stream segregation can be observed in electroencephalographic recordings from electrodes placed on the scalp. For example, Snyder, Alain, and Picton (2006) used the repeating ABA pure-tone sequence developed by van Noorden. They showed that the evoked electrical response to the B tone increased with increasing frequency separation between the A and B tones. The response was also related to the perception of streaming: The response was greater the more often the tones were perceived by the participants as forming separate streams (i.e., A A A A A A . . . and B B B . . .). These responses related to frequency separation were not affected by attention. However, a separate component of the electrophysiological response to the ABA pattern increased as the sequence progressed, and *was* dependent on attention, reducing when the participants ignored the sequence. This is similar to the effects of attention on the build-up of streaming described in Section 10.3.6. Overall, these results may reflect two different streaming mechanisms: One automatic and based on frequency separation, and one affected by attention that builds up over time. Localization analysis suggests that in both cases the enhanced neural responses originated in the region of Heschl's gyrus.

These and similar results may have been based on the spectral differences between the pure tones, promoting segregation dependent on cochlear frequency analysis as in the Beauvois and Meddis model. However, a functional magnetic resonance imaging study used ABA patterns of complex tones with unresolved harmonics filtered into the *same spectral region* (similar to the stimuli of Vliegen & Oxenham, 1999), eliminating spectral cues. Increases in activity related to the difference in fundamental frequency between the A and B tones were observed in primary auditory cortex, and in secondary auditory cortex, outside Heschl's gyrus (Gutschalk, Oxenham, Micheyl, Wilson, & Melcher, 2007). These results suggest that auditory cortex, or earlier centers, may perform a general streaming analysis, even when there is no frequency separation.

10.4 SUMMARY

I have divided the description of auditory scene analysis into *simultaneous grouping* (i.e., assigning frequency components that occur simultaneously to different sources) and *sequential grouping* (i.e., assigning sequences of sounds to different sources). However, in most situations with more than one sound source, we are probably doing both: Following a sound sequence over time *and* separating out the sound components corresponding to the source we are interested in when they coincide with those from another source or sources (see Figure 10.13). The auditory system uses a number of different types of information for separating sounds, and the use of these cues is based on our implicit knowledge of the way sounds, and sound sources, normally behave in the environment. Segregation and grouping mechanisms involve the auditory system deciding, effectively, how likely it is that a particular set of sound waves entering the ear comes from the same source.

1   *Simultaneous* grouping involves the allocation of the different frequency components provided by the cochlea to the correct sound source. *Onset* cues (frequency components that start together are grouped together) and

"Can I   g e t   you a   dr i   n   k?"

"T h is is   a   re a lly good   p a r   t y"

Figure 10.13 The waveforms of two sentences spoken concurrently. Each sentence is given a different shade (black or gray). Extracting one of these sentences involves the segregation and grouping of simultaneous components (when the waveforms overlap) and the formation of a sequential stream.

harmonicity cues (frequency components that form a harmonic series are grouped together) are the main cues for simultaneous grouping.

2   The location of simultaneous frequency components does not contribute substantially to their grouping or segregation. Rather, simultaneous grouping may occur before a location is assigned to the group.

3   Sequential grouping involves the allocation of a temporal sequence of sounds to the correct sound source. Sounds are grouped into a sequential stream on the basis of similarity in periodicity (i.e., frequency or fundamental frequency), spectral balance, level, and location.

4   Sequential sounds with different characteristics (e.g., frequency or spectral balance) are more likely to be grouped together if the transitions between them are smooth rather than abrupt.

5   If a continuous sound is briefly interrupted by another, more intense, sound, the auditory system restores perceptually the obscured part of the continuous sound. Even complex features, such as parts of words, can be restored by reference to the acoustic and semantic context.

6   Sequential streaming is not entirely automatic. At least some types of streaming require attention. An attended sequence may form a separate perceptual group (figure) from the sounds from all the unattended sources (ground), which are largely undifferentiated.

7   Neuroimaging results suggest that streaming has occurred by the level of the auditory cortex.

10.5   READING

The classic work:

Bregman, A.S. (1990). *Auditory scene analysis: The perceptual organization of sound.* Cambridge, MA: Bradford Books, MIT Press.

Useful overviews are provided in the following chapters:

Darwin, C. J., & Carlyon, R. P. (1995). Auditory grouping. In B. C. J. Moore (Ed.), *Hearing* (pp. 387–424). New York: Academic Press.
Dyson, B. J. (2010). Auditory organization. In C. J. Plack (Ed.), *Hearing* (pp. 177–206). Oxford: Oxford University Press.

For a discussion of the role of pitch in grouping:

Darwin, C. J. (2005). Pitch and auditory grouping. In C. J. Plack, A. J. Oxenham, A. N. Popper, & R. R. Fay (Eds.), *Pitch: Neural coding and perception* (pp. 278–305). New York: Springer-Verlag.

For an account of perceptual restoration by the expert:

Warren, R. M. (2008). *Auditory perception: An analysis and synthesis.* Cambridge, UK: Cambridge University Press.

11 SPEECH

Despite the rise of e-mail, text messaging, Facebook, and Twitter, speech remains the main means of human communication in those (admittedly rare) moments when we are away from our computer terminals and smartphones. Through speech, we can express our thoughts and feelings in a remarkably detailed and subtle way. We can allow other people an almost immediate appreciation of what is going on in our heads. The arrival of speech had a dramatic effect on our development as a species and made possible the cultures and civilizations that exist in the world today. For humans, speech is the most important acoustic signal, and the *perception* of speech the most important function of the auditory system.

The peripheral auditory system breaks sounds down into different frequency components, and the information regarding these components is transmitted along separate neural frequency channels. Chapter 10 shows how the auditory system uses this analysis to separate out from a complex mixture the components originating from the sound source of interest. However, we do not *perceive* a sound as a collection of numerous individual components. We usually hear a unified whole that in many cases has a particular identity and meaning, such as a word. This chapter describes the complex processes that underlie the identification of auditory objects, using the perception of speech as an example. We discover that sound identification does not depend solely on the physical characteristics of the stimulus but also depends on cognitive factors and context. The identification of sounds is largely an *interpretation* of the acoustic information that arrives at our ears.

11.1 SPEECH PRODUCTION

Speech is produced by forcing air from the lungs past the vocal folds, which are two bands of muscular tissue in the larynx (see Figure 11.1 and Figure 11.2). The vocal folds vibrate at a frequency of about 120 Hz for a male speaker and about 220 Hz for a female speaker, giving the sound its *fundamental frequency*, which we hear as a *pitch*. We are able to vary the frequency of vocal fold vibration by the use of muscles in the larynx. The action of the vocal folds on the airflow from the lungs is to produce a periodic sequence of pressure pulses: in other words, a complex tone with a rich set of harmonics that sounds like a buzz. The sound coming from the vocal folds is then modified by structures in the throat, mouth, and nose (the *vocal tract*), giving the sound its characteristic *timbre*. These

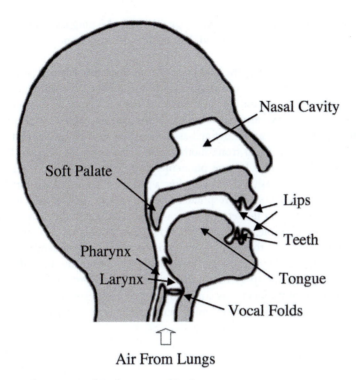

Figure 11.1 The anatomy of the human vocal tract.

Figure 11.2 A complete cycle of vocal fold vibration, viewed from the larynx. Successive time frames are illustrated from left to right. For a female speaker, the entire cycle would take about 4.5 ms. Based on photographs in Crystal (1997).

modifications are controlled by mobile *articulators* in the mouth and throat: the *pharynx, soft palate, lips, jaw,* and *tongue*. By moving the articulators, mainly the tongue, to different positions, we can produce different vowel sounds, which are characterized by their spectra.

It may be instructive at this stage to produce a few vowel sounds yourself. Try mouthing "a" (as in "far"), "e" (as in "me"), "i" (as in "high"), "o" (as in "show"), and "u" (as in "glue"). Say the vowels successively for a few seconds each, and concentrate on what is happening in your mouth. You should be able to feel your tongue and lips moving around as you switch between the different sounds. Now try to produce the same sounds while keeping everything in your mouth completely still. This should demonstrate the importance of the articulators in speech.

In addition to shaping the vocal tract to produce the different vowels, the articulators can also cause constrictions in the vocal tract, preventing or restricting the release of air, and we hear these as *consonants*. Speech is essentially a sequence of complex tones (vowel sounds) that are interrupted by consonants.

The word *phoneme* can be defined as the smallest unit of speech that distinguishes one spoken word from another in a given language (e.g., in English, "mad" and "bad" differ by one phoneme, as do "hit" and "hat"). Phonemes are indicated by a slash before and after a letter or a symbol. Unfortunately, there is not a one-to-one correspondence between a normal written letter and a given phoneme, and the letter does not necessarily match the symbol for the phoneme. For example, "tea" is made up of two phonemes: /t/ and /i/. To add to the confusion, there isn't even a one-to-one correspondence between a given acoustic waveform and a given phoneme. Phonemes are defined in terms of what we *perceive* the speech sound to represent in a word. However, it is still useful to think of phonemes as corresponding to vowel sounds and consonant sounds in most cases. We now examine in more detail the characteristics of some of these phonemes.

11.1.1 Vowels

As described previously, vowels are complex tones with characteristic spectra. The relative levels of the harmonics depend on the vowel sound that is being produced. Figure 11.3 shows the waveforms and spectra of two vowel sounds. We can see from the figure that each spectrum consists of a series of harmonics and that there are broad peaks in the spectra, each consisting of many harmonics. These peaks are called *formants*. The formants are numbered: F1, F2, F3, and so on, the first formant having the lowest frequency. Different vowel sounds are characterized by the frequencies of the various formants. Formants correspond to resonances in the vocal tract, which behaves like a pipe that is open at one end (see Sections 3.1.3 and 3.1.4). The size and shape of the cavities in the mouth and throat determine the resonant frequencies that will be present, and these properties are affected by the positions of the articulators, especially the tongue. In other words, the spectrum of the vowel sound, and hence the *identity* of the vowel sound, depends on the positions of the articulators.

During free-flowing speech, the articulators are moving almost constantly between the shape required for the last speech sound and the shape required for the next speech sound. This means that, for the speech we hear in our everyday lives, there is not a stable spectrum for each vowel sound. As the articulators move, so the formants move. Figure 11.4 is a spectrogram of the author saying "ee-ah-ee-ah-ee-ah-ee-ah." Note how the second formant glides down and up as the vowel changes from "ee" (/i/) to "ah" (/a/) and back again. These *formant transitions* (movements of the peaks in the spectrum) are also important when we consider consonants.

Figure 11.3 The waveforms and spectra of two vowels, both with fundamental frequencies of 100 Hz, showing the positions of the formants (F1, F2, and F3). Also illustrated in each case are the positions of the articulators in a cross-section of the vocal tract.

11.1.2   Consonants

Consonants are associated with *restrictions* in the flow of air through the vocal tract, caused by a narrowing or closure of a part of the vocal tract. Consonants can be categorized in terms of *manner* of the constriction that occurs. *Stop consonants* or *plosives* (e.g., /p/ and /t/) are associated with a complete constriction – that is, a total interruption in the flow of air. *Fricatives* (e.g., /s/ and /v/) are caused by very narrow constrictions, leading to a noisy burst of sound. *Approximants* (/w/ and /r/) are produced by partial constrictions. *Nasals* (/m/ and /n/) are produced by preventing airflow from the mouth and by allowing air to flow into the nasal passages by lowering the soft palate (which acts as a valve).

Figure 11.4 A spectrogram for the utterance "ee-ah-ee-ah-ee-ah-ee-ah." The frequency transitions of the second formant are represented by the dark band oscillating up and down the vertical frequency axis. This image, and the other nonschematic spectrograms in the chapter, were generated using the marvelous Praat program written by Paul Boersma and David Weenink (www.praat.org).

Consonants can also be categorized in terms of the *place* at which the constriction occurs (the *place of articulation*). For example, *bilabial plosives* (/p/ and /b/) are produced by causing a complete constriction at the lips. A narrow constriction between the tongue and the teeth produces a *dental fricative* (the "th" in "think"). Finally, consonants can be categorized into *voiced* or *unvoiced*, depending on whether the vocal folds are vibrating around the time of constriction. For instance, /b/ is voiced, /p/ is not, and we can hear the difference between these sounds even though the manner and place of articulation is the same.

The different ways of producing consonants lead to a variety of different features in the sound that is being produced. Because of the complete closure of the vocal tract, stop consonants are associated with a brief period of silence followed by a burst of noise as the air is released. Fricatives are associated with a noisy sound as the constriction occurs. In addition, consonants modify the vowel sounds before and after they occur. As the articulators move to produce the consonant, or move from the consonant position to produce the subsequent vowel, the shape of the vocal tract, and hence the formant frequencies, change. This creates formant transitions that are characteristic of the place of articulation. The frequency transitions of the first two formants for the utterances "ba" and "da" are illustrated in Figure 11.5. Note that the frequency movement of the second formant is very different for the two consonants. Second formant transitions are important in speech identification.

11.1.3 Prosody

A vowel sound is a complex tone and therefore has a distinct fundamental frequency, determined by the rate of vibration of the vocal folds. Although it is possible for us to speak in a monotone – that is, with a constant fundamental

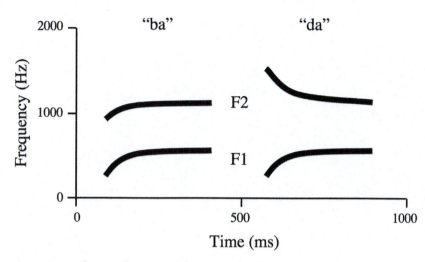

Figure 11.5 A schematic illustration of the frequency transitions of the first two formants in the utterances "ba" and "da."

frequency – we usually vary the fundamental frequency as we speak to give expression and additional meaning to our utterances. (It should be no surprise to learn that monotonic speech sounds monotonous!) The *intonation contour* of an utterance is the variation in the fundamental frequency over time. For example, it is possible for some utterances to change a statement into a question by changing the intonation contour. In particular, questions that can be answered yes or no often end on a rising intonation, whereas statements are more flat. Figure 11.6 shows the spectrograms and the variations in fundamental frequency for the utterance "I'm going to die" expressed both as a statement (top panel) and as a question (bottom panel). Another important use of intonation is to stress or accent a particular syllable, by increasing or decreasing the fundamental frequency on the stressed syllable. Overall increases or decreases in fundamental frequency, or in the *extent* of fundamental frequency variation, can convey emotions such as excitement or boredom (e.g., monotonous speech has no variation in fundamental frequency and gives the impression of boredom or depression). Variations in fundamental frequency are also used, of course, for singing. By carefully controlling the vibration of our vocal folds, we can produce tones with specific fundamental frequencies that can be used to produce musical melodies.

In addition to variations in fundamental frequency, variations in *level* can provide expression. We use increases in level to emphasize individual syllables, words, or entire phrases. Stressing words in this way can give extra meaning to the utterance ("I want to kiss you" versus "I want to kiss *you*"). When we are angry, we tend to raise the levels of our voices. Finally, we can use variations in *tempo* to convey meaning. If we speak quickly, this conveys urgency. A lowering in tempo can be used to stress a part of the utterance, and so on. Taken together, the variations in the intonation, level, and tempo of speech are called *prosody*.

Figure 11.6 Spectrograms for the utterance "I'm going to die" as a statement (top panel) and as a question (bottom panel). The white dots show the positions of the formants. The left-to-right lines on the plots show the variation in fundamental frequency with time (the *y*-axis for this curve is shown on the right).

11.2 PROBLEMS WITH THE SPEECH SIGNAL

11.2.1 Variability

Speech is intelligible at a rate of 400 words per minute, which corresponds to a rate of about 30 phonemes per second (Liberman, Cooper, Shankweiler, & Studdert-Kennedy, 1967). Because the articulators take time to move between the locations required for different phonemes, it follows that the shape of the vocal tract is changing almost continuously. Very rarely is there a one-to-one mapping between a particular phoneme and a particular speech sound, even for slow speech. As demonstrated by the spectrograms in Figure 11.4 and Figure 11.6, in free-flowing speech a vowel sound is not a static pattern of spectral peaks but is constantly changing as the articulators in the vocal tract move between the position corresponding to one speech sound and the position corresponding to the next speech sound. This is called *coarticulation*.

Coarticulation implies that the sound waveform corresponding to a particular phoneme is heavily modified by the nature of the phonemes before and after. For example, if a vowel such as /a/ is preceded by a nasal consonant such as /m/, the onset of the vowel will have a slightly nasal quality. To produce /m/, the soft palate is lowered to open the airflow to the nasal passages, and the soft palate is still being raised while the subsequent vowel is being produced. Another example is taken from Liberman et al. (1967). Figure 11.7 shows schematic spectrograms for the utterances "di" and "du." Note that the second formant transitions associated with the phoneme /d/ are very different for the two utterances. This is because as the /d/ phoneme is produced (by a constriction between the tongue and the upper gum), the lips have already formed into the shape necessary for the production of the subsequent vowel. It follows that there is no single set of formant transitions that defines the phoneme /d/. Stop consonants may sometimes be characterized by the sound that occurs immediately after the closure is released: The gross spectrum of the first 20 ms or so is roughly independent of the adjacent vowel and may provide an invariant cue (Blumstein & Stevens, 1979). In general, however, phonemes are more clearly defined in terms of the place and manner of the intended articulations (effectively, the commands to the muscles in the vocal tract of the speaker) than they are by the sounds themselves.

Not only are the acoustic characteristics of individual phonemes very much dependent on the phonemic context, but also the sound waves that correspond to a particular written phrase may vary dramatically between presentations.

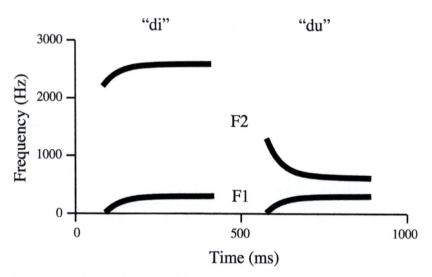

Figure 11.7 A schematic illustration of the frequency transitions of the first two formants in the utterances "di" and "du." Notice that the acoustic features that correspond to the /d/ phoneme are very different for the two utterances. Based on Liberman et al. (1967).

Individual differences in the shape of the vocal tract will affect the spectrum of the vowel. The most obvious differences are between men, women, and children. The frequencies of the first three formants in the /i/ phoneme (as in "me") are about 270, 2300, and 3000 Hz in men; about 300, 2800, and 3300 Hz in women; and about 370, 3200, and 3,700 Hz in young children (Howard & Angus, 2001). However, the vocal tract characteristics for individual men, women, and children will vary compared to the norm for each group. The way speech sounds are produced also varies depending on the particular accent of the speaker. The way I (as a speaker of standard southern British English) pronounce the word "about" is different from the way a Canadian pronounces this word, which sounds to me like "a boat." The individuality of accent and vocal tract characteristics means that we can usually recognize a friend, family member, or media personality just from the sound of his or her voice, and this implies that speech sounds differ markedly between individual speakers.

Furthermore, a *single individual* may show great variability in the way he or she speaks a given phrase from one time to another. We may speak slowly at one time, rapidly at another time ("did you want to" becomes "djawanna"); we may be shouting at one time, whispering (in which the vocal folds are kept almost closed so that the airflow is turbulent and noisy rather than periodic) at another time; we may vary the pronunciation in more subtle ways to apply a particular emphasis to what we are saying. Any slight changes in the way we produce an utterance (and much of the variation may be unintentional) will result in differences in the sound waves that propagate from our mouths.

The huge variability of speech has important consequences for the auditory mechanisms that interpret this information. We have to be able to appreciate that the same words are being spoken for each presentation of a given utterance, even though the sound waves entering our ears may be very different from one presentation to the next. Because there is not a one-to-one correspondence between the speech sounds we hear and the phonemes, syllables, or words that form the intended utterance of the speaker, the brain must be flexible in the way that it interprets the acoustic information. These issues are discussed further in Section 11.3.3.

11.2.2 Corruption and interference

In many listening situations, the speech information is altered or degraded in some way. Even if there are no other sound sources, the speech waveform may be modified by the reverberation characteristics of the room we are in. Delayed reflections may be combined with the original speech, effectively blurring the temporal transitions. Alternatively, the speech may be modified spectrally: If we are having a conversation over a telephone (which filters the speech between about 300 and 3000 Hz) or listening to a tinny radio with small loudspeakers. Also, the speech waveform may suffer distortion such as peak clipping by overloaded transmission systems (microphones, amplifiers, loudspeakers, etc.), which can create a very noisy, degraded signal.

We often listen to a speaker in an environment in which other sound sources are present. As described in Chapters 5 and 10, the auditory system is very good at separating out the sounds of interest from interfering sounds, but it is not perfect. When the interfering sounds are high enough in level, they can completely or partially mask the speech waveform. A door slam or a cough can mask a portion of an utterance, as can peaks in a fluctuating background (e.g., the speech from another speaker). The rumble of a car engine may mask the low-frequency part of the speech spectrum. Speech can be rendered completely unintelligible by the deafening music at a rock concert. In many situations, however, we are able to understand what is being said even though only a portion of the speech signal is audible. How is it possible that we can understand speech quite clearly when much of the signal is lost or obscured?

11.3   SPEECH PERCEPTION

11.3.1   The redundancy of speech

With due respect to the remarkable abilities of the human brain, the reason that the speech signal can withstand such abuse and still be intelligible is that there are many different sources of relevant information in the speech waveform. In ideal listening conditions, the speech signal has *much more information* than is necessary to identify an utterance. In ideal listening conditions, the speech signal contains a great deal of *redundant* information. This can be illustrated by examining the effects of removing different types of information from the speech signal.

First, the spectrum of speech can be severely butchered without affecting intelligibility. Speech can be low-pass or high-pass filtered, to contain only components below 1500 Hz or only components above 1500 Hz, and still be understood clearly. "Everyday speech" sentences band-pass filtered between 1330 and 1670 Hz (1/3-*octave* filter, with 96-dB/octave skirts) can also be identified with almost 100% accuracy (Warren, Riener, Bashford, & Brubaker, 1995). When we consider that the frequencies of the first three formants cover a range from about 300 Hz to over 3000 Hz across different vowels and that the second formant alone varies between about 850 and about 2300 Hz across different vowels for a male speaker, it is clear that speech is intelligible even when the formant frequencies are poorly defined in the acoustic signal. On the other hand, the frequency and amplitude modulations of the formants can provide a great deal of information on their own. Speech can be constructed by adding together three pure tones, with frequencies corresponding to the first three formants of natural speech (see Figure 11.8). Such *sine-wave speech* has a very strange quality but is reasonably intelligible if listeners are made aware that the sounds are supposed to be speech (Remez, Rubin, Pisoni, & Carrell, 1981). This suggests that the words in an utterance are well encoded in terms of formant frequencies and formant transitions, without the harmonic structure or voicing cues that are present in natural speech.

Spectral information can also be reduced by "smearing" the spectral features using digital signal processing, so the sharp formant peaks are blurred across the spectrum and are less prominent. Baer and Moore (1993) used spectral smearing to simulate the effects of the reduced frequency selectivity associated with cochlear hearing loss. Even when the smearing was equivalent to having auditory filters *six times* broader than normal (very poor frequency selectivity; see Figure 11.9), listeners were still able to identify key words in sentences with

Figure 11.8 Sine-wave speech. The spectrogram for the utterance "where were you a year ago," constructed from just three pure tones with frequencies and amplitudes matched to those of the first three formants of the original speech. Based on Remez et al. (1981).

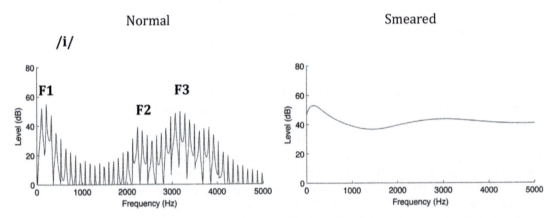

Figure 11.9 The spectrum for the vowel /i/, shown unprocessed (left panel) and spectrally smeared to simulate auditory filters six times broader than normal (right panel). Although the spectral information is severely degraded, smeared speech is intelligible in the absence of interfering sounds.

near-perfect accuracy. However, when the speech was presented in a background noise, spectral smearing had a much more detrimental effect. Listeners with cochlear hearing loss report particular problems with understanding speech in background noise (see Section 13.3.4). Another example of the effects of a reduction of spectral information is when speech is processed to contain just a few usable frequency channels. Shannon, Zeng, Kamath, Wygonski, and Eke-lid (1995) divided natural speech into a number of different frequency bands, using band-pass filters. The temporal envelope of the speech in each band was used to modulate a narrowband noise with the same bandwidth. Hence, each band only contained temporal information about the speech in that frequency region. Only four such bands (0–800 Hz, 800–1500 Hz, 1500–2500 Hz, and 2500–4000 Hz) were necessary for listeners to achieve almost perfect sentence recognition in a quiet background environment.

These experiments show that, provided information about temporal fluctuations is preserved, spectral information can be very radically reduced without affecting intelligibility. Conversely, provided spectral information is preserved, temporal information can be reduced with little effect on intelligibility. Drullman, Festen, and Plomp (1994) removed temporal fluctuations faster than about 4 Hz and found little effect on the intelligibility of sentences presented in a quiet environment. The syllable rate in the speech stimuli they used was approximately 4 Hz. In conditions with a noise interferer, however, modulation frequencies up to 16 Hz contributed to intelligibility. This latter result and the reduced intelligibility of spectrally smeared speech in background noise reported by Baer and Moore (1993) serve to emphasize the fact that information that is redundant in ideal listening conditions may be useful when conditions are more difficult.

Because the speech waveform contains a great deal of redundant information, it can withstand a fair amount of degradation and interference and still be intelligible. If one source of spectral information is lost or reduced (e.g., information from low frequencies), then the brain can rely more on other sources of spectral information (e.g., information from high frequencies). Furthermore, the brain can combine information from isolated spectral regions to improve intelligibility. Warren et al. (1995) found that speech filtered into a narrow frequency band with a center frequency of either 370 or 6000 Hz was almost unintelligible. However, when these two bands were presented together, the number of words identified correctly more than doubled.

The redundancy of speech extends to the phonemes and words that build up an utterance. If a phoneme or word is obscured, we can often reconstruct the missing segment based on the other phonemes or words in the utterance. Miller and Licklider (1950) reported about 80% correct identification of individual words when as much as 50% of the speech was removed, by periodic interruptions with phoneme-sized silent intervals. An example of how the identity of one word may be inferred from the meaning of other words in a sentence is provided in Section 11.3.3. We often use more words than are strictly necessary to convey the meaning we intend. We also adjust the clarity of our speech knowing that the listener will exploit the redundancy. For example, when someone says "a stitch in time saves nine," the word "nine" is often not clearly articulated because the speaker assumes that listeners will be able to predict the final word from the other words in the sentence. On the other hand, if the utterance is "the number that you will hear is nine," then "nine" is clearly articulated by the speaker because it is not predictable from the other words in the sentence (Lieberman, 1963).

11.3.2   Which features are important to the auditory system?

That we can identify speech when different characteristic features are selectively degraded or removed implies that our brains are sensitive to many different sources of information in the speech waveform. We are flexible in our ability to use the different features of the speech code, and this helps us when conditions are less than ideal. Figure 11.10 illustrates some of the detailed spectral and temporal information in a typical utterance, albeit one pronounced more slowly and carefully than is usual for conversational speech.

Figure 11.10 An illustration of the spectral and temporal information in the speech signal. The top left panel shows the spectrogram for the utterance "a good speech." The spectrogram covers 1.5 seconds and 0–5000 Hz. The bottom left panel shows the spectrum of the speech at different times. For each plot, level increases from right to left. Notice the broad peaks corresponding to formants during the vowel sounds and the increase in high-frequency energy during the "s" and "ch" sounds. The top right panel shows the temporal envelope of the speech (the level changes as a function of time) in different frequency bands centered on 1000, 2000, and 4000 Hz. Although the envelope varies between frequency regions, providing information about formant transitions among other things, the stop consonants (/d/ and /p/) result in dips in level across all frequency regions.

Spectral information is clearly important in speech perception (as it is in the identification of other sounds, such as musical instruments). The experiment of Shannon et al. (1995) described in Section 11.3.1 implies that at least some frequency selectivity (at least four channels) is required for perfect intelligibility even in ideal conditions. The positions of the formants are the most important cues for vowel identity, and the formant transitions, particularly the second formant transition, are important in the identification of consonants (Liberman et al., 1967). In addition, the gross spectrum of the sound produced within about 20 ms of the release of a stop consonant (e.g., whether the spectrum is rising or falling with increasing frequency) may provide an invariant cue to the identity of the consonant (Blumstein & Stevens, 1980). Some other consonants, such as the fricative /s/, are associated with a characteristic burst of high-frequency noise (see Figure 11.10).

The peripheral auditory system provides the spectral analysis necessary to identify these features with high resolution (see Chapter 5). We also know that the auditory system is very sensitive to differences in spectral shape (Section 6.4.2). Leek, Dorman, and Summerfield (1987) investigated the effects of spectral shape on vowel identification using vowel-like harmonic complex tones. They presented the first 30 harmonics of a complex tone with a fundamental frequency of 100 Hz. All the harmonics had the same level, except for three pairs of harmonics (e.g., harmonic numbers 2 and 3, 20 and 21, and 29 and 30) that had a slightly higher level than the rest, to simulate three formant peaks. Four such vowels were synthesized, and listeners were asked to identify which vowel was being played. They could identify the vowel with 85% accuracy when the formant harmonics had a level just 2 dB above that of the harmonics in the background. In other words, vowels can be identified with reasonable accuracy when the formants correspond to spectral bumps of just 2 dB. When the spectral contrast is greater, the auditory system is very good at detecting differences in formant frequency. Two vowels can be discriminated from each another when the only difference between them is a 2% disparity in the frequency of a single formant (Kewley-Port & Watson, 1994).

Speech is very *dynamic* – the characteristics of the waveform are constantly changing. This is demonstrated by the formant transitions (changes in the spectrum over time that produce level fluctuations in particular frequency regions) and also by the level fluctuations that are associated with consonants. The constrictions in the vocal tract that produce consonants cause temporal modulations in the level of the speech waveform (see Figure 11.10). Stop consonants, in particular, involve a complete closure of the vocal tract and, therefore, a brief period of silence followed by a rapid increase in amplitude. The utterance "say" can be made to sound like "stay" by introducing a brief (e.g., 10 ms) period of silence after the /s/. The auditory system exhibits high temporal resolution (see Chapter 8): We can detect changes in the level of a sound lasting only a few milliseconds. We are also highly sensitive to modulations of a sound and can detect amplitude modulation at low modulation depths (see Section 8.2.1). This high temporal resolution allows us to process the variations in the speech waveform over time. Together, the acute spectral and temporal processing of the auditory system provide us with a very detailed representation of the *spectro-temporal* aspects of speech (Figure 11.11), which is encoded in terms of the firing rates and firing synchrony of neurons in the auditory system (see Chapters 4 and 6).

Finally, much of speech is voiced and periodic, and the auditory system is able to extract this periodicity (see Chapter 7). We can follow the intonation contour of speech to extract an additional layer of meaning from an utterance. In some "tone" languages, such as the Chinese languages Mandarin and Cantonese, variations in fundamental frequency affect the identity of spoken words. Tones are not used in this way in English, but some consonants are differentiated by the *voice onset time*, the time after the constriction when the vocal folds start vibrating. /p/ and /b/ are distinguished in this way, although both consonants are produced by a closure of the lips, for /b/ the vocal folds are vibrating around the time of closure, and for /p/ there is a short delay (around 30–100 ms) between closure and the onset of voicing. Try whispering "pea" and "bee" and you will notice that, without the voicing cues, the sounds are indistinguishable.

This brief overview of the perceptually important characteristics of speech suggests that the auditory system is well matched to the speech signal. That is expected, because the speech production system evolved to make use of our hearing mechanisms, and (to a lesser extent) vice versa. The auditory system

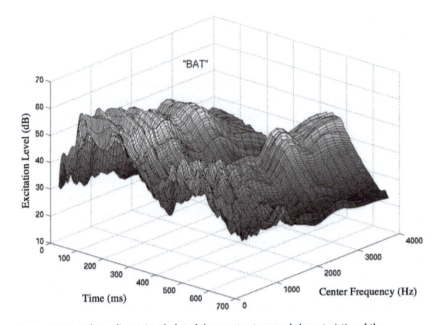

Figure 11.11 A three-dimensional plot of the spectro-temporal characteristics of the utterance "bat," processed to simulate the spectral and temporal resolution of the auditory system (a *spectro-temporal* excitation pattern). This figure is a straight copy of Figure 8.7, and the analysis is based on data from spectral and temporal masking experiments. Although some information is lost (e.g., the high-frequency, unresolved, harmonics during the vowel /a/), the auditory system preserves a very detailed representation of the speech signal.

can exploit the rich speech code because it is highly sensitive to the spectral and temporal features of complex sounds.

11.3.3   What are the units of speech perception?

The phoneme is defined as the smallest unit of speech that distinguishes one spoken word from another in a given language. Is it the case, therefore, that speech perception is a matter of the brain identifying each phoneme that we hear one by one, thereby constructing the intended utterance? The answer is an emphatic no. We can identify a given vowel pronounced clearly on its own by virtue of the locations of the formant frequencies. However, coarticulation and variability ensure that it is much harder to identify a vowel plucked from free-flowing speech, in the absence of the speech sounds preceding and following. Using Dutch vowels, Koopmans-van Beinum (1980, cited in Plomp, 2002) found that the formant frequencies of a given vowel from the *same speaker* vary markedly between occurrences in free conversation. Identification errors for individual vowel sounds extracted from free speech increased by a factor of six (to 67% errors) compared to when the vowels were pronounced on their own. Using a different approach, Harris (1953) constructed new words using the phonemes extracted from different words pronounced naturally. These constructed words were not interpreted according to the supposed phonemic "building blocks" of which they were made. For example, the "w" from "wip" might be combined with "up" to produce a new word. However, listeners do not hear this new word as "wup" because the consonant "w" is pronounced differently when speakers are asked to produce "wip" and "wup" as whole words. As is the case for most consonants, the "w" sound is not independent of the following speech sounds.

Furthermore, the identity of a given phoneme depends on the voice quality and dialect of the speaker. Ladefoged and Broadbent (1957) varied the formant frequencies in a synthetic utterance, to simulate speakers with different vocal tract characteristics. They synthesized the introductory sentence "Please say what this word is" and followed this by a test word that could be identified as "bit," "bet," "bat," or "but." The perceived identity of the vowel in the test word depended, not on its absolute formant frequencies, but on its formant frequencies in *relation to* the formant frequencies of the vowels in the introductory sentence. For example, the *same sound* could be identified as "bit" if one version of the introductory sentence was used but as "bet" if another version of the introductory sentence was used. The finding implies that we calibrate our interpretation of vowels according to the overall voice quality and dialect of the speaker.

Results such as these (and there are many more; see Warren, 2008, and Plomp, 2002) suggest that our brains do not search for the characteristics of individual phonemes in the speech waveform but process sounds over a longer period of time, recognizing the temporal transitions that are associated with coarticulation, and even calibrating for the individual speaker's voice characteristics. Plomp (2002) argues that our obsession with describing speech in terms of a succession of phonemes is related to our familiarity with the written alphabet. We associate phonemes quite closely with letters, and this causes us to think about speech as a sequence of clearly defined phoneme-sized units. The reality, in terms of the speech waveform, is quite different.

The sounds associated with phonemes are too variable to be identified individually during free speech. But what about words? Could the brain have a feature detector that "lights up" whenever the complex pattern of acoustic characteristics that corresponds to a particular word is presented? If so, the utterance could be constructed by identifying each word in turn (e.g., Cole & Jakimik, 1978, cited in Grosjean, 1985). Unfortunately, it seems that this plausible account may be mistaken. We can, of course, quite easily identify words when they are spoken clearly on their own. A word extracted from free conversation, however, may not be recognized so easily. Miller, Heise, and Lichten (1951) found that words extracted from free-flowing speech in a background noise and presented individually are less easily identified than the same words presented in their original context (i.e., in a complete sentence). Grosjean (1985) used a "gating" technique, in which the listener was initially presented with only the first part of a sentence, up to the start of a target word. On subsequent presentations, more and more of the sentence was played, and for each presentation, listeners were required to identify the target word. In this way, Grosjean could determine how much of the sentence was required for accurate identification of the target. Grosjean reported that for an utterance such as "I saw a bun in the store," monosyllabic words such as "bun" may not be identified accurately until after the onset of the *subsequent* word in the sentence. The finding that words after the target are sometimes required for identification implies that words are not always identified in a strict sequence, as suggested by some models of word recognition.

When a word is partially obscured by another sound, we may need to use the preceding and following words to reconstruct the degraded information. As described in Section 10.3.5, Warren (1970) reported an experiment in which the first part of a word in a sentence was replaced by a cough and listeners were asked to identify the damaged word. The word that listeners reported hearing depended on the subsequent words in the sentence. If the sentence was "it was found that the *eel was on the shoe" (where the * represents the missing speech and location of the cough), then listeners reported hearing "heel." If the sentence was "it was found that the *eel was on the table," then listeners reported hearing "meal." This is an example of perceptual restoration. The experiment shows that, in conditions where the speech signal is degraded, the brain can use the *meaning* of subsequent words, not only to determine the identity of degraded words, but also to reconstruct the *sensation* of uninterrupted speech: Restored phonemes are perceptually indistinguishable from "real" phonemes (Warren, 2008). In experiments such as the one reported by Warren, listeners find it difficult to identify exactly when in the utterance the cough occurred, suggesting that the restored phoneme is heard as if it were actually present.

The experiments described in this section demonstrate quite clearly that speech perception is more than just the sequential identification of acoustic features. It is misleading, therefore, to talk about the "units" of speech perception. In some cases, the brain needs to take a *holistic* view and consider the possible meanings of the whole sentence as it tries to determine the identities of the constituent words. Speech perception is therefore a combination of the "bottom-up" analysis of the acoustic features and the "top-down" influence of cognitive processing. By combining the information, the brain arrives at an interpretation of an utterance that is consistent with the raw acoustic features and also with the meaning of the utterance as a whole.

11.3.4   Visual cues

We can understand speech quite easily over the telephone or over the radio. This does not imply, however, that speech perception is solely dependent on acoustic information. Most people think of lipreading as a coping strategy adopted by listeners with hearing impairment. However, when we can see the speaker's face, we all use the cues from lip movements to complement the acoustic information. The importance of lip movements is illustrated dramatically by the McGurk effect (McGurk & MacDonald, 1976). If a listener is presented with the sound "ba-ba" while the lips of a speaker are silently mouthing "ga-ga," then the listener hears the utterance "da-da," which is a compromise between the visual information and the acoustic information (Figure 11.12). If the eyes of the listener are closed, then the perception becomes "ba-ba" (i.e., just the acoustic information). What I find remarkable about this effect is the strength of the auditory sensation. It is hard to believe when you are watching the speaker's lips that you are being played the same sound as when your eyes

Acoustic:

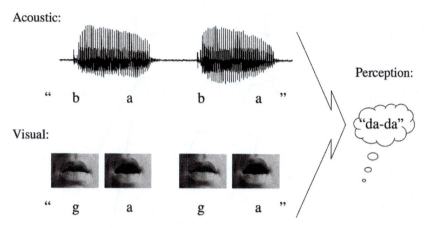

Figure 11.12 The McGurk effect. If the sound "ba-ba" is played at the same time as the listener sees the lip movements for "ga-ga," then the listener hears the utterance as "da-da," a combination of the acoustic and visual information.

are closed. What we imagine to be purely auditory sensations are clearly influenced by visual information.

11.4   NEURAL MECHANISMS

11.4.1   The representation of speech in the ascending auditory pathways

Recordings from the auditory nerve have revealed how speech sounds are represented at the earliest stage in the neural pathway. Sachs and Young (1979) recorded from cat auditory nerve fibers, with a range of characteristic frequencies, in response to artificially synthesized vowel sounds. In this way, using recordings from multiple neurons, they provided a measure of the representation of the spectrum of each vowel in the auditory nerve. They found that the plot of neural firing rate against characteristic frequency gave a fair representation of the formant frequencies when the sound level was low. However, when the sound level was increased, the high spontaneous rate fibers (which include most of the fibers in the auditory nerve, see Section 4.4.2) saturated. Since these fibers were now firing nearly maximally whether they were tuned to a formant peak or were in between two peaks, there was little variation in firing rate with characteristic frequency, and the formants were not well represented (Figure 11.13). This is an example of the "dynamic range problem" in intensity coding we encountered in Section 6.3.2.

Now we know that speech sounds do not become harder to identify as sound level is increased, so something must be providing the missing information at moderate-to-high levels. One possibility is that the low spontaneous rate fibers, which do not saturate at low levels (see Section 4.4.2), may represent formant peaks at moderate-to-high levels. Indeed, Sachs and Young (1979) found that these fibers provided a clearer representation of the formants at high levels than

Figure 11.13 A schematic illustration of the recordings of Sachs and Young (1979) from the cat auditory nerve, showing auditory nerve firing rate as a function of characteristic frequency in response to the vowel sound /I/ presented at different overall sound pressure levels (34, 54, and 74 dB SPL). The measure "normalized rate" is the firing rate of the fiber (minus the spontaneous rate), divided by the saturation rate of the fiber (minus the spontaneous rate). In other words, normalized rate is a measure of the firing rate of the fiber relative to its overall range of possible firing rates. Notice that the formant peaks (illustrated by arrows) are less well defined at 74 dB SPL than at 34 dB SPL.

was the case for the high spontaneous rate fibers. However, the rate-place code is not the only way in which stimuli are represented in the auditory nerve. There is also the phenomenon of phase locking, in which the temporal aspects of sounds are encoded by neural firing synchronized to the fine structure or envelope of basilar membrane vibration (Section 4.4.4). In Section 6.3.4, it was described how the intensity of sounds may be encoded by these synchronized firing patterns. Young and Sachs (1979) found that nerve fibers tended to phase lock to the formant frequencies close to their characteristic frequencies, even when the fibers were saturated in terms of overall firing rate. Hence, the formant frequencies were well represented in the temporal code even when the rate-place code provided poor information. They argued that the pattern of temporal coding as a function of characteristic frequency could provide a strong representation of the spectrum of vowel sounds in the auditory nerve; one that is robust to changes in level.

Whatever the mechanism, at the level of the cochlear nucleus in the brainstem, the dynamic range problem seems to be solved to some extent. For example, the "chopper" neurons in the ventral cochlear nucleus (see Section 4.5.1.1) provide a robust representation of vowel formants in terms of firing rate as function of characteristic frequency. This representation degrades much less with sound level than is the case in the auditory nerve (Blackburn & Sachs, 1990).

Further up the auditory pathway, in the inferior colliculus, thalamus, and auditory cortex, some neurons respond to "features" in the spectrum (such as formants), and to particular rates of temporal modulation (Schnupp, Nelken, & King, 2011). These neurons may help to represent the particular spectro-temporal modulations of the speech signal, which are vital for identification (see Section 11.3.2).

Carney et al. (2015) have proposed another way in which the speech spectrum may be represented in the brainstem, based on saturation in the auditory nerve and on the properties of modulation-sensitive neurons in the inferior colliculus. They argue that the variation of low-frequency fluctuations in auditory nerve firing rate across characteristic frequency provides a robust representation of the spectrum of speech sounds, one that is relatively invariant with level and robust to the presence of background noise. The idea is that most auditory nerve fibers tuned to peaks in the spectrum (for example, vowel formants) will be saturated, and hence the fluctuations in firing rate in response to envelope fluctuations (for example, at the fundamental frequency of the vowel) will be small; when a neuron is saturated, variations in stimulus amplitude have little effect on firing rate. In contrast, auditory nerve fibers tuned away from the spectral peaks will not be saturated, and the fluctuations in firing rate (for example, at the fundamental frequency of the vowel due to beating between the harmonics) will be larger. So in the auditory nerve, spectral peaks are associated with small fluctuations in firing rate, and dips between peaks are associated with large fluctuations in firing rate. This contrast is then enhanced and translated by the inferior colliculus neurons, which vary their firings rates based on the strength of fluctuations they receive from earlier in the auditory pathway. In other words, the representation of spectral features based on the degree of fluctuations across characteristic frequency in the auditory nerve is converted into a representation in terms of firing rate across characteristic frequency in the inferior colliculus.

11.4.2   Speech processing in the cortex

Electrical stimulation during surgery to the brain has been used to disrupt neural processing in different cortical regions in the left hemisphere while patients perform speech tasks of varying complexity (see Boatman, 2004, for a review). The idea is that if a brain region is important in performing a particular task, stimulating that region to produce a "functional lesion" will cause a reduction in performance. These studies reveal that simple discriminations of speech stimuli (for example, determining whether two speech sounds are identical or different) can only be disrupted by stimulation near the auditory cortex, whereas identification of phonological features such as rhymes and the initial speech sounds in words is, in addition, disrupted by stimulation to adjacent areas on the temporal lobe and a nearby region of the frontal lobe. Identification of the meaning of words and sentences is disrupted by any stimulation in a wider region of the temporal lobe, frontal lobe, and parietal lobe. In other words, there may be a *hierarchy* of speech processing in the brain, starting close to the auditory cortex, and spreading to adjacent regions as the complexity of processing increases from simple discriminations to analysis of meaning (Schnupp et al., 2011). Early stages in the hierarchy of processing are necessary for the correct function of later stages but not *vice versa*. This is why disrupting processing in the region of auditory cortex disrupts all subsequent processing of phonology and meaning, but simple discriminations are not disrupted by stimulation to areas remote from auditory cortex.

Two areas of the brain thought to be involved in higher order speech processing deserve mention, although their functions are perhaps beyond what would be considered purely auditory processing. Both areas are normally confined to the left hemisphere, suggesting that the left hemisphere is "dominant" for language function. Damage to Broca's area (in the frontal lobe) is associated with disrupted speech production and damage to Wernicke's area (centered on the posterior part of the temporal lobe) is associated with disrupted speech comprehension, suggesting that populations of neurons in these areas are involved in speech production and comprehension respectively.

11.5   SUMMARY

I hope that the discussion of speech perception in this chapter has convinced you that the identification of sounds is more than just the recognition of a stable set of acoustic features. As a hearing researcher, I am used to dealing with precisely controlled stimuli in the laboratory. In the real world, however, variability is the order of the day. To identify sounds in the absence of a fixed set of acoustic features, the brain must take account of the context in which those sounds are heard, both the acoustic context and the semantic context. Sound identification goes beyond what we normally consider to be the function of the auditory system per se. Having said this, it is also clear that the auditory system is able to make good use of the purely acoustic information that is available in the sounds that are important to us. The spectro-temporal nature of the speech signal is well suited to the detailed spectral and temporal processing of the auditory system.

1   Normal speech is produced by spectral and temporal modifications of the sound from a vibrating source. The periodic sound produced by forcing air from the lungs past the vibrating vocal folds is modified by the shape of the vocal tract, which is controlled by the positions of articulators such as the tongue and the lips.

2   Vowels are complex tones with spectral peaks (formants) corresponding to resonances in the vocal tract. Consonants are produced by constrictions in the vocal tract.

3   As the vocal tract changes smoothly from the production of one phoneme to another, the positions taken by the articulators are influenced by the positions needed for the phonemes before and after (coarticulation). It follows that the sound associated with a particular phoneme is highly variable. Variability also arises from the differing voice characteristics of different speakers. Even the same speaker does not produce the same speech waveform for each articulation of an utterance.

4   Speech is highly resistant to corruption and interference. Speech can be greatly modified spectrally or temporally, or can be partially masked by other sounds, and still be intelligible. This is because there are many sources of information in the speech signal. The auditory system is sensitive to the

complex spectral and temporal cues in speech and can make best use of the limited information in difficult listening conditions.

5   Speech perception is more than just the sequential identification of acoustic features such as phonemes and words. *Context* is very important, and the identity given to individual words may depend on both the acoustic properties and the *meaning* of preceding and following words. An utterance is perceived *holistically*, and the interpretation of acoustic features depends on the meaning of the utterance as a whole, just as the meaning depends on the acoustic features (both *top-down* and *bottom-up* processing).

6   Context extends beyond the auditory domain. Visual information from lip-reading influences the speech sounds we hear. What we may experience as a purely auditory sensation is sometimes dependent on a combination of auditory and visual cues.

7   Speech stimuli are represented in the auditory nerve by the firing rates and temporal firing patterns of neurons as a function of characteristic frequency. Some neurons in the brainstem and cortex may be tuned to particular spectral and temporal "features" in the speech signal. There appears to be a hierarchy of speech processing from the auditory cortex to adjacent cortical areas as the speech analysis becomes more complex.

11.6   READING

Darwin, Moore, and Warren provide good overviews of speech perception:

Darwin, C. (2010). Speech perception. In C. J. Plack (Ed.), *Hearing* (pp. 207–230). Oxford: Oxford University Press.

Moore, B. C. J. (2012). *An introduction to the psychology of hearing* (6th ed.). London: Emerald. Chapter 9.

Warren, R. M. (2008). *Auditory perception: An analysis and synthesis* (3rd ed.). Cambridge, UK: Cambridge University Press. Chapter 7.

I also found Plomp's book both clear and insightful:

Plomp, R. (2002). *The intelligent ear: On the nature of sound perception*. Mahwah, NJ: Lawrence Erlbaum. Chapters 4 and 5.

For a general approach to sound identification:

Handel, S. (1995). Timbre perception and auditory object identification. In B. C. J. Moore (Ed.), *Hearing* (pp. 425–461). New York: Academic Press.

For a discussion of neural mechanisms:

Schnupp, J., Nelken, I., and King, A. (2011). *Auditory neuroscience: Making sense of sound*. Cambridge, MA: MIT Press. Chapter 4.

12 MUSIC

After speech, music is arguably the most important type of sound stimulus for humans. But music remains something of a mystery. It seems to satisfy no obvious biological need, yet it has the power to move us in ways that few other forms of human expression can. Music is strongly linked to our emotional response and can evoke feelings of sadness, happiness, excitement, and calm. Why do certain combinations of notes and rhythms have the ability to affect us in this way?

Music is composed of sound waves, and as such it is analyzed and processed, at least initially, in the same ways as all the other sounds that enter our ears. Musical instruments have different timbres, the perception of which depends on the frequency-selective properties of the ear described in Chapter 5. A large part of music involves melody and harmony, and this depends on the mechanisms for analyzing pitch described in Chapter 7. Music also involves rhythm and timing, and this depends on the auditory mechanisms for analyzing the temporal characteristics of sounds described in Chapter 8. Finally, music is often highly complex, with many different instruments and melodies weaving together. Analyzing this complex scene relies on the mechanisms of grouping and segregation described in Chapter 10.

In this chapter, I will discuss the perception of music in relation to what we have learned so far in the book about the mechanisms of hearing. I will also provide a brief introduction to "higher level" processes such as memory and emotion. Finally, I will describe some of the theories that have been proposed to explain the most puzzling aspect of the story: Why music exists at all.

12.1 WHAT IS MUSIC?

We might think that we have a pretty good idea of what is music; we generally know it when we hear it. But music is actually quite difficult to define. In his famous dictionary, Samuel Johnson defined "musick" as "the science of harmony" or "instrumental or vocal harmony" (Johnson, 1768), a definition that assumes music is a consequence of sound production by tonal instruments such as the violin. However, recent composers have transformed our ideas regarding the sorts of sounds that can be regarded as musical. The innovative composer Edgard Varèse (1883–1965) defined music simply as "organized sound" (Goldman, 1961). This could include anything from a melody played by a flute to the combined sound of a waterfall and a train. The online resource dictionary.com defines music as "an art of sound in time that expresses ideas and emotions in significant forms through the elements of rhythm, melody, harmony, and color." This seems to be a fairly comprehensive definition, although the use of the word "color" is a little ambiguous. In what follows, I am going to err on the conservative side and start by focusing on the building blocks of what might be considered "traditional Western music," in particular the aspects related to pitch (melody and harmony) and the aspects related to time (tempo, rhythm, and meter).

12.2 MELODY

12.2.1 Musical notes and the pitch helix

A musical note can be defined as a sound that evokes a pitch (e.g., a complex tone with a specific fundamental frequency) or, alternatively, as a symbolic representation of such a sound (e.g., the note "A," or a symbol used in standard musical notation). There are certain restrictions on the range of fundamental frequencies that are commonly used. In Western music, the permitted notes have *specific fundamental frequencies*, with adjacent notes separated by a *musical interval* of a *semitone*, which is about a 6% change in fundamental frequency. Notes are given standard labels: A, A♯/B♭, B, C, C♯/D♭, D, D♯/E♭, E, F, F♯/G♭, G, G♯/A♭. The ♯ symbol represents *sharp* (a semitone above the note given by the letter or symbol) and ♭ represents *flat* (a semitone below the note given by the letter or symbol). *Equal temperament* tuning (such as that used to tune a piano) is based on a *constant frequency ratio* (about 1.06:1) between adjacent notes separated by a semitone. In this type of tuning, A♯ and B♭ are the same note, as are C♯ and D♭, D♯ and E♭, and G♯ and A♭. But for an instrument that can play a continuous range of fundamental frequencies (such as the violin or trombone), A♯ and B♭ (etc.) can have slightly different fundamental frequencies, depending on the key the piece is in (see Section 12.2.2).

The reason for this is that mathematically "perfect" harmony, which leads to a pleasing sensation of consonance (see Section 12.3.2), is based on *simple ratios* between the fundamental frequencies of the notes. Unfortunately, the combinations of those ratios regularly used in Western music don't correspond to a simple set of discrete fundamental frequencies. So, for example, the ratio between C♯ and A (a major third) should be 5:4, the ratio between F and D♭ (also a major third) should be 5:4, and the ratio between F and A (a minor sixth) should be 8:5. Unfortunately, $5/4 \times 5/4 = 25/16$, which isn't quite equal to 8/5! This means that choosing fundamental frequencies based on the right ratios for a major third and a minor sixth starting from A will lead to the wrong ratio for the major third starting from D♭ if C♯ and D♭ are forced to have the same fundamental frequency. Equal temperament tuning is a compromise system in which the ratios aren't perfect but close enough across the range of intervals to sound reasonably pleasant.

The 12 notes that have distinct letter labels (including sharps/flats) cover an octave – that is, a doubling in fundamental frequency. If the fundamental frequency is doubled, the letter representing the note stays the same. Notes with the same letter label (and hence whose fundamental frequencies differ by a power of two: 2, 4, 8, etc.) are said to have the same *chroma*, and perceptually they appear to have a strong similarity or association; a melody is considered to be in the same musical key if it is played using the same sequence of notes an octave higher. A more precise labeling of the note is sometimes given by specifying the octave using a number, so the note A2 has double the fundamental frequency of A1 and half the fundamental frequency of A3. The pitch associated with the absolute fundamental frequency (taking into account both chroma and octave changes) is described as the *pitch height*. So A1 and A2 have the same chroma but different pitch height, while D3 and E3 differ in both chroma *and* pitch height. Notice that it is possible to change pitch height without changing chroma (by moving up or down in octave jumps) but that it is not possible to change chroma without changing pitch height.

The idea that the perception in some way cycles with each octave increase in pitch height can be represented by the *pitch helix* (Shepard, 1982). The pitch helix is a three-dimensional plot, in which chroma is plotted going around a two-dimensional circle and pitch height is plotted vertically (Figure 12.1, left panel). This produces a rising spiral as we move systematically from low notes to high notes. In Figure 12.1, notice how notes with the same chroma (A1, A2, and A3

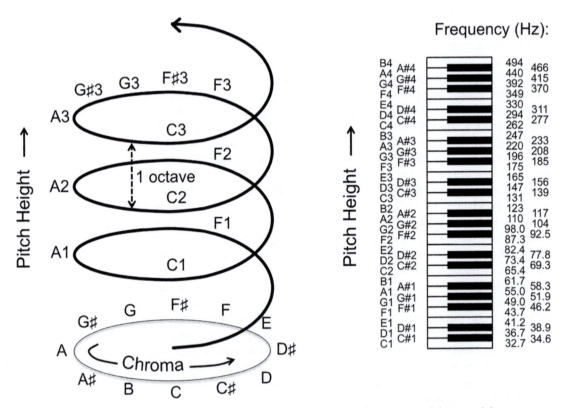

Figure 12.1 The left panel shows the pitch helix. Chroma is shown as a circle at the bottom, and the vertical dimension is pitch height. The spiral shows how chroma and pitch height change as the fundamental frequency of the note is steadily increased. Note that the viewpoint is above the spiral for illustrative purposes – the spiral is continuously rising in terms of pitch height. The right panel shows how pitch height increases in terms of the keys on a piano keyboard. The fundamental frequency of each note (in Hz) is shown on the right.

have the same chroma, and F1, F2, and F3 have the same chroma) are all aligned vertically, mapping on to the two-dimensional chroma circle at the bottom.

Although representations such as the pitch helix are based on the *relative* frequencies of the notes, in order for musicians to be able to accompany each other easily (particularly for instruments such as the piano for which retuning is a major undertaking), there is an agreed international standard tuning ("concert pitch") in which the note A4 has a fundamental frequency of 440 Hz (Figure 12.1, right panel). This standard has varied over the years, and slight deviations are still common for different orchestras and ensembles.

Is there a good physical, or perhaps *physiological*, reason why our perception cycles in this way as we go up in pitch height? Tones an octave apart certainly share some common features (Figure 12.2). First, consider the periodicity of the waveforms. The waveform of a tone with a fundamental frequency of 440 Hz (A4) repeats 440 times a second, with a periodicity of 2.3 ms (1/440). But a tone with a fundamental frequency of 880 Hz (A5) also repeats every 2.3 ms, although this covers two cycles of the waveform (each cycle has a period of 1.14 ms, 1/880). So tones an octave apart share a common periodicity (Figure 12.2, left panel). Unsurprisingly, the distributions of time intervals between spikes in auditory nerve recordings show maxima, not just at the period of the fundamental frequency of complex tones, but also at multiples of this period (Cariani & Delgutte, 1996). In addition, there are *spectral* similarities between tones an octave apart. The harmonics of an 880 Hz tone (880 Hz, 1760 Hz, 2640 Hz, etc.) are all components of the harmonic series of a 440-Hz tone (Figure 12.2, right panel). Hence, auditory pitch mechanisms based on the timing of nerve impulses or on the patterning of harmonics (see Section 7.3)

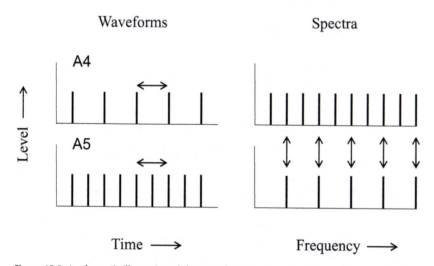

Waveforms   Spectra

A4

A5

Level ⟶

Time ⟶   Frequency ⟶

Figure 12.2 A schematic illustration of the waveforms and spectra of two notes separated by an octave (e.g., A4 and A5). For illustrative purposes, the waveforms shown are artificial *pulse trains*, consisting of regular sequences of almost instantaneous pressure impulses (see also Figure 2.13, top panel). The double-headed arrows show the common periodicity (left panel) and the common harmonics (right panel).

may well respond similarly to tones an octave apart. Evidence for this is that in pitch-matching experiments, participants sometimes make "octave errors": judging that tones whose fundamental frequencies are an octave apart have the same pitch or assigning a tone to the wrong octave. For example, tones containing only higher, unresolved, harmonics (see Chapter 7) are often judged to be an octave higher than tones containing only resolved harmonics, despite having the same fundamental frequency (Patterson, 1990).

There are also some hints that the perceptual distinction between chroma and pitch height may have a basis in how these attributes are processed in the auditory pathway. Results from a functional magnetic resonance imaging study suggest that changes in chroma and changes in pitch height may be represented in separate brain regions: Changes in chroma anterior to primary auditory cortex and changes in pitch height posterior to primary auditory cortex (Warren, Uppenkamp, Patterson, & Griffiths, 2003). In addition, it is known that presenting a tone reduces the electrical response in the auditory cortex (measured using electroencephalography, or EEG) to a subsequent tone with the same fundamental frequency. This is an example of neural adaptation (see Section 4.4.2). It has been shown that this adaptation also occurs when the second tone is an *octave above* the first (e.g., B2 followed by B3; Briley, Breakey, & Krumbholz, 2012). This suggests that the *same neurons* are responding to two tones an octave apart. When the two tones differ in chroma (e.g., B2 followed by F3), the response to the second tone is greater (the adaptation is less), suggesting that distinct populations of neurons are activated by two tones when they differ in chroma. Overall, the EEG results suggest that some neurons in auditory cortex show tuning to a characteristic chroma, regardless of octave (in other words, regardless of the overall pitch height). So there may be some neurons tuned to A (regardless of octave), some to A♯, some to B, and so on.

12.2.2 Musical scales and melody

A melody is a sequence of musical notes; in other words, it is a sequence of fundamental frequencies. To play a musical melody, you need an instrument that can produce periodic sound waves at a range of fundamental frequencies, by virtue of a controlled regular oscillation of some part of the instrument, such as the strings on a guitar. For the perception of melody and harmony, the *relative* fundamental frequencies of the notes are most important, not their absolute frequencies. If the ratios (i.e., musical intervals) between successive notes stay the same, the starting fundamental frequency of "Twinkle, Twinkle, Little Star" could have any value within the range of frequencies perceivable as pitch, and we would still recognize the tune.

A scale is a sequence of notes in ascending or descending order. The full selection of 12 notes (A to G♯) forms the chromatic scale. A melody using a free selection of notes from the chromatic scale tends to sound rather avant-garde and not particularly melodious to most people. However, these notes can be organized in other ways: into *scales* incorporating a reduced set of notes that tend to work well together. The first note in a scale is called the *tonic*. This is particular for the musical *key*, which specifies both the tonic note and the harmonic context, which can be *major* or *minor*. Hence, there are 24 keys, two (major and minor) for each of the notes in the chromatic scale. In Western music, the dominant scales are the *diatonic* major and minor, both of which contain seven notes. Hence, a melody using a diatonic major or minor scale contains a maximum of seven distinct chroma.

A diatonic scale in the key of C major contains the notes C, D, E, F, G, A, and B (the white keys on the piano; Figure 12.3, top panel). E and F are separated by a semitone, as are B and C. The other pairs of successive notes are all separated by two semitones. Hence, the intervals in semitones between the notes in the diatonic C major scale are 2-2-1-2-2-2-1 (assuming that we end on the C an octave above the starting note). Intervals are also specified in terms of the *degree* of the note in the diatonic scale, degree being the number of the note in the scale starting from the tonic. For example, a major third is the interval from the tonic to the third note in a major scale (C to E, in C major), which is an interval of four semitones. The diatonic C minor scale contains the notes C, D, E♭, F, G, A♭, and B♭. The intervals for this scale are 2-1-2-2-2-1-2. Notice that the minor third (tonic to third note in a minor scale) has an interval of three semitones. Another example is the minor pentatonic, associated with blues music. In the key of E♭ minor, the pentatonic scale contains the five notes E♭, G♭, A♭, B♭, and D♭ (the black keys on the piano; Figure 12.3, bottom panel). The intervals for this scale (whatever the tonic) are 3-2-2-3-2. A remarkable list of *dozens* of scales,

C major scale

E♭ minor pentatonic scale

Figure 12.3 Two musical scales. The notes are shown in "staff" musical notation and as letters. The arrows show the correspondence of the notes to the keys on a piano (the white keys in the case of C major and the black keys in the case of E♭ minor pentatonic).

all based on a C tonic, can be found at https://en.wikipedia.org/wiki/List_of_ musical_scales_and_modes. It must be emphasized that the "rules" governing which notes can and cannot be played in a scale are often broken by composers to produce tension and interest by adding a "wrong" note into a melody (Tan, Pfordresher, & Harré, 2010).

The tonic note in a scale is considered to be the most *stable* (e.g., the C in a C major scale) and provides a sense of "home" or resolution for the melody line. Other notes in a scale have varying degrees of stability. In the diatonic C major scale, the most stable notes after the tonic are E and G (the third and fifth notes). As a sequence of notes is played, the melody evokes a feeling of *tension* when the note is unstable and *relaxation* or *resolution* when the note is stable. Furthermore, the brain tends to anticipate a resolution of the sequence on a stable note. If this does not happen, then the effects can be disconcerting. You can try this by humming the chorus of a popular tune without the last note ("Twinkle, twinkle, little star, how I wonder what you . . ."). Can you feel the tension and lack of resolution? The opening melody phrase for "Twinkle, Twinkle, Little Star" in C major has the notes C-C-G-G-A-A-G–F-F-E-E-D-D-C (Figure 12.4). Without the final C, the melody sounds as if it is poised on the edge of a step (the unstable D), waiting to jump down to the stable tonic. The rise and fall of tension produced by stable and unstable notes, and from the fulfillment and violation of expectation, is an important component of our emotional response to music (Dowling, 2010).

Why do some notes from the chromatic scale fit well together in particular groups such as a diatonic scale, and why are some notes in the scale stable and others unstable? Part of the answer is that through repeated exposure to certain scales and note combinations, we build up an implicit knowledge of the tonal structure of music in our culture, and hence we become familiar with certain sequences of notes (Tillmann, Bharucha, & Bigand, 2000). However, another part of the answer is that notes forming one of the standard scales tend to harmonize well together; they sound good when combined. This is especially true of the most stable notes in the scale. The three most stable notes in C major, C, E, and G, form the C major *triad* (Figure 12.5) and sound good when played together, as do the notes of the C minor triad: C, E♭, and G. Possible reasons why some note combinations are pleasant and stable and others are unpleasant and unstable will be discussed in Section 12.3.2.

The general point is that the key of a piece of music, established through melodies and harmonies, provides a *tonal context* that favors certain notes and certain note combinations. For example, if the context of C major is first established by presenting a C major triad, listeners tend to judge successive pairs of stable

Figure 12.4 The melody for the first phrase of "Twinkle, Twinkle, Little Star."

C major triad

Figure 12.5 The C major triad presented as a chord and as a melody, illustrating the two "directions" of harmony and melody.

notes within the diatonic scale of C major (C, E, and G) as more similar to each other than they are to unstable notes within the scale (D, F, A, and B; Krumhansl, 1979). Furthermore, notes within the scale (C, D, E, F, G, A, and B) tend to be judged as more similar to each other than they are to notes outside the scale (C♯, D♯, F♯, G♯, and A♯). An interesting aspect of this is that notes such as C and C♯ are much closer to each other in terms of fundamental frequency than C and G, yet further apart perceptually in the context of the C major key.

12.2.3 Melodic contour

Melodic contour refers to the overall pattern of the frequency changes in a temporal sequence of notes, whether the fundamental frequencies are rising, falling, or staying the same. In other words, C-F-C-E has the same contour (up-down-up) as D-E-C-D. The shape of the melodic contour is important to the way we perceive melodies (Tan et al., 2010). A performance error that results in a change in the contour of a melody (e.g., if the note is higher than the previous note when it should be lower) is more noticeable than an error that preserves the contour. Melodies with different intervals between notes are sometimes identified as the same if they have the same melodic contour. This can occur if the melodies are "atonal" (i.e., not corresponding to any particular key; Dowling & Fujitani, 1971) or if one melody is a "scalar transposition" of the other melody within a particular key (Dowling, 1978). A scalar transposition involves a shift of a constant number of notes (or scale steps) within the same musical scale (e.g., C4-E4-G4 to E4-G4-B4 in C major). Scalar transpositions change the intervals between notes but preserve the melodic contour.

Melodies are often based around a specific set of notes in a particular scale. But there also tend to be regularities in the melodic contour: certain *trajectories* of notes that are more common than others. One of the most popular types of contour is the "arch," in which the melody rises to a midpoint then falls again. The first phrase of "Twinkle, Twinkle" is an example of this, climbing from C to A (in C major) then back again (see Figure 12.4). This type of contour can give a pleasing sense of tension and resolution as the melody moves away from the tonic and then back again. Melodies in Western music also tend to have small intervals between successive notes. Large changes are rare, and hence can be used to grab attention and provide emphasis: a *musical accent* (Jones, 1987). Recall also that we find it easier to group together the notes in melodies if the variations in frequency are small (see Section 10.3.1). If a melody is composed of a sequence of large frequency jumps, it will tend to break apart into several separate melodies and lose its coherence. Another example of regularity in the melodic contour is that large intervals between notes (large changes in frequency) are more likely to be ascending (i.e., increasing in frequency) and small intervals are more likely to be descending (Vos & Troost, 1989). "Somewhere Over the Rainbow" is an example of this, where the melody starts with an ascending octave jump then gradually meanders back down.

12.3   HARMONY

12.3.1   Harmony and chords

Harmony refers to the combination of notes to produce *chords*. A chord is a simultaneous combination of two or more notes. Chords with two notes are called *dyads*, chords with three notes are called *triads*, chords with four notes are called *tetrads*, and so on. The study of harmony is concerned with the principles underlying the perceptual effects of combining notes in chords. In a sense, melody and harmony represent two different directions in music, with reference to standard musical notation. Melody is concerned with the *horizontal* sequence of notes over time, whereas harmony is concerned with the *vertical* sequence of notes at a single time (see Figure 12.5).

12.3.2   Consonance and dissonance

When two or more notes with different fundamental frequencies are played together, the effects of the combination can be consonant (sounding *pleasant* or *resolved*) or dissonant (sounding *unpleasant* or *unresolved*). These perceptual effects contribute greatly to the emotional power of a piece of music. The perception of consonance or dissonance depends on the musical intervals (frequency ratios) between the notes that are played. Figure 12.6 shows the results of an experiment in which listeners were asked to rate their preference for pairs of synthetic tones played together (dyads), as a function of the musical interval between the two tones. Notice that some intervals are given a high pleasantness rating (e.g., the perfect fifth, for which the frequencies are in the ratio 2:3; C and G in the key of C major). Others are given a low pleasantness rating (e.g., the tritone, for which the frequencies are in the ratio 5:7; C and F♯ in the key of C major). Incidentally, the tritone has been called the "*Diabolus in Musica*" (literally, "devil in music") because of its satanic sound, a sound utilized to great effect by Jimi Hendrix in the opening riff of "Purple Haze." The most consonant musical interval is the octave, with a ratio of 1:2. A rule of thumb is that if the notes have a relatively simple frequency ratio, then the effects are consonant, while if the frequency ratio is more complex, the effects are dissonant. Why should this be?

Two main hypotheses have been proposed to explain why we hear some note combinations as consonant and others as dissonant (Terhardt, 1974). Both

Figure 12.6 The results of an experiment showing pleasantness ratings for combinations of two notes (dyads) as a function of the musical interval between them. Data are from McDermott et al. (2010).

hypotheses are based on the patterning of the harmonics of the notes in the combination. Each note is a complex tone with a series of harmonics that are integer (whole number) multiples of the fundamental. For a note with a fundamental frequency of 110 Hz (the note A2), harmonics of 110, 220, 330, 440, 550, 660, . . . Hz will be present (continuous black lines in Figure 12.7a). To produce a perfect fifth, the note A2 would be combined with the note E3, which has a fundamental frequency of 165 Hz and harmonics of 165, 330, 495, 660, . . . Hz (dashed gray lines in Figure 12.7a). Notice that some harmonics are shared between the two notes. In addition, all the components in the chord are harmonics of a single fundamental frequency of 55 Hz (shown by the dotted line in Figure 12.7a). For the tritone (Figure 12.7b), however, the harmonics do not coincide (at least not over this frequency range) and do not form a clear harmonic series. One hypothesis, therefore, is that chords sound consonant when the harmonics are close to a *single harmonic series* and dissonant when the harmonics are not close to a single series.

The other hypothesis concerns how the harmonics interact in the cochlea. Figures 12.7c and 12.7d illustrate the representations in the cochlea of the perfect fifth and the tritone respectively, plotted as excitation patterns (see Section 5.4.4). When a dissonant chord such as the tritone is played, several pairs of harmonics from the individual notes have frequencies that are similar but not the same. These harmonics will interact at a single place on the basilar membrane (i.e., in a single auditory filter) to produce a modulated waveform (*beats*; see

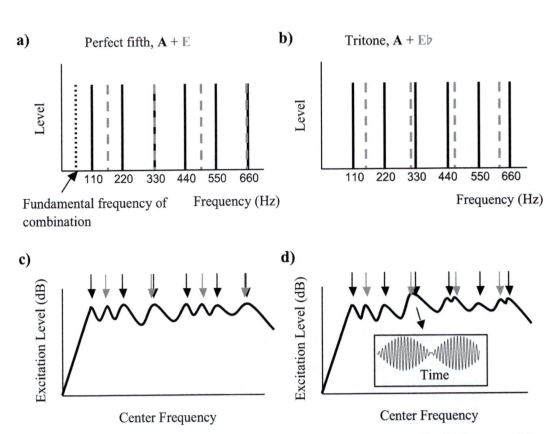

Figure 12.7 The spectra of consonant and dissonant chords and their representations in the cochlea. (a) The spectra of the two notes in a perfect fifth dyad. The harmonics for the note A are shown by the black lines, and the harmonics for the note E are shown by the dashed gray lines. The dotted line shows the fundamental frequency of the combination. (b) The spectra of the two notes in a tritone dyad. The harmonics for the note A are shown by the black lines, and the harmonics for the note E♭ are shown by the dashed gray lines. (c) A schematic excitation pattern for the perfect fifth dyad. Arrows show the locations of peaks corresponding to harmonics. (d) A schematic excitation pattern for the tritone dyad. The plot in the box shows a schematic time waveform for the vibration of the place on the basilar membrane responding to the third harmonic of the note A and the second harmonic of the note E♭. The waveform shows amplitude modulation (beats) caused by the interaction of the two harmonics.

Section 2.5.1). This is illustrated by the plot of the temporal pattern of basilar membrane vibration in the box in Figure 12.7d. For modulation rates between about 15 and 300 Hz, we perceive the beats as a rough sensation (Zwicker & Fastl, 1990). Therefore, dissonant chords may sound unpleasant because they involve more beating between harmonics in the cochlea, an idea that goes back to von Helmholtz (1863). Consistent with this hypothesis is the finding that, for two simultaneous pure tones, consonance increases when the tones are separated by an interval greater than the bandwidth of the auditory filter, suggesting that dissonance depends on the tones interacting within an auditory filter (Plomp & Levelt, 1965).

An ingenious experiment by McDermott, Lehr, and Oxenham (2010) may have resolved this issue. In addition to measuring preference for consonant and dissonant intervals, they also measured preference for nonmusical stimuli in which harmonicity and beating were manipulated independently. They showed that individual preference ratings for consonant and dissonant intervals correlated with individual preference ratings for harmonicity, but not with individual preference ratings for beating. Hence, it is possible that the perception of consonance depends on how close the combination of components is to a single harmonic series rather than on the degree of beating between closely spaced components in the chord. In the experiment of McDermott and colleagues, the preference for harmonic frequencies was stronger in people with experience playing musical instruments, suggesting that learning also plays a role.

There is a good ecological reason why humans might have a preference for harmonic series. Many natural sounds are produced by objects that vibrate periodically, producing complex tones with a series of harmonics. Recall from Chapter 10 that harmonicity is one of the main cues we use to separate out sounds that occur together. Being able to group together harmonics that form a single series allows us to separate sounds in a combination. Hence, if two notes do not combine to form a sequence of frequency components that is close to a single series, this may signify that the notes do not belong together. This suggests that our preference for consonant intervals may in part be a side effect of the adaptation of the auditory system to the acoustic properties of objects in the environment (Plack, 2010).

Even though harmony may be based on harmonicity, which relates to the spectral distribution of harmonics, it is possible that this information is coded temporally, using neural phase locking. In Chapter 7 we saw how a temporal code can be used across the different harmonics of a complex tone to represent fundamental frequency, and this same code may underlie our perception of harmony. In support of this hypothesis, Bones, Hopkins, Krishnan, and Plack (2014) found that the strength of preference for consonant over dissonant dyads correlated with the relative strength of phase locking in the brainstem to those same dyads across individual listeners, measured using the EEG frequency-following response technique (see Sections 7.2.3 and A.3.2). In other words, listeners who had a stronger perceptual distinction between consonant and dissonant dyads also had a greater difference between these dyads in their neural phase locking. This provides some evidence that harmony perception is based on a temporal code.

To summarize, the tonal aspects of music can be divided into melody, the sequence of notes over time, and harmony, the combination of notes at a single time. The construction of melody and harmony is based on loose constraints, comparable to grammar in language. These constraints depend on the key, scale, and harmonic context and on aspects of the melodic contour. Sticking to the "rules," however, can produce music that is simplistic and boring, and composers often break these conventions to create tension and excitement.

12.4 TIMING

Melody and harmony are only a part of music. Of equal importance are how the notes and chords are arranged in time and how notes at particular times are stressed. In Western music, there is usually an underlying *tempo, rhythm,* and *meter* of a piece, which cause the brain to organize the musical events into temporal patterns and sequences. These three components together form the *metric structure* of music.

12.4.1   Tempo

A *beat* in music can be thought of as the tick of a clock (or metronome) in a musical piece, the basic unit of stress in time. It is not required to have a note or other musical event at each beat, and there may well be several events between two beats, but there is a sense that the time of each beat has a perceptual emphasis. The tempo of a musical piece is the rate at which beats occur and is usually measured in beats per minute (bpm). The tempo is also the rate at which we tend to tap our feet, or clap our hands, to the music.

The range of tempi that we can perceive in a musical way is limited from about 60 to 300 bpm (Drake & Botte, 1993). For tempi below about 60 bpm, the events are heard separately, and the sense of a fused temporal pattern is lost. For tempi greater than about 300 bpm, the sense of coherence is also lost, or the brain will tend to organize the pattern of notes into a tempo of half the rate. Interestingly, individual listeners each have a preferred tempo. When asked to tap at a comfortable rate, people tend to tap at about 100 bpm, but this varies a little between individuals: The preferred tempo for an individual seems to be related to the rate at which they *walk* (Fraisse, 1982). Perhaps predictably, younger people prefer faster tempi than do older people (McAuley, Jones, Holub, Johnston, & Miller, 2006). Hence, there may be basic physiological reasons why we like to organize music according to particular tempi. In addition to constraints on tempo, there are additional constraints on the *rate of notes* in a melody that can be perceived coherently (remember that each note doesn't necessarily have to correspond to a beat). If the rate is greater than about six notes per second or slower than about one note per second, we have difficulty recognizing a familiar tune (Warren, Gardner, Brubacker, & Bashford, 1991). Older listeners have more difficulty recognizing fast melodies than younger listeners, perhaps related to the slower overall neural processing speed in older people (Andrews, Dowling, Bartlett, & Halpern, 1998).

It has been suggested that our perception of temporal regularities such as musical tempo may depend on *self-sustaining oscillators* in the brain (Large & Jones, 1999). These internal oscillators can *tune in*, or *synchronize* to temporal regularities in the music. If the tempo of a piece changes, then the rate of oscillation will change so that the oscillators are synchronized with the new tempo. These oscillators may be part of the mechanism that allows us to experience a regular sequence of beats over time and to perceive any complex temporal patterns that are present in the music in the context of the underlying beat. They may also allow us to *anticipate* when the next beat or beats will occur, which is crucial for musicians and dancers alike.

12.4.2   Rhythm

A rhythm is characterized by a repeating temporal pattern of sounds and silences. While tempo refers to the *absolute* rate at which beats occur, rhythm generally refers to the *relative* time intervals between the onsets of musical events, which can be expressed as a ratio. The simplest ratio is 1:1, which is a constant time interval, for example, the driving kick drum rhythm in modern dance music. More interesting options are available, however. For example, one time interval between notes or percussive sounds may be twice as long as the subsequent interval, producing the "shuffle" or "swing" ratio of 2:1. Some examples of simple rhythms are illustrated in Figure 12.8. Of course, much more complicated rhythms can be produced, and it is even possible to have several rhythms occurring at the same time (*polyrhythms*), a characteristic of some African music.

According to the definition used here, tempo and rhythm are independent. Rhythm is the temporal patterning of events, while tempo determines the *rate* at which these patterns occur. Two pieces of music can have the same rhythm at two different tempos or two different rhythms at the same tempo. However, rhythm is also sometimes used to refer to both the relative timing of events *and* their absolute rate. Indeed, the definition of rhythm varies widely even among experts (Tan et al., 2010).

12.4.3 Meter

The final component of the temporal organization of music is *meter*. In terms of music notation, meter refers to the organization of beats into *bars* (or *measures*), with the first beat in each bar often having more stress. Meter is indicated

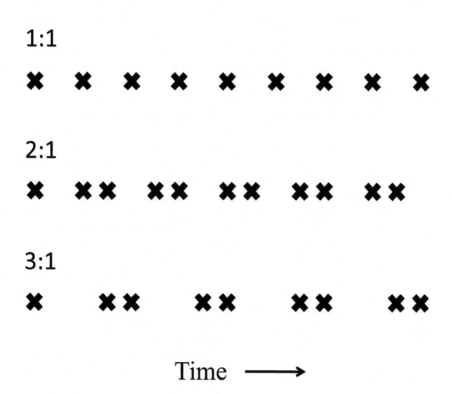

Figure 12.8 Three simple rhythms.

Figure 12.9 Three common time signatures.

by a time signature and vertical bar lines that show where one bar ends and another begins (see Figure 12.9). The time signature has two numbers arranged vertically. The upper number is the number of beats in the bar, and the lower number is the "note value," which determines the relative duration of each beat. For example, 4/4 has four beats in each bar, and each beat is a quarter note (a crotchet). You can perceive this time signature as **one**, *two, three, four;* **one,** *two, three, four,* and so on, with a stress every four beats. The time signature 6/8 has six beats in each bar, and each beat is an eighth note (a quaver). Popular music is almost invariably in 4/4, although there are some exceptions. The song "Money" by Pink Floyd is mostly in 7/4. Waltz music is typically in 3/4 (**one,** *two, three;* **one,** *two, three,* etc.).

However, meter can be defined more generally as the timing of stressed or accented beats in music. Musicians communicate the tempo, rhythm, and meter of a piece by stressing (emphasizing) certain beats, for example, by using a higher level or longer duration for notes at the beginning of a measure than for other notes in the melody. In addition, note onsets tend to occur *more frequently* at metrically accented points (Palmer & Pfordresher, 2003). A period of silence before an event also gives it an emphasis. For example, "A A A pause A A A pause, etc." causes the A note after the pause to be emphasized. The rhythm or meter of a piece of music can also be emphasized by percussive sounds that produce stress at different times (such as the bass drum, snare drum, and hi-hat in rock music). However, these aspects, which can be specified in musical notation, are only part of the story. A major problem with computer-generated music is to make the expression of the piece sound "human" or "natural" rather than rigid and robotic. Beyond the precise prescriptions of musical notation, expert human players use subtle timing variations to add *expression* to the piece. Level variations over time can also be used to produce a more dynamic, expressive performance. Expression can also come from the way the player delivers each note, varying the timbre of the sound that is produced by the instrument.

12.4.4   Bases of time perception in music

What are the reasons why music tends to be organized into particular temporal patterns, and why are certain tempi and rhythms pleasurable? One possibility is that musical time is based on movement. Recall that people's preferred tempi are related to the rate at which they walk (Fraisse, 1982), and this may also drive our preferences for certain rhythms. Dancing is also based on the link between bodily movement and tempo, rhythm, and meter. Even if we don't have the confidence to strut our stuff on the dance floor, we usually enjoy tapping our feet or clapping our hands in time with musical tempi and rhythms. Indeed, even passive listening to music activates areas of the brain involved in the production of movement (Janata & Grafton, 2003). The association between musical time and movement may be made in infancy. Infants who are bounced up and down according to different rhythmic patterns show preference for audio versions of the same rhythms (Phillips-Silver & Trainor, 2005). This may reflect an early developing neural connection between the auditory system (which responds to the rhythms in music) and the vestibular system (which responds to the rhythmic movements in bouncing and dancing).

Another possible influence on musical rhythm is *language*. Of course, much music contains singing, and it is perhaps not surprising that the prosody of a language, the pattern of stressed and unstressed syllables, is reflected in the rhythm of songs. However, there is also evidence for a correlation between the rhythmic structure of a language and the rhythmic structure of *instrumental* music composed by native speakers of the language (Patel & Daniele, 2003). For example, spoken English contains alternating contrasts between syllables that are long (stressed) and those that are short (unstressed). For example, compare the short first syllable "to" with the long second syllable "day" in "today." Intriguingly, instrumental compositions by English-speaking classical composers such as Elgar also contain strong contrasts between the durations of successive notes. Spoken French, on the other hand, consists of syllables with less variable durations, and this may be a reason why French instrumental music (e.g., works by Debussy) tends to contain more similar durations for successive notes than English instrumental music. It seems possible that composers, consciously or unconsciously, incorporate linguistic rhythms into their music (Patel & Daniele, 2003).

12.5   MUSICAL SCENE ANALYSIS

When listening to a musical performance, the auditory system has the task of separating out sound components that originate from different sources and grouping together sound components that originate from the same source, as is generally true of auditory scenes (Chapter 10). "Source" in this case might refer to a single musical instrument. However, the auditory system is also able to separate out different musical parts played on a single instrument, for example, the accompaniment and melody parts being played together on a piano. So a single instrument may produce several separable melodic or chordal sequences. The perception of music is strongly dependent on the gestalt principle of "figure and ground" (Section 10.3.6), with attention often being focused on the main melody part (the figure), while the accompaniment forms the background. It is quite possible, however, to switch attention between different parts in the music, and a skilled listener (e.g., the conductor of an orchestra) is able to switch attention at will to any one of the different parts in a complex score.

As described in Chapter 10, auditory grouping mechanisms can be divided into those involved in *simultaneous* segregation and grouping and those involved in *sequential* segregation and grouping. In music, many of the sound sources (instruments) produce periodic sounds, and so harmonicity cues (Section 10.2.2) can be used for simultaneous grouping. As described in Section 10.2.1, differences in relative onset time between instruments, due to slight departures by each musician from the precise notation, can be particularly important for simultaneous segregation of musical parts. Musical examples were used throughout Chapter 10, and I will not rehearse these discussions in detail here. Instead, I will focus on how our perception of music over time (sequential streaming) depends on the grouping mechanisms described in Chapter 10.

12.5.1   Music and streaming

Sequential streaming (Section 10.3) is essential to our perception of music. Much of the power of music derives from our ability to follow a musical melody over time – to appreciate the phrasing in the rise and fall of the notes and the way they interact in different ways with the harmonic context (e.g., the different chords that are played in the accompaniment). Section 10.3.1 describes how fundamental frequency is a very strong cue to streaming. When two or more melodies are played together in different registers (different ranges of fundamental frequencies), it is fairly easy to attend to one melody and consign the other melodies to the background. When the fundamental frequencies of the notes overlap (in the absence of other cues for segregation), then they are hard to separate. Conversely, if the jumps in fundamental frequency in a single sequence are too great, the melody can split into two. For example, some fingerpicking styles on the guitar involve alternation between low and high strings, resulting in the perception of both a high-register (treble) melody and a low-register (bass) melody.

Spectral cues, perceived as differences in timbre, are also very important in musical streaming. The sounds from different instruments often have different spectral characteristics (see Section 10.3.2). Recall that Van Noorden (1975; see also Bregman, 1990) showed that two complex tones with the *same* fundamental frequency were heard as two different streams if the harmonics occupied difference frequency regions. So interleaved melodies from a violin and a flute might be separated in terms of the timbres of the instruments even if they occupy the same range of fundamental frequencies.

Spatial cues (Section 10.3.3) greatly enhance the quality of a musical experience due to the use of these cues by the auditory system to separate out the different instruments. A stereo reproduction over two loudspeakers often sounds much clearer than a mono reproduction over a single loudspeaker. Level differences between the loudspeakers can be used to separate out the different instruments and hence the different musical parts. A live performance, particularly one in which the instruments are not simply combined in a stereo mix over the

PA, offers richer spatial cues, with interaural time differences coming into play. Finally, being able to *see* the gestures of the musicians as they play helps to segregate the sound sources by allowing us to match up, in time, each sound with the movement on the instrument that made it (Dowling, 2010).

12.6   CULTURE AND EXPERIENCE

One of the most remarkable aspects of music is that seemingly abstract combinations of sounds have the power to move us to tears or cause incredible feelings of excitement and elation. However, the reasons why an individual might respond in a particular way to a piece of music are highly complex. The response may depend in part on *universal* associations, common across all individuals and cultures, which may be based on innate predispositions (Peretz, 2006). One such example might be the association of a high tempo with happiness and excitement. However, there are also associations that are constructed by the personal experience of music over an individual's lifetime. For many aspects of music perception, these influences are quite hard to disentangle.

Past experience is clearly an important component of our reaction to music. We tend to enjoy familiar tunes and familiar styles of music more than tunes and styles that are unfamiliar to us. The emotional state evoked by a piece of music depends to some extent on the unique associations we have had between the same or similar pieces of music and emotional events. For example, we may feel sad because a particular song reminds us of a dead relative who used to sing the song at home. There are also different musical cultures that influence our individual preferences, through exposure not just to the music itself but also to the culture that surrounds the music (social identity, fashion, politics, etc.). Different musical cultures can exist *within* a particular society (think rap music and opera) and, of course, *between* societies (Chinese music, Indian music, etc.). This chapter has focused on traditional Western music, and certain sections would have been somewhat different from the perspective of, say, Arabic music, whose tonal system divides the octave into 24 rather than 12 tones. Each culture has a set of explicit or implicit rules covering the tonal and temporal aspects of music (scales, rhythmic patterns, etc.), and our repeated experience of music reinforces these rules and influences our interpretation and emotional reaction to a music piece. In effect, we learn a *musical grammar*, partly specific to our culture. Much of the emotional impact of events within a piece of music relies on the confirmation or violation of these grammatical rules (McDermott, 2009).

Memory for music also influences our perceptions over much shorter time scales. Section 12.2.2 describes how our memory of the tonal context of a piece influences our perception of notes and chords. Within a piece of music, composers will often play on our memory for a musical melody or "theme" by starting a piece with a strong theme and then developing the theme with slight variations to add surprise and interest. Composers rely on our memory for the basic structure of the theme to provide the context in which these variations are played out (Jones, 1987). The repetition of melodic patterns helps give us a sense that the musical piece forms a coherent whole.

12.6.1 Absolute pitch

A few individuals have *absolute* or "perfect" pitch, which is the ability to name a musical note they hear without any other reference. For example, if you were to sing a random note to someone with absolute pitch, the person would be able to tell you that the note is, say, B ♭ . The person may also be able to sing a written note at the correct fundamental frequency, without any other cues. Absolute pitch is related to musical training during a critical period in childhood and is most prevalent among those who started training before the age of 7 (Deutsch, Henthorn, Marvin, & Xu, 2006). Absolute pitch is thought to be very rare in North America and Europe among the general population, although the prevalence among accomplished musicians may be about 15% (Baharloo, Johnston, Service, Gitschier, & Freimer, 1998). Interestingly, among music conservatory students, absolute pitch is more prevalent in speakers of tone languages such as Mandarin Chinese (Deutsch, Dooley, Henthorn, & Head, 2009). Tone languages depend on differences in fundamental frequency, and on fundamental frequency transitions, to distinguish words.

People with absolute pitch must have a stable representation of a pitch or pitches in their memories, which they can use as standard references to compare with the pitch of any sound in the environment. However, they must also have a way of *labeling* the pitch that they experience (e.g., as the note B ♭). Hence, absolute pitch may depend on the association of *labels* (musical or linguistic) with different *pitches* during a critical phase of development. It is now thought by some authors that most of us may possess some absolute long-term memory for pitch but without the ability to produce the appropriate musical label. For example, when asked to sing familiar songs, people without absolute pitch usually produce melodies within one or two semitones of the original key (Levitin, 1994). People with no musical training can also identify popular themes that are played to them in the original key compared to versions that are shifted by one or two semitones (Schellenberg & Trehub, 2003). It is possible, therefore, that most of us have a good long-term memory for pitch but that the ability to label individual notes requires training during a critical period in early childhood.

12.7 WHY DOES MUSIC EXIST?

Although it is hard to determine when music was first played or sung, there is an archaeological record of musical instruments dating back at least 36,000 years (d'Errico et al., 2003). It is highly likely that music in some form existed long before then, played on instruments that haven't survived, haven't been found, or haven't been conclusively identified as musical instruments. Music is an ancient phenomenon that arose well before the advent of agriculture and civilization. We have seen how some aspects of music are related to the way the auditory system analyzes sounds in general, most notably pitch and harmony. However, knowing this doesn't really answer the central question of why music exists. Why do we humans, uniquely in the animal kingdom, spend so much of our time producing or listening to sounds that seem to have very little significance in terms of our survival?

12.7.1   Evolutionary hypotheses

One possibility is that music is in our genes – that humans have a collection of genes that in some way promotes this particular form of expression. If it is assumed that at least some aspects of our propensity to make and listen to music are genetically determined, then there are two main options: That music is a by-product of other evolved traits or that it confers some direct evolutionary advantage.

For a genetic trait to be successful, it must increase the ability of the organism to survive to maturity and reproduce, so that the genes involved become increasingly common in subsequent generations. It is conceivable that music has no real significance for reproduction in itself. Music could just be a by-product (technically, an *exaptation*) of other mechanisms that do confer direct advantages on individuals, such as those underlying language. For example, musical pitch perception may be "parasitic" on cognitive mechanisms that evolved to process the intonation contour in speech (Peretz, 2006). Music may be an "auditory cheesecake" (Pinker, 1997), in the sense that evolutionary mechanisms favored preferences for fat and sugar but did not select for cheesecake itself. Evidence against this view is that there are cases of individuals with normal or exceptional general cognitive abilities in domains such as language and intelligence who are nonetheless musically inept, being unable to sing, dance, or recognize music. This condition, termed *congenital amusia*, can exist despite formal musical training (Peretz et al., 2002). However, the perception of subtle differences in the intonation contour of speech may be affected in amusic patients (Hutchins, Gosselin, & Peretz, 2010). This suggests that there is at least some overlap in the cognitive processes involved in pitch perception for music and speech.

Alternatively, it has been suggested that music may have a more direct adaptive significance, or at least may have had an adaptive significance in the past. The propensity for music making may be a genetic trait that spread throughout the population over many generations because it increased the chances that individuals with the trait would reproduce successfully. Could our ability to produce and respond to music be an evolutionary adaptation, in the same way as our upright postures and large brains were successful adaptations?

One hypothesis is that music making promotes social cohesion, perhaps in part because of the tendency for music to encourage synchronization between individuals playing together in a group (Huron, 2001). Early music making might have been as simple as using sticks and rocks to bang out rhythms or communal singing. This may have helped synchronize the mood of the group, preparing them to act in unison, for example, when hunting or building shelters. Greater group success would enhance the reproductive success of individuals within it, leading to the genes that promoted such behavior being passed on through the generations.

Another explanation was suggested by the evolutionary psychologist Geoffrey Miller (2000). He proposed that music making, and other art forms, might have evolved as a form of sexual display. The primitive musician communicated to potential mates, through their skill and effort, that they had "good genes" that would result in successful offspring. Hence, music might have had, and perhaps still does have, the same function as the bizarre constructions made by male bowerbirds to attract females. In both cases the behavior indicates to potential mates that the underlying genetic material of their would-be partner is healthy, through the skill and effort needed to create the work – be it an elaborate decorative nest in the case of bowerbirds or a piece of music in the case of humans.

12.7.2   Evidence that music is innate

Although entertaining and thought provoking, these evolutionary hypotheses amount to little more than speculation. Whatever their plausibility, it is very hard to test the ideas empirically. What we can do instead is look for evidence that some aspects of music behavior are innate (possessed at birth), which would suggest a genetic origin. Despite the cultural differences described in the previous section, there do appear to be some constants (Peretz, 2006). For example, most cultures use stable musical scales. These scales have specific intervals between notes, octave equivalence, and a tonal hierarchy of stable and unstable notes (see Section 12.2). Importantly, music making in general appears be a *universal* phenomenon. Music has emerged spontaneously in all human societies. There is a link between all humans in music behavior, just as there is for genetically determined behaviors such as eating, drinking, talking, and sex (McDermott, 2009).

There is also evidence from perceptual experiments with infants, whose musical experience is limited and hence whose behavior is less influenced by experience than is the case for adults. These experiments show that some perceptual abilities are present from an early age (McDermott, 2009), including the ability to distinguish melodies when the notes are rearranged in time, but not when the notes are transposed to a different key. Hence, infants may have an innate ability to respond to relative pitch. However, it has also been shown that adults can recognize transpositions in contours defined by *loudness* and *brightness* (spectral balance) and can match contours in one dimension with another (McDermott, Lehr, & Oxenham, 2008). The ability to encode the relative magnitude of acoustic features extends to more than just pitch. Hence, this ability may be a general feature of sound processing in humans, not limited to music (McDermott, 2009). Overall, there is evidence that *some* aspects of music behavior are innate, but the evidence is far from conclusive at present.

12.8   SUMMARY

As the ancient Greeks understood, much of music is highly mathematical, being based on frequency ratios and regular patterns of timing. The complexity of music arises from combinations of basic mathematical "rules" of melody, harmony, and temporal structure. In this chapter, I have tried to explain how some of these musical rules might be a natural consequence of the way the auditory system processes sounds. However, we have also seen that music is a cultural phenomenon. Experience and expectation are important components of our emotional response to music. The extent to which our perception of music is determined by factors based on experience and on those that are genetically determined is yet to be resolved.

1   Western music can be divided into those aspects related to *pitch* (melody and harmony) and those aspects related to *time* (tempo, rhythm, and meter).

2   Musical *notes* are tones with specific fundamental frequencies. Changing from one note to another produces changes in *chroma* and *pitch height*. Chroma repeats with each doubling in fundamental frequency (an octave increase), while pitch height increases continuously with increases in fundamental frequency. This relation can be represented by the *pitch helix*. The constancy of chroma for octave changes in frequency reflects the strong perceptual similarity of notes an octave apart, which is possibly related to the neural mechanisms of pitch processing.

3   A *melody* is a sequence of notes over time. Notes for a melody are usually chosen from a particular *musical scale* – a subset of the total available notes. Notes within a scale have different degrees of stability, determined by their relation to the *tonic* note in the scale. Tension and resolution can be produced in melodies by moving between unstable and stable notes. The *melodic contour*, the overall shape of the melody, is also very important for determining the character and musical success of the melody.

4   *Harmony* refers to the simultaneous combination of notes into chords. When the ratios between the fundamental frequencies of the notes are simple, the chord evokes a feeling of pleasantness and resolution, and the chord is said to be *consonant*. When the ratios are more complex, the chord evokes a feeling of unpleasantness and tension, and the chord is said to be *dissonant*. Recent research suggests that the perception of consonance may be dependent on the similarity of the combination of notes to a single harmonic series.

5   Musical events such as notes or percussive sounds are usually organized into temporal patterns. *Tempo* refers to the rate of musical beats, *rhythm* refers to the repeating pattern of relative time intervals between the onsets of musical events, and *meter* refers to the grouping of beats into bars or other structures based on stressed beats. Our perception of, and preferences for, particular temporal patterns may be strongly linked to body movements, such as walking, and also to the prosodic rhythms of our native language.

6   The perception of music is strongly dependent on the gestalt principle of *figure and ground*, with our attention being drawn to the main melody line while the accompaniment forms a background. Our analysis of a complex musical scene depends on sequential grouping cues, most importantly *fundamental frequency*, *spectrum*, and *spatial location*. When we can see the performer, grouping is also influenced by visual cues.

7   Cultural experience plays a very important role in shaping our musical preferences and our perception of musical performances. Over our lifetimes, we learn a *musical grammar*, partly specific to our culture, which affects our interpretation of, and emotional reaction to, a musical piece.

8   Despite the differences between cultures, there are also similarities. It is clear
     that music, like speech, is a universal phenomenon for humans, found in
     all cultures and societies. It has been suggested that aspects of our music
     behavior may be genetically determined, although the evidence for this is
     inconclusive.

12.9   READING

An excellent overview is provided by:

Dowling, W. J. (2010). Music perception. In C. J. Plack (Ed.), *Hearing* (pp. 231–248).
    Oxford: Oxford University Press.

The following book is clear and engaging, and was my main resource when
writing the chapter:

Tan, S.-L., Pfordresher, P., & Harré, R. (2010). *The psychology of music: From sound to significance*.
    New York: Psychology Press.

Also, for detailed and extensive coverage:

Deutsch, D. (Ed.). (2012). *The psychology of music* (3rd ed.). San Diego: Academic Press. For
    a discussion of tonal structures in music:
Bigand, E., & Tillmann, B. (2005). Effect of context on the perception of pitch structures.
    In C. J. Plack, A. J. Oxenham, A. N. Popper, & R. R. Fay (Eds.), *Pitch: Neural coding and per-
    ception* (pp. 306–352). New York: Springer-Verlag.

For a discussion of the evolutionary origins of music:

Huron, D. (2001). Is music an evolutionary adaptation? *Annals of the New York Academy of
    Science, 930,* 43–61.

13 HEARING IMPAIRMENT

Hearing impairment is the most common physical disability in the West and one of the most significant public health burdens. About one in six adults in the United States report having a hearing loss. This is expected to rise to about one in five over the next two decades as the average age of the population increases, since hearing impairment is highly prevalent in the elderly.

Speech is the main means of human communication, particularly important at social events and in the classroom. Unfortunately, hearing impairment is often most troublesome in environments in which there is background noise, for example, at a social gathering. Sufferers tend to feel uncomfortable at such events, as they find it hard to communicate easily. They feel embarrassed asking people to repeat what they just said or to speak up. A consequence is that people with hearing impairment often avoid such events and become socially isolated. Noise levels in the classroom can be very high indeed (often compounded by poor architectural design), and children with hearing loss can struggle to understand what the teacher is saying and to interact with their peers to enhance learning. Learning outcomes for children with hearing loss are worse than for children with normal hearing, and this is a major waste of human resource.

Although this chapter will provide an overview of the different types of hearing impairment, the focus will be on hearing loss due to damage or dysfunction of the cochlea, as this is the most common cause of hearing impairment. I will describe the physiological bases of hearing impairment and the relations between the physiological disorders and perception. I will also provide an overview of the techniques that can be used to diagnose hearing loss and the options that are available to correct for hearing loss (albeit to a limited extent).

13.1 WHAT IS HEARING IMPAIRMENT?

Hearing impairment can be defined broadly as an impaired ability to perceive sounds compared to the ability of a normally hearing person. However, *clinical* hearing loss has a stricter definition, one used by most audiologists (the health care professionals specializing in hearing and balance disorders). The clinical definition relates to the absolute threshold for detecting pure tones at different frequencies. If absolute thresholds are abnormally high, in other words, if the person cannot hear some quiet sounds that a normally hearing person would be able to hear, they are said to have a hearing loss.

13.1.1   The audiogram

An *audiogram* is a plot of hearing threshold (the smallest detectable sound level) against frequency for pure tones. Threshold is usually measured in dB HL ("hearing level"), with 0 dB HL defined as no hearing loss. In other words, hearing threshold is expressed *relative to* the expected threshold for someone with no hearing loss: If someone has an absolute threshold of 0 dB HL at all frequencies, they have no hearing loss. Thresholds higher than 0 dB HL indicate hearing loss. The audiogram is usually plotted with increasing hearing loss in the downward direction (i.e., in the reverse direction to the absolute threshold curve shown in Figure 6.1). Normal hearing is indicated by a horizontal line at 0 dB HL. Example audiograms are shown in Figure 13.1.

Hearing loss is often described in terms of defined ranges of threshold elevation; for example, *slight* (16–25 dB HL), *mild* (26–40 dB HL), *moderate* (41–55 dB HL), *moderately severe* (56–70 dB HL), *severe* (71–90 dB HL), and *profound* (above 91 dB HL; Clark, 1981). These terms can be used for each frequency tested. However, it is common to quantify the overall hearing loss by averaging the loss (in dB HL) at frequencies of 500, 1000, and 2000 Hz. This is known as a *pure-tone average* (PTA) hearing loss. For example, someone with a threshold of 40 dB HL at 500 Hz, 50 dB HL at 1000 Hz, and 60 dB HL at 2000 Hz has a moderate loss (PTA = 50 dB HL). Examples of different severities of loss from normal to severe are shown in Figure 13.1.

Hearing loss can also be described as *unilateral* or *bilateral* depending on whether one or both ears are affected, and *symmetrical* (in which the severity and pattern of hearing loss across frequency is similar in the two ears) or *asymmetrical* (in which the severity and pattern of hearing loss across frequency is different in the two ears). So, for the example shown in Figure 13.1 (right panel), the patient has an asymmetrical hearing loss at high frequencies, moderate in the left ear, and severe in the right ear.

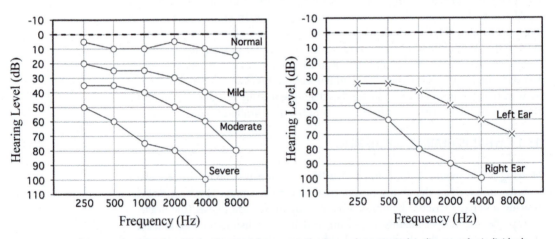

Figure 13.1 Audiograms plotted as hearing level against frequency. The figure shows typical audiograms for individuals with different degrees of hearing loss, from within the normal range to severe (left panel). Also shown are audiograms for the left and right ears of an individual with an asymmetrical loss (right panel). In each case, the horizontal dashed line shows the normal-hearing reference (0 dB HL).

13.1.2 Clinical and subclinical loss

The distinction between the broad definition of hearing impairment and the clinical definition is important. Someone with hearing loss might have a difficulty hearing quiet sounds at particular frequencies, and this is often associated with difficulties in processing sounds above hearing threshold, such as detecting speech in noise. However, it is also the case that someone might have difficulties with some sorts of sound discriminations while having a normal audiogram. That person would be described as having clinically normal hearing, but they would still experience a hearing impairment. Impaired perception of sound with a normal audiogram is sometimes called *subclinical* hearing loss, and this is currently a hot topic in research, as I describe in Section 13.3.5.

13.1.3 What does "deaf" mean?

The term "hearing impaired" is a bit of a mouthful. Wouldn't it be easier just to use the common word "deaf"? While "hearing impaired" is a clear, inclusive description that covers everything from mild loss to total inability to hear, the meaning of "deaf" is a bit more slippery. Sometimes it is used to cover all degrees of hearing loss; in other cases, it might be used only to describe someone who has very little or no hearing ability. So someone might say that she is "a bit deaf" in her left ear, meaning that she has a hearing loss but is not yet profoundly impaired. Clinically, it is usual to describe someone as being hearing impaired if the loss is partial and to use the term "deaf" only if the loss is profound.

13.2 TYPES OF HEARING IMPAIRMENT

13.2.1 Conductive hearing loss

Conductive hearing loss, as the name suggests, refers to hearing loss caused by a problem with the conduction of pressure variations (sound waves) from the outer ear to the cochlea. Problems with conduction can occur at several places. The ear canal may become blocked, for example, due to build-up of earwax or foreign objects (small toys sometimes find their way into the ear canals of young children). The eardrum may be perforated, for example, due to trauma or rapid changes in pressure between outer and middle ear (scuba diving is a common culprit). Also, fluid build-up in the middle ear may disrupt the normal vibration of the eardrum and ossicles. *Otitis media* means inflammation of the middle ear, usually caused by infection, and is a common cause of temporary hearing loss in children. Inflammation is associated with fluid build-up, leading to a conductive loss. Fluid may also build up in the middle ear because the Eustachian tube (see Section 4.1.2) is partially blocked, preventing the normal draining of fluid. The lining of the Eustachian tube can swell in response to allergies, irritants, and respiratory infections such as colds. Fluid build-up is itself one of the main causes of infection, as bacteria become trapped in the middle ear. All of these causes can lead to a reduction in the efficiency of sound transmission to the cochlea, and hence increased absolute threshold. However, the effects are akin to turning down the volume on an amplifier. As the cochlea and the auditory nervous system are not affected directly, the processing of sounds is unaffected.

13.2.2   Sensorineural hearing loss

Sensorineural hearing loss is hearing loss that arises from dysfunction of the cochlea, the auditory nerve, or the auditory pathways in the brain. Sensorineural hearing loss is the most common type of hearing loss and is particularly prevalent in the elderly. The most common underlying cause of sensorineural hearing loss is damage or dysfunction of the hair cells in the cochlea. Damage to the inner hair cells can result in a loss of sensitivity, while damage to the outer hair cells reduces sensitivity and frequency selectivity and leads to an abnormally steep growth of loudness with level. These effects are considered in more detail in Section 13.3. However, it is important not to overlook causes of hearing impairment in the auditory nervous system. Most dramatically, a tumor on the vestibular portion of the eighth cranial nerve (strictly speaking, a *vestibular schwannoma*, but also sometimes called an *acoustic neuroma*) can cause a unilateral hearing loss due to damage to the auditory portion of the nerve. Diseases of the nervous system (e.g., multiple sclerosis, in which the fatty insulating sheaths surrounding nerve fibers are damaged) can also impact on auditory neural processing. It is also becoming clear that the auditory nerve can be damaged by noise exposure and that this may have subclinical effects that have an influence on perception. This topic is explored in Section 13.3.5. These are just a few examples of neural damage that may affect hearing. Some types of dysfunction of the inner hair cells or auditory nerve can lead to deficits in temporal coding in the nerve due to a reduction in the precision of phase locking. This is called *auditory neuropathy* (Zeng & Djalilian, 2010).

A *mixed hearing loss* is simply a conductive loss in combination with a sensorineural loss. Hence, transmission of sounds to the cochlea is impaired, as well as the processing of sounds by the cochlea or the auditory nervous system.

13.2.3   Congenital hearing loss

Congenital hearing loss refers to a hearing loss that is present at birth. This may be identified during the newborn hearing screen (see Section 13.5.3). Congenital hearing loss may be conductive or sensorineural and may be caused by genetic or nongenetic factors. There are many different genes that are important for the normal function of the auditory system, and mutations that affect the normal expression of these genes can cause hearing loss. Many of these mutations have a wide range of effects on health beyond hearing. Nongenetic factors that can cause congenital hearing loss include maternal infection and trauma during birth.

13.3   COCHLEAR HEARING LOSS

13.3.1   Physiological bases and causes

Cochlear hearing loss is the most common form of hearing impairment, particularly prevalent in the elderly, and is mainly associated with damage or dysfunction of the inner or outer hair cells. The inner hair cells are responsible for converting the vibrations of the basilar membrane into neural impulses that are carried to the brain by the auditory nerve (see Chapter 4). The outer hair cells are responsible for amplifying the vibration of the basilar membrane in a frequency-specific way to increase tuning (see Chapter 5). Put simply, inner hair cell damage reduces the sensitivity of the ear to basilar membrane vibration, while outer hair cell damage reduces the amplitude and frequency selectivity of basilar membrane vibration. Both types of damage can cause an increase in hearing threshold. The main causes of hair cell damage are exposure to loud noise, ototoxic drugs (i.e., drugs that are damaging to the ear), and the progressive effects of age itself.

Noise-induced hearing loss is a common condition, due to our reckless desire to expose our ears to sound levels well beyond their design parameters. In the past, the problem was largely industrial noise. For example, the deafening automated looms in nineteenth-century cotton mills in the North of England produced severe hearing loss in the workers. Now that health and safety regulations limit the effective exposure in the workplace, one of the main problems is thought to be recreational noise. In a recent project, we measured noise levels in bars and clubs in Manchester in the United Kingdom and found average exposure to be almost 100 dB(A) (Howgate & Plack, 2011). The longer the duration of exposure, the greater is the chance of permanent damage. Any exposure greater than an average of 85 dB(A) over an 8-hour period is considered to be potentially harmful to hearing. Some rock concerts and dance clubs have levels well in excess of this. In addition, the use of high volumes in personal music players such as iPhones may be having a damaging effect on the hearing of the younger generation (Peng, Tao, & Huang, 2007). It must be said, however, that although extreme exposures (for example, firearm use without protection) are almost certainly damaging, the evidence for a link between normal recreational exposure and hearing loss is somewhat mixed (Carter, Black, Bundy, & Williams, 2014).

Excessive noise can disrupt the stereocilia of the hair cells, causing a breakup of the normal regular arrangement and damage to tip links, which can be permanent. Overstimulation of the metabolism of the hair cells can also cause damage to the cell. Noise exposure tends to affect thresholds in the frequency region to which the ear is most sensitive. However, recall that at high levels the best frequency of each place on the basilar membrane is lower than it is at low levels (Section 5.2.1). In other words, an intense tone at, say, 4000 Hz might have its greatest effect on a region of the cochlea tuned to 6000 Hz at low levels. This means that noise damage has the greatest effect on threshold at frequencies slightly higher than the most sensitive portion of the absolute threshold curve, with most damage occurring between about 4000 and 6000 Hz. This produces a characteristic "notch" in the audiogram at these frequencies (Figure 13.2, left). As we will see in Section 13.3.6, thresholds often return to normal after a recovery period, but the damage can be permanent and accumulates with repeated exposure, which is one reason why hearing loss is found to increase with age.

Drugs that are harmful to hearing include many commonly prescribed medications, for example, aminoglycoside antibiotics, platinum-containing chemotherapy drugs, loop diuretics, and nonsteroidal anti-inflammatory drugs (Zeng & Djalilian, 2010). Even aspirin, the seemingly innocuous hangover cure,

Figure 13.2 Audiograms for an individual with a noise-induced hearing loss (left panel) and for an individual with Ménière's disease (right panel).

can cause hearing loss if taken at the maximum recommended dosage, although the effects are usually temporary.

Presbycusis is a general term used to describe sensorineural hearing loss due to aging. Such hearing loss is usually greatest at high frequencies. A survey in the United Kingdom revealed that 81% of people in the age range 71–80 years had an average hearing loss between 4000 and 8000 Hz greater than 40 dB (Davis, 1995). Age-related hearing loss is characterized by a steeply sloped audiogram, with higher thresholds at high frequencies. Above the age of about 60, low-frequency thresholds also tend to increase (Morrell, Gordon-Salant, Pearson, Brant, & Fozard, 1996). The "mild" and "moderate" audiograms in Figure 13.1 (left panel) are typical for individuals with presbycusis.

For those who have experienced high levels of noise exposure over the lifetime, high-frequency loss may be caused mainly by the damage or loss of hair cells at the basal end of the basilar membrane, with damage being greater for the outer hair cells than for the inner hair cells (Schmiedt, 2010). However, another cause of presbycusis is a reduction in the electric potential of the endolymph fluid in the scala media (the *endocochlear potential*; Section 4.2.1). The *stria vascularis* is a structure on the lateral wall of the cochlea that pumps potassium ions into the scala media. The ability of the stria vascularis to maintain the endocochlear potential in this way is thought to decline in old age (Schmiedt, 2010). This is broadly analogous to a car's battery slowly dying and becoming less effective as it gets older. Recall from Chapter 4 that the transduction process depends on the flow of positively charged potassium ions from the scala media into the hair cells. If the electric potential and potassium concentration of the endolymph are reduced, the driving force that pushes potassium ions into the hair cells becomes weaker, and sensitivity decreases. A reduction in the endocochlear potential affects sensitivity at all frequencies but has the largest effects at high frequencies.

Some diseases can cause cochlear hearing loss, for example, autoimmune disorders and (in extreme cases) diabetes. Ménière's disease is a disorder of the inner ear affecting hearing and balance. Ménière's disease is associated with vertigo, hearing loss, and tinnitus. Ménière's disease may be caused by excessive pressure due to an excess of endolymph. The pressure interferes with the normal transduction process and can damage the tissues in the inner ear. Ménière's disease is associated with a hearing loss at low frequencies (Figure 13.2, right panel).

13.3.2   Characteristics of cochlear hearing loss

Damage to the inner hair cells results in a loss of sensitivity to sounds, increasing the absolute threshold for sounds in the affected frequency region of the cochlea. The effects of outer hair cell dysfunction are more complex. Remember from Chapter 5 that the outer hair cells are not involved directly in the transduction process. Instead, they provide a level- and frequency-selective amplification of the vibration of the basilar membrane (the *active mechanism*). By amplifying the basilar membrane response to low-level sounds by about 50 dB, outer hair cells improve our sensitivity (and reduce the absolute threshold) for sounds by about 50 dB. The amplification is greatest at low levels and decreases to zero for levels above about 90 dB SPL. This gives rise to the shallow growth of loudness with level, so a 10 dB increase in level (a factor of 10 in intensity) causes only a doubling in loudness (see Section 6.2.3). Finally, outer hair cells in the basal regions of the cochlea amplify sounds on a frequency-selective basis at each place on the basilar membrane, so only frequencies close to the characteristic frequency of each place receive amplification. This greatly enhances the sharpness of tuning of each place on the basilar membrane (see Section 5.2.5).

How would we expect a loss of outer hair cell function to affect the perception of sounds? Well, first we'd expect a loss of sensitivity due to loss of amplification of low-level sounds. We'd also expect the rate of growth of loudness with level to increase, since the basilar membrane vibration to low-level sounds would be reduced by outer hair cell damage, but the response to high-level sounds would be unaffected (since the response to high-level sounds is not affected by outer hair cells even in healthy ears). Finally, we would expect a reduction in *frequency selectivity*: The ability of the ear to separate out the different frequency components of sounds. We will examine each of these in turn.

13.3.2.1   Loss of sensitivity
Damage to inner or outer hair cells can result in a loss of sensitivity to quiet sounds. This will show up as a threshold elevation on the audiogram. Typically, high frequencies are affected first, leading to a sloping audiogram (see Figure 13.1). A *dead region* is a region of the cochlea in which there are no (or very few) functioning inner hair cells or auditory nerve fibers. Effectively, the vibration of the basilar membrane in a dead region is not transmitted to the brain. However, it may still be possible to detect sounds with frequencies within the range of characteristic frequencies covered by the dead region. This is because, provided the sound level is sufficiently high, the vibration of the basilar membrane will spread to regions of the cochlea outside the dead region, in which there are functioning hair cells and nerve fibers (Figure 13.6, left panel). Hence, the audiogram cannot be used reliably to diagnose the presence of dead regions, and instead a specialist test is used (see Section 13.5.4).

13.3.2.2   Loudness recruitment

Damage to the outer hair cells results in an abnormally rapid growth in loudness with level, called *loudness recruitment*. This can be measured using loudness estimation techniques, in which participants are required to give a number or category judgment based on their perception of the loudness of a sound. Figure 13.3 shows the growth in loudness with level for a listener with a cochlear hearing loss. The normal loudness growth function is also illustrated. Notice how the normal and impaired growth functions meet at the highest level tested. In other words, for this individual, a 1000 Hz tone at about 85 dB SPL would be just as loud as for a listener with normal hearing.

Loudness recruitment arises because of the change in the slope of the response function of the basilar membrane with damage to the outer hair cells. In effect, the nonlinearity provided by the active mechanism is reduced, and the basilar membrane response becomes more *linear*, completely linear in the case of complete outer hair cell loss. We saw this in Chapter 5 when we looked at the effects of outer hair cell loss on direct measures of the basilar membrane response. Figure 5.5 shows the response of the basilar membrane of a chinchilla both before and after the animal died. Before death, the response function is shallow (*compressive*), reflecting the amplification of low-level sounds by the outer

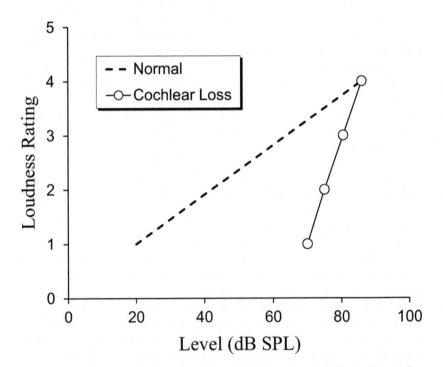

Figure 13.3 Loudness as a function of sound level at 1000 Hz for an individual with a 40-dB cochlear hearing loss at this frequency. The normal loudness growth function is shown by the dashed line. The figure illustrates the reduction in loudness at medium levels, and the rapid growth in loudness with level (loudness recruitment), for an ear with cochlear loss compared to a normal ear. Data are from Moore, Johnson, Clark, and Pluvinage (1992).

hair cells (see Figure 5.6). Outer hair cells require a supply of oxygen and other nutrients to function. After death, the response function is much steeper and linear, reflecting the passive response of the basilar membrane in the absence of outer hair cell activity. The dead chinchilla can be regarded in this respect as an "animal model" of the effects of complete loss of outer hair cell function.

13.3.2.3 Reduction in frequency selectivity

Damage to outer hair cells also results in a reduction in frequency selectivity. In other words, the damaged cochlea has a reduced ability to separate out the different frequency components of sounds. The effects on frequency selectivity can be measured using the masking techniques described in Chapter 5, in partic- ular, psychophysical tuning curves and the notched noise technique. Figure 13.4 shows a comparison between psychophysical tuning curves measured from the normal and impaired ears of a single listener with a unilateral cochlear hearing loss. Notice how the tuning curve in the impaired ear is much broader than in the normal ear. Measured using the notched-noise technique, auditory filter equivalent rectangular bandwidths (see Section 5.4.3) can be over four times larger for listeners with a moderately severe cochlear hearing loss compared to normal-hearing listeners (Moore, Vickers, Plack, & Oxenham, 1999).

The outer hair cells are responsible for the nonlinear basilar membrane response of the healthy ear. Hence, other effects of damage to the outer hair

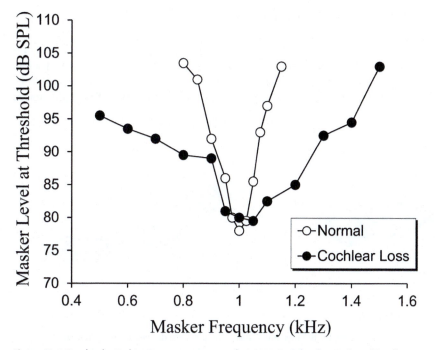

Figure 13.4 Psychophysical tuning curves measured at 1000 Hz using forward masking for the normal and impaired ears of a listener with unilateral cochlear hearing loss. The tuning curve is much broader (less frequency selectivity) in the impaired ear. Data are from Moore and Glasberg (1986).

cells include a reduction in suppression and distortion. Damage to the inner or outer hair cells also implies that the efferent feedback loop described in Section 5.2.5.1 will not operate normally. If there is a reduced signal from the cochlea due to loss of sensitivity, then the strength of the efferent signal will also be reduced. Furthermore, if the amplification of the outer hair cells is already reduced due to damage, then the effect of outer hair cell inhibition by the efferent pathway will be less.

Using computational modeling, we can simulate the effects of a reduction in sensitivity, abnormal loudness growth, and a reduction in frequency selectivity on the neural representation of everyday sounds such as speech. Figure 13.5 shows two *spectro-temporal excitation patterns* for the utterance "baa." Recall that these patterns are generated using a sophisticated model of processing on the basilar membrane, followed by temporal smoothing by the temporal window (Section 8.1.5). The left panel of Figure 13.5 shows the normal representation, with no hearing loss. The right panel shows a simulation of the effects of outer hair cells loss in the base of the cochlea (high center frequencies). There are two obvious effects of the loss. First, the excitation at high center frequencies is reduced because of the loss of amplification by the outer hair cells. Second, the resolution of the third formant of the "aa" sound is much reduced, so a clear peak becomes a shallow hump. This is a consequence of the reduction in frequency selectivity and shows that the formant would be less easily identified for a listener with cochlear hearing loss.

13.3.3   Effects on pitch perception

In Section 7.2.1, I describe how the frequency of pure tones could be represented by a *place code*, based on the excitation pattern in the cochlea, or by a *temporal code*, based on neural phase locking. We would expect the place code to be disrupted in listeners with cochlear hearing loss on account of the reduction in

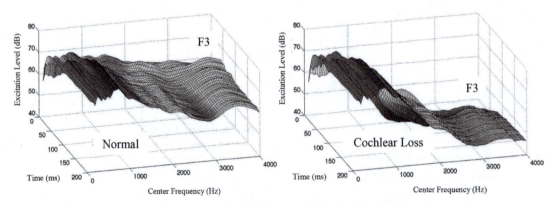

Figure 13.5 Spectro-temporal excitation patterns for the utterance "baa." The plots are derived from a model that simulates the internal neural representation of the sound for an ear with normal hearing (left panel) and for an ear with outer hair cell loss in the base of the cochlea (right panel). The representation of the third formant (F3) is indicated on the plots. The figure illustrates the reduction in sensitivity and frequency selectivity that are both a consequence of cochlear damage.

frequency selectivity. Indeed, listeners with cochlear hearing loss generally show higher frequency discrimination thresholds for pure tones (Moore & Carlyon, 2005). Importantly, however, there seems to be a poor correlation between measures of frequency discrimination for pure tones and measures of frequency selectivity, such as psychophysical tuning curves (Tyler, Wood, & Fernandes, 1983). This is not consistent with an explanation based on a place code.

A complication here is that aspects of the aging process, distinct from the loss of sensitivity, may have an effect on the representation of pitch. Aging is associated with a reduction in the precision of neural phase locking and the neural representation of the temporal fine structure (see Section 4.4.4) of sounds (Hopkins & Moore, 2011). We have shown that pure-tone frequency discrimination thresholds correlated independently with the precision of neural phase locking measured using an electrophysiological technique, which deteriorated with increasing age, and auditory sensitivity measured by hearing thresholds (Marmel, Linley, Plack, Carlyon, & Gockel, 2013). It is possible that, for older hearing-impaired listeners, the deterioration in frequency discrimination is a result of both a deficit in temporal coding and a decrease in frequency selectivity. There is also evidence that the reduction of neural temporal coding with age degrades the perception of musical harmony (Bones & Plack, 2015).

Cochlear hearing loss is sometimes associated with a shift in the pitch of pure tones. For example, listeners with a unilateral or asymmetrical hearing loss will tend to perceive different pitches in the two ears, a phenomenon called diplacusis. Often, the pitch is shifted upward in the impaired ear (Moore & Carlyon, 2005). Diplacusis may result from outer hair cell damage. Loss of the active mechanism will mean that each place on the basilar membrane will be tuned to a lower frequency than normal (see Section 5.2.1 and Figure 5.1). Hence, a tone with a given frequency will maximally excite a more basal region of the basilar membrane than normal. Since more basal sites represent higher frequencies in the normal ear, a place coding explanation of pitch predicts higher pitches in the impaired ear. However, there are substantial individual differences in the pitch shifts observed. There are also other pitch abnormalities in listeners with cochlear loss that cannot be explained easily by place coding, such as abnormally large shifts in pitch with increasing sound level (Burns & Turner, 1986).

If the frequency of a pure tone is well within a dead region, its pitch tends to be abnormal or unclear (Huss & Moore, 2005). In one case reported by Huss and Moore, a unilaterally impaired listener had only a narrow surviving region between 3000 and 4000 Hz in the impaired ear (i.e., all the other frequency regions were "dead"). This listener pitch matched a 500 Hz tone in the bad ear to a 3750 Hz tone in the better ear! These results suggest that an abnormal place-based, or tonotopic, representation of frequency in the auditory system can have a strong effect on pitch.

Listeners with cochlear hearing loss also tend to have higher fundamental frequency discrimination thresholds for complex tones compared to young normal-hearing listeners (Moore & Carlyon, 2005). A reduction in frequency selectivity leads to reduced harmonic resolution (see Section 7.2.2). Hence, low-numbered harmonics that would normally be resolved may be unresolved for the impaired ear. Since complex tones containing just unresolved harmonics produce high discrimination thresholds for normal-hearing listeners, it might be expected that there would be an effect of cochlear hearing loss on pitch discrimination. However, just as with pure tones, the picture is not simple: There is only a weak correlation between fundamental frequency discrimination and frequency selectivity, and there is evidence for a deterioration in fundamental frequency discrimination with age even for listeners with near-normal hearing (Moore & Peters, 1992). As with pure tones, the pitch discrimination results for complex tones may reflect deficits in both place coding and temporal coding.

13.3.4   Effects on speech perception

The perceptual deficits we can observe for esoteric laboratory stimuli are revealing. But what are the effects of cochlear hearing loss on the perception of stimuli that are most important to individuals in their everyday lives, most significantly, speech stimuli? Clearly, if the loss of sensitivity due to cochlear damage is such that some parts of the speech signal are simply inaudible, then this may have an impact on the ability to understand an utterance (Moore, 2007). Since high-frequency hearing is usually most affected, perception of phonemes containing high-frequency energy, such as the fricatives (e.g., /s/), will be affected more than perception of vowels, for which the main formant information is in lower frequency regions.

In addition, speech perception relies on spectral processing, for example, to identify the formant peaks in the spectrum that identify vowel sounds (see Chapter 11). A reduction in frequency selectivity will tend to "blur" the spectrum, resulting in less resolution of the formants (see Figure 13.5). The effects of a reduction in frequency selectivity on speech perception are hard to measure in quiet, as the speech signal is highly redundant (see Section 11.3.1), and there is usually more than sufficient information in even the blurred spectral representation of a damaged cochlea. However, it is a different story when speech recognition is measured in a background noise. Frequency selectivity helps us to *separate out* the speech components from the noise components, and a reduction in frequency selectivity can have a big effect on performance in noisy environments. Recall from Section 11.3.1 the study by Baer and Moore (1993) that used signal processing to smooth the spectrum of speech stimuli to simulate the effects of a reduction in frequency selectivity. They presented their stimuli to normal-hearing listeners so that they could investigate the effects of a reduction in frequency resolution without a reduction in sensitivity or abnormal loudness growth (deficits that would have been confounds if they had tested hearing-impaired listeners). They observed that spectral smoothing had a small effect on speech identification in quiet but had a large effect on performance in background noise at low signal-to-noise ratios. Hence, good frequency selectivity seems to be important when listening to speech in background noise.

It is no surprise that hearing-impaired individuals often report great difficulty in identifying speech in noisy environments, such as at a party or in a noisy restaurant, or even when having a conversation while a TV is on in the background. These are confirmed by laboratory studies of speech perception in background noise and with competing talkers, in which listeners with cochlear hearing loss generally perform much worse than do listeners with normal hearing (Moore, 2007). Unfortunately, even the best hearing aids cannot compensate for the loss of frequency selectivity. Even when they use a hearing aid, hearing-impaired individuals often feel awkward, and socially isolated, due to an inability to communicate easily in social situations. This can have a catastrophic effect on the quality of life for these individuals.

13.3.5   Damage to the auditory nerve and subclinical hearing loss

Recent experiments have provided somewhat alarming evidence that noise exposure may do more than just damage the hair cells. In a seminal study (Kujawa & Liberman, 2009), mice were exposed to a 100 dB SPL noise for two hours, a relatively low exposure compared to some rock concerts. The absolute sensitivity of their hearing was tested using electrophysiological techniques and found to have returned to almost normal after two weeks. There was also no loss of inner or outer hair cells. However, when the mice were dissected and their cochleae examined using advanced microscopy, it was found that they had lost over half of the synapses between inner hair cells and auditory nerve fibers at some frequencies! This disorder is called *cochlear synaptopathy*. It is thought that prolonged high-level release of the neurotransmitter glutamate by the inner hair cells during the noise exposure had damaged the postsynaptic neurons, causing a loss of synapses. Over the year following exposure, at least some of the disconnected nerve fibers degenerate, although some synapses may repair. Subsequent research in guinea pigs (Furman, Kujawa, & Liberman, 2013) suggests that the fibers damaged by noise exposure are mainly the type with low spontaneous rates and high thresholds (see Section 4.4.2), rather than those with high spontaneous rates and low thresholds which that may be responsible for the detection of low-level sounds.

An important and disturbing implication of these findings is that the human auditory system may accumulate substantial damage due to noise exposure, *without affecting the audiogram*. Such a hearing loss has been described as *subclinical* or "hidden" (Schaette & McAlpine, 2011). In other words, a person might have clinically normal hearing and pass the usual audiometric screening, while suffering from a massive reduction in effective neural transmission from the cochlea to the brainstem. However, at the time of writing, the evidence for cochlear synaptopathy in humans with normal audiograms is somewhat mixed. Some studies suggest an effect of noise exposure history on electrophysiological measures of auditory nerve activity (e.g. Bramhall, Konrad-Martin, McMillan, & Griest, 2017), while others show no effect (e.g. Prendergast, Guest et al., 2017). It is possible that human ears are "tougher" than rodent ears, and that they develop synaptopathy only at very high noise levels – high enough to also produce hair cell damage that shows up in the audiogram. Noise exposure aside, there is histological evidence from mice and humans that aging is associated with loss of synapses and nerve fibers (Viana et al., 2015).

What effects might nerve fiber loss have on hearing ability? Well, clearly we don't need all our nerve fibers to have good sensitivity to quiet sounds. This is not too surprising, as we probably just need a few fibers responding to a sound for the brain to register that a sound has occurred. Instead, we might expect to see a problem in the processing of complex sounds at sound levels above absolute threshold. For these tasks, the more information that is passed up the auditory nerve, the better. So losing a large proportion of your auditory nerve fibers may be expected to affect complex discrimination tasks, such as the vital one of identifying speech in background noise. However, recent studies have found no effect of lifetime noise exposure on speech in noise identification, or other behavioral tasks, for listeners with normal audiograms (e.g. Prendergast, Millman et al., 2017). It may be that such listeners just haven't lost enough fibers to affect performance substantially. Theoretical analyses suggest that losing even a half of nerve fibers might result in only a marginal decrease in discrimination performance, too small to be measured reliably (Oxenham, 2016).

One aspect of hearing that may be particularly affected by synaptopathy is the representation of precise temporal information in the auditory nerve. Loss of fibers may reduce the overall precision of phase locking, which relies on combining information from different fibers (see Section 4.4.4). However, again, the evidence for a connection between noise exposure, synaptopathy, and temporal coding is mixed at present (Prendergast, Millman et al., 2017).

As described in Section 13.3.3, the aging process itself may cause a deterioration in neural temporal coding. This could be due to a combination of cochlear synaptopathy, dysfunction of auditory nerve fibers, and dysfunction of neurons in the central auditory pathways. In particular, myelin, the insulating sheath that surrounds neurons in the auditory nerve and the central auditory system and greatly increases the speed of transmission of action potentials, deteriorates with age. The resulting differences in conduction speed across neurons could lead to a loss of synchronization and an impairment in temporal coding (Peters, 2002). There is evidence that the deficits in neural synchronization associated with age may affect pitch perception and sound localization, which rely on precise coding of the temporal fine structure of sounds (Hopkins & Moore, 2011).

Subclinical hearing loss may also arise from selective inner hair cell dysfunction. As with loss of synapses, loss of a substantial proportion of functioning inner hair cells may not have much effect on the audiogram but could affect sound discrimination. In a study in mice, Schrott, Stephan, and Spoendlin (1989) showed that 70% of inner hair cells could be lost with only moderate threshold elevation, provided that the loss in hair cells was evenly spread across the cochlea.

Taken together, these findings suggest that, in the future, audiologists may have to look beyond the audiogram to identify damage to the auditory system. In particular, electrophysiological tests may be useful to identify neural dysfunction (see Section 13.5.2).

13.3.6   Temporary cochlear hearing loss

Given the discussion on subclinical loss in the previous section, it is questionable whether any damage to the auditory system is completely reversible. However, noise-induced hearing loss as characterized by the audiogram often recovers completely a few hours, days, and sometimes weeks after exposure. "Temporary threshold shift" is the term used to describe a temporary elevation in hearing threshold after exposure to loud noise. Immediately after exposure, thresholds may be elevated considerably, sometimes by as much as 40 dB. However, thresholds often return to normal after a recovery time. As with permanent noise-induced hearing loss, temporary threshold shifts after exposure to a broadband noise tend be greatest between about 4000 and 6000 Hz. Noise-induced tem-porary threshold shifts may be largely caused by damage to the outer hair cells (Howgate & Plack, 2011).

13.4 TINNITUS AND HYPERACUSIS

13.4.1 Tinnitus

Tinnitus is defined as the perception of a sound in the absence of an external sound. The internally generated sensation is often perceived as a high-frequency hiss or whistle, which is more audible when environmental noise levels are low (e.g., at night). Most of us have experienced *temporary* tinnitus, perhaps due to listening to loud music. However, for about 5–15% of people, particularly the elderly, the tinnitus sensation is *constant*. For about 1–3% of people, tinnitus can be a serious condition, leading to sleepless nights and communication problems, dramatically reducing quality of life (Eggermont & Roberts, 2004). There is a big drive at the moment to find ways to mitigate the effects of tinnitus, although a real cure may be a long way off.

Tinnitus is most commonly associated with cochlear hearing loss due to noise exposure or aging, and the perceived frequency of the tinnitus corresponds to the frequency region of the loss. Tinnitus can also be associated with conduc-tive hearing loss. However, the correlation with hearing loss is far from perfect. Some people with *clinically normal hearing* have tinnitus, possibly as a consequence of exposure to loud sounds (Guest, Munro, Prendergast, Howe, & Plack, 2017). Conversely, some listeners with a clinical hearing loss do not have significant tinnitus. It has been suggested that tinnitus is sometimes caused by auditory nerve damage after noise exposure, such as that which may underlie one type of subclinical hearing loss (see Section 13.3.5). This would explain why some lis-teners with clinically normal hearing have tinnitus (Schaette & McAlpine, 2011), although the evidence for this is mixed at present (Guest et al., 2017).

Because tinnitus is subjective, it is hard to measure, and this creates problems for researchers trying to determine its physiological basis. It is clear that tinnitus is a consequence of abnormal neural activity of some kind. One hypothesis is that hair cell loss, or the loss of auditory nerve fibers, reduces the strength of the signal traveling to the brainstem. Auditory neurons in the brainstem compensate by effectively increasing the amplification of the signal from the auditory nerve (Norena, 2011; Schaette & Kempter, 2006). Unfortunately, the increase in *central gain* has the unwanted side effect of increasing the level of spontaneous neural activity, and the abnormally high levels of "neural noise" lead to the perception of a sound. However, tinnitus is a complex phenomenon and may also result from other forms of neural reorganization (Eggermont & Roberts, 2004).

13.4.2 Hyperacusis

Hyperacusis is a diminished tolerance of sounds, which may seem uncomfort-ably loud even at moderate levels. Like tinnitus, hyperacusis is associated with noise damage, and the two often co-occur (Baguley, 2003), which suggests that there may be a common mechanism underlying both disorders. Like tinnitus, hyperacusis may be a consequence of *neural hyperactivity* caused by an increase in central gain (Norena, 2011). A recent study used functional magnetic resonance imaging to measure brain activity in participants with clinically normal hearing, some of whom experienced tinnitus or hyperacusis. In response to a noise stimulus at 70 dB SPL, the participants with hyperacusis showed *abnormally high activity* in the auditory midbrain and thalamus. Participants with tinnitus and participants with hyperacusis *both* showed increased activation in the auditory cortex compared to participants with no tinnitus and normal sound level tolerance (Gu, Halpin, Nam, Levine, & Melcher, 2010).

13.5   DIAGNOSIS

13.5.1   Pure tone and speech audiometry

The standard test for hearing impairment is *pure-tone audiometry*, which is used to produce the audiogram. Pure-tone audiometry is also the first test we perform on new participants for our laboratory experiments to screen them for hearing loss. Ideally, the subject is seated in a sound-attenuating room, and sounds are played over headphones. The test is performed using an *audiometer*, a device that can produce pure tones at a range of frequencies and sound levels. A typical set of frequencies for the test might be 250, 500, 1000, 2000, 3000, 4000, 6000, and 8000 Hz. At each frequency, the tone is played to one ear, and the subject indicates by pressing a button if he or she can hear the sound. The sound level is adjusted up and down until a level is found at which the sound can be detected on about 50% of trials. This is taken as the threshold for that frequency. The procedure is repeated for the other ear.

To determine how much of the elevation in threshold is due to a conductive loss, stimuli can be also delivered by a bone vibrator attached to the *mastoid bone* (just behind the pinna). This bypasses the middle ear to stimulate the cochlea via bone conduction of sound. Since both cochleae will be stimulated by vibrating just one mastoid, noise can be presented over headphones to the ear not being tested to mask the signal in that ear. If the thresholds for sounds over headphones are elevated compared to the bone-conduction thresholds by an "air-bone gap" of more than 10 dB (after both have been normalized to normal hearing), this is indicative of a conductive hearing loss.

Pure-tone audiometry tells us about the sensitivity of an ear to quiet sounds, but this may not predict the impairments experienced in everyday life, in particular, a diminished ability to detect speech. To test this, *speech audiometry* can be used, for example, to determine the lowest level at which a listener can identify 50% of the two-syllable words.

13.5.2   Tympanometry, otoacoustic emissions, and electrophysiology

Several diagnostic tests reveal important information about the physiological causes of a hearing loss, without requiring a behavioral response. *Tympanometry* measures the way in which the eardrum reflects sounds. A low-frequency tone is played, and the *tympanometer* measures the amount of sound that is reflected depending on the air pressure in the ear canal, which is also controlled by the tympanometer. The technique is used to diagnose disorders of the eardrum and the middle ear, conductive losses that often change the stiffness of the middle ear and lead to abnormal sound reflection. The tympanometer can also be used to measure the *acoustic reflex*, the contraction of the stapedius muscle in response to high-level sounds, by measuring the resulting change in stiffness. Conductive, cochlear, and neural disorders may all result in abnormal reflex characteristics.

We came across *otoacoustic emissions* in Section 5.2.6. If sounds are played to the ear, then the ear may in turn emit sounds, producing a sort of echo. Remember that otoacoustic emissions are dependent on the function of the *outer hair cells*. Hence, otoacoustic emissions can be used as a clinical test of outer hair cell function. Otoacoustic emissions can be recorded using a sensitive microphone placed in the ear canal. The stimulus is either a click (to produce *transient-evoked* otoacoustic emissions) or pairs of tones (to produce *distortion product* otoacoustic emissions). Absence of emissions implies either damaged outer hair cells or a conductive loss in the middle ear.

Finally, *electrophysiological* recordings of the activity of the auditory nervous system can be made by attaching electrodes to the scalp. The *auditory brainstem response* is a recording made in response to a click or brief tone burst (see Section A.3.1). Peaks in the recording at different time delays after the stimulus reflect activity at different stages in the auditory pathway, from the auditory nerve to the inferior colliculus. Hence, in addition to being a test of middle ear and cochlear function, the auditory brainstem response can provide information on neural processing. For example, auditory neuropathy is identified by normal otoacoustic emissions (suggesting normal cochlear function), together with an absent or abnormal auditory brainstem response. Other electrophysiological recordings can probe different aspects of auditory processing, such as the response of the hair cells or of neurons in the auditory cortex.

13.5.3 Newborn hearing screening

In many countries, newborn babies are now routinely screened for hearing loss. A universal program (i.e., screening *all* babies) was implemented in some U.S. states from the 1990s and in England in 2006. Screening normally occurs within a few months of birth. It is important to identify hearing problems early so that appropriate intervention can be made (e.g., hearing aids or cochlear implants) to minimize disruption to language development. Clearly, it is difficult for very young babies to be tested using a behavioral procedure such as pure-tone audiometry – they can't be instructed to press a response button! Hence, nonbehavioral tests need to be used. The initial screen measures either transient-evoked or distortion product otoacoustic emissions to assess the function of the cochlea. The auditory brainstem response may also be used as an additional measure of hearing loss and to assess the integrity of neural processing in the brainstem.

The use of otoacoustic emissions to screen millions of babies worldwide represents the triumphant final stage in a scientific journey from the initial discovery of otoacoustic emissions by David Kemp in the 1970s to their clinical implementation in the 2000s. This story is also an important illustration of the length of time that it can take to translate basic scientific findings into important clinical benefit.

13.5.4   Testing for dead regions

As described in Section 13.3.2.1, a dead region is region of the cochlea without functioning inner hair cells or auditory nerve fibers. However, at high levels, the vibration of the basilar membrane in response to a pure tone will spread to regions of the cochlea outside the dead region, in which there are functioning hair cells and nerve fibers. Hence, it is difficult to detect the presence of a dead region using pure-tone audiometry alone. A frequency region in the audiogram with a large hearing loss may reflect a dead region, but it may also be caused by, for example, loss of outer hair cells and partial loss of inner hair cells. In order to diagnose dead regions, Brian Moore and colleagues have developed the TEN test (Moore, Glasberg, & Stone, 2004; Moore, Huss, Vickers, Glasberg, & Alcantara, 2000).

TEN stands for "threshold-equalizing noise," which is a wideband noise that is spectrally shaped to give a *constant masked threshold* for a pure tone presented in the noise for someone with normal hearing. If the frequency of the tone falls within a dead region, however, then the threshold in TEN will be *abnormally high*. Why should this be? Let's assume that, without any noise, a tone with a frequency within the dead region is detected by activity at a place in the cochlea just outside the dead region (i.e., at a place with functioning inner hair cells and auditory nerve fibers). Now, the wideband TEN has frequency components close to the characteristic frequency of the place, whereas the tone within the dead region is far removed in frequency and will produce relatively little activation at that place. Hence, when the TEN is present, the activity produced by the tone will be *strongly masked* (Figure 13.6, right panel). This means that the threshold for the

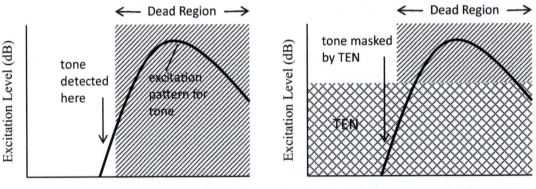

Figure 13.6 Schematic excitation patterns for a pure tone presented within a dead region (the dead region is indicated by the diagonal shading). The left panel shows the situation in quiet. In this case, due to spread of excitation along the basilar membrane, the tone can be detected at a center frequency just below the dead region (in other words, in a region of the cochlea apical to the dead region). The right panel shows the situation when TEN is added (shown by the hashed shading). Notice that the region in which the tone could be detected in quiet is now *masked by the noise*. However, for a listener without a dead region, the tone would be easily detected at the place in the cochlea tuned to the frequency of the tone (compare the excitation level at the peak of the tone's excitation pattern to the level of the noise). Based on Moore (2004).

tone will be much higher than it would be if the tone could be detected at the place in the cochlea tuned to the frequency of the tone.

13.6   MANAGEMENT OPTIONS

13.6.1   Hearing aids

A hearing aid is an electronic device that amplifies the sound delivered to the ear canal. Hearing aids can be used to manage the effects of mild to severe hearing loss. The device consists of a microphone, an electronic circuit powered by a battery, and a miniature loudspeaker. The microphone and electronic components are usually located in a small plastic case behind the ear (these devices are called *behind-the-ear* hearing aids), and the loudspeaker delivers the sound by a plastic tube from the case to the ear canal, via an individually fitted earmold. Alternatively, the loudspeaker is located in the ear canal and receives an electronic signal from the case. Another variant is the *in-the-ear* aid, in which all the components are fitted in the concha and ear canal. Although in-the-ear aids can be less visible, they are more expensive and can be damaged by a build-up of moisture in the ear.

If the patient has a conductive or mixed loss, the middle ear can be bypassed by using a hearing aid to vibrate the mastoid bone via a surgically implanted titanium post. The cochlea is stimulated via bone conduction. These devices are called *bone-anchored hearing aids*.

One problem in correcting for cochlear hearing loss arises from loudness recruitment (Section 13.3.2.2). Although a hearing-impaired listener may have a reduction in sensitivity to quiet sounds, loudness grows much more rapidly with level than is the case for a normal-hearing listener. At high levels, a sound may be as loud, or almost as loud, to the impaired listener as it would to a normal hearing listener (see Figure 13.3). If we just amplify equally across all sound levels, applying a *linear gain*, low-level sounds may be audible but high-level sounds will be much too loud (Figure 13.7, left panel)! Hence, modern hearing aids use *automatic gain control* to amplify low-level sounds more than high-level sounds (Figure 13.7, right panel). In this way, the hearing aid is partly mimicking the action of the outer hair cells in a normal ear to produce a *compressive* input-output function (see Chapter 5).

Modern hearing aids use digital electronics, providing great flexibility in the processing that can be done prior to delivering the sound to the user. In particular, sounds can be amplified and compressed independently in different frequency bands. So if you have a high-frequency loss, the amplification can be delivered just to those frequencies. Digital hearing aids also allow the parameters of the hearing aid (e.g., the amount of amplification and compression at each frequency) to be programmed by the audiologist using a computer, according to the characteristics of an individual's hearing loss (mainly based on the individual's audiogram).

Although hearing aids can restore sensitivity to quiet sounds and provide a more normal growth of loudness with level, they fail to correct for the third main characteristic of cochlear hear loss – the reduction in frequency selectivity. The problem is that, no matter how sounds are processed before they are delivered to the ear, we cannot get around the fact that two components that are close

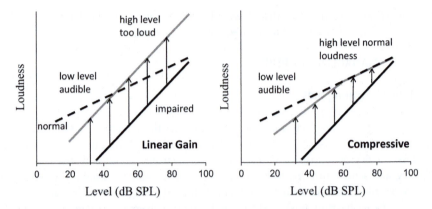

Figure 13.7 A schematic illustration of why a hearing aid with linear amplification is not a good management option for cochlear hearing loss and how compressive amplification (automatic gain control) produces a better result. On each plot, the dashed line shows loudness as a function of level for a normal ear, and the continuous black line shows loudness for an ear with cochlear loss, which exhibits a steep growth in loudness with level (loudness recruitment). The arrows show the effects of gain at each level, and the gray line shows the loudness growth function after amplification. The left panel shows the effects of linear amplification (constant gain) on the loudness function. Although low-level sounds are now more audible, high-level sounds are too loud. By providing more amplification at low levels than at high levels (right panel), a more normal loudness function can be produced.

together in frequency will not be separated out by the impaired cochlea. In a sense, the impaired cochlea is an impassable barrier to delivering normal tonotopic information to the auditory nerve. This means that even with a hearing aid, the impaired listener will have difficulty perceptually separating sounds that are played together. Hence, hearing aids are not very effective in correcting for one of the main problems experienced by hearing-impaired listeners: The inability to understand speech in noisy environments.

13.6.2 Cochlear implants

A *cochlear implant* is a surgically implanted device that provides a treatment for severe to profound hearing loss. If the normal cochlear transduction process is severely impaired, usually because of extensive damage to the hair cells, the patient may not benefit from conventional aids that just amplify the acoustic signal. Instead, the aim is to bypass the hair cells entirely and stimulate the auditory nerve directly using electrical impulses. Over 300,000 people worldwide have received cochlear implants, and the numbers are growing.

A cochlear implant is composed of a number of components. Externally, there is a *microphone* that responds to sounds, a *speech processor* that separates the signal into different frequency channels (in the same way, but with less specificity, as the normal cochlea), and a *transmitter coil*, located behind and slightly above the ear, which transmits the signal across the skin using electromagnetic induction. The signal is picked up by a *receiver* secured in bone beneath the skin, which converts the signal into electrical impulses that are carried by a cable to the cochlea. Running around the cochlea in the scala tympani is the final part of the cochlear implant: an *array of electrodes* (typically, 22 electrodes) that stimulate the auditory nerve fibers at different locations in the cochlea. Because of the frequency separation processing provided by the speech processor, each electrode receives information from a different band of frequencies in the sound. In this way, the spectrum of the sound is represented tonotopically in the auditory nerve, in the same general way as it is in normal healthy hearing.

However, the cochlear implant delivers limited information about sounds compared to that available to a normal-hearing person, for a number of reasons (Moore & Carlyon, 2005). First, the frequency selectivity for a cochlear implant is generally poor. This is not just because the low number of electrodes means that there are just a few independent frequency channels compared to arguably several hundred in normal hearing. Even if more electrodes were used, the spread of current between each electrode and the auditory nerve means that it is not possible to limit the stimulation from each electrode to a precisely defined group of neurons in the tonotopic array. Second, there is a problem called *tonotopic misalignment*. The electrode array is inserted in the basal end of the cochlea and, for most devices, does not reach far around into the apex of the cochlear spiral. This means that the full spectrum of the sound is delivered to neurons that would normally code only high frequencies. Third, the temporal information delivered by the implant is dissimilar to the normal pattern of phase locking in the healthy auditory nerve. Finally, and perhaps most significantly, if there is a period of deafness before implantation, there may be changes in the nervous system due to the lack of prior stimulation that will limit the effectiveness of the implant. For example, there will often be degeneration in the auditory nerve, which may result in dead regions in the cochlea. In addition, the central auditory nervous system may reorganize leading to an abnormal representation of stimuli in the cortex (Giraud, Price, Graham, & Frackowiak, 2001).

Disordered pitch perception is one of the main perceptual deficits experienced by implant users. Now, one might think that a regular pattern of electric pulses, directly stimulating the auditory nerve, would provide excellent temporal information for pitch (see Chapter 7). However, even discrimination of the rate of electrical impulses delivered by the device (equivalent to frequency or fundamental frequency discrimination) is much poorer for cochlear implant users than is pure-tone frequency discrimination for normally hearing listeners. Rate-discrimination thresholds range from about 2% to 18% for a baseline rate of 100 impulses per second, and thresholds become much higher at higher rates (Moore & Carlyon, 2005). Most cochlear implant users are completely unable to detect changes in rate for baseline rates above about 300 impulses per second. One possible explanation is that a match between the rate of stimulation and the normal characteristic frequencies of the neurons stimulated is necessary for good pitch perception (see Section 7.3.3). Tonotopic misalignment means that this is not usually possible for stimulation by a cochlear implant. The same problem may be why normal-hearing listeners show poor pitch discrimination for unresolved harmonics (see Figure 7.8), where the envelope repetition rate does not match the characteristic frequency of the place of stimulation.

Despite these limitations, cochlear implants usually restore good speech identification in quiet and are particularly successful for deaf infants who are implanted at a young age. Recall in Section 11.3.1 that the speech signal is highly redundant and that only a few independent frequency bands are necessary for good performance. Hence, the patient can generally get by with the limited spectral information provided by the implant, *unless there is significant background noise*, in which case performance will be poor. This is just what we saw in Section 13.3.4 for normal-hearing listeners when the spectrum of the stimulus was smoothed to simulate reduced frequency resolution (Baer & Moore, 1993). The cochlear implant also gives poor outcomes for the perception of tonal music, because the pitch information is weak (usually too poor to allow discrimination of notes a semitone apart).

13.6.3   Brainstem and midbrain implants

For a cochlear implant to work, the patient must have a functioning auditory nerve. Howver, some patients do not have an auditory nerve, sometimes because the nerve is destroyed during surgery to remove a vestibular schwannoma. To provide hearing for these patients, we have to move to the brainstem and deliver electrical stimulation to the cochlear nucleus (*auditory brainstem implant*) or to the inferior colliculus (*auditory midbrain implant*). Speech perception for brainstem and midbrain implant users is generally poor, but there are some exceptions, and the devices usually deliver sufficient information to facilitate lipreading (Schwartz, Otto, Shannon, Hitselberger, & Brackmann, 2008). The poor outcomes are perhaps not surprising, as the more neural stages that are bypassed, the less normal processing is available. We don't have a good idea what type of stimulation we should be giving to brainstem and midbrain implants, and this is an active area of research. Comparatively few patients have received these devices to date.

13.7   SUMMARY

The chapter has provided an overview of the causes, perceptual consequences, and management options for hearing impairment. Although we now have a fairly clear idea of the nature of cochlear hearing loss, the most common form of hearing impairment, we still cannot fully correct for the deficits.

1   Hearing impairment is one of the most significant public health burdens. Since speech perception is impaired, this can have a dramatic effect on quality of life, particularly for the elderly who are most affected.

2   Hearing loss is usually characterized clinically by the *audiogram*, a plot of hearing threshold against frequency. Hearing loss can be divided into *conductive*, which is a disruption in the transmission of sound from the outer ear to the cochlea, and *sensorineural*, which is due to dysfunction of the cochlea or auditory nervous system.

3   Cochlear damage is the most common cause of hearing impairment, usually resulting from dysfunction of the hair cells, in particular the *outer hair cells*.

Cochlear damage results mainly from the combined effects of *exposure to loud noises*, *ototoxic drugs*, and the progressive effects of *aging*. Cochlear hearing loss is particularly prevalent in the elderly, a condition called *presbycusis*, which is characterized by a progressive decrease in sensitivity to high-frequency sounds with increasing age.

4   Inner hair cell damage may cause a loss in sensitivity. Extensive inner hair cell loss may lead to a *dead region* in the cochlea in which information about basilar membrane vibration is not transmitted to the brain. Outer hair cell damage leads to a reduction in the active amplification of basilar membrane vibration, which results in a *loss in sensitivity*, an abnormally rapid growth in loudness with level called *loudness recruitment*, and a reduction in *frequency selectivity*.

5   Cochlear hearing loss is associated with *impaired pitch perception*, which may be a consequence of a combination of deficits in *place coding* and *temporal coding*. Importantly, cochlear hearing loss also results in *impaired speech perception*, particularly in noisy environments.

6   Recent research suggests that exposure to loud noises can cause auditory nerve degeneration without necessarily affecting sensitivity to quiet sounds. This *subclinical hearing loss* may affect neural temporal coding and complex sound discrimination.

7   *Tinnitus* is the perception of sound in the absence of external sound. Tinnitus is associated with noise-induced and age-related hearing loss but can also occur in individuals with clinically normal hearing as defined by the audiogram. Tinnitus may result from neural reorganization, in particular an increase in *central neural gain* to compensate for a peripheral dysfunction.

8   Hearing loss is usually identified using *pure-tone audiometry*, although a range of diagnostic techniques are available. These include *tympanometry* to identify conductive losses, the recording of *otoacoustic emissions* to assess outer hair cell function, and *electrophysiological techniques* to investigate neural processing.

9   Mild to severe hearing loss can be managed with *hearing aids*, which amplify the sound entering the ear canal to restore sensitivity. *Level compression* is used to restore audibility without making the sounds uncomfortably loud. However, hearing aids cannot compensate for reduced frequency selectivity, which is one of the main causes of poor speech perception in noise. Profound hearing loss can be managed with *cochlear implants*, *brainstem implants*, and *midbrain implants*, which stimulate the auditory nervous system directly.

13.8   READING

This chapter provides a terrific introduction:

Zeng, F.-G., & Djalilian, H. (2010). Hearing impairment. In C. J. Plack (Ed.), *Hearing* (pp. 325–348). Oxford: Oxford University Press.

For a wide-ranging overview of cochlear hearing loss, you can't beat:

Moore, B. C. J. (2007). *Cochlear hearing loss: Physiological, psychological, and technical issues* (2nd ed.). Chichester, UK: Wiley.

For a clinical perspective:

Bess, F. H., & Humes, L. E. (2008). *Audiology: The fundamentals* (4th ed.). Philadelphia: Lippincott Williams & Wilkins.

14 CONCLUDING REMARKS

The final chapter of this book is intended as a summary (of sorts) of the previous chapters, highlighting some of the main findings of hearing research over the last hundred years or so. There is also a little amateur philosophy of science and pointers to some of the many holes in our knowledge that future researchers will doubtless fill.

14.1 IN PRAISE OF DIVERSITY

We can investigate hearing using many different techniques. Cell biologists study the functioning of hair cells and neurons down to a molecular level. Physiologists measure basilar membrane vibration, neural activity, and other physiological functions, often in animals, although some physiological techniques can be used with human participants (e.g., electroencephalography and functional magnetic resonance imaging). Psychophysicists study the behavior of conscious human listeners to determine the relations between sounds and sensations. All these different approaches contribute to our understanding of hearing, and the snobbishness that is sometimes associated with advocates of one particular approach is misplaced. We need techniques that explore the different aspects of auditory perception to understand hearing as a whole. We also need different *levels* of explanation. We can understand the transduction process in hair cells at a very low level of explanation, which involves protein filaments and ion channels, and this knowledge has practical value, particularly in our search for the underlying causes of hearing impairment. On the other hand, although we may assume that all of our sensations are dependent on the electrical and chemical activity of cells in the brain, we may never be able to understand complex mechanisms such as auditory scene analysis in terms of the activity of individual neurons. Instead, we may have to be content with explanations of the general processes that are involved, based mostly, perhaps, on behavioral experiments. These explanations may be supported by mathematical and computational models that generate precise predictions that can be tested empirically (a requirement for a truly scientific theory).

This book aims to provide an account of human perceptions and, as such, is biased toward behavioral aspects and away from physiological aspects. However, I hope it is clear that the disciplines of psychophysics and physiology are heavily interdependent, and in many cases the techniques from the different disciplines are used to study the same mechanisms. For example, in Chapter 5, I describe how both physiological and psychophysical techniques can be used to measure frequency selectivity. The techniques are complementary. The physiological techniques provide detailed information about the response of the basilar membrane in nonhuman mammals such as the chinchilla and the guinea pig. We cannot obtain this type of information about humans, yet the psychophysical techniques can measure the effects of frequency selectivity on our *perceptions*. Taken together, the results suggest that the response of the basilar membrane determines the frequency selectivity of the whole auditory system. Similarly, Chapter 7 describes how the mechanisms of pitch perception can be illuminated using physiological recordings from neurons and psychophysical tasks such as frequency discrimination. If the goal is to understand our perceptions, then we need to know what these perceptions are before we can understand how the responses of neurons may relate to these perceptions. At the same time, we would not have a good understanding of pitch if we did not appreciate that neurons can code periodicity in terms of synchronized firing patterns (phase locking).

The different disciplines can work together to develop theories at the *same* level of explanation, as well as provide evidence appropriate to different levels of explanation. I find this an attractive aspect of research in this area, and I very much enjoy my discussions and collaborations with auditory physiologists.

14.2   WHAT WE KNOW

By way of a summary, I have tried to list below some of the most important findings described in the previous chapters. These are findings that are well established in the literature and form part of the core knowledge of auditory science. I would like to believe that most (if not all) researchers in the field would agree with these conclusions.

1   Sounds are broken down into their constituent frequency components by the basilar membrane in the cochlea. The analysis is enhanced by the action of the outer hair cells, which sharpen the tuning and lead to a compressive growth of basilar membrane velocity with respect to sound pressure.

2   The vibrations on the basilar membrane are transduced into electrical activity by the inner hair cells. The vibrations are represented in terms of the firing rates, and the phase-locked temporal firing patterns, of neurons in the auditory nerve. Information from different places along the basilar membrane travels to the brain in separate neural frequency channels.

3   Our sensation of loudness is related to the total activity of the auditory nerve. It is probably derived from a combination of the firing rates of neurons across characteristic frequency. The compressive response of the basilar membrane results in a compressive growth of loudness with sound level and provides the auditory system with a wide dynamic range.

4   Our sensation of pitch is related to the repetition rate of the sound waveform. Pitch is probably dependent, at least in part, on the phase-locked neural firing patterns, which are probably converted into a firing-rate code

in the brainstem. The low-numbered harmonics that are resolved by the cochlea are dominant in the determination of pitch.

5   The auditory system is very "fast" and can follow changes in sounds with a resolution of the order of milliseconds. The auditory system can also combine information over several hundred milliseconds in order to improve discrimination.

6   Our ability to judge where a sound is coming from relies on two main cues: interaural time differences and interaural level differences. The former are probably extracted in the medial superior olive in the brainstem, by neurons that receive input from both ears at different relative delays. The direction-specific spectral modifications of the pinna resolve ambiguities and allow us to estimate the elevation of the sound source.

7   The segregation of sounds that occur simultaneously involves the assignment of the frequency components separated by the cochlea to the different sound sources. The main cues for the segregation of simultaneous sounds are onset differences and differences in fundamental frequency or harmonicity. A sequence of sounds over time is grouped on the basis of similarity in periodicity, spectral balance, level, and location. The auditory system can restore perceptually sounds that are interrupted by other sounds.

8   Speech is identified using a number of different cues, particularly spectral peaks and temporal fluctuations that are well represented in the auditory system. Speech is very redundant, and this helps us to understand speech that is degraded or that is subject to interference from other sounds. Speech sounds are also very variable, and the brain takes account of the acoustic, visual, and semantic context before it identifies an utterance. Speech perception is therefore a combination of the bottom-up analysis of acoustic features and the top-down influence of context.

9   The perception of music is based on an underlying "musical grammar" of mathematical relations between the frequencies of notes and the timing of musical events. The grammatical rules act as partial constraints on how musical events are combined across frequency and time and determine whether certain combinations produce feelings of tension or release. However, music is very flexible, and composers often break the rules to add interest to a piece. The musical grammar we develop as individuals, and the associations between different sounds and different emotional reactions, is partly dependent on culture and experience, but there may also be genetic factors.

10 Hearing impairment can occur due to dysfunction at any stage in the auditory system, although the most common cause is damage to the hair cells in the cochlea. Damage to the inner hair cells affects sensitivity, and damage to the outer hair cells causes a reduction in sensitivity, an abnormally rapid growth in loudness with level, and a reduction in frequency selectivity. The

perceptual effects of outer hair cell damage can be understood in terms of the action of the outer hair cells on basilar membrane vibration. Hearing aids can restore sensitivity and loudness growth to some extent but cannot compensate for the reduction in frequency selectivity, which affects the ability to understand speech in background noise.

14.3   WHAT WE DON'T KNOW

The topic of this section could probably justify a volume in itself. As you may have realized from reading the other chapters in this book, our degree of certainty about auditory processes declines from the peripheral to the central auditory system. We have a reasonable understanding of the transduction process, but we are still quite vague about how the auditory brainstem and the auditory cortex work. From a psychophysical perspective, as the stimuli and the processing become more complex, it becomes harder to relate our sensations to the characteristics of the sound waves entering our ears. As Chapter 11 demonstrates, the difficulty is particularly acute with regard to high-level functions such as speech perception.

I focus on those questions that follow directly from the discussions in the book to narrow the scope a little. These are just some of the missing links that prevent me from providing an adequate explanation of many of the phenomena that characterize human hearing.

1   How and why is the activity of the outer hair cells modulated by the efferent connections from the brain?

2   How is the firing rate (or possibly firing synchrony) information from the high and low spontaneous rate fibers combined to produce the sensation of loudness? How and where does the auditory system make comparisons of level across frequency and across time?

3   How is the perception of pitch dependent on the combination of temporal and place information? How and where is the information combined across frequency, to give us the sensation of a single pitch when we listen to complex tones?

4   What limits the temporal resolution of the auditory system? What are the neural mechanisms involved in the integration of information over time?

5   How is the information from interaural time differences combined with that from interaural level differences and the modifications of the pinnae, to give us (in most cases) a unified sense of sound location?

6   What are the neural mechanisms that underlie the segregation of sounds, and how do these mechanisms interact with other auditory processes, such as those involved in pitch perception and sound localization? How do

attentional mechanisms change the representation of sounds so that we can follow a unified sequence of sounds over time?

7   How and where is the information from basic auditory processes (such as those involved in the perception of spectral shape, temporal modulation, and periodicity) combined with contextual information to determine the identity of a sound?

8   Why does music exist? In particular, does music have an evolutionary function?

9   How and why does subclinical neural damage affect our perceptions? How and why does aging affect hearing? Can hearing aids and implants be improved sufficiently to restore normal hearing?

These are just a few of the large number of fundamental questions about hearing that remain to be answered. The good news is that progress is being made, and as the reference section demonstrates, many important discoveries have been made in the last few years. As we uncover the ear's remaining secrets, I like to think that there will be a few surprises in store.

APPENDIX: RESEARCHING THE EAR

Hearing research covers a wide range of scientific disciplines. Physical acoustics tells us about the characteristics of sounds and how they propagate and interact with objects. It tells us about sound waves reaching the ear from a given sound source: about the nature of the stimulus, in other words. Physical acoustics also helps us understand how sounds are modified by structures in the ear. The biological processes involved in hearing can be studied in many ways and at different levels of detail. At a low level, cell biology tells us about the machinery of cells in the auditory system, including the special molecules that cause the unique behavior of these cells. For understanding the overall function of the auditory system, however, two disciplines dominate: psychophysics and physiology.

A.1 HUMAN PSYCHOACOUSTICS

Auditory psychophysics, or *psychoacoustics*, is the psychological or behavioral study of hearing – *behavioral* in that the participant is required to make a response to the sounds that are presented. As the name suggests, the aim of psychoacoustic research is to determine the relation between the *physical* stimuli (sounds) and the *sensations* produced in the listener. That we measure the *behavioral* responses of listeners is essentially why psychoacoustics is regarded as a branch of psychology, although many of the problems addressed by psychoacousticians have little to do with the popular conception of psychology. As we have seen throughout the book, psychoacoustic techniques can be used to study very "physiological" processes, such as the mechanical processes underlying the separation of sounds in the cochlea.

It is possible that the term "psychoacoustics" was first coined by T. W. Forbes when he described the research his team was conducting in the United States during World War II (Burris-Meyer & Mallory, 1960). A secret government project was set up to investigate, in part, the potential of acoustic weapons. To the disappointment of warmongers everywhere, the team was unable to produce anything close to an acoustic death beam, although it did develop a sound system for broadcasting propaganda from aircraft.

In a psychoacoustic experiment, paid participants are asked to make a response based on sounds that are played to them over headphones, loudspeakers, or in the case of cochlear implant research, electrical signals that are transmitted to the implant. Most of these experiments take place in sound-attenuating rooms to isolate the participant from external noise. For experiments on spatial hearing, sounds may be presented from loudspeakers at different locations in an *anechoic room*, in which the walls, floor, and ceiling are covered in special material to absorb sounds and minimize reflections. There are broadly speaking two different types of measurement that we can make.

A.1.1 Measuring perceived magnitude

First, we can ask the participant to make a subjective response corresponding to the *perceived magnitude* of some aspect of the sound that they hear. For example, the participant might give a numerical judgment of the loudness of a sound, of the pleasantness of a musical chord, or of the direction of a sound source. These techniques often use rating scales in which the response is constrained to a number of predetermined options. In the case of loudness, for example, the participant might be asked to rate a sound as either very soft, soft, moderately loud, loud, or very loud. Or the participant might have to indicate how loud is the sound on a numerical scale going from, say, 1 to 5. Another example is a spatial hearing task, in which listeners may be required to point or indicate on a computer from which direction a sound originates. These are all examples of *magnitude estimation* tasks. We could alternatively provide the participant with a number representing a target ratio between the perceived magnitudes of some aspect of two sounds. The participant would then be asked to vary some aspect of one sound (e.g., sound level) using a controller until it appears to be that ratio greater than a reference sound on a particular perceptual dimension (e.g., twice as loud). This is an example of a *magnitude production* task. Finally, the participant may be asked to vary some aspect of one sound so that it *matches* perceptually the other sound. An example is the loudness-matching task that is used to produce equal loudness contours (see Section 6.2.2).

Tasks such as these allow us to estimate the perceptual magnitude of physical quantities such as level, fundamental frequency, spatial location, and so on. In addition to being of practical use, these measurements help us understand how the physical aspects of sounds are represented in the auditory nervous system.

A.1.2   Measuring discrimination performance

Second, we can ask the participant to *discriminate* (i.e., to detect a difference) between two or more sounds or between a sound and silence in the case of measurements of absolute hearing threshold. For example, on each *trial* of an experiment, participants might be presented successively with two tones with different fundamental frequencies and have to indicate, by pressing a button on a response box or a key on a computer keyboard, which one has the higher pitch. The order of the stimuli is randomized so that participants cannot get the right response just by pressing the same button every time. This is an example of a *two-interval, two-alternative forced-choice task*, because there are two observation intervals in which stimuli are presented, and the participant is forced to choose one of these (see also Figure 6.5 and Figure 8.1). It is possible to have any number of observation intervals and alternatives. Three-interval, three-alternative is also popular, with the participant picking which of three sounds is different or the "odd one out" (again, the interval containing the "correct" stimulus would be randomized). You can also have different numbers of intervals and alternatives. For example, a three-interval, two-alternative forced-choice task might have an initial sound that is always the same and then two subsequent sounds, one of which is different from the initial sound. The participant would have to try to pick which of the two subsequent sounds was different from the initial sound. You can even have one interval with two alternatives, for example, if just one sound is presented and the participant has to decide if it contained just noise or a noise and a pure tone. This is an example of a yes/no task, as the response is either "yes" the tone is present or "no" it is not. Discrimination tasks are often accompanied by feedback after every trial, perhaps by a light on the response box or computer screen, indicating whether the response was correct or which interval contained the correct sound. Feedback helps the participant learn the cues in the sound to which he or she needs to attend to achieve good performance.

Discrimination tasks such as these are very powerful. By presenting a number of trials, we can measure the percentage correct for a particular discrimination, to determine how discriminable are the two sounds. This allows us to create a *psychometric function* (Figure A.1), which is a plot of performance as a function of the physical difference between the sounds (e.g., frequency difference, or the level of a pure tone in a noise). Discrimination tasks also allow us to measure the *just-noticeable difference* between two sounds. This is often done using an *adaptive* technique in which the task is made harder the more correct responses are made and easier the more incorrect responses are made. A popular example of this is the *two-down, one-up* procedure, in which the task is made harder for every two consecutive correct responses and easier for every one incorrect response.

Let's take an example of how this might work (Figure A.2). Say we wanted to find the smallest detectable level of a pure tone in a masking noise. We might use a two-interval, two-alternative task, in which one interval contains the noise and one interval contains the noise plus the tone. Initially, the tone would be set at a level at which it is easily detectable so that the participant would pick the interval with the tone almost every time. However, every two successive correct responses would cause the level of the tone for the next trial to be reduced by, say, 2 dB. Eventually, the participant would not be able to detect the tone and

Figure A.1 A typical psychometric function for a two-alternative discrimination task, showing percent correct responses as a function of the difference between the sounds. Chance performance (50%) is shown by the horizontal dashed line.

Figure A.2 An example of an adaptive track, showing the level of a tone in noise as a function of trial number. The correctness of the participant's response on each trial is indicated by a tick (correct) or cross (incorrect). For every two *consecutive* correct responses, the level of the tone is decreased, making the task harder. For every incorrect response, the level of the tone is increased, making the task easier. As the experiment progresses, the level of the tone oscillates around threshold (defined, e.g., by 70.7% correct responses). Threshold is indicated by the horizontal dashed line.

he or she would pick the wrong interval. Then the level of the tone would be increased and performance would improve. Over a block of trials, a plot of the level of the tone against trial number (an *adaptive track*) would show that the level of the tone varied up and down around the threshold of discrimination as the participant's responses varied from correct to incorrect. By averaging the level of the tone at the *turnpoints* or *reversals* in the track (changes in direction of the track from decreasing to increasing tone level, and vice versa), we can obtain a threshold value for the tone in the noise. For a two-down one-up procedure, this corresponds to the level at which the tone would be correctly detected on 70.7% of trials.

We could of course measure other types of discrimination threshold using the same technique. For example, we could reduce or increase the difference between the fundamental frequencies of two complex tones to measure the smallest detectable difference in fundamental frequency. Discrimination performance can also be estimated from the measures of perceived magnitude described in Section A1.1 by recording the variability of responses. If the variability is high, this implies that the internal representation is not very precise and hence that discrimination is poor. As described in several chapters of the book, psychophysical thresholds can give us a great deal of information about how the auditory system works, from measuring frequency selectivity using masking experiments to measuring the discrimination of speech stimuli.

A.2 SIGNAL DETECTION THEORY

Signal detection theory is the conceptual framework that is used to interpret the results of discrimination experiments. The idea is that discriminating between two sounds is not usually all or nothing. In other words, there is a not usually an absolute physical limitation to discrimination, above which the sounds are always discriminated and below which it is impossible to discriminate. Instead, as the physical difference between two sounds is decreased, the *probability* of producing a correct response decreases continuously until there is no physical difference between the sounds in which case performance is at chance (equivalent to guessing). In the case of a two-alternative task, chance is 50% correct (one in every two trials correct by guessing). In the case of a three-alternative task, chance is 33% correct (one in every three trials correct by guessing). As described in Section A1.2, the psychometric function is a plot of percentage correct as a function of the physical difference (Figure A.1). Threshold or the just-noticeable difference is usually defined as the difference that produces a criterion percentage correct, for example, 70.7% in the case of the two-down, one-up adaptive procedure described in Section A1.2.

So why should performance be limited when there is a difference between the stimuli? The answer is that the internal neural representation of a sound is never perfect. There is always some *variability*, or *noise*, in the representation, due to the normal variability in the activity of neurons, and sometimes additionally a variability in the physical stimulus (e.g., in the case of a random noise stimulus). This variability can be described by a *probability density function*, which shows the likelihood that the internal representation will take a particular value in response to a given stimulus. The *area* under the curve between two values on the x-axis is the probability of the internal magnitude falling within this particular *range* of magnitudes (Figure A.3). Hence, it is most likely that the internal representation of a sound will be close to the mean of the distribution of values (corresponding to the peaks of the functions in Figure A.3). However, there is a small probability that the internal representation will be considerably lower or higher than the mean (near the tails of the functions). The area under the *whole curve* is 1, since there is a probability of 1 (i.e., certainty) that the internal representation will take some value.

Now, consider the case we examined earlier of a two-alternative task in which the participant is required to detect a tone in a background noise. One interval contains the noise, and one interval contains the noise plus the tone. On *average*, the noise plus the tone will have a higher internal representation (e.g., a higher neural firing rate) than the noise (compare the peaks of the functions in Figure A.3). However, because there is some variability in neural activity, on some trials (just by chance) the internal representation might be greater for the noise than it is for the noise plus the tone (illustrated by the downward-pointing arrows in Figure A.3). On these trials, the participant will choose the incorrect interval. The number of errors will be greater if the average difference in the internal representations is reduced (e.g., by reducing the level of the tone) or if the variability in the representations (the width of the functions in Figure A.3) is increased. The internal neural variability is dependent on the participant, and usually beyond the control of the experimenter, but it might be increased if the participant is distracted, or decreased after a period of training.

The discrimination index, d-*prime* or d′, is defined as the difference between the means of the distributions *divided by* the standard deviation of the distributions (a measure of variability). For a task with a given number of alternatives, d′ can

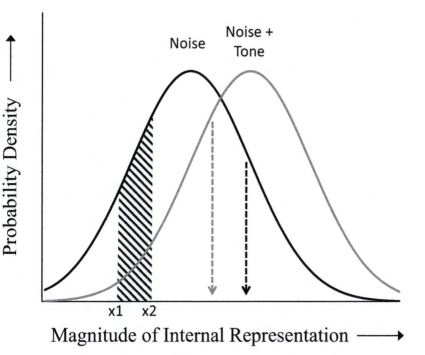

Figure A.3 Probability density functions showing probability density as a function of the magnitude of the internal representation for a noise and a noise to which a pure tone has been added. These are examples of *normal* or *Gaussian* distributions. The peak shows the location of the mean of the distribution. The probability of obtaining an internal magnitude within a particular range is given by the area under the curve between two points on the x-axis. For example, the probability of obtaining an internal magnitude for the noise between x1 and x2 is given by the shaded area. For a two-alternative task, it is assumed that the participant will select the interval that contains the highest magnitude in the internal representation. Because adding the tone shifts the distribution to the right, in the majority of cases, the noise plus the tone will produce the highest internal magnitude. However, on a proportion of trials, just by chance, the noise might produce a greater magnitude than the tone (indicated by the downward-pointing dashed arrows). In this case, the participant will pick the incorrect interval. Notice that the more the functions overlap, the greater the chance of an incorrect response. Hence, the chance of an incorrect response will increase if the means of the distributions are closer together (e.g., if the level of the added tone is reduced) or if the spread of the distributions (the *standard deviation*) is greater (if the variability in the neural representation is increased).

be derived directly from the percent correct score. The higher the percent correct (i.e., the better the performance) the higher the value of d'. Thus, d' is a very useful measure of discrimination performance, and using simple equations it can be used to predict optimum performance on complex discrimination tasks (such as combining information from different sources, e.g., from different places in the excitation pattern or from different points in time; see Section 8.3.2).

A.3 HUMAN ELECTROPHYSIOLOGY

Except in very unusual circumstances, for example, during brain surgery, we are not allowed to stick electrodes into individual neurons in the human auditory system. However, we can make recordings of the electrical activity of *populations* of neurons by attaching electrodes to the scalp. This technique is called *electroencephalography* (EEG). The electric potentials are very small, of the order of microvolts or nanovolts (a nanovolt is a billionth of a volt) in the case of recordings from the auditory system. However, if the background electrical noise is very low, and the sound stimuli are repeated a large number of times and the electrical responses averaged, quite good recordings can be obtained. A detailed discussion of these techniques is contained in the excellent volume edited by Burkard, Eggermont, and Don (2007), and only a brief overview will be provided here.

A.3.1 The auditory brainstem response

The *auditory brainstem response* (ABR) is the electrical response of neurons in the auditory nerve and brainstem when a sound is played. The ABR can be recorded by measuring the electric potential between two electrodes placed on the head, for example, one on the high forehead and one on the mastoid bone behind the ear, although many other configurations (or *montages*) can be used. Sometimes an electrode is inserted into the ear canal (usually a foam insert wrapped in gold foil called a *tiptrode*) to obtain a stronger recording of the auditory nerve response. A third *ground* electrode is also needed for some systems, and can be positioned on the lower forehead. The auditory stimulus is usually a brief click or tone burst, repeated thousands of times to average out any background electrical noise (neural or external) which will not be synchronized to the recordings and hence will tend to cancel across presentations.

The ABR is associated with five distinct peaks or *waves* in the EEG recording over time (Figure A.4, left panel). Each wave corresponds to synchronized electrical activity in populations of neurons, from peripheral sites to more central sites, as the neural signal passes up the brainstem. Waves I and II are thought to originate from the auditory nerve, wave III from the cochlear nucleus, wave IV from the superior olive and lateral lemniscus, and wave V from the lateral lemniscus and inferior colliculus. However, it is probably not the case that each wave represents the response of just one structure, except for the earlier waves that originate from the auditory nerve (Møller, 2006). This is because the ascending auditory pathways are very complex, with extensive parallel connections. I describe in Section 13.5.2 how the ABR can be used for clinical diagnostics. It can also be used for research purposes, as a means of investigating neural function in the auditory nerve and brainstem.

A.3.2 The frequency-following response

The *frequency-following response* (FFR) is an electrophysiological measure of phase locking (see Section 7.2.3). Based on the delay or *latency* of about 6 ms in the onset of the FFR compared to the onset of the stimulus, the FFR is thought to

Figure A.4 Two sound stimuli and their associated ABR and FFR recordings made using electrodes attached to the scalp. For the ABR (bottom left panel), the five characteristic waves are indicated above the curve. For the FFR (bottom right panel), notice how the periodicity in the recording matches the periodicity in the pure tone stimulus (top right panel).

originate mainly from neural activity in the upper brainstem, in the region of the inferior colliculus, although there may be contributions from earlier generators, such as the auditory nerve, cochlear nucleus, and superior olive (Krishnan, 2006), and also the auditory cortex (Coffey, Herholz, Chepesiuk, Baillet, & Zatorre, 2016). The FFR can be measured using the same electrode configurations as used for the ABR. However, unlike the ABR, the stimulus has a longer duration (100 ms or so), again repeated thousands of times to reduce the noise in the response. Also, while the ABR represents the response to the onset of a brief sound, the FFR is a measure of *sustained neural activity*. Neurons in the auditory pathway will tend to phase lock to periodicities in the stimulus, and hence a periodic pattern of stimulation will result in a periodic variation in electric potential (Figure A.4, right panel). Consequently, the spectrum of the FFR typically shows peaks corresponding to the frequency components in the stimulus or to the fundamental frequency or amplitude modulation rate of the stimulus. However, the FFR can be observed only in response to frequencies below about 2000 Hz, perhaps reflecting the upper frequency limit of phase locking in the upper brainstem (Krishnan, 2006).

A.3.3 The auditory steady-state response

Like the FFR, the *auditory steady-state response* (ASSR) is a measure of the sustained activity of neurons and can be recorded using similar electrode configurations.

However, the term ASSR is usually used to refer to the phase-locked response to *modulated tones* at low modulation rates. The ASSR originates mainly from the auditory cortex for modulation rates below about 60 Hz and mainly from the auditory brainstem for rates greater than this. The genius in the ASSR technique is that it is possible to measure the responses in several frequency regions simultaneously. For example, pure tones can be presented at several different frequencies and modulated at *different rates*. By examining the peaks in the spectrum of the ASSR at each of the different modulation rates, it is possible to measure the neural response to each of the modulated tones separately even when they are presented together.

The ASSR can be used in the clinic to estimate hearing thresholds based on the strength of the response to modulated pure tones with different frequencies. By introducing a masking sound to reduce the response to the modulated tone, tuning curves may be measured similar to psychophysical tuning curves to provide an "objective" estimate of cochlear frequency selectivity (Markessis et al., 2009; Wilding, McKay, Baker, Picton, & Kluk, 2011).

A.3.4 Cortical auditory evoked potentials

To investigate neural processing at higher stages in the auditory pathway, we can use electrodes placed around the scalp to measure the electric potentials produced by neurons in the cerebral cortex. Like the ABR, a series of characteristic peaks and troughs in the electric potential can be observed in response to transient auditory stimuli. However, for cortical potentials, these variations are much slower than for the ABR, occurring over a time span of hundreds of milliseconds. The peaks and troughs are given labels, P1, N1, P2, and so on, with P standing for positive electric potential (peak) and N for negative (trough). They may also be designated by the time of occurrence of the peak or trough in milliseconds (P50, N100, P200, etc.).

One popular cortical measure is called the *mismatch negativity*, in which the response to a rare sound in a sequence is compared to the response to a sound that occurs frequently in the sequence. The mismatch negativity is measured from about the time of N1 to the time of P2 (roughly 100–250 ms after the stimulus onset) and reflects the detection of *acoustic change* in the brain. Hence, the mismatch negativity can be used as an electrophysiological measure of sensitivity to differences between sounds, comparable to psychoacoustic measures of discrimination performance.

The brain region generating the cortical potentials can be estimated by comparing the outputs of a large number of electrodes arranged around the scalp using complex mathematics. However, this *source localization* is based on a number of assumptions and may not always reliably identify the neural generators.

A.3.5 Magnetoencephalography

As an alternative to electrophysiology, the *magnetic fields* produced by neurons can be recorded using *magnetoencephalography* (MEG). The participant places his or her head in a fixed tight enclosure containing very sensitive superconducting magnetometers, all located in an electromagnetically shielded room. While MEG and

EEG originate from the same neural processes, MEG is thought to be superior to EEG for some applications because the magnetic field is distorted less than the electric field by the skull and scalp. Hence, MEG provides better source localization than EEG, telling us with more precision where in the auditory pathway the response originates. However, MEG equipment is very expensive, large, and fixed in location. Hence, MEG is performed in relatively few specialized centers, whereas EEG use is widespread.

A.4 FUNCTIONAL MAGNETIC RESONANCE IMAGING

Although EEG and MEG are good at telling us about the neural representations of sounds over time, they provide relatively crude information about *where* in the brain the neural processing is occurring. To answer these questions, we must use an alternative technique that does not depend directly on the electrical response of neurons.

Magnetic resonance imaging (MRI) is a technique often used in medical imaging. MRI uses the magnetic response of hydrogen nuclei (protons) in order to provide three-dimensional images of the internal structure of, for example, the human body. A very powerful magnet causes the protons to line up with the stable magnetic field, and then an additional fluctuating magnetic field is turned on, which causes the protons to flip their magnetization alignment. When they flip back to their resting state after the fluctuating field is turned off, they release electromagnetic radiation that can be detected. The *frequency* of the emitted radiation depends on the strength of the constant field. Hence, by applying a field that varies across space (a *gradient field*), it is possible to calculate where in the body the signal is coming from based on the frequency of the emitted radiation. In addition, the length of time that the protons take to get back to their resting state (the *relaxation time*) varies depending on the tissue in the body, and so it is possible to distinguish between different internal structures.

In terms of understanding the *function* of the auditory system, a variant of the MRI technique called *functional magnetic resonance imaging* (fMRI) is most relevant here. The greater the neural activity in a region of the brain, the more oxygen that is supplied by the blood in that region, in the form of oxygenated hemoglobin. This increases the size of the emitted response in the MRI scanner, an effect called the *blood-oxygen-level dependent* (BOLD) response. Hence, by using gradient fields, fMRI can provide accurate three-dimensional images of brain activity in response to stimulation, but with a relatively poor temporal resolution of several seconds. For example, by comparing the BOLD response to a complex tone (with a pitch) and a noise (without a pitch) matched in spectrum and level, we can make inferences about the location of pitch processing in the auditory cortex (Hall & Plack, 2009). A particular problem with auditory fMRI is that the scanner is very loud, and we don't want the BOLD response to the scanner noise to interfere with the response to the signal of interest. Hence, a technique has been developed to scan intermittently, with each scan measuring the BOLD response after the response to the noise from the previous scan has declined (Hall et al., 1999).

Although fMRI does not have the high temporal resolution of EEG and MEG, it provides much better spatial resolution, down to the order of millimeters.

Hence, EEG, MEG and fMRI can be used to provide complementary information about the time course (EEG or MEG) and location (fMRI) of neural activity. However, like MEG, fMRI requires very expensive equipment, usually located at a permanent site.

A.5 ANIMAL PHYSIOLOGY

At a general level, physiology is concerned with the internal workings of living things – the functions of biological systems. Auditory physiology is concerned with the internal workings of the auditory system: how sound is processed by the cells and structures in the ear and brain. Research is based on direct measurements of the biological systems that underlie hearing. To investigate the detailed function of the auditory system requires *invasive* techniques, which involve some degree of surgery. Hence, these procedures are usually performed on anaesthetized animals or on *in vitro* preparations of tissue that has been removed from an animal. Although the experiments are performed on nonhuman species (typically rodents such as mice, guinea pigs, and chinchillas), the primary goal of these experiments is to improve our understanding of *human* hearing. It is assumed that there are common physiological mechanisms across mammalian species, and hence by studying animal physiology we can make inferences about human physiology.

A.5.1 Measuring the basilar membrane response

Although psychoacoustic experiments can reveal the remarkable ability of human listeners to separate the different frequency components of sounds, it is only by studying animals that we have learned how these abilities depend on the response of the basilar membrane in the cochlea (see Chapter 5). We have also learned from these experiments that the growth of loudness with level is dependent on the compressive response of the basilar membrane.

To measure the highly tuned, compressive response of the healthy basilar membrane, the animal and the cochlea need to be in a good physiological condition so that the outer hair cells are functioning normally. This requires delicate surgery. Modern techniques use *laser interferometry*. The cochlea is opened up and laser light bounced off a reflective surface, for example, tiny glass beads that are placed on the basilar membrane. The reflected light is compared to the original light reflected off a mirror in an optical device called an *interferometer*. The phase of the laser light that returns will depend on the path distance between the laser, the basilar membrane, and the interferometer. Depending on this distance, the light will either *reinforce* or *cancel* the original light. Hence, by measuring the variations in the interference pattern produced when the original light and the light reflected from the basilar membrane are superimposed, it is possible to measure the tiny movements of the basilar membrane.

The base of the cochlea is more accessible surgically than the apex, and only a few attempts have been made to record basilar membrane vibration in the apex. It is not yet clear that measurements of basilar membrane vibration in the apex really reflect the response of a healthy cochlea, since these measurements reveal a more linear response, and less frequency selectivity, than observed in behaving human listeners at low frequencies (see Chapter 5).

A.5.2 Single-unit recordings

Using tiny *microelectrodes*, it is possible to record the electrical response of *single neurons* ("single units") in the auditory system while sounds are played to the animal. The animal is usually anaesthetized throughout the procedure. The microelectrodes have very fine tips and are composed of either a thin glass tube (a glass micropipette) or a metal such as platinum or tungsten. The recordings can be made either by inserting the microelectrode into the neuron or by positioning it nearby. The electrical responses, usually action potentials (spikes), produced by the neuron are amplified and recorded for computational analysis. It is also possible to use arrays of microelectrodes to record from several neurons simultaneously. This helps physiologists to understand how a group of neurons may work together to process the sound. Microelectrodes can also be used to record from the hair cells in the cochlea.

It is common to use sound stimuli that are similar to those used in human psychoacoustic experiments. Physiologists can determine how the neuron *represents* those sounds and, hence, what the function of the neuron might be with respect to auditory perception. Examples of these measurements are provided in many of the chapters in the book. Two of the standard measurements are of the *rate-level function*, which is a plot of the change in firing rate with level, and the *frequency threshold tuning curve*, which is a plot of the level of a pure tone required to produce a criterion increase in firing as a function of the frequency of the tone (see Chapters 4 and 5 for examples).

A.6 ANIMAL PSYCHOACOUSTICS

Physiological recordings in nonhuman mammals provide important information about the fine detail of neural processing. However, it is unlikely that the auditory systems of humans and animals are identical. After all, humans are a separate species that use specialized types of acoustic signals (e.g., speech and music). Our auditory systems have evolved separately from those of the guinea pig and chinchilla. So how do we relate the physiological measurements on animals to the psychoacoustic performance of human listeners?

Animal psychoacoustics, or *comparative psychoacoustics*, provides a "conceptual bridge" between animal physiology, on the one hand, and human perception, on the other (Shofner & Niemiec, 2010). By measuring the ability of behaving animals to respond to, and discriminate, different sounds, it is possible to understand how the physiological mechanisms underlie behavior in the same animals. By comparing results from animal psychoacoustics with results from human psychoacoustics, we can also understand how the physiological mechanisms might give rise to *human* perceptions.

Of course, it is not possible to ask a guinea pig to press a response button. Instead, the animal has to be *trained* to provide a particular response when it hears a particular sound. Typically, the animal is trained to make two responses

(Shofner & Niemiec, 2010). The *observing response* initiates the trial and is used to indicate that the animal is ready to participate. The observing response is also used to position the animal in the correct location for performing the task. The *reporting response* is used by the animal to indicate that it has detected the correct auditory stimulus. For example, for rodents, the observing response might be a lever press and the reporting response a lever release. The observing response is trained first, by rewarding the animal with a food pellet when it presses the lever. Then the reporting response is trained by rewarding the animal for releasing the lever when it hears the correct stimulus played over a loudspeaker. The animal can also be rewarded for *not* releasing the lever on *catch* trials that are silent or that do not contain the correct stimulus. These responses are broadly equivalent to those that might be used by participants in a human psychoacoustic experiment. Once the animal is trained, discrimination performance can be measured in a similar way to that used in human psychoacoustics. Researchers can measure the percent correct responses for a particular discrimination, or they might use an adaptive tracking procedure (typically, one-down, one-up) to estimate threshold.

A.7 ETHICAL ISSUES

When conducting research on humans or animals, we must never forget that we are experimenting on sentient creatures rather than, say, on reagents in a test tube. Animal research is particularly controversial, as animals never participate voluntarily, and they sometimes experience pain or stress. In physiological experiments, the animals are often killed after the experiment. For all experiments on humans or animals, we have to be sure that the experiment is worthwhile. In other words, that the benefits to humans (e.g., treatments for hearing loss) outweigh any pain or discomfort that may be inflicted. In the final analysis, we have to make a decision as a society that such research is justified.

Before conducting experiments on humans or animals, formal approval is required from an independent *ethics committee*, sometimes based at the institution in which the research is conducted. The job of the ethics committee is to make sure that the research is in accordance with legal and ethical guidelines, that any potential pain or psychological injury for the animals or human participants is minimized, that the experiments are safe for the researchers, and that the benefits of the research justify the procedures used. The ethics committee will also ensure that any human participants provide *informed consent* before being tested. This usually means signing a form stating that they agree to participate in the experiment. An information sheet will usually be provided so that the participants are fully aware of the nature of the experimental procedures.

GLOSSARY

absolute threshold	The lowest detectable level of a sound in the absence of any other sounds.
acoustics	The scientific study of sound.
afferent fibers	Nerve fibers that carry information from the sensory receptors to the central nervous system.
amplitude	The value of an oscillating quantity (e.g., sound pressure) at a given time. Also used to refer to the peak amplitude, which is the maximum value attained during a cycle of oscillation.
amplitude modulation (AM)	Variation in the envelope of a sound over time.
audiogram	A plot of absolute threshold as a function of frequency for pure tones.
audiologist	A health care professional specializing in hearing and balance disorders.
auditory brainstem response	An auditory evoked potential generated by a brief click or tone burst, reflecting activity in the auditory nerve and brainstem.
auditory evoked potential	See *evoked potential*.
auditory filter	A band-pass filter reflecting the frequency selectivity of a single place in the cochlea. The peripheral auditory system behaves as an array of auditory filters, each passing a narrow range of frequency components.
auditory nerve	The eighth cranial nerve, carrying information from the inner ear to the brain.
auditory scene analysis	The perceptual organization of sounds according to the sound sources that are producing them.
auricle	See *pinna*.
backward masking	Refers to the situation in which the presence of one sound renders a previously presented sound less detectable.
band-pass filter	A filter that passes a band of frequencies between a lower cutoff frequency (greater than zero) and an upper cutoff frequency.
band-stop, band-reject filter	A filter that removes frequencies between a lower cutoff frequency (greater than zero) and an upper cutoff frequency.
band-stop noise, notched noise	A wideband noise that has a spectral notch (i.e., a frequency band in which the noise is attenuated)
bandwidth	Range of frequencies.
basilar membrane	A thin fibrous membrane extending the length of the cochlea and separating the scala media from the scala tympani.
beat	The basic unit of musical stress in time.
beats	Periodic envelope fluctuations resulting from the interaction of two or more tones of slightly different frequencies.
best frequency	The pure-tone frequency to which a given place on the basilar membrane, or a given neuron in the auditory system, is most sensitive.
binaural	Refers to the use of both ears. A binaural stimulus is one that is presented to both ears.
binaural masking level difference	A measure of the advantage in signal detection that can result from the use of both ears. The binaural masking level difference is the difference in signal threshold between a situation in which the masker and signal have the same level and phase relation at the two ears, and a situation in which the level or phase relation between the masker and the signal differs between the two ears.

brainstem	The base of the brain, located between the spinal cord and the cerebral hemispheres.
center frequency	For a band-pass filter, the center frequency is the pure-tone frequency that produces the largest output. For an auditory filter, the center frequency is considered to be equivalent to the characteristic frequency of a single place on the basilar membrane.
central auditory system	The auditory neural pathways in the brainstem and in the auditory cortex.
cerebral cortex	The outer layer of the cerebral hemispheres.
characteristic frequency	The pure-tone frequency to which a given place on the basilar membrane, or a given neuron in the auditory system, is most sensitive at low stimulation levels.
chord	A combination of two or more notes presented simultaneously.
chroma	A reference to the fundamental frequency of a note, or order of a note, within each octave. Notes separated by an octave have the same chroma.
coarticulation	The tendency for the articulatory processes involved in the production of one phoneme to be influenced by the production of previous and subsequent phonemes.
cochlea	The spiral, fluid-filled tube in the inner ear in which acoustic vibrations are transduced into electrical activity in the auditory nerve.
cochlear implant	A surgically implanted device that provides a treatment for severe to profound hearing loss by stimulating the auditory nerve using electrical impulses.
cochlear synaptopathy	A loss of synapses between inner hair cells and auditory nerve fibers. Associated with noise exposure and aging.
combination tone	One of the additional frequency components (distortion products) that may be generated in the cochlea when two or more frequency components are presented.
comodulation masking release	The reduction in signal threshold that occurs with an amplitude-modulated masker, when additional frequency components, with the same pattern of modulation as the masker, are added to the stimulus.
complex tone	A tone composed of more than one frequency component. For complex tones in the environment, the components are usually harmonically related. Sounds composed of a harmonic series of frequency components are often referred to as complex *tones*, even though they may not evoke a pitch (e.g., if the fundamental frequency is too high).
compression	A reduction in the range of levels of a signal. A compressive system has a nonlinear, shallow growth, with a slope less than one, in output level with respect to input level.
conductive hearing loss	Hearing loss caused by a problem with the conduction of sound from the outer ear to the cochlea.
consonance	The sensation of pleasantness or resolution when certain combinations of notes are presented.
contralateral	Opposite, with reference to the two sides of the body (left and right). The left ear is contralateral to the right ear.
dead region	A region of the cochlea in which there are no (or very few) functioning inner hair cells or auditory nerve fibers.
decibel (dB)	The unit of sound level. The difference between the levels of two sounds in decibels is equal to 10 times the natural logarithm of the ratio of the two intensities.
depolarization	With respect to hair cells and neurons, an increase in the electric potential of the cell from a negative resting potential.
difference limen	See *just-noticeable difference*.
diffraction	The bending of sound waves as they pass the edge of an obstacle.
dissonance	The sensation of unpleasantness or lack of resolution when certain combinations of notes are presented.
distortion	A change in the waveform of a signal as a result of nonlinearity.

dominant region	The range of harmonic numbers for the harmonics that have the greatest influence on the pitch of a complex tone.
dorsal	Toward the back (of the body).
dynamic range	The range of levels over which a system can operate effectively or to a certain standard of performance.
ear canal	The passage in the outer ear that leads to the eardrum.
efferent fibers	Nerve fibers that carry information from the central nervous system to muscles, glands, and in the case of the ear, to the outer hair cells and to the afferent fibers innervating the inner hair cells.
electric potential	Strictly speaking, the energy required to move a unit of positive charge from an infinite distance to a specified point in an electric field. The electric potential is related to the difference between the amounts of positive and negative electric charge. You may be more familiar with the term *voltage*, which is the electric potential expressed in volts. For a 12-volt car battery, there is an electric potential difference of 12 volts between the two electrodes.
endocochlear potential	The electric potential of the endolymph fluid in the scala media.
envelope	The peak (or overall) amplitude of a sound wave as a function of time. Envelope variations are slower than the variations in fine structure.
equal loudness contour	A line joining points of equal loudness on a graph of level against frequency.
equivalent rectangular bandwidth (ERB)	The ERB of a filter is the bandwidth of a rectangular filter (with a flat top and infinitely steep sides) that has the same peak transmission as that filter and has the same area under the curve in intensity units (i.e., that passes the same intensity of a white noise).
evoked potential	An electric potential recorded from the nervous system in response to a stimulus.
excitation pattern	A representation of the auditory system's version of the spectrum. The excitation pattern of a sound is a plot of the output of the auditory filters as a function of center frequency, or the neural activity as a function of characteristic frequency, in response to the sound.
filter	A device for changing the frequency composition of a signal.
fine structure	The individual pressure variations of a sound wave.
formant	A resonance in the vocal tract or the resulting peak in the spectrum of a speech sound.
formant transition	A smooth change in the frequency of a formant.
forward masking	Refers to the situation in which the presence of one sound renders a subsequently presented sound less detectable.
Fourier analysis	A mathematical technique for determining the spectral composition of a waveform.
frequency	The number of periods of a waveform in a given time. Also used to refer specifically to the number of periods in a given time for one of the pure-tone frequency components that make up a waveform. Measured in cycles per second, or hertz (Hz).
frequency channel	A pathway through the auditory system with a constant characteristic frequency. The basilar membrane separates out the different frequency components of a sound spatially, and the information from different places on the basilar membrane is carried from the cochlea through the central auditory system in (to a certain extent) separate frequency channels.
frequency component	One of the pure tones that when added together make up a sound waveform.
frequency-following response	A sustained auditory evoked potential that shows fluctuations synchronized to the fine structure or envelope of a sound stimulus, reflecting neural phase locking.
frequency modulation (FM)	Variation in the frequency of a sound over time.

frequency selectivity	The ability of the auditory system to separate out the frequency components of a complex sound.
frequency threshold curve	A plot of the level of a pure tone required to produce a just-measurable increase in the firing rate of a neuron as a function of the frequency of the tone.
functional magnetic resonance imaging	A technique for measuring neural activity in the brain based on changes associated with blood flow.
fundamental component	The first harmonic of a complex tone.
fundamental frequency	The repetition rate of the waveform of a periodic complex tone; the number of periods of the waveform of a complex tone in a given time.
hair cell	A sensory cell with fine hairlike projections called stereocilia. The auditory sensory receptor cells are hair cells, located within the organ of Corti.
harmonic	One of the pure-tone frequency components that make up a periodic complex tone. The frequency of each harmonic is an integer multiple of the fundamental frequency.
harmony	The combination of notes to produce chords.
hearing aid	An electronic device that amplifies the sound delivered to the ear canal.
hearing impairment	An impaired ability to perceive sounds.
high-pass filter	A filter that passes all frequencies above a specified cutoff frequency.
hyperacusis	A condition characterized by an abnormally low tolerance of moderate- and high-level sounds.
impulse	A sudden change in a quantity, such as pressure (in the case of sounds) or electric potential (in the case of neural impulses or spikes).
impulse response	The waveform at the output of a filter in response to an impulse.
inner ear	The part of the ear that is filled with fluid, including the cochlea (involved in hearing) and the semicircular canals (involved in balance).
inner hair cell	An auditory sensory cell, located in the organ of Corti toward the inside of the cochlear spiral. Inner hair cells are responsible for transducing basilar membrane vibration into electrical activity.
intensity	The sound power passing through a unit area. Measured in watts per square meter (W/m^2).
interaural level difference (ILD)	A difference in the level of a sound at the two ears.
interaural time difference (ITD)	A difference between the arrival times of a sound wave at the two ears.
interspike interval	The time interval between two neural impulses or spikes.
ipsilateral	Same side, with reference to the two sides of the body (left and right).
just-noticeable difference	The difference in a quantity that a listener can just detect at some criterion level of performance (e.g., 71% correct detection).
key	The tonic note and chord (major or minor) that specifies the melodic and harmonic context of a piece of music.
lateral	Toward the side.
level	An intensity ratio expressed in decibels. The level of a sound is its intensity relative to a reference intensity, expressed in decibels.
linear	A linear system is one for which the output magnitude is a constant multiple of the input magnitude, and for which the output in response to the sum of two signals is equal to the sum of the outputs to the two signals presented individually.
loudness	The perceived magnitude of a sound. The perceptual correlate of intensity.

loudness recruitment	An abnormally rapid growth of loudness with level, often experienced by listeners with hearing impairment.
low-pass filter	A filter that passes all frequencies below a specified cutoff frequency.
masker	In a psychoacoustic experiment, the masker is the sound used to make another sound (the signal) less detectable.
masking	Refers to the situation when the presence of one sound (the masker) renders another sound (the signal) less detectable.
medial	Toward the midline.
melody	A sequence of musical notes.
meter	The timing of stressed or accented beats in music.
middle ear	The air-filled space between the eardrum and the cochlea that contains the ossicles.
minimum audible angle	The smallest detectable angular separation between two sound sources relative to the head.
mismatch negativity	A component of the evoked potential in response to a rare deviant stimulus in a sequence of frequent standard stimuli. The mismatch negativity is thought to reflect the detection of change by the brain.
modulation transfer function	The smallest detectable depth of sinusoidal modulation as a function of modulation frequency.
monaural	Refers to the use of one ear. A monaural stimulus is one that is presented to one ear only.
narrowband	A narrowband sound has a small bandwidth.
neuron, nerve cell	A specialized cell that carries information in the form of electrical impulses, and that is the basic functional unit of the nervous system.
neurotransmitter	A chemical messenger used to carry information between different neurons, between sensory cells and neurons, and between neurons and muscle cells.
noise	A sound or signal with a random sequence of amplitude variations over time. Also used to refer to any unwanted sound.
octave	A musical interval characterized by a doubling in fundamental frequency.
organ of Corti	The auditory hair cells and their supporting cells.
ossicles	The three tiny bones (malleus, incus, and stapes) that transmit vibrations from the eardrum to the cochlea.
otoacoustic emissions	Sounds generated by the active mechanism in the cochlea.
outer ear	The external part of the auditory system, including the pinna and the ear canal.
outer hair cell	An auditory sensory cell, located in the organ of Corti toward the outside of the cochlear spiral. Outer hair cells are involved in modifying the vibration of the basilar membrane.
passband	The range of frequency components passed by a filter with little attenuation.
period	The smallest time interval over which a waveform is repeated. The inverse of the frequency. For a sound within the frequency range of human hearing, the period is usually measured in milliseconds (ms).
periodic	Repeating over time.
peripheral auditory system	The outer ear, middle ear, inner ear, and auditory nerve.
phase	The phase of a pure tone is the proportion of a period through which the waveform has advanced at a given time.
phase locking	The tendency of an auditory neuron to fire at a particular time (or phase) during each cycle of vibration on the basilar membrane.
phon	A unit of loudness. The loudness level of a sound in phons is the sound pressure level (in decibels) of a 1-kHz pure tone judged equally loud.

phoneme	The smallest unit of speech that distinguishes one spoken word from another in a given language.
pinna	The part of the outer ear that projects from the head; the most visible part of the ear. Also called the *auricle*.
pitch	That aspect of sensation whose variation is associated with musical melodies. The perceptual correlate of repetition rate.
place coding	A representation of information in terms of the place that is active (e.g., on the basilar membrane or in a neural array).
power	The energy transmitted per unit time. Measured in watts (W).
precedence effect	Refers to the dominance of information from the leading sound (as opposed to delayed or reflected versions of that sound) for the purpose of sound localization.
pressure	The force per unit area. Measured in newtons per square meter (N/m^2).
profile analysis	The perceptual analysis of the shape of the spectrum.
psychoacoustics	The study of the relation between sounds and sensations.
psychophysical tuning curve	See *tuning curve*.
psychophysics	The study of the relation between physical stimuli and sensations.
pulse train	A periodic waveform consisting of a regular sequence of pressure pulses.
pure tone	A sound with a sinusoidal variation in pressure over time.
rate-place coding	A representation of information in terms of the firing rates of neurons and their positions in the neural array.
resolved harmonic	A low-numbered harmonic of a complex tone that can be separated out by the peripheral auditory system.
resonance	The property of a system of oscillating most efficiently at a particular frequency.
rhythm	The repeating pattern of relative time intervals between the onsets of musical events.
sensation level	The level of a sound relative to absolute threshold.
sensorineural hearing loss	Hearing loss that arises from dysfunction of the cochlea, the auditory nerve, or the auditory pathways in the brain.
signal	A representation of information. In a psychoacoustic experiment, the signal is the sound the listener is required to detect or discriminate.
sine wave, sinusoid	A waveform whose variation over time is a sine function.
sone	A unit of loudness that scales linearly with perceived magnitude. One sone is defined as the loudness of a 1-kHz pure tone, presented binaurally in the free field from a frontal direction, at a level of 40 dB SPL.
sound pressure level	The level of a sound expressed relative to an intensity of $10^{-12}\,W/m^2$.
spectral splatter	Frequency components generated when a sound changes level abruptly.
spectrogram	A quasi-three-dimensional representation of the variation in the short-term spectrum of a sound over time.
spectro-temporal excitation pattern (STEP)	A quasi-three-dimensional plot of the output of the temporal window model as a function of the center time of the temporal window and of the center frequency of the auditory filter, in response to a given sound. The pattern is equivalent to a smoothed version of the spectrogram, illustrating the effects of the limited spectral and temporal resolution of the auditory system.
spectrum	The distribution across frequency of the pure-tone components that make up a sound wave.
spectrum level	The level of a sound in a 1-Hz wideband; a measure of spectral density.
spike	An electrical impulse in the axon of a neuron; an action potential.

standing wave   A stable pattern of pressure variations in a space, characterized by points of zero pressure variation and points of maximum pressure variation. A standing wave results from the combination of sound waves with equal frequency and amplitude traveling in opposite directions.

stereocilia   The fine, hairlike projections from hair cells, formed of extrusions of the cell membrane.

suppression   The reduction in the physiological response to one sound caused by the presence of another sound (the suppressor). Often used to refer to the frequency-dependent, nonlinear interaction between two or more frequency components on the basilar membrane.

synapse   A junction between two neurons where information is transmitted between the neurons.

tempo   The rate at which musical beats occur.

temporal coding   A representation of information in terms of the temporal pattern of activity in auditory neurons.

temporal excitation pattern (TEP)   A plot showing the output of the temporal window model as a function of the center time of the window, for a single frequency channel. The temporal excitation pattern is a smoothed version of the envelope of a sound, representing the loss of temporal resolution that may occur in the central auditory system.

temporal resolution   The resolution or separation of events in time.

temporal window   A function that weights and integrates the envelope of a sound over time, to simulate the temporal resolution of the auditory system.

threshold   The magnitude of a quantity (e.g., sound level) that a listener can just detect at some criterion level of performance (e.g., 71% correct detection).

timbre   That aspect of sensation by which two sounds with the *same* loudness, pitch, duration, and ear of presentation can be distinguished. Timbre is often used to refer to the sensations associated with the overall spectral shape of sounds, but timbre is also dependent on temporal factors such as the envelope. Generally (and rather vaguely), timbre refers to the "quality" of a sound.

tinnitus   The perception of sound in the absence of external sound.

tone   Strictly speaking, a sound that evokes a pitch. This definition can be quite loosely applied. For example, *pure tone* is often used to refer to any sound with a sinusoidal waveform, whether or not it evokes a pitch. See also *complex tone*.

tonotopic representation   A system of representation in which the frequency that is presented determines the place (e.g., in a neural array) that is active.

traveling wave   A wave that travels continuously in one direction. The pattern of vibration on the basilar membrane in response to a pure tone takes the form of a traveling wave that travels from base to apex.

tuning curve   In auditory physiology, a plot of the level of a pure tone required to produce a constant response, from a place on the basilar membrane, a hair cell, or an auditory neuron, as a function of the frequency of the tone. In auditory psychophysics (*psychophysical* tuning curve), a plot of the level of a pure tone or other narrowband masker required to mask a pure-tone signal (with fixed level and frequency) as a function of the frequency of the masker.

ventral   Toward the underside (of the body).

vocal folds   A pair of folds in the wall of the larynx that vibrate to produce speech sounds.

vocal tract   The irregular passage from the larynx to the lips and nasal cavities.

waveform   The waveform of a sound is the pattern of the pressure variations over time.

Weber fraction   The ratio of the smallest detectable change in the magnitude of a quantity to the baseline magnitude of that quantity (the magnitude of the quantity before the change was applied).

Weber's law	A general rule of perception stating that the smallest detectable change in a quantity is proportional to the magnitude of that quantity. In other words, Weber's law states that the Weber fraction is constant as a function of magnitude.
white noise	A noise with a constant spectrum level over the entire frequency range.
wideband, broadband	A wideband sound has a large bandwidth.

REFERENCES

American National Standards Institute (2015). *American national standard bioacoustical terminology*. New York: American National Standards Institute.

Andrews, M. W., Dowling, W. J., Bartlett, J. C., & Halpern, A. R. (1998). Identification of speeded and slowed familiar melodies by younger, middle-aged, and older musicians and nonmusicians. *Psychology and Aging*, 13, 462–471.

Arthur, R. M., Pfeiffer, R. R., & Suga, N. (1971). Properties of "two-tone inhibition" in primary auditory neurones. *Journal of Physiology*, 212, 593–609.

Attneave, F., & Olson, R. K. (1971). Pitch as a medium: A new approach to psychophysical scaling. *American Journal of Psychology*, 84, 147–166.

Bacon, S. P., & Viemeister, N. F. (1985). Temporal modulation transfer functions in normal-hearing and hearing-impaired subjects. *Audiology*, 24, 117–134.

Baer, T., & Moore, B. C. J. (1993). Effects of spectral smearing on the intelligibility of sentences in the presence of noise. *Journal of the Acoustical Society of America*, 94, 1229–1241.

Baguley, D. M. (2003). Hyperacusis. *Journal of the Royal Society of Medicine*, 96, 582–585.

Baharloo, S., Johnston, P. A., Service, S. K., Gitschier, J., & Freimer, N. B. (1998). Absolute pitch: An approach for identification of genetic and nongenetic components. *American Journal of Human Genetics*, 62, 224–231.

Bajo, V. M., Nodal, F. R., Moore, D. R., & King, A. J. (2010). The descending corticocollicular pathway mediates learning-induced auditory plasticity. *Nature Neuroscience*, 13, 253–260.

Beauvois, M. W., & Meddis, R. (1996). Computer simulation of auditory stream segregation in alternating-tone sequences. *Journal of the Acoustical Society of America*, 99, 2270–2280.

Békésy, G. (1960). *Experiments in hearing* (E. G. Wever, Trans.). New York: McGraw-Hill.

Bendor, D., Osmanski, M. S., & Wang, X. (2012). Dual pitch-processing mechanisms in primate auditory cortex. *Journal of Neuroscience*, 32, 16149–16161.

Bendor, D., & Wang, X. (2005). The neuronal representation of pitch in primate auditory cortex. *Nature*, 436, 1161–1165.

Bernstein, L. R., & Trahiotis, C. (2002). Enhancing sensitivity to interaural delays at high frequencies by using "transposed stimuli." *Journal of the Acoustical Society of America*, 112, 1026–1036.

Blackburn, C. C., & Sachs, M. B. (1990). The representations of the steady-state vowel sound /e/ in the discharge patterns of cat anteroventral cochlear nucleus neurons. *Journal of Neurophysiology*, 63, 1191-1212.

Blauert, J. (1972). On the lag of lateralization caused by interaural time and intensity differences. *Audiology*, 11, 265–270.

Blauert, J. (1997). *Spatial hearing: The psychophysics of human sound localization*. Cambridge, MA: MIT Press.

Blumstein, S. E., & Stevens, K. N. (1979). Acoustic invariance in speech production: Evidence from measurements of the spectral characteristics of stop consonants. *Journal of the Acoustical Society of America*, 66, 1001–1017.

Blumstein, S. E., & Stevens, K. N. (1980). Perceptual invariance and onset spectra for stop consonants in different vowel environments. *Journal of the Acoustical Society of America*, 67, 648–662.

Boatman, D. (2004). Cortical bases of speech perception: Evidence from functional lesion studies. *Cognition*, 92, 47–65.

Bones, O., Hopkins, K., Krishnan, A., & Plack, C. J. (2014). Phase locked neural activity in the human brainstem predicts preference for musical consonance. *Neuropsychologia*, 58, 23–32.

Bones, O., & Plack, C. J. (2015). Losing the music: Aging affects the perception and sub-cortical neural representation of musical harmony. *Journal of Neuroscience*, 35, 4071–4080.

Bramhall, N. F., Konrad-Martin, D., McMillan, G. P., & Griest, S. E. (2017). Auditory brain-stem response altered in humans with noise exposure despite normal outer hair cell function. *Ear and Hearing*, 38, e1–e12.

Bregman, A. S. (1990). *Auditory scene analysis: The perceptual organization of sound*. Cambridge, MA: Bradford Books, MIT Press.

Bregman, A. S., & Campbell, J. (1971). Primary auditory stream segregation and percep-tion of order in rapid sequences of tones. *Journal of Experimental Psychology*, 89, 244–249.

Bregman, A. S., & Dannenbring, G. (1973). The effect of continuity on auditory stream segregation. *Perception and Psychophysics*, 13, 308–312.

Briley, P. M., Breakey, C., & Krumbholz, K. (2012). Evidence for pitch chroma mapping in human auditory cortex. *Cerebral Cortex*, 23, 2601–2610.

Briley, P. M., Kitterick, P. T., & Summerfield, A. Q. (2012). Evidence for opponent process analysis of sound source location in humans. *Journal of the Association for Research in Otolar-yngology*, 14, 83–101.

Broadbent, D. E., & Ladefoged, P. (1957). On the fusion of sounds reaching different sense organs. *Journal of the Acoustical Society of America*, 29, 708–710.

Brokx, J. P. L., & Nooteboom, S. G. (1982). Intonation and the perceptual separation of simultaneous voices. *Journal of Phonetics*, 10, 23–36.

Bronkhurst, A. W., & Plomp, R. (1988). The effect of head-induced interaural time and level differences on speech intelligibility in noise. *Journal of the Acoustical Society of America*, 83, 1508–1516.

Burkard, R. F., Eggermont, J. J., & Don, M. (2007). *Auditory evoked potentials: Basic principles and clinical application*. Philadelphia: Lippincott Williams & Wilkins.

Burns, E. M., & Turner, C. (1986). Pure-tone pitch anomalies II: Pitch-intensity effects and diplacusis in impaired ears. *Journal of the Acoustical Society of America*, 79, 1530–1540.

Burns, E. M., & Viemeister, N. F. (1976). Nonspectral pitch. *Journal of the Acoustical Society of America*, 60, 863–869.

Burris-Meyer, H., & Mallory, V. (1960). Psycho-acoustics, applied and misapplied. *Journal of the Acoustical Society of America*, 32, 1568–1574.

Butler, R. A., & Belendiuk, K. (1977). Spectral cues utilized in the localization of sound in the median sagittal plane. *Journal of the Acoustical Society of America*, 61, 1264–1269.

Buus, S. (1985). Release from masking caused by envelope fluctuations. *Journal of the Acous-tical Society of America*, 78, 1958–1965.

Buus, S., Florentine, M., & Poulsen, T. (1997). Temporal integration of loudness, loudness discrimination, and the form of the loudness function. *Journal of the Acoustical Society of America*, 101, 669–680.

Carcagno, S., & Plack, C. J. (2011). Subcortical plasticity following perceptual learning in a pitch discrimination task. *Journal of the Association for Research in Otolaryngology*, 12, 89–100.

Cariani, P. A., & Delgutte, B. (1996). Neural correlates of the pitch of complex tones I: Pitch and pitch salience. *Journal of Neurophysiology*, 76, 1698–1716.

Carlyon, R. P. (1994). Further evidence against an across-frequency mechanism specific to the detection of frequency modulation (FM) incoherence between resolved frequency components. *Journal of the Acoustical Society of America*, 95, 949–961.

Carlyon, R. P. (1998). Comments on "A unitary model of pitch perception" [J. Acoust. Soc. Am. 102, 1811–1820 (1997)]. *Journal of the Acoustical Society of America*, 104, 1118–1121.

Carlyon, R. P., Cusack, R., Foxton, J. M, & Robertson, I. H. (2001). Effects of attention and unilateral neglect on auditory stream segregation. *Journal of Experimental Psychology: Human Perception and Performance*, 27, 115-127.

Carlyon, R. P., & Moore, B. C. J. (1984). Intensity discrimination: A severe departure from Weber's law. *Journal of the Acoustical Society of America*, 76, 1369–1376.

Carney, L. H., Li, T., & McDonough, J. M. (2015). Speech coding in the brain: Representation of vowel formants by midbrain neurons tuned to sound fluctuations. Eneuro, 2: ENEURO-0004.

Carney, L. H., Heinz, M. G., Evilsizer, M. E., Gilkey, R. H., & Colburn, H. S. (2002). Auditory phase opponency: A temporal model for masked detection at low frequencies. Acustica, 88, 334–346.

Carr, C. E., & Konishi, M. (1990). A circuit for detection of interaural time differences in the brain stem of the barn owl. Journal of Neuroscience, 10, 3227–3246.

Carter, L., Black, D., Bundy, A., & Williams, W. (2014). The leisure-noise dilemma: Hearing loss or hearsay? What does the literature tell us? Ear and Hearing, 35, 491–505.

Cherry, E. C., & Taylor, W. K. (1954). Some further experiments upon the recognition of speech, with one and with two ears. Journal of the Acoustical Society of America, 26, 554–559.

Chowning, J. M. (1980). Computer synthesis of the singing voice. In J. Sundberg (Ed.), Sound generation in wind, strings, computers (pp. 4–13). Stockholm: Royal Swedish Academy of Music.

Clark, J. G. (1981). Uses and abuses of hearing loss classification. American Speech-Language Hearing Association, 23, 493–500.

Coffey, E. B., Herholz, S. C., Chepesiuk, A. M., Baillet, S., & Zatorre, R. J. (2016). Cortical contributions to the auditory frequency-following response revealed by MEG. Nature Communications, 7, 11070.

Cole, R. A., & Jakimik, J. (1978). Understanding speech: How words are heard. In G. Underwood (Ed.), Strategies of information processing (pp. 67–116). London: Academic Press.

Cooper, N. P., & Guinan, J. J. (2006). Efferent-mediated control of basilar membrane motion. Journal of Physiology, 576, 49–54.

Crystal, D. (1997). The Cambridge encyclopedia of language (2nd ed.). Cambridge, UK: Cambridge University Press.

Culling, J. F., & Darwin, C. J. (1993). Perceptual separation of simultaneous vowels: Within and across-formant grouping by F0. Journal of the Acoustical Society of America, 93, 3454–3467.

Dai, H. (2000). On the relative influence of individual harmonics on pitch judgment. Journal of the Acoustical Society of America, 107, 953–959.

Dallos, P. (1996). Overview: Cochlear neurobiology. In P. Dallos, A. N. Popper, & R. R. Fay (Eds.), The cochlea (pp. 1–43). New York: Springer-Verlag.

Darwin, C. J. (2005). Pitch and auditory grouping. In C. J. Plack, A. J. Oxenham, A. N. Popper, & R. R. Fay (Eds.), Pitch: Neural coding and perception (pp. 278–305). New York: Springer-Verlag.

Darwin, C. J., & Bethell-Fox, C. E. (1977). Pitch continuity and speech source attribution. Journal of Experimental Psychology: Human Perception and Performance, 3, 665–672.

Darwin, C. J., & Ciocca, V. (1992). Grouping in pitch perception: Effects of onset asynchrony and ear of presentation of a mistuned component. Journal of the Acoustical Society of America, 91, 3381–3390.

Darwin, C. J., & Hukin, R. (1999). Auditory objects of attention: The role of interaural time differences. Journal of Experimental Psychology: Human Perception and Performance, 25, 617–629.

Darwin, C. J., Hukin, R. W., & al-Khatib, B. Y. (1995). Grouping in pitch perception: Evidence for sequential constraints. Journal of the Acoustical Society of America, 98, 880–885.

Darwin, C. J., & Sutherland, N. S. (1984). Grouping frequency components of vowels: When is a harmonic not a harmonic? Quarterly Journal of Experimental Psychology, 36A, 193–208.

Darwin, C. R. (1859). On the origin of species by means of natural selection, or the preservation of favoured races in the struggle for life. London: John Murray.

Dau, T., Kollmeier, B., & Kohlrausch, A. (1997). Modeling auditory processing of amplitude modulation. I. Detection and masking with narrowband carriers. *Journal of the Acoustical Society of America, 102,* 2892–2905.

Davis, A. (1995). *Hearing in adults.* London: Whurr.

Delgutte, B. (1990). Two-tone suppression in auditory-nerve fibers: Dependence on suppressor frequency and level. *Hearing Research, 49,* 225–246.

Deutsch, D., Dooley, K., Henthorn, T., & Head, B. (2009). Absolute pitch among students in an American music conservatory: Association with tone language fluency. *Journal of the Acoustical Society of America, 125,* 2398–2403.

Deutsch, D., Henthorn, T., Marvin, E., & Xu, H. S. (2006). Absolute pitch among American and Chinese conservatory students: Prevalence differences, and evidence for a speech-related critical period. *Journal of the Acoustical Society of America, 119,* 719–722.

Dorman, M. F., Cutting, J. E., & Raphael, L. J. (1975). Perception of temporal order in vowel sequences with and without formant transitions. *Journal of Experimental Psychology: Human Perception and Performance, 104,* 121–129.

Dowling, W. J. (1968). Rhythmic fission and perceptual organization. *Journal of the Acoustical Society of America, 44,* 369.

Dowling, W. J. (1973). The perception of interleaved melodies. *Cognitive Psychology, 5,* 332–337.

Dowling, W. J. (1978). Scale and contour: Two components of a theory of memory for melodies. *Psychological Review, 85,* 341–354.

Dowling, W. J. (2010). Music perception. In C. J. Plack (Ed.), *Hearing* (pp. 231–248). Oxford: Oxford University Press.

Dowling, W. J., & Fujitani, D. S. (1971). Contour, interval, and pitch recognition in memory for melodies. *Journal of the Acoustical Society of America, 49,* 524–531.

Drake, C., & Botte, M. C. (1993). Tempo sensitivity in auditory sequences: Evidence for a multiple-look model. *Perception and Psychophysics, 54,* 277–286.

Drullman, R., Festen, J. M., & Plomp, R. (1994). Effect of temporal envelope smearing on speech reception. *Journal of the Acoustical Society of America, 95,* 1053–1064.

Eggermont, J. J., & Roberts, L. E. (2004). The neuroscience of tinnitus. *Trends in Neurosciences, 27,* 676–682.

d'Errico, F., Henshilwood, C., Lawson, G., Vanhaeren, M., Tillier, A.-M., Soressi, M., . . . Julien, M. (2003). Archaeological evidence for the emergence of language, symbolism, and music – An alternative multidisciplinary perspective. *Journal of World Prehistory, 17,* 1–70.

Ewert, S. D., & Dau, T. (2000). Characterizing frequency selectivity for envelope fluctuations. *Journal of the Acoustical Society of America, 108,* 1181–1196.

Feng, L., & Wang, X. (2017). Harmonic template neurons in primate auditory cortex underlying complex sound processing. *Proceedings of the National Academy of Sciences,* E840–E848.

Florentine, M. (1986). Level discrimination of tones as a function of duration. *Journal of the Acoustical Society of America, 79,* 792–798.

Florentine, M., & Buus, S. (1981). An excitation-pattern model for intensity discrimination. *Journal of the Acoustical Society of America, 70,* 1646–1654.

Florentine, M., Fastl, H., & Buus, S. (1988). Temporal integration in normal hearing, cochlear impairment, and impairment simulated by masking. *Journal of the Acoustical Society of America, 84,* 195–203.

Formby, C., & Forrest, T. G. (1991). Detection of silent temporal gaps in sinusoidal markers. *Journal of the Acoustical Society of America, 89,* 830–837.

Fraisse, P. (1982). Rhythm and tempo. In D. Deutsch (Ed.), *The psychology of music* (pp. 149–181). New York: Academic Press.

Furman, A. C., Kujawa, S. G., & Liberman, M. C. (2013). Noise-induced cochlear neuropathy is selective for fibers with low spontaneous rates. *Journal of Neurophysiology*, *110*, 577–586.

Gardner, M. B., & Gardner, R. S. (1973). Problem of localization in the median plane: Effect of pinnae cavity occlusion. *Journal of the Acoustical Society of America*, *53*, 400–408.

Giraud, A. L., Price, C. J., Graham, J. M., & Frackowiak, R. S. (2001). Functional plasticity of language-related brain areas after cochlear implantation. *Brain*, *124*, 1307–1316.

Glasberg, B. R., & Moore, B. C. J. (1990). Derivation of auditory filter shapes from notched-noise data. *Hearing Research*, *47*, 103–138.

Gockel, H. E., Carlyon, R. P., Mehta, A., & Plack, C. J. (2011). The frequency following response (FFR) may reflect pitch-bearing information but is not a direct representation of pitch. *Journal of the Association for Research in Otolaryngology*, *12*, 767–782.

Goldman, R. F. (1961). Varèse: Ionisation; Density 21.5; Intégrales; Octandre; Hyperprism; Poème Electronique. Instrumentalists, cond. Robert Craft. Columbia MS 6146 (stereo). *Musical Quarterly*, *47*, 133–134.

Goldstein, J. L. (1973). An optimum processor theory for the central formation of the pitch of complex tones. *Journal of the Acoustical Society of America*, *54*, 1496–1516.

Grantham, D. W. (1984). Interaural intensity discrimination: Insensitivity at 1000 Hz. *Journal of the Acoustical Society of America*, *75*, 1191–1194.

Grantham, D. W. (1995). Spatial hearing and related phenomena. In B. C. J. Moore (Ed.), *Hearing* (pp. 297–345). New York: Academic Press.

Green, D. M. (1973). Temporal acuity as a function of frequency. *Journal of the Acoustical Society of America*, *54*, 373–379.

Green, D. M. (1988). *Profile analysis*. Oxford: Oxford University Press.

Green, D. M., Kidd, G., & Picardi, M. C. (1983). Successive versus simultaneous comparison in auditory intensity discrimination. *Journal of the Acoustical Society of America*, *73*, 639–643.

Grosjean, F. (1985). The recognition of words after their acoustic offset: Evidence and implications. *Perception and Psychophysics*, *38*, 299–310.

Grothe, B., Pecka, M., & McAlpine, D. (2010). Mechanisms of sound localization in mammals. *Physiological Reviews*, *90*, 983–1012.

Gu, J. W., Halpin, C. F., Nam, E. C., Levine, R. A., & Melcher, J. R. (2010). Tinnitus, diminished sound-level tolerance, and elevated auditory activity in humans with clinically normal hearing sensitivity. *Journal of Neurophysiology*, *104*, 3361–3370.

Guest, H., Munro, K. J., Prendergast, G., Howe, S., & Plack, C. J. (2017). Tinnitus with a normal audiogram: Relation to noise exposure but no evidence for cochlear synaptopathy. *Hearing Research*, *344*, 265–274.

Guinan, J. J. (1996). Physiology of olivocochlear efferents. In P. Dallos, A. N. Popper, & R. R. Fay (Eds.), *The cochlea* (pp. 435–502). New York: Springer-Verlag.

Gutschalk, A., Oxenham, A. J., Micheyl, C., Wilson, E. C., & Melcher, J. R. (2007). Human cortical activity during streaming without spectral cues suggests a general neural substrate for auditory stream segregation. *Journal of Neuroscience*, *28*, 13074–13081.

Hall, D. A., Haggard, M. P., Akeroyd, M. A., Palmer, A. R., Summerfield, A. Q., Elliott, M. R., . . . Bowtell, R. W. (1999). "Sparse" temporal sampling in auditory fMRI. *Human Brain Mapping*, *7*, 213–223.

Hall, D. A., & Plack, C. J. (2009). Pitch processing sites in the human auditory brain. *Cerebral Cortex*, *19*, 576–585.

Hall, J. W., Haggard, M. P., & Fernandes, M. A. (1984). Detection in noise by spectro-temporal pattern analysis. *Journal of the Acoustical Society of America*, *76*, 50–56.

Harris, C. M. (1953). A study of the building blocks in speech. *Journal of the Acoustical Society of America*, *25*, 962–969.

Hellman, R. P. (1976). Growth of loudness at 1000 and 3000 Hz. *Journal of the Acoustical Society of America*, 60, 672–679.

Helmholtz, H. L. F. (1863). *Die Lehre von den Tonempfindungen als Physiologische Grundlage für die Theorie der Musik* [The science of the perception of tones as physiological basis for music theory]. Braunschweig: F. Vieweg.

Hopkins, K., & Moore, B. C. J. (2011). The effects of age and cochlear hearing loss on temporal fine structure sensitivity, frequency selectivity, and speech reception in noise. *Journal of the Acoustical Society of America*, 130, 334–349.

Houtgast, T. (1973). Psychophysical experiments on "tuning curves" and "two-tone inhibition." *Acustica*, 29, 168–179.

Houtsma, A. J. M., & Goldstein, J. L. (1972). The central origin of the pitch of pure tones: Evidence from musical interval recognition. *Journal of the Acoustical Society of America*, 51, 520–529.

Houtsma, A. J. M., & Smurzynski, J. (1990). Pitch identification and discrimination for complex tones with many harmonics. *Journal of the Acoustical Society of America*, 87, 304–310.

Howard, D. M., & Angus, J. (2001). *Acoustics and psychoacoustics*. Oxford: Focal Press.

Howgate, S., & Plack, C. J. (2011). A behavioral measure of the cochlear changes underlying temporary threshold shifts. *Hearing Research*, 277, 78–87.

Huber, A. M., Schwab, C., Linder, T., Stoeckli, S. J., Ferrazzini, M., Dillier, N., & Fisch, U. (2001). Evaluation of eardrum laser doppler interferometry as a diagnostic tool. *Laryngoscope*, 111, 501–507.

Huron, D. (2001). Is music an evolutionary adaptation? *Annals of the New York Academy of Sciences*, 930, 43–61.

Huss, M., & Moore, B. C. J. (2005). Dead regions and pitch perception. *Journal of the Acoustical Society of America*, 117, 3841–3852.

Hutchins, S., Gosselin, N., & Peretz, I. (2010). Identification of changes along a continuum of speech intonation is impaired in congenital amusia. *Frontiers in Psychology*, 1, 236.

Ingard, U. (1953). A review of the influence of meteorological conditions on sound propagation. *Journal of the Acoustical Society of America*, 25, 405–411.

Janata, P., & Grafton, S. T. (2003). Swinging in the brain: Shared neural substrates for behaviors related to sequencing and music. *Nature Neuroscience*, 6, 682–687.

Jeffress, L. A. (1948). A place theory of sound localization. *Journal of Comparative and Physiological Psychology*, 41, 35–39.

Jeffress, L. A. (1972). Binaural signal detection: Vector theory. In J. V. Tobias (Ed.), *Foundations of modern auditory theory* (pp. 351–368). New York: Academic Press.

Jesteadt, W., Bacon, S. P., & Lehman, J. R. (1982). Forward masking as a function of frequency, masker level, and signal delay. *Journal of the Acoustical Society of America*, 71, 950–962.

Johnson, D. H. (1980). The relationship between spike rate and synchrony in responses of auditory-nerve fibers to single tones. *Journal of the Acoustical Society of America*, 68, 1115–1122.

Johnson, S. (1768). *A dictionary of the English language: In which the words are deduced from their originals, explained in their different meanings* (3rd ed.). Dublin: Thomas Ewing.

Jones, M. R. (1987). Dynamic pattern structure in music: Recent theory and research. *Perception and Psychophysics*, 41, 621–634.

Joris, P. X., & Yin, T. C. T. (1992). Responses to amplitude-modulated tones in the auditory nerve of the cat. *Journal of the Acoustical Society of America*, 91, 215–232.

Kemp, D. T. (1978). Stimulated acoustic emissions from within the human auditory system. *Journal of the Acoustical Society of America*, 64, 1386–1391.

Kewley-Port, D., & Watson, C. S. (1994). Formant-frequency discrimination for isolated English vowels. *Journal of the Acoustical Society of America*, 95, 485–496.

Klump, R. G., & Eady, H. R. (1956). Some measurements of interaural time difference thresholds. *Journal of the Acoustical Society of America, 28*, 859–860.

Koffka, K. (1935). *Principles of gestalt psychology.* New York: Harcourt, Brace.

Kohlrausch, A., Fassel, R., & Dau, T. (2000). The influence of carrier level and frequency on modulation and beat-detection thresholds for sinusoidal carriers. *Journal of the Acoustical Society of America, 108*, 723–734.

Koopmans-van Beinum, F. J. (1980). *Vowel contrast reduction: An acoustic and perceptual study of Dutch vowels in various speech conditions* (Unpublished doctoral thesis). University of Amsterdam.

Krishnan, A. (2006). Frequency-following response. In R. F. Burkhard, M. Don, & J. Eggermont (Eds.), *Auditory evoked potentials: Basic principles and clinical application.* Philadelphia: Lippincott Williams & Wilkins.

Krishnan, A., Xu, Y., Gandour, J., & Cariani, P. (2005). Encoding of pitch in the human brainstem is sensitive to language experience. *Cognitive Brain Research, 25*, 161–168.

Krumhansl, C. L. (1979). The psychological representation of musical pitch in a tonal context. *Cognitive Psychology, 11*, 346–374.

Kujawa, S. G., & Liberman, M. C. (2009). Adding insult to injury: Cochlear nerve degeneration after "temporary" noise-induced hearing loss. *Journal of Neuroscience, 29*, 14077–14085.

Ladefoged, P., & Broadbent, D. E. (1957). Information conveyed by vowels. *Journal of the Acoustical Society of America, 29*, 98–104.

Langner, G., & Schreiner, C. E. (1988). Periodicity coding in the inferior colliculus of the cat. I. Neuronal mechanisms. *Journal of Neurophysiology, 60*, 1799–1822.

Large, E. W., & Jones, M. R. (1999). The dynamics of attending: How people track time-varying events. *Psychological Review, 106*, 119–159.

Leek, M. R., Dorman, M. F., & Summerfield, A. Q. (1987). Minimum spectral contrast for vowel identification by normal-hearing and hearing-impaired listeners. *Journal of the Acoustical Society of America, 81*, 148–154.

Leshowitz, B. (1971). Measurement of the two-click threshold. *Journal of the Acoustical Society of America, 49*, 426–466.

Levitin, D. J. (1994). Absolute memory for musical pitch: Evidence from the production of learned melodies. *Perception and Psychophysics, 56*, 414–423.

Liberman, A. M., Cooper, F. S., Shankweiler, D. P., & Studdert-Kennedy, M. (1967). Perception of the speech code. *Psychological Review, 74*, 431–461.

Licklider, J. C. R. (1951). A duplex theory of pitch perception. *Experientia, 7*, 128–133.

Licklider, J. C. R. (1956). Auditory frequency analysis. In C. Cherry (Ed.), *Information theory* (pp. 253–268). New York: Academic Press.

Lieberman, P. (1963). Some effects of semantic and grammatical context on the production and perception of speech. *Language and Speech, 6*, 172–187.

Litovsky, R. Y., Colburn, H. S., Yost, W. A., & Guzman, S. J. (1999). The precedence effect. *Journal of the Acoustical Society of America, 106*, 1633–1654.

Markessis, E., Poncelet, L., Colin, C., Coppens, A., Hoonhorst, I., Kadhim, H., & Deltenre, P. (2009). Frequency tuning curves derived from auditory steady state evoked potentials: A proof-of-concept study. *Ear and Hearing, 30*, 43–53.

Marmel, F., Linley, D., Plack, C. J., Carlyon, R. P., & Gockel, H. E. (2013). Subcortical neural synchrony and absolute thresholds predict frequency discrimination independently. *Journal of the Association for Research in Otolaryngology, 14*, 757–766.

McAlpine, D., & Grothe, B. (2003). Sound localization and delay lines – Do mammals fit the model? *Trends in Neurosciences, 26*, 347–350.

McAuley, J. D., Jones, M. R., Holub, S., Johnston, H. M., & Miller, N. S. (2006). The time of our lives: Life span development of timing and event tracking. *Journal of Experimental Psychology: General, 135*, 348–367.

McDermott, J. H. (2009). What can experiments reveal about the origins of music? *Current Directions in Psychological Science*, 18, 164–168.

McDermott, J. H., Lehr, A. J., & Oxenham, A. J. (2008). Is relative pitch specific to pitch? *Psychological Science*, 19, 1263–1271.

McDermott, J. H., Lehr, A. J., & Oxenham, A. J. (2010). Individual differences reveal the basis of consonance. *Current Biology*, 20, 1035–1041.

McGill, W. J., & Goldberg, J. P. (1968). A study of the near-miss involving Weber's law and pure-tone intensity discrimination. *Perception and Psychophysics*, 4, 105–109.

McGurk, H., & MacDonald, J. (1976). Hearing lips and seeing voices. *Nature*, 264, 746–748.

McNicol, D. (2004). *A primer in signal detection theory*. Mahwah, NJ: Lawrence Erlbaum.

Meddis, R., & Hewitt, M. (1991). Virtual pitch and phase sensitivity of a computer model of the auditory periphery. I: Pitch identification. *Journal of the Acoustical Society of America*, 89, 2866–2882.

Meddis, R., O'Mard, L. P., & Lopez-Poveda, E. A. (2001). A computational algorithm for computing nonlinear auditory frequency selectivity. *Journal of the Acoustical Society of America*, 109, 2852–2861.

Miller, G. A. (1947). Sensitivity to changes in the intensity of white noise and its relation to masking and loudness. *Journal of the Acoustical Society of America*, 19, 609–619.

Miller, G. A., Heise, G. A., & Lichten, W. (1951). The intelligibility of speech as a function of the context of the test materials. *Journal of Experimental Psychology*, 41, 329–335.

Miller, G. A., & Licklider, J. C. R. (1950). The intelligibility of interrupted speech. *Journal of the Acoustical Society of America*, 22, 167–173.

Miller, G. F. (2000). *The mating mind: How sexual choice shaped the evolution of human nature*. New York: Doubleday.

Mills, A. W. (1958). On the minimum audible angle. *Journal of the Acoustical Society of America*, 30, 237–246.

Møller, A. R. (2006). Neural generators for auditory brainstem evoked potentials. In R. F. Burkhard, M. Don, & J. Eggermont (Eds.), *Auditory evoked potentials: Basic principles and clinical application*. Philadelphia: Lippincott Williams & Wilkins.

Møller, A. R. (2013). *Hearing: Anatomy, physiology, and disorders of the auditory system* (3rd ed.). San Diego: Plural Publishing.

Moore, B. C. J. (1973). Frequency difference limens for short-duration tones. *Journal of the Acoustical Society of America*, 54, 610–619.

Moore, B. C. J. (1995). Frequency analysis and masking. In B. C. J. Moore (Ed.), *Hearing* (pp. 161–205). New York: Academic Press.

Moore, B. C. J. (2004). Dead regions in the cochlea: Conceptual foundations, diagnosis, and clinical applications. *Ear and Hearing*, 25, 98–116.

Moore, B. C. J. (2007). *Cochlear hearing loss: Physiological, psychological, and technical issues* (2nd ed.). Chichester, UK: Wiley.

Moore, B. C. J. (2008). The role of temporal fine structure processing in pitch perception, masking, and speech perception for normal-hearing and hearing-impaired people. *Journal of the Association for Research in Otolaryngology*, 9, 399–406.

Moore, B. C. J. (2012). *An introduction to the psychology of hearing* (6th ed.). London: Emerald.

Moore, B. C. J., & Bacon, S. P. (1993). Detection and identification of a single modulated carrier in a complex sound. *Journal of the Acoustical Society of America*, 94, 759–768.

Moore, B. C. J., & Carlyon, R. P. (2005). Perception of pitch by people with cochlear hearing loss and by cochlear implant users. In C. J. Plack, A. J. Oxenham, R. R. Fay, & A. N. Popper (Eds.), *Pitch: Neural coding and perception* (pp. 234–277). New York: Springer-Verlag.

Moore, B. C. J., & Glasberg, B. R. (1986). Comparisons of frequency selectivity in simultaneous and forward masking for subjects with unilateral cochlear impairments. *Journal of the Acoustical Society of America*, 80, 93–107.

Moore, B. C. J., Glasberg, B. R., & Baer, T. (1997). A model for the prediction of thresholds, loudness, and partial loudness. *Journal of the Audio Engineering Society, 45*, 224–240.

Moore, B. C. J., Glasberg, B. R., Gaunt, T., & Child, T. (1991). Across-channel masking of changes in modulation depth for amplitude-and frequency-modulated signals. *Quarterly Journal of Experimental Psychology, 43A*, 327–347.

Moore, B. C. J., Glasberg, B. R., & Peters, R. W. (1985). Relative dominance of individual partials in determining the pitch of complex tones. *Journal of the Acoustical Society of America, 77*, 1853–1860.

Moore, B. C. J., Glasberg, B. R., Plack, C. J., & Biswas, A. K. (1988). The shape of the ear's temporal window. *Journal of the Acoustical Society of America, 83*, 1102–1116.

Moore, B. C. J., Glasberg, B. R., & Stone, M. A. (2004). New version of the TEN test with calibrations in dB HL. *Ear and Hearing, 25*, 478–487.

Moore, B. C. J., Huss, M., Vickers, D. A., Glasberg, B. R., & Alcantara, J. I. (2000). A test for the diagnosis of dead regions in the cochlea. *British Journal of Audiology, 34*, 205–224.

Moore, B. C. J., Johnson, J. S., Clark, T. M., & Pluvinage, V. (1992). Evaluation of a dual-channel full dynamic range compression system for people with sensorineural hearing loss. *Ear and Hearing, 13*, 349–370.

Moore, B. C. J., & Peters, R. W. (1992). Pitch discrimination and phase sensitivity in young and elderly subjects and its relationship to frequency selectivity. *Journal of the Acoustical Society of America, 91*, 2881–2893.

Moore, B. C. J., & Raab, D. H. (1974). Pure-tone intensity discrimination: Some experiments relating to the "near-miss" to Weber's law. *Journal of the Acoustical Society of America, 55*, 1049–1054.

Moore, B. C. J., & Sek, A. (1996). Detection of frequency modulation at low modulation rates: Evidence for a mechanism based on phase locking. *Journal of the Acoustical Society of America, 100*, 2320–2331.

Moore, B. C. J., Vickers, D. A., Plack, C. J., & Oxenham, A. J. (1999). Inter-relationship between different psychoacoustic measures assumed to be related to the cochlear active mechanism. *Journal of the Acoustical Society of America, 106*, 2761–2778.

Morrell, C. H., Gordon-Salant, S., Pearson, J. D., Brant, L. J., & Fozard, J. L. (1996). Age- and gender-specific reference ranges for hearing level and longitudinal changes in hearing level. *Journal of the Acoustical Society of America, 100*, 1949–1967.

Nelson, D. A., Schroder, A. C., & Wojtczak, M. (2001). A new procedure for measuring peripheral compression in normal-hearing and hearing-impaired listeners. *Journal of the Acoustical Society of America, 110*, 2045–2064.

Nelson, P. C., Smith, Z. M., & Young, E. D. (2009). Wide-dynamic-range forward suppression in marmoset inferior colliculus neurons is generated centrally and accounts for perceptual masking. *Journal of Neuroscience, 29*, 2553–2562.

Norena, A. J. (2011). An integrative model of tinnitus based on a central gain controlling neural sensitivity. *Neuroscience and Biobehavioral Reviews, 35*, 1089–1109.

Ohm, G. S. (1843). Über die Definition des Tones, nebst daran geknüpfter Theorie der Sirene und ähnlicher tonbildender Vorrichtungen [On the definition of the tone, and the related theory of a siren and similar tone producing devices]. *Annalen der Physik und Chemie, 59*, 513–565.

Oxenham, A. J. (2016). Predicting the perceptual consequences of hidden hearing loss. *Trends in Hearing, 20*.

Oxenham, A. J., & Bacon, S. P. (2004). Psychophysical manifestations of compression: Normal-hearing listeners. In S. P. Bacon, R. R. Fay & A. N. Popper (Eds.), *Compression: From cochlea to cochlear implants* (pp. 62–106). New York: Springer-Verlag.

Oxenham, A. J., Bernstein, J. G. W., & Penagos, H. (2004). Correct tonotopic representation is necessary for complex pitch perception. *Proceedings of the National Academy of Sciences, 101*, 1421–1425.

Oxenham, A. J., Micheyl, C., Keebler, M. V., Loper, A., & Santurette, S. (2011). Pitch perception beyond the traditional existence region of pitch. *Proceedings of the National Academy of Sciences, 108*, 7629–7634.

Oxenham, A. J., & Moore, B. C. J. (1994). Modeling the additivity of nonsimultaneous masking. *Hearing Research, 80*, 105–118.

Oxenham, A. J., & Plack, C. J. (1997). A behavioral measure of basilar-membrane non-linearity in listeners with normal and impaired hearing. *Journal of the Acoustical Society of America, 101*, 3666–3675.

Palmer, C., & Pfordresher, P. Q. (2003). Incremental planning in sequence production. *Psychological Review, 110*, 683–712.

Patel, A. D., & Daniele, J. R. (2003). An empirical comparison of rhythm in language and music. *Cognition, 87*, B35–45.

Patterson, R. D. (1976). Auditory filter shapes derived with noise stimuli. *Journal of the Acoustical Society of America, 59*, 640–654.

Patterson, R. D. (1990). The tone height of multiharmonic sounds. *Music Perception, 8*, 203–214.

Peng, J.-H., Tao, Z.-Z., & Huang, Z.-W. (2007). Risk of damage to hearing from personal listening devices in young adults. *Journal of Otolaryngology, 36*, 181–185.

Penner, M. J. (1977). Detection of temporal gaps in noise as a measure of the decay of auditory sensation. *Journal of the Acoustical Society of America, 61*, 552–557.

Peretz, I. (2006). The nature of music from a biological perspective. *Cognition, 100*, 1–32.

Peretz, I., Ayotte, J., Zatorre, R. J., Mehler, J., Ahad, P., Penhune, V. B., & Jutras, B. (2002). Congenital amusia: A disorder of fine-grained pitch discrimination. *Neuron, 33*, 185–191.

Peters, A. (2002). The effects of normal aging on myelin and nerve fibers: A review. *Journal of Neurocytology, 31*, 581–593.

Phillips-Silver, J., & Trainor, L. J. (2005). Feeling the beat: Movement influences infant rhythm perception. *Science, 308*, 1430.

Pickles, J. O. (2013). *An introduction to the physiology of hearing* (4th ed.). Leiden: Brill.

Pinker, S. (1997). *How the mind works*. New York: Norton.

Pisoni, D. B. (1977). Identification and discrimination of the relative onset time of two component tones: Implications for voicing perception in stops. *Journal of the Acoustical Society of America, 61*, 1352–1361.

Plack, C. J. (2010). Musical consonance: The importance of harmonicity. *Current Biology, 20*, R476–R478.

Plack, C. J., & Carlyon, R. P. (1995). Differences in frequency modulation detection and fundamental frequency discrimination between complex tones consisting of resolved and unresolved harmonics. *Journal of the Acoustical Society of America, 98*, 1355–1364.

Plack, C. J., & Drga, V. (2003). Psychophysical evidence for auditory compression at low characteristic frequencies. *Journal of the Acoustical Society of America, 113*, 1574–1586.

Plack, C. J., & Oxenham, A. J. (1998). Basilar-membrane nonlinearity and the growth of forward masking. *Journal of the Acoustical Society of America, 103*, 1598–1608.

Plack, C. J., & Oxenham, A. J. (2005). The psychophysics of pitch. In C. J. Plack, A. J. Oxenham, R. R. Fay, & A. N. Popper (Eds.), *Pitch: Neural coding and perception*. New York: Springer-Verlag.

Plack, C. J., Oxenham, A. J., & Drga, V. (2002). Linear and nonlinear processes in temporal masking. *Acustica, 88*, 348–358.

Plomp, R. (2002). *The intelligent ear: On the nature of sound perception*. Mahwah, NJ: Lawrence Erlbaum.

Plomp, R., & Levelt, W. J. M. (1965). Tonal consonance and critical bandwidth. *Journal of the Acoustical Society of America, 38*, 548–560.

Plomp, R., & Mimpen, A. M. (1968). The ear as a frequency analyzer II. *Journal of the Acoustical Society of America*, 43, 764–767.

Prendergast, G., Guest, H., Munro, K. J., Kluk, K., Léger, A., Hall, D. A., Heinz, M. G., & Plack, C. J. (2017). Effects of noise exposure on young adults with normal audiograms I: Electrophysiology. *Hearing Research*, 344, 68–81.

Prendergast, G., Millman, R. E., Guest, H., Munro, K. J., Kluk, K., Dewey, R. S., Hall, D. A., Heinz, M. G., & Plack, C. J. (2017). Effects of noise exposure on young adults with normal audiograms II: Behavioral measures. *Hearing Research*, 356, 74–86.

Pressnitzer, D., & Patterson, R. D. (2001). Distortion products and the pitch of harmonic complex tones. In D. J. Breebaart, A. J. M. Houtsma, A. Kohlrausch, V. F. Prijs, & R. Schoonhoven (Eds.), *Physiological and psychophysical bases of auditory function* (pp. 97–104). Maastricht: Shaker.

Pressnitzer, D., Patterson, R. D., & Krumbholz, K. (2001). The lower limit of melodic pitch. *Journal of the Acoustical Society of America*, 109, 2074–2084.

Rakerd, B., & Hartmann, W. H. (1986). Localization of sound in rooms III: Onset and duration effects. *Journal of the Acoustical Society of America*, 80, 1695–1706.

Rasch, R. A. (1979). Synchronization in performed ensemble music. *Acustica*, 43, 121–131.

Rayleigh, L. (1907). On our perception of sound direction. *Philosophical Magazine*, 13, 214–232.

Relkin, E. M., & Turner, C. W. (1988). A reexamination of forward masking in the auditory nerve. *Journal of the Acoustical Society of America*, 84, 584–591.

Remez, R. E., Rubin, P. E., Pisoni, D. B., & Carrell, T. D. (1981). Speech perception without traditional speech cues. *Science*, 212, 947–950.

Rhode, W. S., & Cooper, N. P. (1996). Nonlinear mechanics in the apical turn of the chinchilla cochlea in vivo. *Auditory Neuroscience*, 3, 101–121.

Richards, V. M. (1987). Monaural envelope correlation perception. *Journal of the Acoustical Society of America*, 82, 1621–1630.

Ritsma, R. J. (1962). Existence region of the tonal residue I. *Journal of the Acoustical Society of America*, 34, 1224–1229.

Ronken, D. (1970). Monaural detection of a phase difference between clicks. *Journal of the Acoustical Society of America*, 47, 1091–1099.

Rosowski, J. J., & Relkin, E. M. (2001). Introduction to the analysis of middle ear function. In A. F. Jahn & J. Santos-Sacchi (Eds.), *Physiology of the ear* (pp. 161–190). San Diego: Singular.

Ruggero, M. A. (1992). Physiology and coding of sound in the auditory nerve. In A. N. Popper & R. R. Fay (Eds.), *The mammalian auditory pathway: Neurophysiology* (pp. 34–93). New York: Springer-Verlag.

Ruggero, M. A., Rich, N. C., Recio, A., Narayan, S. S., & Robles, L. (1997). Basilar-membrane responses to tones at the base of the chinchilla cochlea. *Journal of the Acoustical Society of America*, 101, 2151–2163.

Sachs, M. B., & Abbas, P. J. (1974). Rate versus level functions for auditory-nerve fibers in cats: Tone-burst stimuli. *Journal of the Acoustical Society of America*, 56, 1835–1847.

Sachs, M. B., & Young, E. D. (1979). Encoding of steady-state vowels in the auditory nerve: Representation in terms of discharge rate. *Journal of the Acoustical Society of America*, 66, 470–479.

Sachs, M. B., & Young, E. D. (1980). Effects of nonlinearities on speech encoding in the auditory nerve. *Journal of the Acoustical Society of America*, 68, 858–875.

Schaette, R., & Kempter, R. (2006). Development of tinnitus-related neuronal hyperactivity through homeostatic plasticity after hearing loss: A computational model. *European Journal of Neuroscience*, 23, 3124–3138.

Schaette, R., & McAlpine, D. (2011). Tinnitus with a normal audiogram: Physiological evidence for hidden hearing loss and computational model. *Journal of Neuroscience, 31,* 13452–13457.

Schellenberg, E. G., & Trehub, S. E. (2003). Good pitch memory is widespread. *Psychological Science, 14,* 262–266.

Schlauch, R. S., DiGiovanni, J. J., & Reis, D. T. (1998). Basilar membrane nonlinearity and loudness. *Journal of the Acoustical Society of America, 103,* 2010–2020.

Schmiedt, R. A. (2010). The physiology of cochlear presbycusis. In S. Gordon-Salant, R. D. Frisina, R. R. Fay, & A. N. Popper (Eds.), *The aging auditory system* (pp. 9–38). New York: Springer.

Schnupp, J., Nelken, I., & King, A. (2011). *Auditory neuroscience: Making sense of sound.* Cambridge, MA: MIT Press.

Schooneveldt, G. P., & Moore, B. C. J. (1987). Comodulation masking release (CMR): Effects of signal frequency, flanking-band frequency, masker bandwidth, flanking-band level, and monotic versus dichotic presentation of the flanking band. *Journal of the Acoustical Society of America, 82,* 1944–1956.

Schouten, J. F. (1940). The residue and the mechanism of hearing. *Proceedings of the Koninklijke Nederlandse Akademie van Wetenschappen, 43,* 991–999.

Schouten, J. F. (1970). The residue revisited. In R. Plomp & G. F. Smoorenburg (Eds.), *Frequency analysis and periodicity detection in hearing* (pp. 41–54). Lieden, The Netherlands: Sijthoff.

Schrott, A., Stephan, K., & Spoendlin, H. (1989). Hearing with selective inner hair cell loss. *Hearing Research, 40,* 213–219.

Schwartz, M. S., Otto, S. R., Shannon, R. V., Hitselberger, W. E., & Brackmann, D. E. (2008). Auditory brainstem implants. *Neurotherapeutics, 5,* 128–136.

Sewell, W. F. (1996). Neurotransmitters and synaptic transmission. In P. Dallos, A. N. Popper, & R. R. Fay (Eds.), *The cochlea* (pp. 503–533). New York: Springer-Verlag.

Shackleton, T. M., & Carlyon, R. P. (1994). The role of resolved and unresolved harmonics in pitch perception and frequency modulation discrimination. *Journal of the Acoustical Society of America, 95,* 3529–3540.

Shackleton, T. M., Meddis, R., & Hewitt, M. (1994). The role of binaural and fundamental frequency difference cues in the identification of concurrently presented vowels. *Quarterly Journal of Experimental Psychology, 47A,* 545–563.

Shailer, M. J., & Moore, B. C. J. (1987). Gap detection and the auditory filter: Phase effects using sinusoidal stimuli. *Journal of the Acoustical Society of America, 81,* 1110–1117.

Shannon, R. V., Zeng, F. G., Kamath, V., Wygonski, J., & Ekelid, M. (1995). Speech recognition with primarily temporal cues. *Science, 270,* 303–304.

Shepard, R. N. (1982). Geometrical approximations to the structure of musical pitch. *Psychological Review, 89,* 305–333.

Shera, C. A., Guinan, J. J., & Oxenham, A. J. (2002). Revised estimates of human cochlear tuning from otoacoustic and behavioral measurements. *Proceedings of the National Academy of Sciences, 99,* 3318–3323.

Shofner, W. P., & Niemiec, A. J. (2010). Comparative psychoacoustics. In C. J. Plack (Ed.), *Hearing* (pp. 145–176). Oxford: Oxford University Press.

Snyder, J. S., Alain, C., & Picton, T. W. (2006). Effects of attention on neuroelectric correlates of auditory stream segregation. *Journal of Cognitive Neuroscience, 18,* 1–13.

Srulovicz, P., & Goldstein, J. L. (1983). A central spectrum model: A synthesis of auditory-nerve timing and place cues in monaural communication of frequency spectrum. *Journal of the Acoustical Society of America, 73,* 1266–1276.

Stevens, S. S. (1957). On the psychophysical law. *Psychological Review, 64,* 153–181.

Stevens, S. S. (1972). Perceived level of noise by Mark VII and decibels (E). *Journal of the Acoustical Society of America, 51,* 575–601.

Summerfield, Q., & Culling, J. F. (1992). Auditory segregation of competing voices: Absence of effects of FM or AM coherence. *Philosophical Transactions of the Royal Society B*, 336(1278), 357–365.

Tan, S.-L., Pfordresher, P., & Harré, R. (2010). *Psychology of music: From sound to significance*. New York: Psychology Press.

Terhardt, E. (1974). Pitch, consonance, and harmony. *Journal of the Acoustical Society of America*, 55, 1061–1069.

Thurlow, W. R., Mangels, J. W., & Runge, P. S. (1967). Head movements during sound localization. *Journal of the Acoustical Society of America*, 42, 489–493.

Tillmann, B., Bharucha, J. J., & Bigand, E. (2000). Implicit learning of tonality: A self-organizing approach. *Psychological Review*, 107, 885–913.

Tyler, R. S., Wood, E. J., & Fernandes, M. A. (1983). Frequency resolution and discrimination of constant and dynamic tones in normal and hearing-impaired listeners. *Journal of the Acoustical Society of America*, 74, 1190–1199.

van de Par, S., & Kohlrausch, A. (1997). A new approach to comparing binaural masking level differences at low and high frequencies. *Journal of the Acoustical Society of America*, 101, 1671–1680.

van Noorden, L. P. A. S. (1975). *Temporal coherence in the perception of tone sequences* (Unpublished doctoral thesis). Eindhoven University of Technology.

Viana, L. M., O'Malley, J. T., Burgess, B. J., Jones, D. D., Oliveira, C. A. C. P., Santos, F., Merchant, S. N., Liberman, L. D., & Liberman, M. C. (2015). Cochlear neuropathy in human presbycusis: Confocal analysis of hidden hearing loss in post-mortem tissue. *Hearing Research*, 327, 78–88.

Viemeister, N. F. (1988). Intensity coding and the dynamic range problem. *Hearing Research*, 34, 267–274.

Viemeister, N. F., & Bacon, S. P. (1988). Intensity discrimination, increment detection, and magnitude estimation for 1-kHz tones. *Journal of the Acoustical Society of America*, 84, 172–178.

Viemeister, N. F., & Wakefield, G. H. (1991). Temporal integration and multiple looks. *Journal of the Acoustical Society of America*, 90, 858–865.

Vliegen, J., & Oxenham, A. J. (1999). Sequential stream segregation in the absence of spectral cues. *Journal of the Acoustical Society of America*, 105, 339–346.

Vos, P. G., & Troost, J. M. (1989). Ascending and descending melodic intervals: Statistical findings and their perceptual relevance. *Music Perception*, 6, 383–396.

Warren, J. D., Uppenkamp, S., Patterson, R. D., & Griffiths, T. D. (2003). Separating pitch chroma and pitch height in the human brain. *Proceedings of the National Academy of Sciences*, 100, 10038–10042.

Warren, R. M. (1970). Perceptual restoration of missing speech sounds. *Science*, 167, 392–393.

Warren, R. M. (2008). *Auditory perception: An analysis and synthesis* (3rd ed.). Cambridge, UK: Cambridge University Press.

Warren, R. M., Gardner, D. A., Brubacker, B. S., & Bashford, J. A., Jr. (1991). Melodic and non-melodic sequences of tones: Effects of duration on perception. *Music Perception*, 8, 277–290.

Warren, R. M., Riener, K. R., Bashford, J. A., Jr., & Brubaker, B. S. (1995). Spectral redundancy: Intelligibility of sentences heard through narrow spectral slits. *Perception and Psychophysics*, 57, 175–182.

Wenzel, E. M., Arruda, M., Kistler, D. J., & Wightman, F. L. (1993). Localization using non-individualized head-related transfer functions. *Journal of the Acoustical Society of America*, 94, 111–123.

White, L. J., & Plack, C. J. (1998). Temporal processing of the pitch of complex tones. *Journal of the Acoustical Society of America*, 103, 2051–2063.

Wightman, F. L., & Kistler, D. J. (1992). The dominant role of low-frequency interaural time differences in sound localization. *Journal of the Acoustical Society of America*, 91, 1648–1661.

Wilding, T., McKay, C., Baker, R., Picton, T., & Kluk, K. (2011). Using the auditory steady state response to record response amplitude curves. A possible fast objective method for diagnosing dead regions. *Ear and Hearing*, 32, 485–497.

Wong, P. C. M., Skoe, E., Russo, N. M., Dees, T., & Kraus, N. (2007). Musical experience shapes human brainstem encoding of linguistic pitch patterns. *Nature Neuroscience*, 10, 420–422.

Woods, W. S., & Colburn, H. S. (1992). Test of a model of auditory object formation using intensity and interaural time difference discrimination. *Journal of the Acoustical Society of America*, 91, 2894–2902.

Yasin, I., & Plack, C. J. (2003). The effects of a high-frequency suppressor on tuning curves and derived basilar membrane response functions. *Journal of the Acoustical Society of America*, 114, 322–332.

Yates, G. K., Winter, I. M., & Robertson, D. (1990). Basilar membrane nonlinearity determines auditory nerve rate-intensity functions and cochlear dynamic range. *Hearing Research*, 45, 203–220.

Yost, W. A., Sheft, S., & Opie, J. (1989). Modulation interference in detection and discrimination of amplitude modulation. *Journal of the Acoustical Society of America*, 86, 2138–2147.

Young, E. D., & Sachs, M. B. (1979). Representation of steady-state vowels in the temporal aspects of the discharge patterns of populations of auditory-nerve fibers. *Journal of the Acoustical Society of America*, 66, 1381–1403.

Zahorik, P. (2002a). Assessing auditory distance perception using virtual acoustics. *Journal of the Acoustical Society of America*, 111, 1832–1846.

Zahorik, P. (2002b). Direct-to-reverberant energy ratio sensitivity. *Journal of the Acoustical Society of America*, 112, 2110–2117.

Zeng, F.-G., & Djalilian, H. (2010). Hearing impairment. In C. J. Plack (Ed.), *Hearing* (pp. 325–347). Oxford: Oxford University Press.

Zheng, J., Shen, W., He, D. Z. Z., Long, K. B., Madison, L. D., & Dallos, P. (2000). Prestin is the motor protein of cochlear outer hair cells. *Nature*, 405, 149–155.

Zwicker, E. (1970). Masking and psychological excitation as consequences of the ear's frequency analysis. In R. Plomp & G. F. Smoorenburg (Eds.), *Frequency analysis and periodicity detection in hearing* (pp. 376–394). Leiden, The Netherlands: Sijthoff.

Zwicker, E., & Fastl, H. (1990). *Psychoacoustics – facts and models*. Berlin: Springer-Verlag.

Zwicker, E., Flottorp, G., & Stevens, S. S. (1957). Critical bandwidth in loudness summation. *Journal of the Acoustical Society of America*, 29, 548–557.

Zwicker, E., & Scharf, B. (1965). A model of loudness summation. *Psychological Review*, 72, 3–26.

INDEX